Children's Encyclopedia

John Farndon

HarperCollins*Children'sBooks*

D1342950

INTRODUCTION

This Children's Encyclopedia is a family guide to a world of knowledge. The enticing design invites the reader to discover a wealth of information about people, ideas, events and the living world.

The aim is to provide easy-to-follow information that will stimulate interest in a variety of topics. The language used speaks directly to children and the information provided can be used either as quick fact-checking in answer to specific questions, or as a source of more detailed project work, at school or at home.

All the information has been authenticated by a team of experts and the aims of children's education have been addressed throughout.

The Children's Encyclopedia is arranged thematically which enables the reader to see the information in a wide context. The contents list provides a guide to the breakdown of the main subject areas, and in addition the extensive index is a valuable source of more detailed listings.

Careful consideration has been given to the presentation of all subjects. In order to make the information more accessible, each subject area is divided into more specific sections which are easy to identify. On each double-page there is a main body of text which provides an overview of the subject. In addition, there are specially designed 'fact panels' which provide more detailed information. Hence the reader can be drawn into interesting facts at a glance. Occasionally the reader will come across a word in *italics*. This signifies the word (often a scientific term) may be new to the reader. The meaning of the word will usually be explained in the text, but may need to be looked up in a dictionary.

Recognizing the importance of stimulating the reader visually, the Encyclopedia is beautifully illustrated and all illustrations have been selected for their ability to convey additional information to the text.

To supplement the main subjects, there is a very useful section at the back of the Encyclopedia based on more general information, such as famous people and highest mountains.

With the Children's Encyclopedia, general knowledge arguments can be easily resolved and readers will discover the excitement and fun of acquiring new information.

CONTENTS

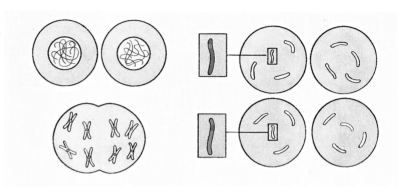

THE LIVING WORLD

THE HUMAN BODY

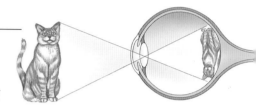

ANIMALS WITH BACKBONES

ANIMALS WITHOUT BACKBONES

PLANTS

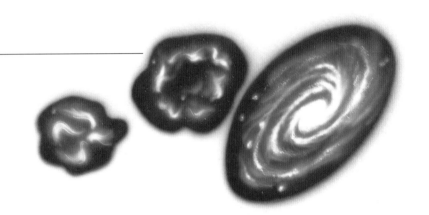

SPACE

THE EARTH

THE AGES OF THE EARTH

THE HUMAN STORY

HISTORY

SCIENCE

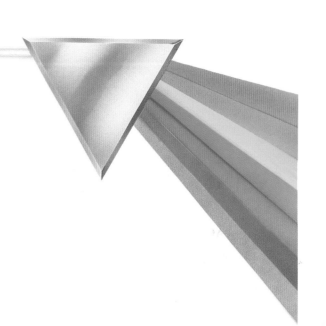

Technology, inventions & discoveries

Society

Places

Information section

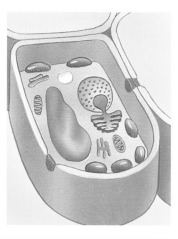

A plant cell contains many of the same organelles (inner structures) as an animal cell, but lacks some such as the lysosome (see below).

PLANT CELLS

Plant cells are enclosed in a rigid membrane of cellulose. Unlike animal cells, plant cells contain small organelles called *chloroplasts*. The chloroplasts are like tiny solar converters, and they enable plants to trap the energy from the Sun in a process called *photosynthesis* (page 57). Plant cells also contain a large space filled with air or water called a *vacuole*.

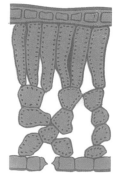

Leaves are built up from rows of interlocking plant cells. All the food the cells need to survive is carried as chemicals dissolved in water, which seeps through the cell walls.

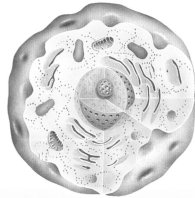

Animal cells have only tiny vacuoles, but many more organelles.

ANIMAL CELLS

Animal cells have softer membranes than plants cells. Like plant cells, they contain a series of tubes called the *endoplasmic reticulum* where important cell chemicals called *enzymes* are made. Unlike plant cells, they have a *lysosome* for waste disposal.

LIVING CELLS

Nearly all living things are built up from tiny parcels called cells. The cells are so small that they can be seen only under a microscope, but each is a living, dynamic chemical factory with its own role to play in the life of the plant or animal.

INSIDE A CELL

A living cell is a squidgy case containing a jelly-like mixture of chemicals called the *cytoplasm*. Cells gain their strength by clumping together with other cells.

Membrane Holding each cell together is a thin skin called the *membrane*. Plant cells have a tough, stiff membrane made of a material called *cellulose*; the soft membrane of animal cells is made of fat dotted with protein. Although it holds the cytoplasm in place, the membrane lets certain chemicals in to feed the cell and lets waste out.

The cytoplasm acts as a storeroom of molecules for the enlargement and repair of structures inside the cell. It surrounds an intricate set of structures called *organelles*. Different cells have different organelles, each with its own function. There are, for instance, sausage-shaped *mitochondria*, which are the cell's factories, and the flattened sacks of the *Golgi bodies*, where protein and carbohydrate are packaged for release from the cell.

The nucleus Most plant and animal cells contain an inner part called a *nucleus*, which is the cell's control centre. The nucleus is surrounded by a nuclear membrane. The nucleus contains the blueprint for an entire new plant or animal (page 9). Cells with a nuclear membrane are called *eukaryotic*. Bacteria are *prokaryotic*, which means they have no nuclear membrane.

BODY CELLS

Your body is made up of many different kinds of cell – round fat cells, plate-like skin cells, box-shaped liver cells and many others. All of them grew from a single cell made by the fusion of a sperm cell from your father and an egg cell from your mother. This one cell contained all the instructions necessary to make you. It divided many times to produce the millions and millions of cells in your body.

So although cells have many shapes and tasks, they all have the same basic structure.

Cells are constantly wearing out and being replaced by new ones. Some last months, some less than a day. Only nerve cells last for a very long time – but once they die, they may never be replaced.

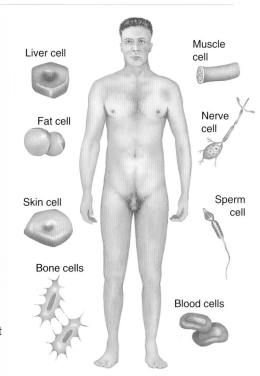

Liver cell

Fat cell

Skin cell

Bone cells

Muscle cell

Nerve cell

Sperm cell

Blood cells

LIFE PLAN

Inside every living cell is a remarkable molecule that contains all the instructions the cell needs to perform its tasks, and all the instructions to make an exact copy of the entire plant or animal. This molecule is called *deoxyribonucleic acid*, or *DNA* for short.

THE GENETIC CODE

Like a computer, DNA carries all these instructions in code. Scientists estimate the tiny DNA molecule in each cell contains enough information to take up the memory of 85,000 small home computers, or fill an entire library holding thousands of books.

Genes The key to the DNA code lies in the sequence of chemical bases (see right) along each strand. These bases are a bit like letters of the alphabet, and the sequence is broken up into 'sentences' called *genes* that provide the instructions to make a particular *protein*. Proteins are the basic material of all living cells.

Proteins are built up from different combinations of chemicals called *amino acids*. All these amino acids are on hand in each cell, so in order to make a certain protein, the DNA must instruct the cell to make the right combination of amino acids.

Codons Bases are arranged in groups of three along each strand of DNA. These groups are called *codons*, and the sequence of the three bases spells out the name of a particular amino acid.

Altogether, there are 64 different ways the four bases can be arranged in groups of three, so there must be 64 different codons. Since there are only 20 amino acids, some codons code for the same amino acid. Three codons act as full stops at the end of each gene to show that the instructions for a particular protein are complete.

THE DNA MOLECULE

The DNA molecule is one of the largest molecules known, weighing 500 million times as much as a molecule of sugar. It is very thin, but very long – if stretched out it would be over 40cm long.

It is usually coiled up like a twisted rope, but is actually made from two thin strands wrapped tightly round each other in a long spiral called a *double helix*. It is a bit like an incredibly long twisted rope ladder. The ropes are made of two alternating chemical groups – sugars and phosphates; the rungs are chemicals called bases, linked by *hydrogen bonds*.

There are four kinds of base in DNA – guanine, adenine, cytosine and thymine. Each of these bases pairs only with one other. Guanine links only with cytosine; adenine only with thymine. This means that the sequence of bases along one strand of the DNA is a perfect mirror image of the sequence on the other strand. So each can be used, like a mould, to make a copy of the other.

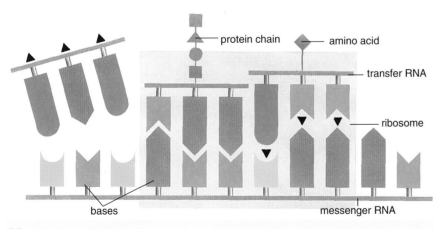

protein chain — amino acid

transfer RNA

ribosome

bases

messenger RNA

MAKING PROTEINS

The DNA is too valuable to use directly as a mould, so when the cell needs a new protein, it sends a special enzyme into the nucleus to get a copy of the right bit of DNA. The copies are made in molecules of a similar chemical called RNA. The copies are called messenger RNA or mRNA.

Back out in the cytoplasm, the mRNA joins up with a body called the ribosome, while another kind of RNA, transfer RNA (tRNA) brings the amino acids. The mRNA then runs through the ribosome, hooking in the right amino acids and stringing them together to make the protein.

DNA is a long double-spiral shaped molecule made from hydrogen, carbon and oxygen. This model shows a tiny section.

MULTIPLYING CELLS

Living cells multiply by splitting in half again and again. This is how all plants and animals grow, and how old cells are replaced when they are worn out.

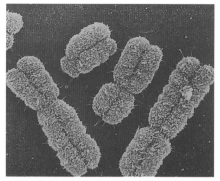

MAKING COPIES

When cells divide, each of the new cells must be identical – and carry the same set of instructions. So before each cell divides, it makes copies of its DNA (page 9) to share between the new cells by a process called *replication*.

When DNA replicates, its two strands gradually unzip, exposing the mirror image sequences of bases (page 9) on each. At once, bases floating around in the cell nucleus, called *free bases*, latch on to each of the exposed strands.

Each of the four kinds of free base finds the right partner on the exposed strand – guanine joining with cytosine, adenine with thymine, and vice versa. In this way, a matching strand is added to each of the exposed strands, creating two identical copies of the original DNA ready for cell division to begin.

MITOSIS

When cells are worn out, new cells are made by *mitosis*. During mitosis, the knots binding the two threads of each chromosome (see right) loosen, and one thread is drawn to each end of the cell. The cell stretches out like a sausage and the threads bunch at each end. The middle slowly narrows until the cell splits to form two new cells.

MEIOSIS

Most animals and plants have two sets of chromosomes in each cell, one from each parent. Before a new life can begin, special *germ cells* with just one set of chromosomes must be made by a process of division and reduction called *meiosis*. The products of meiosis, the germ cells, combine to create a *zygote*, a cell containing the normal two sets of chromosomes.

Chromosome pairs (above) can be seen under a powerful microscope.
A sperm cell combines with an egg cell (below).

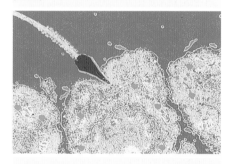

CHROMOSOMES

DNA in the nucleus of a cell is mixed with protein in threads called *chromosomes*. If genes carry a sentence of the genetic code, chromosomes carry a whole book. The number of chromosomes in each cell varies from species to species. Humans usually have 46. When DNA replicates, the two copies of each chromosome are joined at the middle, making an X-shaped pair.

1 Before cell division begins, each DNA strand is replicated to make a series of X-shaped chromosome pairs.

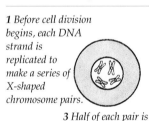

2 The pairs line up across the middle of the cell.

3 Half of each pair is drawn along threads to opposite ends of the cell.

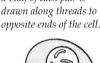

4 A nucleus forms around the cluster of chromosomes at each end of the cell.

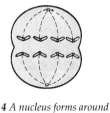

5 The cell finally splits in two between the new nuclei to leave two complete cells.

1 Before the cell divides, the chromosomes in each pair swap genes.

4 The chromosome pairs line up across the middle of each of the two new cells, and then are pulled apart by long threads of protein.

Each chromosome in the germ cells has genes from both parents.

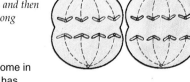

2 The chromosome pairs line up across the middle of the cell.

3 The cell divides, just as in mitosis, to leave two cells with the normal number of chromosomes.

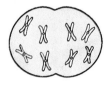

5 Each half of the chromosome pair is pulled to opposite ends of each cell. The two cells then split to form four germ cells, each with half the normal number of chromosomes.

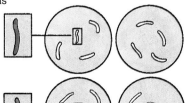

Mitosis (above) is the way cells divide to create new cells to grow or replace those that have worn out. Each new cell gets an identical copy of the original cell's chromosomes.

Meiosis (right) is the way cells divide to create germ cells with half the normal number of chromosomes, ready to combine with other germ cells to start a new life.

HEREDITY

So well does the genetic code work that nearly every plant and animal resembles not only its parents but even its grandparents very closely. This family resemblance is called heredity.

Girls get red–green colour blindness only if the mutant gene is on both their X-chromosomes.

BLUEPRINT FOR LIFE

What is remarkable about the genetic code is that it not only passes on family traits with astonishing accuracy but also allows minor variations, so that no two plants or animals are exactly alike. This is important because it is these subtle differences that allow species to change and develop (page 101).

Boy or girl? The key to heredity is the chromosomes. Humans have 46 altogether. Women have 23 matching pairs; men have only 22 matching pairs, plus two odd ones. It is the odd chromosomes that fix whether a baby will be a boy or a girl, which is why they are called the *sex chromosome*s. One is shaped like an X, one like a Y. Women have sex chromosomes too, only both theirs are matching Xs.

When germ cells are created by meiosis (see left), the number of chromosomes is halved. In a woman, the germ cells will always get an X chromosome, because she has two. In a man, however, half will get an X and half a Y. So when the germ cells combine during fertilization (page 21), it will give the fertilized egg either an X or a Y. If it gives an X, the baby will be a girl; if it gives a Y, it will be a boy.

Genes Humans' other 44 chromosomes come in pairs. In each pair, both chromosomes code for the same thing. Indeed features are coded in exactly the same place on each of the pair, called a *gene locus*. So there are alternative instructions for each feature. Most features are a mixture of the two, but in some cases there can be no compromise (see below).

COLOUR BLINDNESS

Sometimes a gene may be damaged. This is a *mutant gene*. When someone inherits a mutant version of a certain gene on the X sex chromosome, they may not be able to see the number picked out in red dots in this green circle. This is called red-green colour blindness.

MUTATION

The genetic code is remarkably reliable, but every now and then it makes a slip, and a gene *mutates* (changes) as the DNA is copied before cells divide. Mutations are exceptionally rare, and can be beneficial, allowing us to evolve. Occasionally they can cause illness, too.

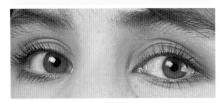

Brown eyes or blue? If both your parents have brown eyes, you may still get blue eyes if the recessive blue-eye gene is expressed.

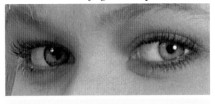

DOMINANT AND RECESSIVE GENES

With some features, one of the pair of genes must win. A gene that always wins, like the gene for brown eyes, is a *dominant* gene; a gene that loses is a *recessive* gene.

A recessive gene will win only if paired with a similar one. The diagram shows how there is a 1-in-4 chance of a child of brown-eyed parents having blue eyes.

ONE GENE OR TWO

Whether your eyes are brown depends on one gene. Many features depend on more than one (*polygene inheritance*).

Mould (above) The mould attacking this apple is a micro-organism called a protoctista.

MICROSCOPIC LIFE

The most abundant forms of life are very small and can only be observed with a microscope. They are found in huge numbers in every habitat on earth. Many live in or on other larger living things. Many forms of micro-organism are carried in the air. Operating theatres, and some factories, use complex filters to keep micro-organisms out.

MICROBES OF ALL KINDS

There is such an enormous range of different microbes that scientists have found it hard to decide how to group them. Microscopic algae and mould are sometimes thought of as kinds of plants, or as part of a separate group called *protoctista*. But blue-green algae are now thought of as bacteria. These bacteria are autotrophic, and all plants evolved from them; all animals probably evolved from heterotrophic bacteria.

The protoctista are also part of a much bigger group of organisms called *protists*, which are dominated by *protozoa*. Like bacteria, protozoa such as amoebas are one-celled organisms, but they are much bigger, and generally live by themselves, floating in water and in many ways behaving like animals – eating, excreting, breathing and moving by pulsating their cell walls. While bacteria are *prokaryotic*, which means they have no nucleus, protozoa are eukaryotic. Some protozoa are parasites of fish and land animals. Amoebas can cause disease called *amoebic dysentery*.

BACTERIA SHAPE

Every bacterium has a rigid cell wall around a soft membrane holding the jelly-like protoplasm and the strands of DNA (page 10). Some also have a flagellum (tail-like structure) to drive them along. Bacteria are often classified according to their shape. Cocci are round, bacilli are rod-shaped, vibrios are curved and spirilla are spiral. Cocci that live in pairs are called diplococci, clusters are staphylococci and chains are streptococci.

BACTERIA

By far the most common of the micro-organisms are bacteria. They have a simple structure, and, under favourable conditions, can multiply at a very rapid rate. However, they have very special requirements. The size of bacterial colonies is controlled by the availability of food, a suitable temperature and other essential environmental factors.

There are many thousands of different bacteria, but they are all made of just one cell. Aerobic bacteria need oxygen to survive; anaerobic bacteria are poisoned by it. Some bacteria are *autotrophic*, which means they can make food for themselves from sunlight or chemicals. Others are *heterotrophic*, which means they survive by feeding off organic matter.

Finding a host Most bacteria cannot move very far by themselves, so most heterotrophic bacteria find a host organism to live on.

Sometimes they get on well with their hosts and the relationship is good for both bacteria and host. This is called a *symbiotic* relationship. There are bacteria in cows' stomachs, for instance, which help break grass into more digestible lumps. Or the bacteria may simply live harmlessly on the host. The bacterium *Escherichia coli* or *E. coli* lives quite harmlessly in your intestine. This is called a *commensal* relationship.

1 Virus approaches the host cell.

2 Virus sticks to the surface of host cell and injects its DNA (genetic material).

3 The virus DNA replicates (copies itself) inside the host cell.

4 New viruses are formed inside the cell.

5 The cell bursts and the viruses spread out.

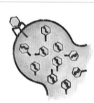

VIRUSES

Viruses are the simplest of all forms of life, but they are so small (100 millionths of a millimetre long) that you can see them only under a powerful electron microscope. Unlike bacteria, viruses are entirely parasitic and cannot multiply outside a host. Indeed, outside a host cell, they are virtually lifeless.

When a virus enters a host cell, it takes over the host's chemical energy and protein-making ability in order to multiply itself. After the virus multiplies, the new viruses burst out of the cell, often leaving it dissolved.

Sometimes, however, bacteria are *parasites* that live inside the host's body, and may damage the host by releasing poisonous chemicals called toxins. A bacterium that causes disease is sometimes called a *pathogen* (see below). Moreover, bacteria that are commensal in one place can be pathogenic in another. *E. coli*, for instance, can cause disease if it gets into your urinary tract.

Although bacteria can cause disease, many are useful. Some break down organic matter, releasing the nutrients to the soil. Some help ferment alcohol for drinks or are used in the cheese-making process. Some help in genetic engineering.

Reproducing Most bacteria multiply simply by splitting again and again and again. Sometimes, bacteria can survive for thousands of years in adverse conditions by creating *spores*.

GENETIC ENGINEERING

Micro-organisms have played a vital role in the development of genetic engineering techniques. The idea of genetic engineering is to change a creature's genetic code to eliminate faults such as inherited diseases, or to create a particular effect.

So far, the most common use of genetic engineering has been to produce

Medicine machine Genetic engineering may mean cows will deliver vital medicines in their milk.

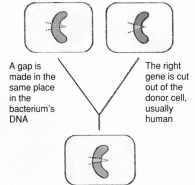

A gap is made in the same place in the bacterium's DNA

The right gene is cut out of the donor cell, usually human

The right gene is inserted in the gap in the bacterium's DNA

medicines cheaply in large quantities. If scientists can identify the gene responsible for making a certain substance, they can insert it into bacteria. Because bacteria multiply rapidly they will manufacture large quantities of the substance very quickly. The *E. coli* bacterium is especially widely used for this.

Insulin for diabetics, *growth hormone* for undergrown children and interferon (used for treating viral infections) are all made this way.

DISEASE AND PATHOGENS

Many pathogens cause *infectious diseases*. When you get an infectious disease, a colony of pathogens such as bacteria, viruses or fungi begins to grow inside your body. As they multiply, they either damage your cells directly, as viruses do, or they release harmful toxins which themselves may harm your cells.

Infection normally activates the body's *immune system*, and many of the symptoms of illness that you feel – such as fever, weakness and aching joints –

are often the effects of your body's immune system's mighty struggle against the invading organisms.

Sometimes, the infection may be spread throughout the body. This is called a *systemic infection*. A cold is an example of a systemic infection. Sometimes the infection may be just in one spot. This is called a *localized infection*. If dirt is allowed into a cut, it may result in a localized infection. This kind of infection can usually be avoided by keeping hands and so on clean.

Tapeworms or cestodes live in the intestine. They usually come from eating uncooked meat or fish.

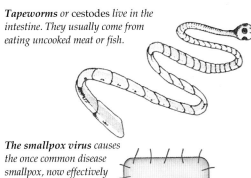

The smallpox virus causes the once common disease smallpox, now effectively eliminated by vaccination.

Cholera bacteria Bacterial infection cannot be prevented by vaccination, and cholera is still common.

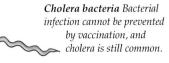

PARASITES

Parasites, such as tapeworms and amoebas, are often to blame for illnesses, such as some kinds of diarrhoea, malaria, sleeping sickness and toxoplasmosis (a disease caught from cats). All parasites are harmful to their host, but some are beneficial to humans. Some bacteria, for instance, help keep down populations of other micro-organisms.

The mumps virus can cause an unpleasant disease called mumps which mainly affects children. It is spread from person to person by droplets of water in the air.

Tobacco mosaic virus Plants are just as susceptible to viral attack as animals. The tobacco mosaic virus can cause havoc in tobacco crops.

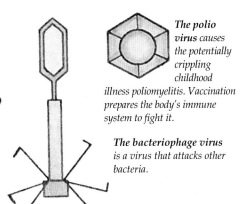

The polio virus causes the potentially crippling childhood illness poliomyelitis. Vaccination prepares the body's immune system to fight it.

The bacteriophage virus is a virus that attacks other bacteria.

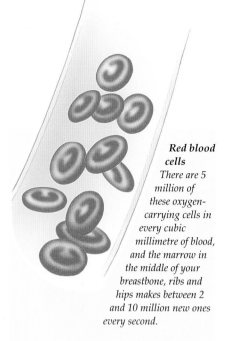

Red blood cells *There are 5 million of these oxygen-carrying cells in every cubic millimetre of blood, and the marrow in the middle of your breastbone, ribs and hips makes between 2 and 10 million new ones every second.*

BREATHING & EATING

Every minute of the day, even while you sleep, your body is hard at work. Your chest is drawing air in and out of your lungs to maintain the oxygen level in your blood. Your heart is pumping oxygen-rich blood from the lungs to the rest of your body. And chemicals are breaking down food in your stomach and gut and changing it into the materials your body needs.

BLOOD

Blood is not simply a red liquid; it is a rich stew of different cells, swept along in a clear, yellowish fluid called *plasma*. The most numerous blood cells are the button-shaped red blood cells. The red blood cells are like rafts ferrying oxygen around the body. The oxygen is held on board by a protein called *haemoglobin*. There are also tiny cell fragments in the blood called *platelets*, which help to plug a leak, such as a cut, and giant white blood cells called *leucocytes*. The white blood cells play a vital role in the body's defence against disease. White cells called *neutrophils*, for instance, swallow intruders. Others, called *lymphocytes*, help to identify intruders.

FUELLING THE BODY

Like a machine, your body needs a constant supply of fuel to grow and keep going, and materials to replace worn-out cells. These come from the air you breathe and the food you eat. They are delivered to every part of your body by the blood, which also carries away waste.

Breathing and blood If you ever stopped breathing, you would very rapidly die. Oxygen from the air is vital to the survival of every cell of the body. Just as fire burns only if there is plenty of oxygen, so cells need oxygen to break down the food they get from the blood. Without oxygen, they would die. Brain cells cannot live for more than a few minutes without oxygen – which is why the brain

can be damaged if the heart stops pumping blood.

When cells break down food, oxygen combines with carbon in the food to make carbon dioxide. Carbon dioxide is breathed out through your lungs.

Your lungs are like hollow trees, with hundreds of branching airways called *bronchioles*. Around the end of each are clustered little air sacs or *alveoli*. It is through the alveoli that oxygen gets into your body. Each is wrapped round with tiny blood vessels. Every time you breathe in, air enters the alveoli. Oxygen passes through their thin walls into the blood and is swept away to the rest of your body. At the same time, unwanted carbon dioxide passes from the blood into the alveoli and is breathed out.

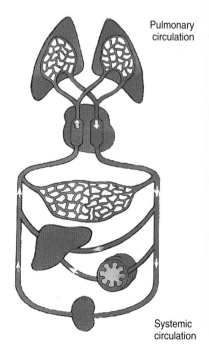

Pulmonary circulation

Systemic circulation

HEART AND BLOOD CIRCULATION

Blood is pumped continually round your body by the heart. It flows out from the heart through large blood vessels called *arteries* that branch into small *arterioles* and then tiny *capillaries*. It flows back to the heart through *venules* that join to form *veins*. Blood is redder in arteries than in veins because it is rich in oxygen.

There are, in fact, two systems of circulating blood in your body, not just one. Each starts and ends at the heart, which is actually two pumps. The left of the heart drives the *systemic circulation*, which carries oxygen-rich blood from the lungs round the body and back. The smaller right side drives the blood on through the lungs and back to your left heart. This is the *pulmonary circulation*.

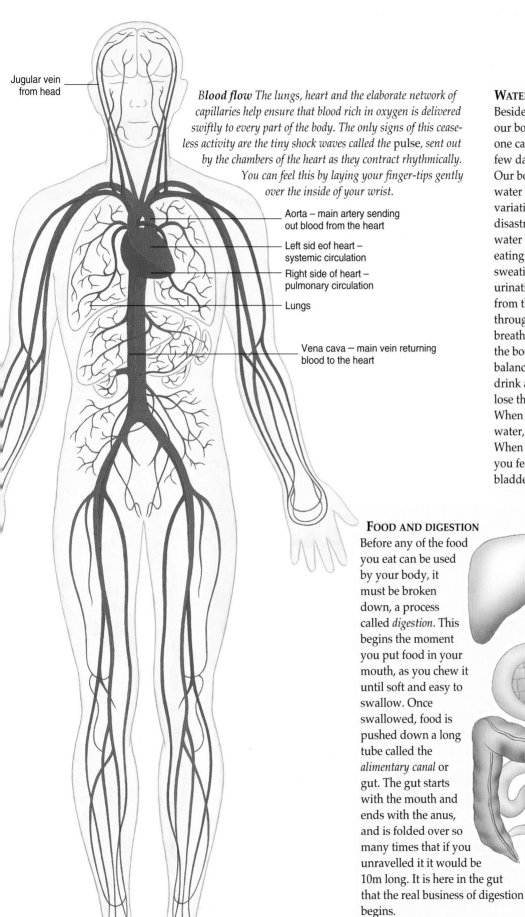

Jugular vein from head

Blood flow The lungs, heart and the elaborate network of capillaries help ensure that blood rich in oxygen is delivered swiftly to every part of the body. The only signs of this cease-less activity are the tiny shock waves called the pulse, *sent out by the chambers of the heart as they contract rhythmically. You can feel this by laying your finger-tips gently over the inside of your wrist.*

Aorta – main artery sending out blood from the heart

Left sid eof heart – systemic circulation

Right side of heart – pulmonary circulation

Lungs

Vena cava – main vein returning blood to the heart

WATER

Besides food and oxygen, our bodies need water; no one can last more than a few days without water. Our bodies are two-thirds water by weight, and a variation of over 5% is disastrous. The body gains water by drinking and eating. It loses it by sweating, breathing and urinating. Water gained from the cells and lost through sweating and breathing stays stable, so the body controls water by balancing the water you drink against the water you lose through urinating. When you need more water, you feel thirsty. When you need to urinate, you feel pressure in your bladder.

FOOD AND DIGESTION

Before any of the food you eat can be used by your body, it must be broken down, a process called *digestion*. This begins the moment you put food in your mouth, as you chew it until soft and easy to swallow. Once swallowed, food is pushed down a long tube called the *alimentary canal* or gut. The gut starts with the mouth and ends with the anus, and is folded over so many times that if you unravelled it it would be 10m long. It is here in the gut that the real business of digestion begins.

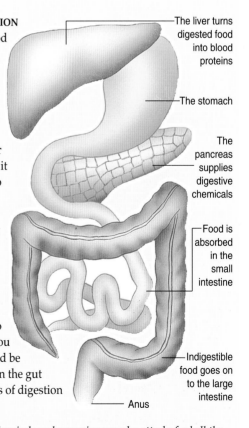

The liver turns digested food into blood proteins

The stomach

The pancreas supplies digestive chemicals

Food is absorbed in the small intestine

Indigestible food goes on to the large intestine

Anus

The gut A barrage of chemicals and squeezing muscles attacks food all the way through the gut. Eventually, it is ready to be absorbed through the gut walls and carried away to the rest of the body in the blood. Food that cannot be digested goes out through the anus.

MOVEMENT & SENSES

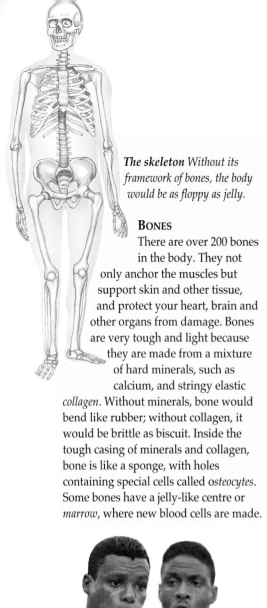

The skeleton Without its framework of bones, the body would be as floppy as jelly.

BONES

There are over 200 bones in the body. They not only anchor the muscles but support skin and other tissue, and protect your heart, brain and other organs from damage. Bones are very tough and light because they are made from a mixture of hard minerals, such as calcium, and stringy elastic *collagen*. Without minerals, bone would bend like rubber; without collagen, it would be brittle as biscuit. Inside the tough casing of minerals and collagen, bone is like a sponge, with holes containing special cells called o*steocytes*. Some bones have a jelly-like centre or *marrow*, where new blood cells are made.

Running, dancing, clapping, smiling and every other movement you make depend on muscles and bones. Muscles are bundles of fibres that tense and relax to move different parts of the body. Bones are the hard parts that anchor the muscles. Your senses supply the brain with a constant stream of information about your surroundings.

MUSCLES

There are two kinds of muscle in your body: muscles that you can control, called *voluntary* muscles, and muscles you cannot control, called *involuntary* muscles. You can control most *skeletal* muscles – that is, the muscles that move parts of your body. The muscles of your heart, and around the gut and blood vessels, work automatically.

Skeletal muscle owes its power to long, thin fibre-like cells, stretching from one end of the muscle to the other. Muscles are bundles of these stringy fibres bound together in a bag or sheath, and attached to bone at either end by tough cords called *tendons*. Some muscles contain just a few hundred fibres; others contain many thousands.

Every muscle fibre is made from thin strands called *myofibrils*. Under a microscope, the strands look striped, which is why this kind of muscle is called *striated* or striped. The stripes are actually alternating filaments of two substances called *actin* and *myosin*, and it is these that are the key to muscle power. At a signal from the brain, the myosin and actin filaments are drawn together, making the muscle shorter. As the muscle shortens, it pulls on the bone, making the movement.

Involuntary muscle is of two kinds: *cardiac* and *smooth*. Cardiac muscle is the muscle in the heart. It beats automatically, though its rate is adjusted by chemical and

HOW MUSCLES WORK

Muscles do everything from the twitching of an eyebrow to a jump in the air. The way they do it is simply by contracting – pulling together two points, such as two bones. Indeed, muscles can only contract, not make themselves longer. So each time a muscle contracts to make a movement, it must be pulled back to its original length by another muscle contracting. This is why many muscles are arranged in pairs – a *flexor* muscle to bend or flex a joint, and an *extensor* to straighten it out again. Not all muscles create movement; some have to contract just to hold something still. *Isotonic* contraction is when a muscle moves something; *isometric* contraction is when it simply holds something still.

Bending your arm In the upper arm, the biceps at the front is the flexor muscle that bends the arm; the triceps at the back is the extensor that straightens it.

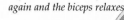

When your arm is straight, the triceps is constricted and feels hard, while the biceps is relaxed and feels soft.

When you want to bend your arm, your brain sends nerve signals to the biceps to contract. The biceps hardens and the triceps relaxes. When you straighten your arm, the triceps contracts again and the biceps relaxes.

HEARING

The flap of skin on the side of your head is only one part of the ear, called the *outer ear*, and simply funnels sound down a tube (the *ear canal*). Inside your head, in the *middle ear*, sounds hit a taut wall of skin called the *eardrum*, shaking it rapidly. As it shakes, it rattles three tiny bones or *ossicles*. Even further inside, in the *inner ear*, is a curly tube full of fluid called the *cochlea*. As the ossicles vibrate, they knock against this tube, making waves in the fluid. Minute hairs waggle in the waves, sending signals along nerves to the brain.

Middle ear
Stapes (Ossicle)
The oval window is the entrance to the inner ear
Cochlea
Outer ear
Ear canal
Eardrum
Malleus (Ossicle)
Incus (Ossicle)
Inner ear

The ear A child can hear sounds quieter than rustling leaves (10 decibels) and louder than a jet engine at close range (140 decibels). Very loud noises are painful.

nervous signals to match demand. Smooth muscle occurs in moving soft tissue inside your body, contracting blood vessels to control blood flow or rippling around the gut to push food through.

SENSES

There are five basic senses to tell you what is going on in the world around you: sight, hearing, touch, smell and taste.

Touch There are touch receptors all over the body. They react to four kinds of feeling – a light touch, steady pressure, heat and cold, and pain – and send a message to the brain via the nerves.

Smell seems to rely on a small patch of *olfactory* receptors inside the top of your nose. The olfactory receptors react to traces of different chemicals in the air. There are over five million of them and they need pick up only a few tiny molecules (page 150) of a substance for you to identify a smell.

Taste is a mixture of different sensations, including smell. Your tongue has an array of different taste receptors, which react to sweet, salty, bitter and sour tastes in food. Sweet detectors are commonest at the tip of the tongue, salty just behind on either side, sour and bitter further back.

DID YOU KNOW?
Walking puts a pressure of 3500 kg/cm² on the thigh bone.
All the muscles in your body could lift a heavy lorry if they all pulled together.
There are over 600 voluntary muscles.
With gentle exercise, the blood system can deliver fresh supplies of oxygen and glucose (sugar) in order to keep muscles going.
Anaerobic exercise means the muscle works so hard that it uses up oxygen faster than it can be supplied.
Aerobic exercise is not so strenuous, and supplies of oxygen can increase with the demand from the muscles.
The eye has 125 million rods and 7 million cones.

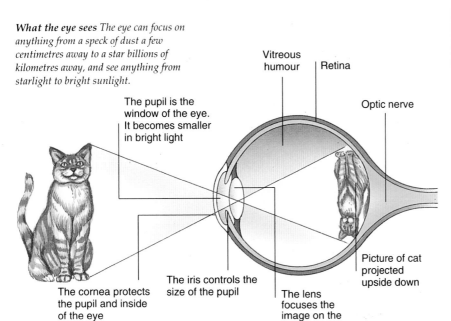

What the eye sees The eye can focus on anything from a speck of dust a few centimetres away to a star billions of kilometres away, and see anything from starlight to bright sunlight.

Vitreous humour
Retina
Optic nerve

The pupil is the window of the eye. It becomes smaller in bright light

Picture of cat projected upside down

The cornea protects the pupil and inside of the eye

The iris controls the size of the pupil

The lens focuses the image on the retina.

SIGHT

Your eyes are two tough little balls filled with a jelly-like substance called *vitreous humour*. Each eyeball is a bit like a video camera. At the front is a *lens* – the dark spot in the middle of each eye. This projects a picture on to the lining of the back of the eye, called the *retina*. The retina is made up of millions of light-sensitive cells called *rods* and *cones* which transmit the picture to the brain via the *optic nerve*. Rods can pick up even very dim light, but cannot tell the difference between colours. Cones distinguish colours, but are not so sensitive to light as rods, which is why we do not see colours well at night. There are three kinds of cone, one sensitive to red light, one to blue and one to green.

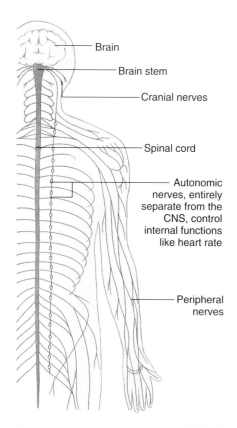

Brain
Brain stem
Cranial nerves
Spinal cord
Autonomic nerves, entirely separate from the CNS, control internal functions like heart rate
Peripheral nerves

BRAIN & NERVES

The human brain is an incredibly complicated network of specialized nerve cells. It produces all your thoughts and controls nearly all your actions by communicating with the rest of the body through the nervous system.

THE BRAIN

The human brain looks rather like a huge walnut, with a wrinkled surface split into two halves. An adult brain weighs about 1.5kg and consists of soft grey-coloured material. Its functions are very complex and provide humans with their intelligence and natural curiosity. There are more than one thousand million nerve cells or *neurones* in the brain, each linked to many others to form a complex network of connections.

Neurones are highly specialized cells. They depend upon other brain cells, called *Schwann cells*, for their supply of nutrients. Schwann cells also provide insulation between the neurones so that the signals can transmit correctly.

The brain requires a good supply of blood to provide the food and oxygen necessary to maintain its activity. If the blood supply is cut off for just a few seconds the person becomes unconscious – permanent damage will be caused if the blood supply is not quickly restored.

AREAS OF THE BRAIN

At first sight, all parts of the brain look much the same. However, closer examination shows that it is divided into many distinct areas. The layout of the brain reflects the way that it evolved – growing out from the *brain stem* at the top of the spinal cord. As the brain developed, its structure became more complex. The brain can be divided into two main parts, the *hind brain* and the *cerebrum*.

The hind brain Basic functions like breathing and heart beat are controlled by this part of the brain. These functions take place without the need to think about them. The *hypothalamus* is an important area of the hind brain. It functions as the body's clock, controlling everyday activities like hunger, thirst and sleeping. The *pituitary*

CENTRAL NERVOUS SYSTEM

The body's nervous system focuses on the *central nervous system* (CNS). This consists of the brain plus the *spinal cord*, which is the bundle of nerves running down the spine. From the central nervous system, tiny threads of nerves branch out all over the body. *Sensory nerves* feed back to the brain signals from the body's sense organs – touch, smell, taste, sight and hearing – telling you what is happening all around you. Then *motor nerves* carry instructions from the brain to prod the muscles into motion.

NERVE CELLS

Signals pass through nerve cells as impulses of electrical energy. Every neurone is made up of a cell body and long thread-like fibres. A nerve contains many nerve fibres, each with its own insulating sheath. Inside the main cell body of every neurone is a nucleus, which controls the activity of the cell. Nerve fibres end in a network of fine branches called *dendrites*, that make contact with dendrites from other cells to form a *synapse*. At each synapse there is a small gap, across which a chemical transmitter passes to take the signal to the next neurone.

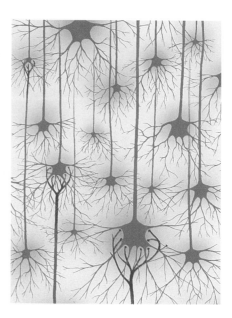

Growing links
Brain cells start dying off from the moment we're born – and are never replaced. But we have so many this does not usually matter. As we grow older and learn, the cells make more and more connections, opening up new pathways for messages through the brain. The picture shows part of the brain of a child at 3 months (far left) and the same part when the child was 24 months (near left).

MEMORY AND PERCEPTION

We remember things in three ways, each lasting a different time. *Iconic memory* is how we remember briefly things we see for a split second. We are not really aware of this memory. The shortest memory we are aware of is *short-term memory*. This stores things for five minutes or so. *Long-term memories* can be stored for days, months or even your entire life. The brain is very selective about what it remembers. Traumatic experiences, even if lasting only a second or so, are often remembered forever. But to transfer a telephone number from short to long-term memory you must rehearse it again and again. Some scientists believe short-term memory activates certain neural pathways while long-term memory involves creating entirely new pathways through the brain.

Young and old (right) *Everything we see is interpreted in the brain, but the brain can be fooled by ambiguous clues. In this picture, for instance, sometimes we see an old woman with only three teeth; at other times we see a young woman with her face turned away. The nose of the old woman becomes the young woman's chin and face; the old woman's eye becomes the young woman's ear.*

gland is located next to the hypothalamus. It controls the production of hormones throughout the body.

The cerebrum The cerebrum is split into two halves or *cerebral hemispheres*. The hemispheres have similar functions, although one (usually the left) is dominant. Communication between the hemispheres is achieved by inter-connecting nerves that form a structure called the *corpus callosum*. The more complex activities of the brain, such as memory, speech and conscious control of movement, go on in the cerebrum. This is where we think.

The wrinkled structure of the cerebral hemispheres increases the surface area to hold a greater number of neurones. Parts of the cerebrum have become specialized to control particular functions. For example, signals from the eyes go to the *occipital lobe*. Information from the ears goes to *Wernicke's area* in the *temporal lobes*. This area enables us to understand language and to make up our replies. Speech is controlled by another part of the brain known as *Broca's area* at the front of the cerebrum.

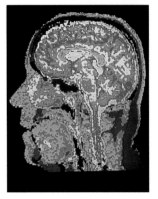

Brain scan This picture of the brain was taken with a special scanner called an MRI (magnetic resonance imaging) scanner. The image has been coloured to show differences in water content.

LOOKING INTO THE BRAIN

One way scientists can study living brains is with thermographs. These are photographs sensitive to heat that show where blood flow is increased – perhaps when an area becomes active.

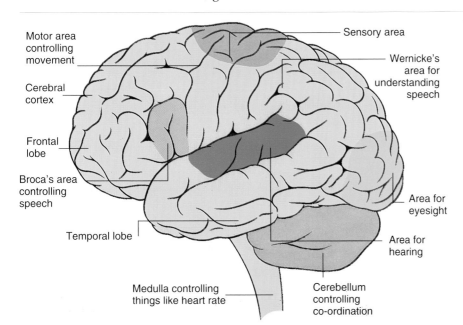

- Motor area controlling movement
- Cerebral cortex
- Frontal lobe
- Broca's area controlling speech
- Temporal lobe
- Medulla controlling things like heart rate
- Sensory area
- Wernicke's area for understanding speech
- Area for eyesight
- Area for hearing
- Cerebellum controlling co-ordination

THE MAP OF THE BRAIN

Throughout the brain there are various areas *associated* with different functions, such as walking or speaking. These areas become active whenever the associated function is going on. Scientists do not fully understand how this association works. Sometimes injury or disease can damage large areas of the brain, including these association areas, with little or no effect. Yet if certain tiny areas are damaged, the effect can be devastating. Moreover, there are large parts of the brain which seem to have no identifiable purpose at all. Some scientists believe these areas gradually come into use as we get older.

GROWING UP & PREGNANCY

Life begins when an egg is fertilized by a sperm. Development of the unborn child is possible because humans have very specialized reproductive systems. Babies require many years of development before they themselves are able to reproduce.

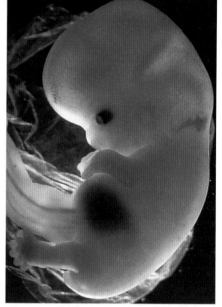

Photograph of a seven-week old human foetus in the mother's womb The foetus measures about 3cm long. Most features are formed, including arms, legs, toes and eyes.

PUBERTY

Puberty refers to the changes that take place in boys and girls to bring about sexual maturity. A biological clock, located inside the brain, decides when the body is ready for these changes to begin and then stimulates the release of chemical signals, called sex hormones, to cause the developments that turn boys into men and girls into women.

The sex hormones cause many changes: girls' periods start, and boys produce sperm. At this stage, boys and girls become more interested in each other. All of the developments that take place during puberty are known as secondary sexual characteristics.

Hormones are powerful chemicals that control or influence particular functions of the body. They are required in very small quantities and are carried in the blood from the glands that produce them to where they have an effect. During puberty, sex hormones cause major changes to take place in the appearance and functioning of the body.

The changes that occur at puberty are a normal part of growing up, although it is not unusual for young people to feel self-conscious and insecure as they develop adult characteristics. An adolescent may experience rapid changes in mood, along with feelings of insecurity and uncertainty, but these emotional happenings are all part of the process of growing up.

Adolescents should understand what is happening to their bodies. A girl has to get used to the physical changes to her body. When her *periods* start she experiences bleeding from her *vagina* for about five days each month. This bleeding is known as *menstruation* and is caused by changes in her *womb*. During a period she must wear either an external pad or an internal tampon to absorb the blood. Many girls do not feel any ill effects during menstruation, but it is not uncommon for some to experience painful cramps and emotional upsets. Boys often start the changes caused by puberty a

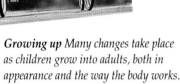

Growing up Many changes take place as children grow into adults, both in appearance and the way the body works.

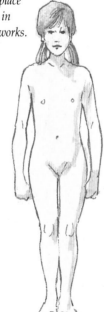

BECOMING A WOMAN

Hormones cause a girl's body to develop into that of a woman. Her hips grow wider to make room for a baby to develop in her womb and to be born through her vagina. Breasts form that, after pregnancy, produce milk to feed the baby. Her ovaries release one or more eggs during each menstrual cycle. She grows hair in her armpits and in the pubic region of her body.

BECOMING A MAN

Hormones cause a boy's body to develop into that of a man. His body becomes muscular and his penis and testes grow larger. His penis, when erect, can enter a woman's vagina to provide sperm from his testes to fertilize an egg. He grows hair on his face and body and his voice becomes deeper.

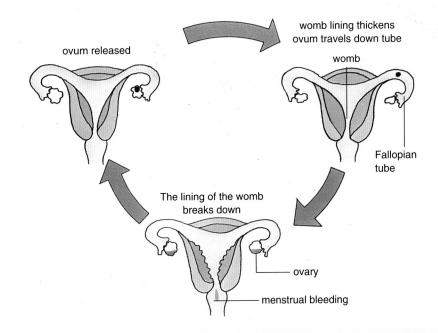

ovum released

womb lining thickens
ovum travels down tube

womb

Fallopian
tube

The lining of the womb
breaks down

ovary

menstrual bleeding

year or two later than girls. A boy's voice will become deeper, hair grows on his body and face and he will start to produce sperm. Adolescent girls and boys have a strong interest in their own sexual development and become more curious about the opposite sex.

Most boys and girls enjoy the process of growing up. They welcome the challenge of gradually becoming more independent and responsible for their own actions. Sexual attractions begin to develop and friendships form with members of the opposite sex.

Young people can reproduce at the end of puberty. The age when this occurs varies but it nearly always happens before boys and girls have left school. In many countries there are laws governing the age when a young person may consent to sexual intercourse. In Britain the minimum age is 16.

It is important to consider all of the possible consequences before engaging in sexual activity with another person. These risks include unwanted pregnancy and the possibility of contracting a sexually transmitted disease such as AIDS. Many adults use contraceptives to enjoy sexual intercourse without the woman becoming pregnant. Some types of contraceptive also reduce the chance of spreading sexually-transmitted diseases.

THE MENSTRUAL CYCLE

The menstrual cycle is a monthly sequence of changes that prepares the female body for conception and pregnancy. This cycle repeats itself about every 28 days until either conception occurs or the child-bearing years end with the *menopause* at about the age of fifty.

Eggs are made and stored in the ovaries of a woman. About every four weeks an egg, sometimes called an *ovum*, matures and moves from the ovary where it was stored, down a *Fallopian tube* to the *womb*. This process is under hormonal control. The lining of the womb is stimulated to produce a thick lining of mucus and blood ready to receive and feed a fertilized egg. If the ovum is not fertilized, the lining of the womb breaks down and the blood flows

The Human Menstrual cycle The diagram above shows the stages of the menstrual cycle. The cycle starts when a girl reaches puberty and continues until she is about fifty years old.

from the body through the *vagina*. This menstrual bleeding, or period, goes on for several days. When the period starts, the hormonal cycle begins again with the development of another ovum.

If the egg is fertilized, the lining of the womb is retained and develops into a special organ called the *placenta*. The placenta allows the exchange of oxygen, food and waste products between the developing baby and its mother. Hormones are produced by the placenta which suppress the normal hormonal cycle and prevent further ovulation and menstruation during pregnancy.

Sexual intercourse in cross-section

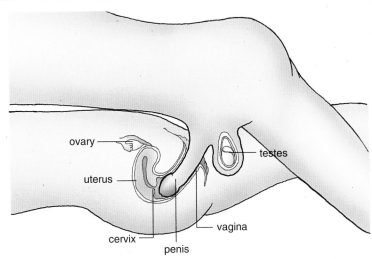

ovary

uterus

cervix

penis

vagina

testes

SEXUAL INTERCOURSE AND PREGNANCY

Fertilization takes place in the Fallopian tubes that connect the ovaries to the womb. For sperms to get to the Fallopian tube, sexual intercourse must take place. The man's penis becomes stiff so that he can insert it into the woman's vagina. The climax of sexual inter-course occurs when semen, a sticky fluid containing sperms, is ejaculated into the vagina. The release of semen is a pleasurable feeling called an orgasm.

The sperms swim into the womb and up the Fallopian tubes. Fertilization occurs if the sperms meet an egg. Although hundreds of millions of sperms are released in an ejaculation, only one is required to fertilize an egg. After fertilization, the egg divides into a ball of cells and passes into the womb, where it continues to develop into a baby.

ANIMALS

Animals are not just furry creatures like cats and hamsters, but all the world's many living creatures. There may be 30 million different kinds altogether, ranging from microscopic parasites that live in people's blood to whales more than 30m long.

COLOURS AND MARKINGS

Animal colourings and markings serve many purposes. Sometimes they attract a mate, like the striking plumage of many male birds. Sometimes they warn that the animal is poisonous, like the bright red of arrow-poison frogs. Sometimes they match the animal's surroundings to hide it from predators – or from its prey. This is called *camouflage*. Ground-nesting birds like the nightjar are mottled brown and are hard for hunters to spot among fallen leaves. Tigers are striped like dry grass so their prey cannot see them until too late. Chameleons can even change their colour to match their backgrounds.

THE ANIMAL KINGDOM

All the world's living things are divided into two huge kingdoms: the animal kingdom and the plant kingdom. What makes plants and animals different is that while plants can make their own food (from sunlight, page 57), animals must find theirs – which means most animals have to move about.

Animals are creatures that are born, grow up and die. They move about, eat and breed and can sense the world around them in a variety of ways – by sight, hearing, touch, smell and taste.

ANIMAL HABITATS

Animals live in an enormous range of places. Each place or *habitat* has its own special combination of animals.

The seas are teeming with animal life, from tiny sea anemones that cling to seashore rocks to worms that live in the black ocean depths where daylight never penetrates. Rivers, streams and lakes have their own animal life too, including many fish and insects.

Yet there is an even richer variety on land. The rainforests of the tropics are swarming with animal

ANIMAL SENSES

Sea creatures rely on smell and taste to tell them of food and danger, detecting tiny particles drifting in the water. Eyesight is less important because water is often cloudy. A sense of balance is important, too, and many creatures have simple balance organs called *statocysts*.

For animals that live on land or in the air, however, sight is usually the most important sense. Animals that hunt – especially birds of prey – often have very sharp eyesight so that they can spot victims far away. Hearing and smell are important, too, and bats 'see' with the echo of their high-pitched squeaks.

ANIMALS WITHOUT BACKBONES

The animal kingdom is divided into animals that have backbones, called *vertebrates*, and those that do not, called *invertebrates*. Invertebrates are usually small creatures like insects – although giant squids can grow to 20m. Some have soft bodies; others are protected by hard shells. Some have a hard flexible casing called an *exoskeleton*.

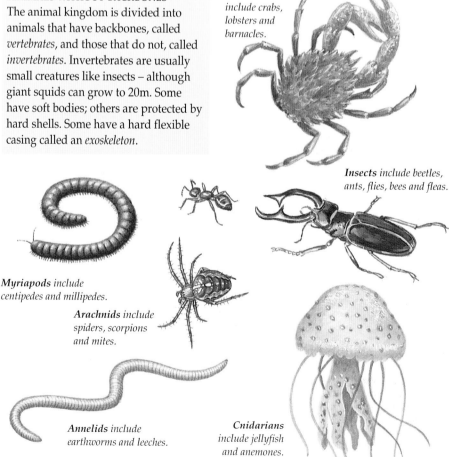

Crustaceans *include crabs, lobsters and barnacles.*

Insects *include beetles, ants, flies, bees and fleas.*

Myriapods *include centipedes and millipedes.*

Arachnids *include spiders, scorpions and mites.*

Annelids *include earthworms and leeches.*

Cnidarians *include jellyfish and anemones.*

life, and thousands of different species or kinds of insects, birds, reptiles, amphibians, mammals and other creatures can be found in just a small area. Open forests and grasslands are rich in animal life too. But animals thrive even in more extreme environments. Yaks survive over 6000m up in the bitter cold of the Himalayan mountains. Insects, spiders and scorpions flourish even in the hottest deserts.

The air, too, has its own abundant and varied *fauna* (animal life) – including birds, insects and even some mammals. Sadly, though, human activity has begun to severely reduce the habitats available to animals. As a result, many creatures that were once common are now very rare, or even *extinct* (have died out completely). Each year, many species of animal disappear forever.

CREATING OFFSPRING

An important part of any animal's life is creating offspring. With most animals there are both males and females, and they have young only when male and female come together. This is called *sexual reproduction*.

For a young animal to be born, a sex cell or *sperm* from the male must join with an egg from the female. This usually involves a male and a female animal mating. But there are other ways. Animals such as marine worms just drop eggs and sperm in the water for them to meet by chance.

A few animals have neither males nor females and reproduce *asexually*. Often a part of the parent animal will simply break off and develop into a new creature. This process is called *budding*. Tiny freshwater creatures called hydra reproduce like this. So do flatworms.

FINDING A MATE
Humans are among the few animals that mate at any time of year; most animals are ready to mate only in spring. Warmer spring weather triggers the production of sperm in males and eggs in females. So in spring, many animals behave in certain ways to try and attract the right mate. This is called courtship.

Courtship displays, especially those of birds, can be elaborate and spectacular. The male capercaillie (a Scottish bird a little like a turkey) gives a raucous cry that can be heard for miles around. Great crested grebes perform a dramatic dance in the water, in which male and female present water plants to each other.

There are other ways to attract mates besides singing and dancing. Many male animals are brighty coloured. Male peacocks, for instance, have brilliantly coloured fan-shaped tails; the peahen's tail is small and brown. Some animals attract mates with scent. Female gypsy moths have a scent that a male can smell 11km away.

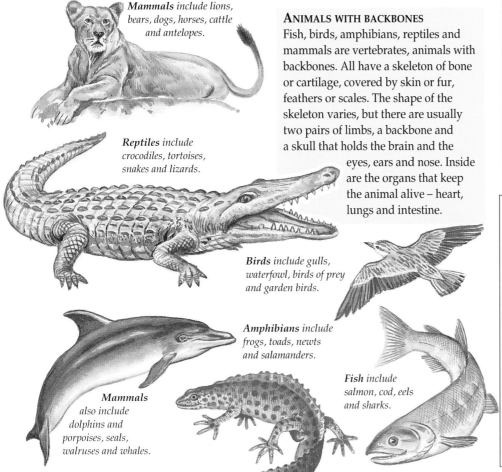

Mammals *include lions, bears, dogs, horses, cattle and antelopes.*

Reptiles *include crocodiles, tortoises, snakes and lizards.*

ANIMALS WITH BACKBONES
Fish, birds, amphibians, reptiles and mammals are vertebrates, animals with backbones. All have a skeleton of bone or cartilage, covered by skin or fur, feathers or scales. The shape of the skeleton varies, but there are usually two pairs of limbs, a backbone and a skull that holds the brain and the eyes, ears and nose. Inside are the organs that keep the animal alive – heart, lungs and intestine.

Birds *include gulls, waterfowl, birds of prey and garden birds.*

Amphibians *include frogs, toads, newts and salamanders.*

Fish *include salmon, cod, eels and sharks.*

Mammals *also include dolphins and porpoises, seals, walruses and whales.*

DID YOU KNOW?
Male bower birds line their bower (nest) with blue shells and flowers and paint it blue with berry juice to attract a mate.
Male monitor lizards have harmless wrestling matches to win a female.
Arctic beetles and Alaskan flies can survive temperatures of minus 60°C.
Owls can hear sounds ten times softer than any human can hear.
Cats' eyes absorb 50% more light than humans', so they see well in the dark.
The Arctic fox turns white in winter to camouflage itself against the snow.
Flatfish can change their colour and marks to match the seabed in seconds.

Wild boar piglets suckle milk from their mother. The piglets have a special stripey camouflage during their early life.

MAMMALS

Mammals come in all shapes and sizes, and live in an enormous variety of different ways. Some live mainly on land; others spend all their lives in water. Some run in the open; others scurry through the undergrowth, climb high in the trees or burrow deep underground. There are mammals in the frozen wastes of the Arctic and in steamy tropical jungles. They range in size from the tiny Etruscan shrew, no bigger than your little finger, to the blue whale – as big as a jumbo jet.

MOTHER'S MILK

Mammals are the only animals to feed their young on milk. It is the perfect food for young mammals – nourishing and warm, and full of special substances that help protect baby animals from disease.

When a mammal becomes pregnant, she starts to make milk at teats on her chest, around her groin or along the underside of her body. When they are born, the babies suck from the teats until they are able to eat solid foods. The number of teats depends partly on the number of babies that may be born at once. Humans and other primates have just two teats on the chest. Wild hogs and pigs, which can have twelve or more babies in a single litter, have seven or more pairs of teats under their bodies. Duck-billed platypuses and other monotremes have no teats, and the milk oozes on to hairs which the young suck.

WARM BLOOD

Mammals can live in so many different ways and places because they are *endothermic* (warm-blooded). This means their bodies are always at just the right temperature for body processes to work well. *Ectothermic* (cold-blooded) creatures such as reptiles thrive only if the weather is warm enough; mammals can get on in all kinds of weather. So mammals such as the puma, an American big cat, can happily live everywhere from the tropical forests of Peru to the snowy plains of Patagonia.

The temperature of our bodies is always within a degree or so of 36.9°C, except when we are ill, and most mammals keep their body at much the same temperature. The blood temperature of a three-toed sloth, though, can vary between 24.4°C and 37.6°C.

But to keep as warm as this, mammals have to eat frequently. This is why mammals are often less able to survive in deserts than reptiles, which can live on much less food. To get through the winter, when food is scarce, some mammals go into a deep sleep called *hibernation*, and their body temperature drops dramatically.

BEING BORN

All mammals begin life as an egg inside their mother's body, but only a few mammals, known as *monotremes* – such as the Australian duck-billed platypus – actually lay eggs like a bird. Many Australian mammals, such as kangaroos, wallabies, koalas and opossums, are *marsupials*. This means they have a pouch on their tummy for their young. Marsupials' babies are very tiny indeed when they are born and cannot survive in the open – a

---

DID YOU KNOW?

A single pair of rabbits could produce a family of 33 million offspring in 3 years if all the young survived to breed.
The aye-aye lemur of Madagascar has fingers like toothpicks which it uses to pick insects out of dead wood.
Bushbabies can leap up to 6m between trees.
Macaque monkeys in northern Japan have learned to keep warm in winter by bathing in hot volcanic springs.
Big ears such as those of elephants and jack rabbits help keep them cool.
Red kangaroos can jump up to 9m.

KEEPING WARM, KEEPING COOL

Biological mechanisms keep mammals' bodies at just the right temperature automatically – but mammals must protect themselves from extremes of heat and cold. Thick fur and layers of fat or blubber act like a coat to *insulate* mammals from the cold, and keep them warm in winter. When it is very cold, most mammals curl up, seek shelter or shiver to generate warmth in their muscles. Humans keep cool by sweating, but furry animals cannot do this. Instead, they lose heat by hanging out their tongues and panting.

Polar bears survive the bitter cold of the Arctic winter because they are kept warm by their thick fur coats, and the layer of fat beneath.

baby kangaroo or 'joey' is barely 2.5cm long, smaller than your thumb. After it is born, a baby marsupial crawls into its mother's pouch and stays there until it is big enough to survive in the open air.

Most mammals, however, including dogs, pigs and elephants, stay inside their mother's body until they are fully developed, nourished by food carried in the mother's blood. They are called *placental* mammals, because the young are fed inside the womb through a special organ called a *placenta*, which provides all the food they need to grow.

Pregnancy All mammals produce babies sexually, which means the mother becomes pregnant only after a male and a female have mated. The time between mating and birth, called the *gestation period*, varies from mammal to mammal. The larger the animal, the longer gestation tends to be and the fewer babies are born. Rabbits are born just one month after mating, and seven or eight baby rabbits may be born at once. In giraffes, the mother gives birth to a single baby after 17 months pregnancy. In African elephants, pregnancy lasts 22 months. Humans and other primates come halfway between rabbits and elephants, with a gestation period of nine months or so.

Dogs pant to keep cool, lolling their tongues so that moisture from their breath evaporates from the surface and draws heat from the blood.

PRIMATES

Humans, apes, monkeys, lemurs and tree-shrews all belong to a group of mammals called *primates*. Most are adapted to living in trees and have hands with fingers and feet with toes for gripping branches. Apes, including chimpanzees and gorillas, are our closest relatives in the animal world. Their bodies are a similar shape, and, like us, they have long arms and fingers and toes for gripping. Some apes are very clever and use tools such as sticks and stones to help get food. Monkeys such as baboons and marmosets are similar to apes but usually have a tail to help them balance as they swing through the trees. Some, like woolly monkeys, have a *prehensile* tail which they can use for gripping.

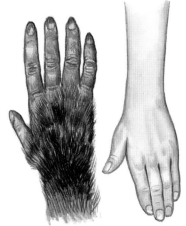

Handy creatures Primates such as chimpanzees (left) and humans (right) have hands with four fingers and a thumb.

Gorillas are the biggest of all apes, weighing up to 225kg and standing up to 2m tall. But they are largely gentle and eat only leaves and shoots. Mountain gorillas are very rare and live only in scattered areas throughout central Africa.

Chimpanzees remind us of ourselves with their sense of fun and expressive faces. They live in African forest and grassland. Although they sleep in crude nests in the trees, they spend most of their lives on the ground, walking on all fours.

Baboons live on the ground and run on all fours like a dog. They have powerful dog-like jaws and fang-like teeth.

25

MAMMALS SMALL & LARGE

The biggest land mammals of all are the elephants, rhinoceroses and hippopotamuses of tropical Africa and Asia. Yet there are very few of them. The most numerous mammals tend to be the smallest, including mice, rats and other rodents, and rabbits and hares. There are more house mice in the world than any other single mammal, except humans.

RABBITS AND HARES

Rabbits and hares are found all over the world, and owe some of their success to their huge families. A female rabbit may have 20 young in a year. Hares usually live above ground, escaping enemies through sheer speed – the European brown hare can run at 60km/h – and they are born above ground, usually in long grass, with their eyes open and their body covered in fur, ready to face the dangers of the world. Rabbits, however, protect themselves by digging elaborate burrows, and baby rabbits are born blind and naked but safe below ground.

SHREWS

Shrews are very tiny creatures that look rather like mice, but they have long snouts and very short legs. The Etruscan shrew is one of the smallest mammals in the world, barely longer than your little finger. Shrews are very active, fidgety creatures that eat up to three times their own weight in 24 hours. Some are so nervous that a loud thunderclap can make them die of fright. All the same, if shrews meet each other when out hunting, they let out a shrill squeal and leap into a violent wrestling match.

When they are young, some shrews follow their mothers in a train, each hanging on with its teeth to the rump of its brother or sister in front.

RODENTS

There are more species of rodent in the world than all other mammals put together. Altogether, there are some 1800 kinds. What makes them different from other small mammals is their strong teeth. All rodents have two pairs of razor-sharp front teeth for gnawing nuts and berries and a set of ridged teeth in their cheeks for chewing. Like fingernails, the pairs of front teeth, called *incisors*, grow all the time. Only constant gnawing keeps them the same length.

There are three main kinds of rodent: rats and mice; squirrels and beavers; porcupines and guinea pigs.

Squirrels and beavers Squirrels are a little like mice and rats, but have a big bushy tail and live in trees. They are well known for their habit of hoarding nuts in autumn to provide a food store for the winter. In Asia there are giant flying squirrels that can glide for over 450m between tree tops.

Beavers are among the biggest of rodents. They live in water, and gnaw through small trees to provide wood to dam streams. In the pond behind the dam, they build their homes, called *lodges*.

Porcupines and guinea pigs In the Americas, porcupines are small creatures that live in trees. They have sharp claws and are covered in short, spiny quills which act as a defence against predators. In the rest of the world, porcupines are larger creatures that live in underground runs and have long quills.

Guinea pigs are furry South American rodents very popular as pets. Wild guinea pigs live in burrows on the fringes of forests, and hunt at night. They are much more lively than domestic guinea pigs. Capybaras are like guinea pigs, but they are the biggest of all rodents, weighing up to 50kg. They live in large groups on river banks and plunge into the water when predators such as jaguars approach.

RATS AND MICE

Rats and mice are by far the most common of all rodents, and no other mammal has adapted so well to living alongside humans. There is barely a city in the world without its rats and mice. In fact, they are generally thought of as pests, for they eat crops and damage buildings with their gnawing and tunnelling. Brown rats will gnaw even through metal to get at food. Worse still, rats carry diseases such as typhus and bubonic plague.

Rats can reach 50cm from nose to tail.

Mice and rats have long thin tails, pointed noses, whiskers and beady black eyes.

ELEPHANTS

Elephants are the largest of all land mammals, growing to nearly 4m tall and often weighing over 7000kg. They have a remarkable trunk, like a very long nose, called a *proboscis*, and this is useful for all kinds of tasks. An elephant can use its trunk to grasp branches, leaves, fruit and shoots and put food in its mouth. It can also suck up water to squirt into its mouth to drink or over its body to keep cool. An elephant can even use its trunk as a snorkel when swimming across deep rivers.

Elephants also have huge ears which they stretch out to keep cool. The ears provide a large surface for body heat to escape from. Unfortunately, elephants' great ivory tusks are so valuable that hunters have killed them in huge numbers. There are now less than half a million elephants altogether in Africa.

There are two kinds of elephant: African and Asian (Indian). The picture above shows a family of African elephants. African elephants are noticeably larger than Asian elephants and their ears and tusks are larger, too. The African elephant also has two 'fingers' on the tip of its trunk to help it pick up objects; the Asian elephant has only one.

RHINOS AND HIPPOS

Rhinoceroses are big, tough-skinned animals that live in Africa and southern Asia. Right in the middle of their heads, they have a horn or two made of compacted hair. Black and white African rhinos and the smaller Sumatran rhino have two horns each; Indian and Javan rhinos have just one. Rhino horn is believed by some people to have magical properties. As a result, thousands of rhinos have been slaughtered for their horns and they are now in danger of becoming extinct.

Hippopotamuses are huge, pig-like creatures that live in Africa. They have enormous heads and the biggest mouths of any land mammal. When a hippo yawns, it opens its mouth wide enough to swallow a sheep, but it eats only grass. Hippos spend their days wallowing in rivers or swamps, and usually feed only at night. A hippo's eyes, ears and nose are all on the top of its head, so they remain above water even when the rest of the body is completely submerged.

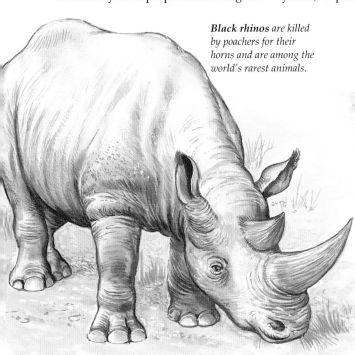

Black rhinos are killed by poachers for their horns and are among the world's rarest animals.

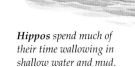

Hippos spend much of their time wallowing in shallow water and mud.

DID YOU KNOW?
The Indian elephant can live to be over 70 years old.
A white rhino's horn can grow to over 1.5m long.
Elephant tusks can grow to almost 3.5m long.

MAMMALS IN ALL PLACES

Mammals are very adaptable creatures, but they each have their own preferred habitat, and every major habitat, from deep oceans to arid deserts, has its own particular range of mammals.

MAMMALS OF THE AIR

Birds are not the only creatures that can fly. Bats can fly, too, but their wings are leathery skin rather than feathers. During the day, bats sleep, hanging upside down. At night they fly off in search of food, finding their way in the dark by emitting a series of high-pitched clicks. The way these sounds bounce back off insects, rocks and other obstacles helps the bats locate exactly where they are. Bats are the only mammals that can really fly, but flying squirrels and flying lemurs can glide huge distances from tree to tree.

WHERE MAMMALS LIVE

Which mammals live where depends on a variety of factors, including the range of food to be found, the easiest way to move about and the shelter available. But the two most important influences are usually climate and plant life.

Scientists divide the world into five major regions, each of which has its own particular range of animals. The regions nearly coincide with the world's major land masses. In the northern half of the world is the Holarctic region, which includes all of northern Asia and Europe and North America. The Neotropical region covers Central and South America. The Ethiopian region covers southern Arabia and all but the very northern edge of Africa. The Oriental region includes India, China and South East Asia. The Australasian region includes Australia, New Guinea, New Zealand and southern Indonesia.

Within these regions, different species of mammal have slowly evolved to suit a particular climate or range of plant life. So the tropical grasslands in the Ethiopian region of Africa, for instance, contain a different range of mammals to those in Neotropical South America. Large creatures such as antelopes and giraffes (see below) are common on the African grasslands. The mammals of the South American grasslands, such as the pampas deer and a rodent called the capybara, are much smaller. Similarly, African grassland hunters include lions and leopards; those in America are tiny pampas cats, foxes and skunks.

SAVANNA MAMMALS

The tropical grasslands or *savanna* of Africa are among the world's most spectacular wildlife habitats. Vast herds of grass-eating animals can be seen here, including zebras, buffaloes and many kinds of antelope, such as gazelles, impala, hartebeest and wildebeest. They are hunted by lions, cheetahs and leopards. There are bigger mammals, too, such as hippos, rhinos, elephants and giraffes – not to mention the many birds, including ostriches.

Giraffes' long necks enable them to reach leaves high up in trees.

Impala spend most of their life grazing, but can leap and run very fast to escape lions.

Zebras' stripey markings make them much harder for predators to spot.

Lions find plenty of prey among the grass-eaters.

MAMMALS OF THE SEA

Many mammals live in the sea. Seals, walruses and sea cows have fur and *blubber*, a thick layer of fat, to keep them warm. Whales, dolphins and porpoises have only blubber.

Whales, dolphins and porpoises are together known as *cetaceans*. Many are among the most intelligent and gentle of all creatures. They can stay under water for some time, but cannot breathe there and must come up for air every now and then. Some whales, such as the sperm whale and the orca, or killer whale, have teeth. Others, such as the humpback whale, have no teeth. Instead they have special sieves in their mouth called *baleens* and feed by straining small prawn-like creatures called krill through them.

Seals, sea lions and walruses are strong, agile swimmers but, unlike cetaceans, they can live on land. Once ashore they tend to waddle around awkwardly. In spring and summer, thousands of seals crowd together in vast colonies to breed.

Dolphins are exceptionally friendly, playful and intelligent creatures. They are believed to talk to each other by an elaborate language of clicking sounds.

Seals have a streamlined shape which enables them to swim very fast. But on land, where they breed, they are very slow. Most seals eat fish, squid and krill, but the leopard seal will eat penguins and other seals.

Walruses live on beaches near shallow waters at the edge of the polar ice in the Arctic. They live mainly on shellfish. Adult male (bull) walruses can weigh up to 1400kg.

Killer whales and other toothed whales are fearsome hunters, feeding on seals, porpoises and penguins, as well as fish. They will even attack young or injured blue whales, the biggest creatures that ever lived.

DESERT MAMMALS

Deserts are hard places for mammals to live. They are very dry and often very hot too. But there are mammals well-adapted to these conditions. The addax – a large antelope of the Sahara desert – gets all its water from its food, so never needs to drink. Kangaroo rats conserve water by eating their own droppings. Lack of shelter can also be a problem for desert mammals, especially as deserts can swing from scorching days to cold nights. Some mammals, like naked mole rats, live underground all the time. Gundis, African creatures like guinea pigs, hide among rocks during the day, coming out in the morning and evening.

Lizards survive in the desert by sheltering during the heat of the day and expending little energy.

Camels can store enough food and fluids for days in the humps of fat on their backs. They also have huge stomachs for taking in lots of grass and water when available. There are two kinds of camel: one-humped dromedaries or Arabian camels; and two-humped, shaggy Bactrian camels.

The fennec fox survives in the north African desert by resting in a burrow by day and hunting only at night. Its large ears help to keep it cool by radiating heat.

FOOD CHAINS

All animals depend on other living things for food, and each forms part of an endless chain, with each link feeding on another. In one chain, a caterpillar eats a leaf, a bird eats the caterpillar, a fox eats the bird, then when the fox dies, bacteria help decompose its body into substances that will be taken up by plants. If a link is lost, the effects may be felt throughout the chain. So, if the plants on which the caterpillar feeds are destroyed, not only the caterpillar is threatened but the bird and fox too.

MAMMALS & FOOD

Mammals depend on other living things for their food, some eating mainly plants, some eating mainly animals. Mammals that usually eat only plants are called *herbivores*. Those that eat mostly animals – that is, meat – are called c*arnivores*. *Omnivores* eat both plants and animals. *Insectivores* eat insects.

HERBIVORES

Some herbivorous mammals are very choosy. The koala bear, for instance, eats only the leaves of 12 kinds of eucalyptus. Others will eat almost any plant if they have to. Herbivorous mammals either *graze*, eating mainly grasses, or *browse*, eating mainly leaves, bark and buds of bushes and trees.

The most common herbivores are the *ungulates*, including horses, rhinos, tapirs and *artiodactyls* (see below). Ungulates are large grazing mammals with hooves and long legs – perfect for running across grasslands to escape hunting animals. The hooves enable them to run very fast on the tips of their toes, without their heels touching the ground.

CARNIVORES & INSECTIVORES

Some meat-eating animals, such as hyenas, eat *carrion* (meat left by others), but most are hunters. They usually have keen senses to find their prey, strong and agile bodies to catch it and sharp teeth and claws to kill it. Meat is very nourishing compared to vegetation, so while herbivores tend to eat all the time, carnivores can usually rest a while after a meal – and save their energy for hunting their next victim.

Most carnivores are either a kind of dog or a kind of cat. The dogs include wolves, jackals and coyotes. Bears, too, are similar to dogs, but they tend to be omnivores rather than carnivores.

Insectivores are animals that eat

DID YOU KNOW?

Pygmy shrews lose body heat so rapidly because of their small size that they must eat up to three times their own weight in food every day.

The Australian numbat has 52 teeth, more than any other mammal – yet, strangely enough, it has no need of them, for it eats by licking up termites and swallowing them whole.

Springbok antelopes once roamed the plains of southern Africa in herds 150km long and 100 million strong.

The okapi of Zaire is the giraffe's only living relative. Its tongue is so long that it can lick its own eyes clean.

Elephants eat more than a quarter of a tonne of plant food every day.

Vampire bats do suck blood. Usually they feed on cattle, but they have been known to attack humans, where they bite the big toe.

Deer are browsers, feeding mainly on leaves. Like cows, they are ruminants – that is, they chew the cud.

ARTIODACTYLS

Unlike horses, rhinos and tapirs, artiodactyls have an even number of toes. Pigs, hippos, camels, and cows are artiodactyls. All but pigs and hippos 'chew the cud', like cows. This means they chew food again after first partially digesting it in a special stomach.

Buffaloes belong to a large family of artiodactyls called bovids, which includes cows and antelopes. Male bovids have big horns which they sometimes use to defend themselves.

Brown bears, *including grizzly bears, are found all across northern Europe and Asia and in north west America.*

insects, although most eat other small animals too, but they are not really hunters like the big cats. They are usually fairly small creatures with pointed snouts and sharp teeth, like shrews, hedgehogs and moles.

OMNIVORES

Most mammals eat both plants and animals from time to time. Bears – except for polar bears – will eat almost anything. But only primates (page 25), including humans, are truly omnivorous.

ENDANGERED WILDLIFE

Sabre-toothed cats, woolly mammoths and woolly rhinos (page 109) are just some of the many kinds of mammals that have become extinct. But ecologists now feel that the effects of human activity may be driving many more to extinction. They are convinced that a few species of mammal are dying out each year already. But what they fear more is that as the plants on which they are dependent disappear, so more and more species of mammals will face extinction in the near future. The plight of giant pandas is already well known. Pandas live in three small mountain forest areas in western China and there may be less than 500 left. The bamboo plant which they eat flowers only once every 30 years. There is now so little bamboo that if it fails to flower at the right time, the pandas will be left without a source of food. The koala bears of Australia, too, were once threatened with extinction – not only because of disease and because they were hunted for their fur but because many of the eucalyptus trees they eat have been cut down. Both the trees and koalas are now strictly protected and numbers are picking up again.

Koalas look like bears but they are marsupials, carrying their young in a pouch.

The giant pandas *of China have a special pad on their front paws, called a sixth finger, for holding bamboo stems. The bamboo shoots they eat are not very nutritious, so pandas have to spend 10-12 hours a day feeding.*

BIG CATS

Lions, tigers, cheetahs, leopards and pumas are all kinds of cat, known as big cats. They are found all over the world, except in Australasia. All are deadly hunters, slinking quietly up on their prey, then pouncing or pursuing it. Their sharp claws inflict terrible wounds on the victim – as do their powerful jaws and razor-sharp *fangs* (teeth). Most big cats hunt on their own, except for lions, which live in groups called *prides*. The lionesses (female lions) do most of the hunting, and often hunt together for antelopes, zebras and even young giraffes.

Male lions *are easily recognizable by their huge manes. There is usually just one adult male in each pride, and he always eats before the lionesses and the cubs. When a young male lion grows up he has to fight the older male – and the loser will leave the pride.*

Cheetahs *are the fastest mammals, able to run at 100km/h.*

BIRDS

From soaring eagles to swooping swifts, most birds are completely at home in the air, where they can fly around and glide as easily as fish swim in the sea. But what makes them different from every other creature is their unique coat of feathers. Not all birds are able to fly, but they all have feathers.

Nestlings Newly hatched chicks are very vulnerable and must rely on their parents to keep them warm, to protect them from predators and to feed them. The parents of most insect-eating birds have to make as many as 25 trips every hour to gather food. Some birds, such as Great tits, may give their young more than 400 meals each day!

Most young birds grow very quickly indeed. A young robin weighs about two grams when it hatches, but within about eleven days it is more or less fully grown.

FEATHERS

Feathers not only keep a bird warm, but also enable all but a few to fly. Feathers are very light, yet are linked together with hooks called *barbs* to make wings strong enough to lift the bird into the air. Wrens have about 1000 feathers; a swan has over 20,000.

A bird's feathers are usually set in rows all over its body. On the wings there are two rows of *flight feathers*: large *primary* feathers at the tips and smaller *secondary* feathers along the rear edge. On top (above and below the wing) are rows of smaller *coverts* and even smaller *contour* feathers.

Every kind of bird has its own particular pattern and colour of feathers, called its *plumage*, and this is often the easiest way of identifying a bird. Some birds, like the wren, have plain brown plumage to make them less easy for predators to spot. Others, like parrots and peacocks, have brilliant, shimmering colours.

TOWN AND GARDEN BIRDS

Many of the small birds you see in cities once lived in fields and woodland. As human activity reduces their natural *habitats* (home areas), many have adapted to life in towns and gardens.

A few birds of prey – the kestrel, black kite, tawny owl and great horned owl – have adapted well to city life. But most city birds belong to the huge group called *passerines* or perching birds. There are over 5000 different passerines, but all are quite small and have a foot with three front toes and one hind toe – ideal for perching. Most build nests, from the plain, cup-shaped nests of thrushes and blackbirds to the more elaborate nest of the long-tailed tit.

Feral pigeons, found in nearly every park and city square, are descended from the wild rock dove.

Magpies are notorious thieves, stealing jewellery and other shiny objects which they hide or bury.

Robins are among the most familiar of all garden birds, with their bright red breasts.

Sparrows find warm nesting sites in old buildings. Their strong bills are good for cracking seeds.

Starlings feed by day in the countryside, and swoop into cities at dusk to roost (sleep) on ledges of high buildings.

Wrens may be tiny but they are very energetic - easily identified by the way they bob here and there looking for insects.

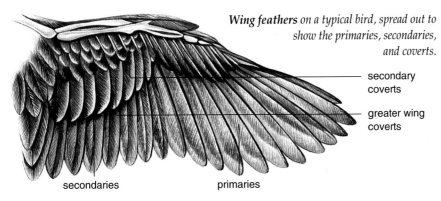

Wing feathers on a typical bird, spread out to show the primaries, secondaries, and coverts.

secondary coverts

greater wing coverts

secondaries   primaries

BEAKS AND BILLS

Instead of a mouth, birds have a hard beak or bill. Beaks are adapted for many tasks – some for building nests, some for breaking nuts, some for catching insects, some for extracting worms from deep mud. The shape depends largely on the kind of food the bird eats. Birds of prey have hooked bills for tearing flesh. Ducks have broad, flat bills for sifting food from water. Seed-eating birds have short pincer-like beaks for cracking seeds. Swifts and swallows have gaping beaks for catching insects in flight.

EGGS AND NESTS

Birds (unlike most mammals) do not give birth to babies. Instead, they lay eggs with hard shells, then sit on them to keep them warm while the baby bird develops inside. The *embryo* grows inside the egg by feeding on the yolk. Then when it is big enough it hatches by pecking through the shell with its beak.

Most birds lay their eggs in a nest. Magpies, jays and many other birds build nests in trees from twigs. Warblers build nests in grass. Sand martins dig out burrows in sandy banks. Robins nest in any hole they can find, whether it is a crack in a wall or an old teapot.

Most newly-hatched birds are naked and helpless, but soon grow a covering of soft feathers called *down*. They stay in the nest, and are fed by their parents until they are ready to learn to fly or are strong enough to fend for themselves.

The South American Andean condor is the world's biggest bird of prey, with wings 3m long from tip to tip. Condors prefer to scavenge dead and dying creatures, but they sometimes attack healthy animals as big as deer.

The bald eagle eats fish, which it snatches from rivers. It is the national symbol of the USA. It is not really bald but has white feathers on its head.

Owls like this barn owl hunt by night, using their eyes and ears to pinpoint creatures such as mice.

Vultures do not hunt, but soar above the ground looking for dead and dying animals (carrion).

Merlins and other falcons are often trained to fly from a falconer's wrist to catch small birds and animals.

BIRDS OF PREY

Many of the most majestic birds are hunters, preying upon other birds, fish and small mammals. They are generally strong fliers with sharp eyes, powerful claws or talons and a hooked beak. There are some 280 kinds of birds of prey or *raptors*, including kestrels, hawks, falcons, eagles and vultures. Some have become very rare as intensive farming has deprived them of their natural prey – and also because they are such attractive targets for hunters and egg collectors. Birds of prey lay only one or two eggs at a time, and so are very vulnerable to attacks. The Californian condor, for instance, is not only one of the world's largest birds; it is also one of the rarest and may even be extinct in the wild.

Bird migration *Many birds fly to different places at certain times of year. This journey is called migration. When winter hits the north, many birds fly far south to the warmth of the tropics where food is more plentiful. Some birds, such as warblers and birds of prey, migrate alone, but birds such as starlings, pigeons and godwits move in vast flocks. No bird flies further than the Arctic tern. This remarkable bird lives in the Antarctic when it is summer there, then flies all the way to the Arctic to catch the summer again – a round trip of 40,000km.*

Gulls are the best known of all seabirds, though many spend much of their lives inland. Most are scavengers.

SEA BIRDS

Many species of bird live near the sea, feeding on the shore, or diving for fish in the sea. Most have webbed feet for swimming, waterproof plumage and sharp bills for gripping slippery fish. Albatrosses, shearwaters and petrels spend nearly all their lives at sea, landing only to nest. They are all superb fliers, able to fly enormous distances. They are also brilliant navigators. One Manx shearwater from Wales was released in the USA, 5000km away. It took just 12 days to find its way home. Gannets, cormorants and diving petrels are the champion divers, plunging straight down into the sea to catch fish.

Puffins live in burrows on the shore. They can hold up to 11 fish in their big bills at once.

HOW BIRDS FLY

With their feathers and wings and light, hollow bones, birds are perfectly adapted for flight. They usually fly in one of two ways: by gliding with the wings held almost still, and by flapping their wings up and down. Birds fly at anything from 40 to 100km/h, but may fly very fast indeed to escape danger or pursue a prey. Peregrine falcons can plunge down on a victim at over 130km/h. The fastest flier of all is the spine-tailed swift, which can reach speeds of over 160km/h.

WATER BIRDS

Millions of birds live near fresh water or by estuaries, feeding on the wealth of animal and plant life there. Many, like curlews and redshanks, have long legs for wading in shallow water. Some, like oystercatchers, have long, thin beaks for probing into mud and sand for food. Waterfowl, such as ducks, geese and swans, have webbed feet and long, agile necks for reaching down into the water.

Swans are the largest waterfowl. They have long necks and feed on water plants and animals.

Pelicans have a huge soft pouch beneath their beaks, which they use to scoop fish.

Mallards are dabbling ducks, which means they up-end in the water to feed.

Gliding flight is much less effort for a bird than flapping, and birds that stay in the air a long time tend to be the best gliders. Only birds with long wings can glide, for short wings do not give enough lift. Birds of prey are usually good gliders, hanging in the air as they search for food with their sharp eyes. So too are swifts, gulls and gannets. Albatrosses, petrels and shearwaters have long narrow wings that enable them to soar upwards on rising currents of warm air called *thermals*. Often, birds circle up and up in a

Herons, storks and flamingoes are tall wading birds with long beaks and necks.

Kingfishers perch over water and make flashing dives for fish, which they toss in the air and swallow headfirst.

Geese often graze on grass, and fly in V-formation, filling the air with their noisy honking.

thermal, then glide slowly down until they find another thermal to carry them up again. In this way, they can cover huge distances without once beating their wings. Albatrosses are especially good at this kind of gliding (called *dynamic soaring*) and can keep it up for many days on end.

Flapping flight Most birds flap their wings to fly, and even birds that mainly glide flap their wings to take off and land. Powerful muscles in the bird's breast pull the wings up and down. For the downstroke, the primary feathers close together and push the air down and back, thrusting the bird up and forward. For the upstroke, the primaries part to let air flow through as the wings gently rise, ready for another downstroke. Birds such as vultures flap only slowly. Hummingbirds flap their wings so fast – 50 times a second or more – that they disappear in a blur of movement.

Toucans of the South American forests use their big gaudy beaks to push through thick foliage to get at fruit and insects.

Scarlet macaws are noisy birds, with big hooked beaks so strong they can crack open even Brazil nuts.

Hummingbirds hover in the air and dip their long beaks into flowers to drink their nectar.

TROPICAL BIRDS

Many of the world's most beautiful birds live in tropical forests. In New Guinea and Australia, there are birds of paradise and lyre birds with magnificent tail feathers. In South America, there are brilliantly coloured cotingas like the Peruvian cock-of-the-rock, toucans, and over 300 kinds of tiny jewel-like hummingbirds. And all over the tropics, there are noisy, colourful parrots, such as macaws, cockatoos and budgerigars. Not all tropical birds are so colourful; plain-looking hornbills, ovenbirds, honeybirds, sunbirds and flowerpeckers thrive too on the abundant insect and plant life of the tropical forest.

FLIGHTLESS BIRDS

Not all birds can fly. Penguins, for instance, use their short, stubby wings for swimming. Ostriches, emus, rheas, cassowaries and kiwis walk or run everywhere. In fact, ostriches can run at speeds of 60km/h, faster than a racehorse. Flightless birds are often very large, but have very small wings, used only for balancing and display. As a group, they are sometimes called *ratites*, although scientists are not certain how closely related they are to each other.

Adelie penguins are so well-adapted to the cold that they can breed even in the bitter chill and darkness of an Antarctic winter.

Kiwis are found only in New Zealand. They are hen-sized and feed mainly at night on insects and berries.

Emus are inquisitive birds. They feed on fruit and insects but are known to steal coins and keys.

Cassowaries are wary, aggressive birds, active mainly at night. They are found in New Guinea and Australia.

Ostriches are the world's largest birds, reaching almost 2.5m tall and weighing up to 150kg.

Penguins can stand really cold conditions, and many live in huge colonies called rookeries along the Antarctic coast. They are agile swimmers, using their wings as flippers to push them through the water, and steering with their webbed feet. They can also leap high out of the water to land on an ice bank. But on land they can only waddle clumsily or toboggan along on their bellies.

REPTILES

Reptiles are scaly-skinned creatures such as crocodiles, lizards, tortoises and snakes. They are among the most ancient of all backboned land animals, and are found all over the world's warmer regions, on land and in water. Reptiles are especially well-adapted to survive in hot deserts.

LIZARDS

Lizards are the most varied of all reptiles and there are some 3700 species. Although most live in the warm tropics and subtropics, lizards inhabit a wide range of different environments. There are land lizards, tree lizards, water lizards and even flying lizards. The largest lizard of all is the Komodo dragon, which grows up to 3m long. The smallest are geckos just a few centimetres long.

Like most reptiles, lizards are hunters and can move very quickly. But they often stay completely still for hours as they warm up in the sun before starting to hunt. If a lizard is caught by the tail, the tail will usually break off, confusing the attacker. But a new tail will grow in its place in about eight months. Like other reptiles, most female lizards lay eggs, which they bury in the soil or hide under rocks until ready to hatch.

HOT AND COLD

Reptiles are often said to be cold-blooded. This does not mean their blood is always cold; it just means they are only as warm or as cold as their surroundings. Warm-blooded creatures such as mammals stay equally warm however hot or cold it is – but they must eat frequently to stay warm. Reptiles can survive on very little food, but must continually shuttle between warm and cold places to avoid getting too hot or too cold. So they adjust their lifestyle according to changes in their surroundings.

Reptiles such as lizards spend hours basking in the sun, soaking up its warmth and gaining energy to hunt. Once they are warm enough, they scurry off to find food, rest in the shade for a while, then bask again. At night or when it is cold, they sleep – although geckos (tropical lizards) and some snakes are active on warm nights.

At cool times of year, reptiles are active only at midday, when it is fairly warm. When it is hot, they retreat to the shade and emerge only in the cool of the evening.

SCALY SKIN

Reptiles may sometimes look slimy, but their scaly skin is perfectly dry. Indeed, it keeps a reptile's body

DID YOU KNOW?

The thorny devil lizard of Australia is covered in vicious-looking thorns and spines and has the scientific name Moloch horridus, but is actually quite harmless.

Chameleons catch insects by shooting out a long sticky tongue in less than 0.04 seconds.

The most poisonous land snake of all is the Australian taipan. Its venom glands hold enough poison to kill 200 people.

Turtles and tortoises live to a great age. One giant turtle found in Mauritius in 1766 lived 152 years.

Giant tortoises were once kept on board ships to provide fresh meat for sailors on long voyages.

TURTLES AND TORTOISES

Turtles and tortoises (known together as *chelonians*) cannot be mistaken for any other creature. They live inside an armoured shell of bony plates. On their back is a dome of plates called a *carapace*; on their belly is a flat *plastron*. This armour has just two holes in it: one for the turtle's head and front legs, and one for its tail and back legs. So effective is the protection the shell gives that chelonians have no need to move fast.

Most chelonians live in warm parts of the world and some hibernate in winter if brought to a cold country. There are both land and sea species. The biggest land species is the giant tortoise, which grows up to 1.5m long; the biggest turtle is the leatherback, which grows up to 2.5m and weighs over 800kg. Chelonians eat both plants and animals, but they have no teeth – just jaws with very sharp edges.

Greek tortoises and Hermann's tortoises were once so popular as pets that they are now very rare in the wild.

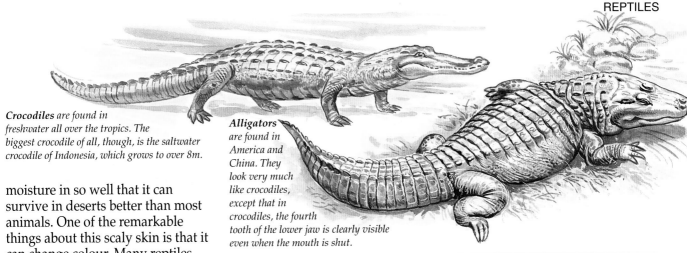

Crocodiles are found in freshwater all over the tropics. The biggest crocodile of all, though, is the saltwater crocodile of Indonesia, which grows to over 8m.

Alligators are found in America and China. They look very much like crocodiles, except that in crocodiles, the fourth tooth of the lower jaw is clearly visible even when the mouth is shut.

moisture in so well that it can survive in deserts better than most animals. One of the remarkable things about this scaly skin is that it can change colour. Many reptiles turn a darker colour when basking in order to absorb the sun's warmth better. Chameleons can change colour to match their background and avoid being spotted by predators.

Unlike mammals, reptiles grow all through their lives, but their skin does not. Every now and then, they must shed or *slough* their skin to reveal a soft new one underneath. Snakes slough off all the old skin in a single piece.

CROCODILES AND ALLIGATORS

Crocodiles, alligators, caymans and gharials are together called crocodilians. Creatures very like them lived 200 million years ago. They are the nearest we get to a live dinosaur today.

They live in warm freshwaters and swamps in the tropics of Africa, Asia, Australia and America. They are hunters, and lie in wait for animals that come to drink at the water. When crocodilians seize a victim, they drag it into the water. There they stun the animal with a blow from their powerful tail and drown it.

Like all reptiles, crocodilians adjust their life to the weather. In the morning, they crawl on to the bank or a sandbar and bask in the sun to warm up. When it gets too hot, they slip back into the water and cool off before sunbathing again in the cooler afternoon sun.

SNAKES

Snakes are long, thin, legless reptiles. Most live in warmer regions, but some adders live inside the Arctic Circle. With no legs to grasp victims, snakes kill their prey in other ways. Constrictors such as pythons wrap themselves around the animal and stop it breathing. Venomous snakes such as cobras stun or kill it with *venom* (poison). The venom is made in special salivary glands and injected into victims through fangs – though a few snakes can spit venom. Snakes hunt their prey by sight, sound or smell. They have no ears, but pick up sound vibrations from the ground. They smell with their tongue, which picks up minute particles floating in the air as it flickers in and out.

Adders are venomous snakes found in Europe. They lie in wait for their prey, bite it, wait for it to die and then swallow it.

The boa constrictor kills its victims by squeezing them until they suffocate. Boas grow up to 5.5m long, but some constrictors are even bigger. The anaconda of America is up to 11m long.

Eggs Like all reptiles, young snakes come from eggs. In some snakes the egg develops inside the mother. But in most the eggs are laid, then hidden out of sight in hollow trees, under stones or in dung heaps. The mother usually abandons the eggs and lets them fend for themselves. The only exceptions are snakes like the mother rat snake, which stays near her eggs, keeping them warm with her sun-warmed body.

Rattlesnakes are venomous American snakes. They get their name from the way they rattle their bony tails.

The axolotl *stays forever a tadpole, yet lives 25 years, as long as an adult tiger salamander.*

AMPHIBIANS

Amphibians are creatures such as frogs, toads, newts and salamanders that live both on land and in the water. Most begin life in the water as *larvae* (tadpoles) that hatch from huge clutches of eggs called *spawn*. But they soon grow legs and develop lungs for breathing air – though some breathe through their skins. Then they can live on land as well.

FOREVER YOUNG

Some salamanders never grow up. They remain as tadpoles all their lives and yet are still able to reproduce – a phenomenon known as *neoteny*. The best-known example is the axolotl, which lives in freshwater lakes around Mexico City. The axolotl stays a tadpole all its life because the water it lives in lacks iodine. Without iodine, the axolotl cannot metamorphose (change) into an adult salamander and simply grows bigger. Scientists have found that if they inject iodine into an axolotl's thyroid gland, it completes its development and turns into a tiger salamander.

The olm is another amphibian that stays a tadpole all its life. It lives in permanent darkness in streams in the Carniola caves of Slovenia. Unlike the axolotl, the olm never changes into an adult, however much the thyroid is stimulated, and scientists believe it is a relic from the days before amphibians crawled out of the water and on to the land.

LIFE ON LAND AND IN WATER

The word 'amphibian' means 'both lives' and perfectly describes the lives of amphibians. They start life in the water as eggs, which must be laid in water because, unlike reptiles' eggs, they are not waterproof. On land, the eggs would simply dry out.

The egg does not hold enough food for the embryo to develop fully, so the eggs hatch into tadpoles at an early stage. The tadpoles have gills like fish (see page 40) and live entirely under-water, feeding greedily and growing rapidly. As they develop, the tadpoles grow legs and lungs and *metamorphose* (change) into adults able to live on land.

Even adult amphibians, however, can never stray far from water. Unlike reptiles, which have a waterproof skin that allows them to survive in hot, dry places, amphibians lose water through their skins, so they must always stay in moist environments.

AMPHIBIAN ORIGINS

Until the end of the Devonian period some 360 million years ago, fishes were the only creatures with backbones. But about this time, the first amphibians evolved from fishes with lobe-shaped fins, grew legs and lungs, and started to crawl out of the water.

These early amphibians were very different from modern

NEWTS AND SALAMANDERS

Newts and salamanders may look like lizards, but they are true amphibians, beginning life as tadpoles in the water, and living on land in damp woods only as adults. Newts live in the temperate regions of the world. In the cold of winter, they hibernate under logs and stones on land. When spring comes, they head for ponds and calm fresh water to breed. Salamanders live in warmer climates so have no need to hibernate, but spend more time on land, sheltering under logs.

Smooth newts always return to the same stretch of water to breed.

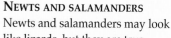

Palmate newts *breed in lakes high up in the Pyrenean mountains between France and Spain.*

Black salamanders *live in the Alps up to 3200m, and hunt for insects after dusk.*

Tiger salamanders, *found in North and Central America, are the adult form of the axolotl.*

amphibians. They were much larger and looked like a cross between a fish and a lizard with smooth skin. Like the salamanders and newts of today, these early amphibians had tails left over from their watery origins. Frogs and toads eventually lost the tail, making it easier to move on land.

Scientists think that these creatures initially evolved because the huge oceans of the Devonian period gradually dried out, creating swamps and leaving fish high and dry. Those fish that could breathe in air with their swim-bladders survived much better, and over millions of years the lobe-shaped fins gradually changed into limbs.

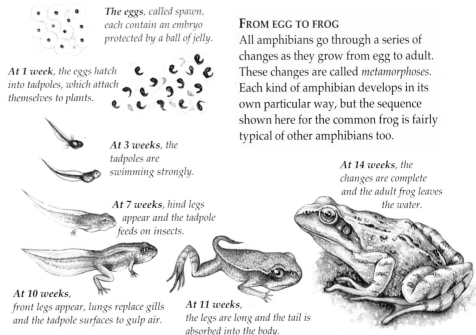

The eggs, called spawn, each contain an embryo protected by a ball of jelly.

At 1 week, the eggs hatch into tadpoles, which attach themselves to plants.

At 3 weeks, the tadpoles are swimming strongly.

At 7 weeks, hind legs appear and the tadpole feeds on insects.

At 10 weeks, front legs appear, lungs replace gills and the tadpole surfaces to gulp air.

At 11 weeks, the legs are long and the tail is absorbed into the body.

At 14 weeks, the changes are complete and the adult frog leaves the water.

FROM EGG TO FROG

All amphibians go through a series of changes as they grow from egg to adult. These changes are called *metamorphoses*. Each kind of amphibian develops in its own particular way, but the sequence shown here for the common frog is fairly typical of other amphibians too.

FROGS AND TOADS

Neither frogs nor toads have tails as adults, but they have long, strong back legs to help them jump huge distances. They also have strong front legs to withstand the shock of landing. Frogs are the better jumpers, but toads are better adapted to life on land, with thicker, wartier skins that retain moisture better.

Both toads and frogs are meat-eaters, able to catch fast-moving insects by darting out their long, sticky tongues. They escape from predators themselves by jumping, or in some species, by exuding poison from glands on their skin. Some poisons are relatively harmless, others are lethal.

Green tree frogs live mostly in trees and do not return to water even to breed. Big fingers and toes aid grip when jumping from twig to twig.

The common frog, like all frogs, has two big swivelling eyes to help judge distances when jumping and catching flies.

The common toad exudes a white poison from the parotid gland behind its eyes.

Looking after eggs

Many frogs and toads have unusual ways of looking after their eggs. With the midwife toad, for instance, it is not the mother who cares for the eggs but the father. He gathers up strings of eggs as they are laid, winds them round his back legs and carries them around until they are ready to hatch. With Darwin's frog, found in Australia, the male watches the eggs for signs of life, then gulps in a dozen or so and keeps them in the safety of the croaking sac of his throat. Soon they hatch and hop out of his mouth.

FISH

Fish are animals that live almost anywhere there is water – in rivers and lakes, and in the oceans. There are over 21,000 different species – more than all other vertebrates put together – ranging from the tiny pygmy goby, just 8mm long, to the whale shark, over 15m long.

Safe colours Some fish are brightly coloured or have striking markings, but most are camouflaged – that is, coloured to match their surroundings.

COLOURING

Many fish are in constant danger of being eaten by other fish or by birds, so they are often coloured to blend in with their surroundings, which hides them from predators' eyes. The backs of fish that live near the surface of the open sea are blue like the surface of the sea, while river perch are marked with bars that make them difficult to see amongst weeds. Most fish can actually change colour to match the background. Some tropical fish can change almost instantly from yellow to scarlet or from red to green.

BREATHING

Fish are well adapted to life underwater. Like us, they must breathe oxygen to survive. But they breathe through *gills*, not lungs. These enable them to get all the oxygen they need from the water – although a few fish can breathe in air. Gills are rows of feathery brushes – usually four – just inside the back of the fish's head, in a cavity called the *gill chamber*. To get oxygen, the fish gulps water through its mouth into the gill chamber. The gills absorb oxygen from the water, and then flaps called *gill covers*, on the side of the fish's head, open to let the water out again.

SWIMMING

Most fish have long, streamlined bodies perfect for slipping through the water, and fins for swimming. Usually, fish have at least one *dorsal* fin along the back, a tail or *caudal* fin and an *anal* fin underneath. They also have two pairs of identical fins near the front: one pair just behind the gills, called the *pectoral* fins, and one pair just below, called the *pelvic* fins.

Typically, a fish propels itself through the water by curving its body and swinging its tail fin from side to side. To stop, steer and move up or down, it waggles its pectoral and pelvic fins. The dorsal

SHARKS AND RAYS

Sharks are the most ferocious fish in the sea. There are over 250 kinds, some quite small, but nearly all sharks are hunters, with a mouth full of rows of razor-sharp teeth. Fortunately, most prey on fish. Only 12 species are dangerous to humans.

Most fish have skeletons of bone, but a shark's skeleton is made of a rubbery substance called cartilage, like the cartilage in your nose. Sharks also have gill slits on their heads rather than gill covers – typically five on each side.

Like sharks, rays and skates are cartilaginous, but while sharks are long and thin, most rays are broad and flat, with giant pectoral fins extending either side like aeroplane wings. They have eyes on the top of their head and often a sting in their long, slender tail. To breathe, they draw in water through two *spiracles* (holes) on top of their head.

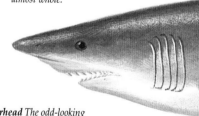

The great white shark is the most dangerous of all sharks. It can grow up to 9m in length and can swallow a person almost whole.

Hammerhead The odd-looking hammerhead shark has eyes and nostrils at the end of its 'hammer', which can be up to 1m wide. It is dangerous to humans, but survives mainly by eating stingrays, which it can devour whole.

Sharks' teeth Most sharks have many rows of large, sharp teeth and powerful jaws that enable them to bite through almost anything. As the outer rows of teeth wear out or break, the inner rows move forward to replace them.

fin helps to keep it balanced and upright.

Fast, powerful swimmers such as swordfish and tuna tend to have a long, forked tail fin and sharply curved pectorals. Slower swimmers, such as bowfins, have much shorter and blunter fins.

Staying afloat To keep them afloat, many fish have a special air bag inside their bodies called a *swim bladder*. Without this, they would have to swim all the time to avoid sinking. Sharks and rays have no swim bladder, so they drift to the bottom of the sea whenever they stop swimming.

Just as the air in a lifejacket helps a person stay afloat, so gas in the swim bladder helps a fish float at a particular depth in the water. As the fish swims deeper, the extra pressure of water squeezes the gas in the bladder. To avoid sinking, the fish inflates the bladder with extra gas made in its blood. When the fish swims higher again, this extra gas is let out. All these adjustments are made

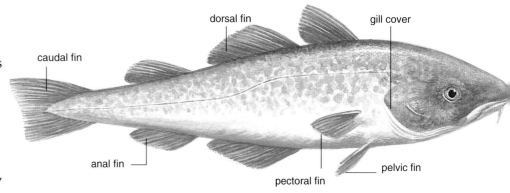

Scales, gills and fins Most fish have long, streamlined bodies covered in overlapping bony plates called scales, gills for breathing, and various fins to help them swim. The fish shown here is a cod, but most fish have a similar range of fins.

automatically by the fish's nervous system.

In some fish, the swim bladder does not only keep the fish afloat. In lungfish, for instance, the bladder acts as a lung. Lungfish live in tropical rivers and the bladder enables them to breathe air when they are stranded on the mud in the dry season. Some catfish can make noises with their bladder – just like a set of bagpipes. A few species of fish communicate with each other by using sounds from their bladder.

DID YOU KNOW?
An African catfish called a clariid can breathe air through a kind of lung and survive days out of water as it wriggles from lake to lake.
Flying fish can glide over the sea for over 400m and soar up to 6m above the waves.
The archerfish of South East Asia shoots down flying insects by spitting a jet of water up to 1m.
The stonefish has spines so poisonous that a single sting can kill a person in minutes.

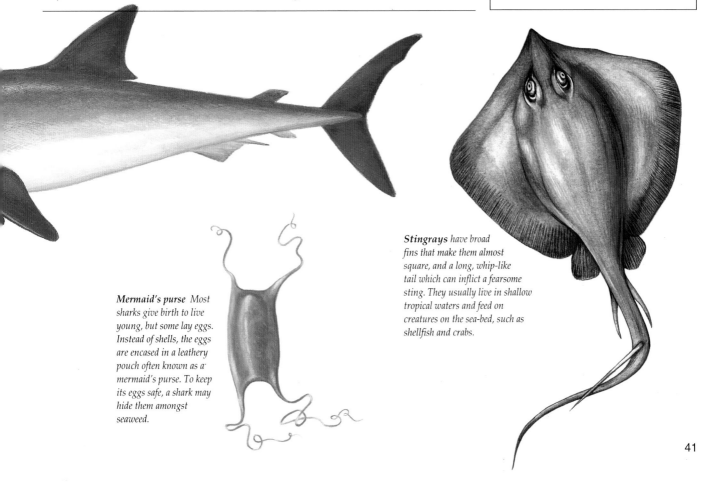

Mermaid's purse Most sharks give birth to live young, but some lay eggs. Instead of shells, the eggs are encased in a leathery pouch often known as a mermaid's purse. To keep its eggs safe, a shark may hide them amongst seaweed.

Stingrays have broad fins that make them almost square, and a long, whip-like tail which can inflict a fearsome sting. They usually live in shallow tropical waters and feed on creatures on the sea-bed, such as shellfish and crabs.

Coelacanths are often described as living fossils, and were once thought to have been extinct for 70 million years. Fossils of lungfish like them date back nearly 400 million years.

LAMPREYS AND HAGFISH

The first animals with backbones were fish with neither jaws nor scales. Fish like these first appeared over 450 million years ago. Now there are only two kinds: lampreys and hagfish. Lampreys are long, thin fish that live in the sea, but swim up rivers to lay their eggs. They are parasites, latching on to other fish with a ring of horny teeth. A lamprey's mouth is like a sanding disc with sharp teeth that it uses to rasp into its victim's skin to suck its blood. Hagfish are slimy, eel-like fish that scavenge on dying fish, boring into their bodies like a drill and eating away the flesh until nothing is left but skin and bone.

DID YOU KNOW?

The elephant-nosed mormyrid of the Congo River in Africa has a snout like an elephant's trunk, which it uses to suck up food from the mud. It also sends out an electric current to help find its way.

The electric catfish can give an electric shock of up to 400 volts.

Swallower fish are almost all mouth and can swallow fish twice their own size in their stretchy stomach.

An ocean sunfish can lay over 50 million eggs at once.

Male deep-sea angler fish are a tiny fraction of the size of the female. To mate, he hangs on to her with his teeth – for so long that he eventually becomes lost in her giant body.

SEA FISH

Nearly two-thirds of all fish live in the sea. Some sea fish live in *tropical* waters, where the water is always warm. Others live in *temperate* waters, where the water is neither warm nor cold. Temperate waters off northeast North America and northwest Europe provide rich fishing grounds for fish such as herring and cod. The biggest, fastest-swimming fish live near the surface of the open ocean, far from land. Fish like these can often migrate vast distances to spawn or find food. But there are many smaller fish living some way below the surface. Flatfish and eels live on the sea-bed. And in the dark ocean depths are weird fish like the deep-sea angler, which gets its name from the glowing bulb it dangles in front of its mouth to attract prey, like bait on an angler's rod.

Mackerel (right) are related to tuna and are some of the fastest swimmers in the sea.

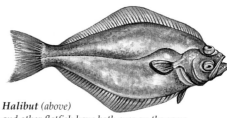

Plaice (above) spend nearly all their life lying on their side on the sea-bed.

Halibut (above) and other flatfish have both eyes on the same side of their bodies.

TROPICAL FISH

The warm waters of the tropics are rich in fish life, especially in shallows around coral reefs. Beautiful, brilliantly coloured fish like angelfish and butterfly fish teem among the coral reefs of the Indian and Pacific oceans and the Caribbean. But some of the world's most dangerous fish lurk in tropical waters too. Not only are there powerful predators, such as barracudas, moray eels and sharks, but also highly poisonous fish, such as turkey fish, lionfish and stonefish. Along the back of a lionfish are 18 beautiful long spines – but each carries a deadly venom. Stepping on the spines of a stonefish can cause such extreme pain that victims can die of shock.

Damsel fish are common in both tropical and warm temperate waters.

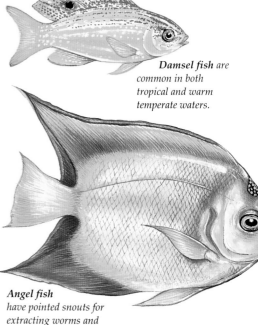

Angel fish have pointed snouts for extracting worms and shellfish from crevices.

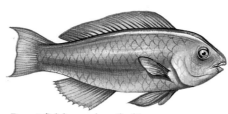

Parrot fish have a sharp 'beak' for grazing on coral.

Butterfly fish feed on buds of coral, nipping off their heads.

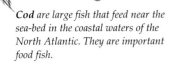

Cod are large fish that feed near the sea-bed in the coastal waters of the North Atlantic. They are important food fish.

Tuna grow up to 700kg and are very important food fish, caught widely for canning.

Herring often live in huge shoals, millions strong, especially in the Atlantic and Indian oceans.

Swordfish and marlin are big fish that live near the surface of the open ocean. They can swim at speeds of up to 80km/h.

Conger eels are long, snake-like fish that haunt crevices in rocky reefs and wrecks.

Moray eels are among the most common of all eels. They are fearsome predators that grow up to 3m long and feed on small fish and shrimps.

FRESHWATER FISH

Fish are found in nearly every stream, pond and lake in the world. A few fish, like salmon and eels, spend some of their life in both freshwater and seawater, but most freshwater fish cannot survive in the salty sea water. Some, such as trout and grayling, prefer fast-flowing streams like those flowing from chalk downland. Slow-flowing rivers and lakes are the home of tench, rudd and carp. Here, large predatory pike often lurk in the weeds. Shoals of fish feed on floating plankton, or take insects from the surface, while common bream and barbel graze on the bottom, eating insect larvae, worms and molluscs.

Sea trout are solitary hunters, preying on small fish and water creatures.

Carp were originally an Asian fish, probably brought to Europe by the Romans, and they prefer warm water. Carp can live over 40 years.

Roach are found in lakes and slow-flowing rivers.

Minnows are among the smallest of freshwater fish, rarely growing more than 90mm long. Large shoals can often be seen in cool, clear upland rivers.

Perch are hunters of lowland lakes and slow-flowing rivers, where they lie in wait for their prey among water plants.

Salmon spend most of their life in the sea, but eventually swim into a river to return to the place where they were spawned. On the journey upstream they battle against strong currents and leap up waterfalls and rapids. When they reach the spawning ground, they mate. The female lays her eggs in the gravel, then male and female drift down river to die.

FARM ANIMALS

Pork chops and steaks, butter and milk, shoes and woollen pullovers – these and many other things come from animals kept on farms, such as cattle, sheep, goats, pigs and hens. All farm animals were once wild, but about 10,000 years ago people began to capture and *domesticate* (tame) them to provide a ready supply of meat, milk, eggs, fur, wool and leather. Since then, farmers have bred farm animals to make them bigger and meatier, for example, or to give more milk. Now there are many hundreds of breeds, each known for a special quality.

SHEEP AND GOATS

Sheep and goats were first domesticated over 10,000 years ago and are farmed almost everywhere – sometimes in huge numbers, as on the Australian plains, sometimes on small hill farms in remote regions. *Hairy sheep* are kept for milk and meat (lamb and mutton), *woolly sheep* for wool. Some sheep give coarse wool which is good for carpets. Others, like the Merino, give fine wool for jumpers. Sheep and goats are often kept in dry or mountainous areas because they are not only fairly agile, but also have strong jaws and are able to survive on tough, short grass.

CATTLE

The first cattle were domesticated from the auroch 9000 years ago. Now there are billions around the world and many different breeds. They provide not only meat, but also milk – from which butter, cheese and yoghurt are produced – and leather. Oxen pull ploughs and carts.

Female cattle reared for milk are called *dairy cows* and are kept for up to 10 years. Dairy cows usually give birth to a

FOOD AND FODDER

There are now more than twice as many farm animals in the world as humans – more than 14 billion all told. All these animals need over 3 billion hectares of land to graze on – twice the area used for growing crops. Animals can feed on grass and other plants inedible to humans, so in hot, dry countries, and in mountain regions, animals make the most of land where crops will not grow. However, in many places farm animals graze on good crop land – and they are fed over 40 per cent of

calf each year, then provide milk at least twice each day for 10 months. They are often milked with special machines attached to their udders. Since they give richer milk if they eat good grass, dairy cows are usually kept on lush meadows. Most male calves are reared for their meat (beef). Beef cattle are bred to grow quickly and are usually slaughtered as soon as they are fully grown.

the world's cereal crop. In many of the world's richer countries, farm animals consume 75 per cent of the grain harvest. A cow has to eat ten calories of grain to give one calorie of steak, so many people argue that raising so many animals wastes the world's farming land. If this grain went to people, not animals, they say, fewer people would go hungry.

MODERN LIVESTOCK REARING

In the richer countries of the world, the 20th century has seen dramatic changes in the way farm

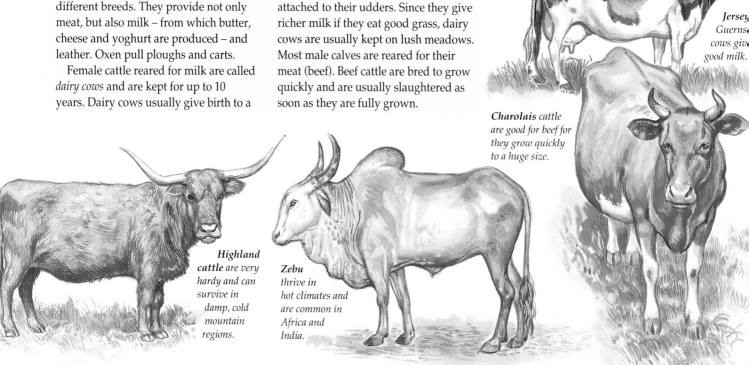

Jersey and *Guernsey cows give good milk.*

Charolais cattle are good for beef for they grow quickly to a huge size.

Highland cattle are very hardy and can survive in damp, cold mountain regions.

Zebu thrive in hot climates and are common in Africa and India.

animals are reared. Many animals are now made pregnant by *artificial insemination* – that is, with sperm collected from the male, deep frozen, then injected into the female's womb. Artificial insemination means that one bull can father thousands of calves – even after the bull is dead. Totally new breeds are also being created by genetic engineering (page 13).

In richer countries, drugs are now widely used in farming. Animals are not only vaccinated to protect them against disease, but are also given regular doses of antibiotics. They may be fed growth hormones and other chemical additives to make them grow quickly. Some people worry that the effects of these drugs might harm the animals.

Factory farms Many farm animals are now reared in *factory farms*, where they are kept in specially controlled buildings to make them grow quickly. Many people say that this is cruel, but farmers insist it is the only way to produce the large quantities of meat and other products we demand.

POULTRY

Poultry are birds farmed for their eggs, meat or feathers, such as hens, turkeys, ducks and geese. Sometimes hens scratch around for insects and seeds in farmyards and fields and lay their eggs – usually one every day or two – in a small coop (hut). These are *free-range* hens. In Europe and North America, most hens are now crowded into row upon row of boxes called *batteries* inside a heated building where they are fed and watered, and waste and eggs are collected, completely automatically. Even for free-range hens, conditions may be very crowded.

BUFFALOES, DEER AND OTHERS

Cattle, sheep and goats, pigs and poultry are not the only farm animals. In India and South East Asia, for instance, water buffalo are widely kept, partly for meat and milk and partly for pulling ploughs and carts. In Africa, Asia and South America, asses and mules are kept for carrying things and to turn water wheels. Deer were once hunted for their meat, called *venison*, and now they too are sometimes farmed. Reindeer are large deer with antlers that live in the cold regions of Eurasia and North America. They were first domesticated 1500 years ago in Lapland and Siberia, where they are used to provide transport, meat, milk and clothing.

PIGS

Pigs are kept for their meat and their skins, which give fine leather. Their hair is often used for artists' brushes. Pigs were once allowed to roam woodlands, rooting for worms, roots and shoots. Now pigs in Europe and North America are usually raised on factory farms. Here they are fed special nutrients which help them to gain over 0.5kg a day.

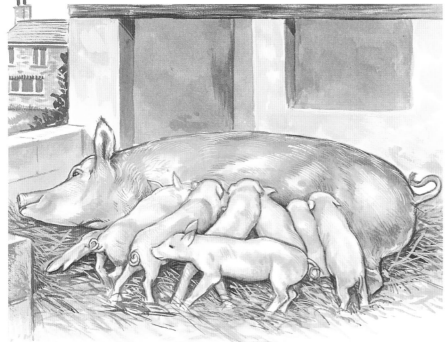

> **DID YOU KNOW?**
> **The average European cow** gives almost 5000 litres of milk in ten months – that is, over 16 litres a day.
> **Battery hens** lay 250 eggs a year.
> **In the USA**, people eat about 110kg of meat each year; in the UK, they eat about 75 kg; in China they eat about 23kg; in India, they eat just 1.1kg.

PETS

People have enjoyed the company of animals for thousands of years. Dogs were tamed to help with hunting over 12,000 years ago, and since then cats, birds, horses, guinea pigs, and many other animals have been adopted as pets – some species for companionship, some for their appearance. Each has its own particular quality.

BIRDS

Birds have always made popular pets for the beauty of their plumage or their singing. Mynah birds and parrots often mimic human speech. One very talkative African grey parrot is said to have known more than 800 words. Only larger birds, such as waterfowl, have been completely domesticated, though. Most smaller birds, such as canaries and budgerigars, must normally be kept in a cage. Budgerigars are Australian parakeets. In the wild, they nest in a hole they dig in mallee scrub and line it with rotten wood. Canaries are descendants of the wild serin finch or canary of the Canary Islands. Their brightly-coloured plumage comes from selective breeding.

LOOKING AFTER PETS

Some pets, like cats and dogs, were first domesticated long ago, and these generally make the best pets. Other pets are just wild creatures that have been caught and caged. Thousands of parrots, for instance, are netted in the wild each year to be sold as pets. Wild creatures like this are never entirely happy away from their natural environment.

Whether domesticated or wild, pets need careful looking after. Pet owners must know just what their pets need in the way of food, housing and exercise. Dogs and other pets must also be trained when young to behave in a safe, obedient way and to avoid soiling the house or street.

PEDIGREES

Over the centuries, many pets – dogs and cats especially – have been bred to bring out certain qualities, and there are now scores of breeds, all very different from their wild ancestors, and often very different from other breeds. Since all dogs are from the same species, a dog of one breed can mate with a dog of another. The puppies of two dogs of different breeds are called *mongrels*. The most valuable dogs and cats, however, are *pedigrees* – dogs and cats with parents and ancestors all known for sure to be of the same breed. Dog and cat shows, where pure pedigree animals compete, are very popular.

DID YOU KNOW?

Miniature Yorkshire terriers often weigh less than 500g when fully grown.

The heaviest dog breed is the St Bernard, which often weighs 90kg.

Cocker spaniels originated in 14th century Spain, which is why they are called spaniels. Cocker spaniels were used by hunters to flush out woodcocks.

Chihuahuas are named after the Mexican state of Chihuahua. The Aztecs are thought to have believed them holy.

A female cat is called a queen. A group of cats is called a clowder.

A female dog is called a bitch. A group is called a kennel.

Tabby cats may get their name from the Attab district of Baghdad, now capital of Iraq, where a certain kind of striped silk was made in the Middle Ages.

DOGS

Domestic dogs are all descended from wild wolves and jackals, but only the German shepherd looks anything like its ancestors. There are now 130 or more breeds, from giant Afghan hounds to tiny chihuahuas. Not all dogs are pets. Many are trained to do jobs, such as herding sheep, guarding property, and guiding blind people. These are called *working dogs*. *Sporting dogs*, including hounds, gun dogs and terriers, were originally bred to help hunters, but most are pets now. The smallest dog breeds are called *toy dogs*.

Spaniels like this springer spaniel originated in Spain. They make very good sporting dogs and pets.

The dachshund's name is the German for badger hound.

Terriers were bred as sporting dogs. This is a cairn terrier.

UNUSUAL PETS

People keep all kinds of animals as pets besides dogs, cats and birds – from fleas to elephants. While most people like harmless, friendly pets, some like to keep highly dangerous creatures – poisonous snakes, such as cobras; poisonous spiders, such as the black widow; aggressive dogs, such as the pit bull terrier, and even big cats and bears. For almost every animal, it seems, there is someone willing to adopt it as a pet. Keeping an unusual pet, though, is not easy, for there are rarely any books to show how to look after it properly. Unusual pets are also generally wild creatures, and most would be far better off in their own natural environment.

Golden hamster

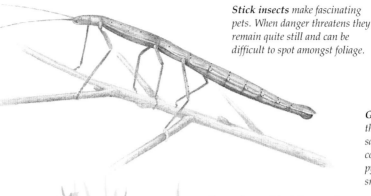

Stick insects make fascinating pets. When danger threatens they remain quite still and can be difficult to spot amongst foliage.

Terrapins and tortoises used to be very popular pets in northern Europe and the USA, but there are now so few left in the wild that they are no longer imported.

Garter snakes like this one make much safer pets than boa constrictors and pythons, or poisonous snakes, such as cobras.

CATS

The first domestic cats were wild African bushcats, tamed by ancient Egyptians thousands of years ago. Yet cats show some of their wild ancestry even today. They are deadly hunters – strong and agile, with keen senses and sharp claws – and often catch mice and birds. Unlike many breeds of dog, they can be highly independent of their owners.

There are now more than 500 million cats around the world and dozens of different kinds, from common tabbies and tortoiseshells to highly valuable pedigree breeds such as the Siamese, with its intense blue eyes, the Russian blue, with its soft, seal-like coat of blue-grey, and the Abyssinian, with its red-brown banded coat and yellow eyes.

Cat litter Most female cats are ready to be mothers by the time they are ten months old – although many are neutered to prevent them breeding. Female cats are usually pregnant for about nine weeks or so, and then give birth to a litter of between 2 and 5 kittens – though a litter of as many as 19 has been recorded. Newborn kittens are helpless – blind, deaf and furless. They begin to hear quite soon, but their eyes may stay closed for a week or more, and they only start to crawl after a fortnight. For the first two months of their lives, kittens feed only on their mother's milk, which they suck from teats on her underside. Eventually, though, they are 'weaned' off the milk and on to solid food. A month later, the mother cat is ready to mate again.

47

INSECTS

Insects may seem tiny, but there are more of them than all other animals put together, and they were around long before the dinosaurs. There are over 1,000,000 known species, from minute flies to huge beetles, and they are so adaptable that they are found nearly everywhere on Earth, even the coldest and hottest places.

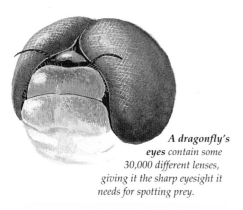

A dragonfly's eyes contain some 30,000 different lenses, giving it the sharp eyesight it needs for spotting prey.

EYES AND ANTENNAE

Insects see with two large *compound* eyes. This means they do not have just one lens in each eye as we do, but many. In the eyes of worker ants there may only be six lenses, but in dragonflies there are 30,000. The more lenses in its eyes, the better an insect sees. In fact, most insects see anything further than a metre away as a blur, but can rapidly spot movement from almost any direction.

Insects use their antennae to sense the world in a variety of ways. Most use them mainly for smelling and feeling. Hairs on the antennae are sensitive to even the slightest air current. Insects such as mosquitoes hear with their antennae, because minute hairs on the antennae are waggled by sound waves. Ants, bees and wasps use their antennae to taste things.

AN INSECT'S BODY

Insects usually have six legs and a body divided into three parts – head, thorax and abdomen. The body is encased in a shell so tough that an insect has no need of bones – which is why the shell is called an *exoskeleton*. The exoskeleton is made mainly of a substance called *chitin* (say 'kite-in') and consists of 20 or so rings. These may be fused together into a rigid shell, or hinged to make the body flexible.

Unlike bones, the exoskeleton does not grow. Instead, it is discarded and replaced with a new, larger one every now and then – a process called moulting. When an insect moults, it crawls out of its old shell, then takes in air to blow up the new shell like a balloon, while it is still soft.

Head An insect's head is very different from that of any other animal and consists mainly of mouth parts, eyes and antennae.

Insects can feed on almost anything, including other insects, plants, blood, nectar, paper, wood and even sweat. The shape of the mouth parts depends on the way the insect eats. Insects that chew their food, such as beetles, cockroaches and grasshoppers, have a pair of strong jaws called *mandibles* and a pair of slightly weaker jaws just below called

Inside an insect, showing the breathing system, blood circulation and digestive system.

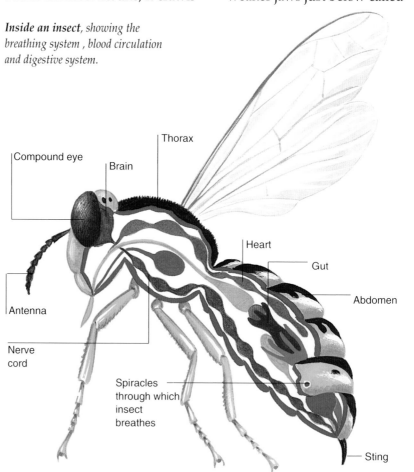

Compound eye

Brain

Thorax

Heart

Gut

Abdomen

Antenna

Nerve cord

Spiracles through which insect breathes

Sting

DID YOU KNOW?

The world's longest insect is the giant stick insect of Indonesia, which grows up to 330mm long.

The world's smallest insect is the fairy fly, only 0.2mm long.

Leaf-cutter ants in South America grow a crop of fungus on rotting leaves they carry into their nests.

An ant can lift 50 times its own weight – like you lifting a lorry!

A flea can jump 300mm – like you jumping 200m in the air!

A queen termite's body swells to 1000 times its original size when full of eggs.

Insects have been frozen solid and survived.

Dragonflies beat their wings just 25 times a second, while midges beat them 40 times as fast. Even so, dragonflies can fly at 60km/h.

maxillae. Insects that suck plant juices or animal blood, such as bedbugs, flies and butterflies, suck through a long tube like a drinking straw, called a *proboscis*.

Thorax The thorax is in the middle and is packed with strong muscles that move the legs and wings attached to the outside. Fleas and grasshoppers have long, strong back legs for jumping. Bees have legs with a pocket to pick up pollen from flowers. Most adult insects have wings and can fly. Flies and mosquitoes have two wings, but some insects have four.

Abdomen The abdomen, at the rear, holds all the insect's digestive system and its sex organs. In the abdomen of many female insects there is a special organ called an *ovipositor*, through which they can inject eggs into soil, wood, seeds and even the bodies of animals. The ovipositor of wasps, bees and ants has developed into a poisonous sting.

Blood and circulation Insects do not have lungs for breathing like mammals. Instead, they breathe through holes in their sides called *spiracles*, which are linked to tiny air tubes called *tracheae*. In other animals, oxygen from the air is carried around the body in blood. In insects, the tracheae take it directly to where it is needed. The blood that fills the body carries only food and may be green, red, yellow or clear.

LIFE CYCLE

When they are adults, mammals look much the same as when they are born, but insects may change so much that you hardly recognize them as being the same creatures. All begin life as an egg, but change as they grow in one of three ways.

Moulting To grow, an insect casts off its old shell completely to inflate a new soft one formed underneath.

The simplest pattern is followed by silverfish, springtails and other wingless insects. Every time these insects moult, they get bigger but look the same.

The next pattern is followed by insects such as grasshoppers and mayflies. The young are called nymphs and look much like adults except that they have no wings. After a few moults, however, the wings appear, small at first, but getting larger with each moult.

Insects such as butterflies, beetles and flies change dramatically through life, from egg to larva to pupa or chrysalis to adult. This change is called *metamorphosis* and is shown in detail on page 50. Larvae of different insects have different names. Those of butterflies are caterpillars; those of flies maggots, those of beetles grubs, and those of mosquitoes wrigglers.

Grasshoppers 'sing' (stridulate) by rubbing their hind legs across their closed fore wings.

The praying mantis is a large carnivorous insect that gets its name from its habit of standing in wait for prey with its front legs folded together as if in prayer.

Ladybirds are a kind of beetle. They feed on aphids, and make good, natural controllers of these pests.

Wasps have a distinct narrow waist. Female wasps can paralyse prey with the sting in their tail.

Beetles are the largest group of insects. There are over 250,000 different kinds.

The stag beetle, one of the largest beetles, is a predator, but its horns are used mainly for wrestling other stag beetles.

INSECT ORDERS

Insects come in an amazing variety of shapes, sizes and colours. Scientists find thousands of new species each year and believe millions are yet to be found. Insects are divided into *orders*. The order *Lepidoptera* includes all butterflies and moths. *Coleoptera* includes beetles. *Diptera* includes flies and mosquitoes.

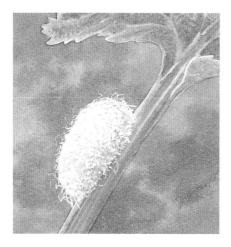

SILK

More than 2000 years ago, the Chinese discovered that certain caterpillars make a fine, light thread that can be woven into one of the most beautiful of all materials, silk. Most moth caterpillars make silk. It oozes as a fluid from glands beneath their mouth, then hardens into a thread. Caterpillars use the thread to spin the cocoons in which they change into an adult moth. With most caterpillars, the cocoon is made from short lengths of thread glued together, but the mulberry silkworm caterpillar makes its cocoon from a single thread up to 1km long. This thread can be retrieved only by softening the cocoon in hot water, killing the pupa. Silkworms are extinct in the wild, but are reared on special farms where the mulberry trees on which they live have been planted.

DID YOU KNOW?

Hairstreak butterflies have a false head on their hind wings. Birds peck at this, leaving the real head alone.
Male queen butterflies stroke the female's antennae with hair brushes on their abdomen to prepare her for mating.
Tiger moths emit high-pitched clicks at night to warn bats they taste bad. Woolly bear moths are edible but emit the same clicks.
The biggest butterfly is the Queen Alexandra's birdwing, which has wings up to 28cm across.
Butterflies sip nectar from flowers through a straw-like tube called a proboscis.

BUTTERFLIES & MOTHS

Butterflies and moths are among the most beautiful of all insects and their fluttering flight gives us plenty of time to see the often vivid colours of their large wings. The order of butterflies and moths is called *Lepidoptera*, and it is one of the largest and most varied orders of insects. There are over 100,000 species.

BUTTERFLY OR MOTH?

Butterflies and moths are found all over the world in an enormous range of different places. Tropical forests have the richest variety, but there are lepidopterans in fields, in woods, on grassland, in deserts and high on mountains right up to the snowline. Among the smallest is the dwarf blue of Africa, which has wings less than 1cm across. One of the biggest is the Atlas emperor moth, with wings up to 30cm across.

The distinction between butterflies and moths is far from clear cut, but there are a number of differences. Most butterflies have brilliantly coloured wings and fly only during the day. They also have slim, hairless bodies and a pair of clubbed antennae. Most moths, however, are usually more drab in colour and fly only at dusk or at night. They also tend to have plump, hairy bodies and straight antennae. When it's resting, you can usually tell a butterfly from a moth by the way the butterfly folds its wings up; a moth spreads them flat.

SCALY WINGS

Lepidopterans get their name from the minute scales on their wings (from the Greek *lepis*, meaning

---

1 Egg Some butterflies lay 300 eggs at a time; some lay just one. They are usually laid on plants that provide food after hatching.

2 Larva Caterpillars are hungry eaters, chewing their way rapidly through leaves. As they grow, they keep bursting out of their skins to reveal a new one, since the skin itself cannot grow.

LIFE CYCLE

Few insects change so much during their life cycle as a butterfly or moth. It begins life as an egg, then hatches into a long wiggly larva called a *caterpillar*. The caterpillar eats leaves greedily and grows rapidly. When it is big enough, the caterpillar makes itself a case, which may be either a *cocoon* or a *chrysalis*. For some time the case seems quiet, but inside the caterpillar is *metamorphosing* (changing) into a moth or butterfly. When it is ready, it breaks out and flies away.

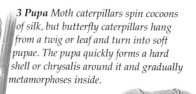

3 Pupa Moth caterpillars spin cocoons of silk, but butterfly caterpillars hang from a twig or leaf and turn into soft pupae. The pupa quickly forms a hard shell or chrysalis around it and gradually metamorphoses inside.

4 Metamorphosis It takes anything from a few days to a year for the pupa to turn into an adult. At last, it is ready to break the shell and emerge into the light.

5 Adult The new wings are damp and crumpled, but soon dry out and flatten in the sun. After an hour or so, it is ready to fly away.

scale, and *pteron,* meaning wing). If you touch a butterfly, these scales often rub off as dust. It is the scales that give the wings their vivid colours; underneath the wings are clear like other insects' wings.

Sometimes the colours on the wings help hide the insect from predators. Many moths, for instance, have mottled brown wings and are almost invisible when resting on wood during the day.

Sometimes the bright colours of a butterfly's wings warn a predator that it is poisonous to eat. Or they may mimic another butterfly that is poisonous to eat. The viceroy butterfly mimics the similar-looking monarch in this way. Some butterfly wings have spots that look just like eyes. The owl butterfly of South American rainforests startles predators by suddenly flashing its eyespots.

Wing colours may also attract a mate. The wings of many male lepidopterans have scent glands to attract females as well.

MIGRATING BUTTERFLIES

Butterflies don't look like strong fliers, but species like the painted lady migrate huge distances to escape cold winters. The monarch (above) is the most remarkable. Every autumn, huge clouds of monarchs leave eastern North America and fly south for 3200km to winter in the Mexican mountains. What is amazing is that none of them have made the journey before, for they are barely a month old. Monarchs live only six weeks, and it was their great grandparents that flew north in the spring. Yet the monarchs know just where to go, to the precise tree.

Monarchs in winter When monarchs reach their winter home in the Mexican mountains after their long migration, they huddle together in huge numbers on trees for warmth. There they stay until the following spring, when they all head north again to spend the summer breeding.

KINDS OF BUTTERFLY AND MOTH

Butterflies are just one of the 24 families of lepidoptera; most are moths, such as hawkmoths, burnets and clothes moths. But there are 17,700 known species of butterfly, including skippers, metalmarks and snouts, whites and sulphurs, blues, hairstreaks and coppers, swallowtails, and nymphs. The largest group is the nymphs, of which there are almost 6000 different kinds, including red admirals, viceroys and mourning cloaks. They are sometimes called brush-foot butterflies because they have brush-like hairs on their short front legs which help them locate food. Skippers are not true butterflies for they have plump, hairy bodies like moths and hooked antennae.

Swallowtails are found all over the world but are most common in the tropics, where they grow up to 25cm across.

Moon moths come from South East Asia. They fly mainly at night.

Peacock butterflies are brush-foots. They have four eyespots on their brilliantly coloured wings, which they flash to frighten off predators.

Holly blue caterpillars make a sweet liquid called honeydew, which ants milk.

Orange tips have bright orange tips to their wings.

Leopard moths are night fliers, often seen fluttering round street lights, to which they are attracted.

Red admirals often migrate huge distances. Some have been known to fly across the Atlantic in 12 days.

SPIDERS, SCORPIONS, WORMS & SNAILS

The world is full of many tiny creatures besides insects. There are snails and slugs that creep along the ground, worms that burrow underground, and many more. Some, like insects, belong to a huge group of little creatures called *arthropods*, which also includes spiders and other arachnids, centipedes, and woodlice.

Orb webs are beautiful circular webs strung between branches or other supports in the flight path of insects. Orb web spiders build a new web every night, eating the old one to save protein.

HOW SPIDERS HUNT

Different species of spider have different methods of catching their prey. Many weave silken nets called webs. Some are simple tube-shaped webs inside holes, others are elaborate *orb* webs. The web is usually sticky, so any insects flying into it are stuck fast.

Spiders such as tarantulas and sun spiders crush their victims with their powerful fangs, but most species use their poisonous bite to kill or disable their prey. Some spiders, such as the black widow and funnel-web spiders, have a bite so poisonous that it can be fatal to humans.

Not all species of spider make webs. Some catch their prey by dropping a silk net on them. Others, such as the Australian trapdoor spider, ambush their prey from a burrow with a carefully-fitting and well-camouflaged flap. Hunting spiders stalk their prey and leap on them from a distance.

ARACHNIDS

Arachnids are small, scurrying creatures that look a little like insects, but they have eight legs, not six, and their bodies have only two parts. Arachnids also have a pair of 'arms' called *pedipalps* and a pair of fangs called *chelicerae*. There are over 70,000 different kinds of arachnid, including spiders, scorpions, harvestmen, ticks and mites.

Spiders are found in nooks and crannies almost everywhere in the world. They are most abundant where there is plenty of vegetation, but you can encounter spiders in the darkest cellars and down the deepest mines, as well as high on mountains. Spiders are hunters, feeding mainly on insects and other arthropods – though a few large 'bird-eating' species, or *tarantulas*, occasionally eat lizards and small rodents. Unlike other hunting animals, spiders generally have poor eyesight. They usually have eight simple eyes, not the compound eyes of insects, and hunt by 'listening' to vibrations in the ground, which they pick up with their legs. Jumping spiders, wolf spiders and ogre-faced spiders are exceptions, having very keen eyesight.

Ticks and mites are very tiny, but they can be real pests, bringing sickness to humans, animals and plants. Ticks are blood-suckers, and their bite may not only irritate but also infect their victim with organisms that cause disease. Typhus and spotted fever are transmitted this way. Red spider mites and other sap-sucking mites can harm fruit trees and other greenhouse plants. Scabies mites can make people itch, and house-

LIFE IN THE SOIL

Soil is one of the richest of all wildlife habitats, teeming with tiny creatures. Scientists estimate that there are 2.5 million spiders in the soil beneath every hectare of pasture land, as well as 25 million insects and 1500 million mites – and if you weighed all the worms in the soil beneath a field of sheep they would weigh more than the sheep. All these creatures play a vital part in maintaining the soil structure and in recycling nutrients. Worms air soil by burrowing through it, and improve its texture by eating and then excreting it. Bacteria help to turn rotting plant and animal matter into soil nutrients essential for plants.

Thorn-backed spider (left) from South America.

Woodlice chew their way through tough twigs and leaves. Like sea crabs, they are crustaceans.

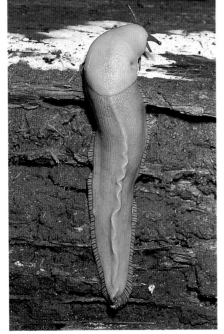

Banana slug *Slugs are gastropods, like snails, but they have no shell. They feed at night, eating roots and leaves, which is why they are pests.*

SCORPIONS

Fossil scorpions have been found in rocks over 400 million years old, and there are now 1200-1300 different species. Nearly all live in hot countries. Many inhabit rainforests, but they also thrive in deserts. Like spiders, scorpions have eight legs, but their pedipalps have developed into two huge pincers for gripping their prey. Their long arched tail has a poisonous sting in the end, usually used to subdue larger prey. Humans can be killed by the sting of some scorpions such as the Durango scorpion of Mexico and the North African variety of a scorpion known as the fat-tailed scorpion.

Scorpions detect their victims through vibrations in the ground – then tear them apart with their pincers.

dust mites can bring on asthma attacks in some people. But mites are also helpful, playing a vital role in recycling nutrients in the soil. Even house-dust mites clean up dead skin.

CENTIPEDES AND MILLIPEDES

These are long, wriggling creatures with many legs. Centipedes have fewer legs, just one pair on each segment of their bodies; millipedes can have up to 200. Centipedes are hunters with powerful jaws to devour insects, worms and grubs.

Most millipedes are herbivores, living on dead plants.

SNAILS AND SLUGS

Snails and slugs have soft, squidgy bodies. Snails are protected by a hard shell on their backs. When danger threatens, a snail can slip inside its shell. Slugs and snails are not arthropods but *gastropods*, which means 'stomach foot', because they seem to slide along on their stomachs. As they crawl along, they ooze a trail of slime to ease their way over the ground.

DID YOU KNOW?

The biggest spider is the Theraphosa leblondi, a bird-eating spider from South America. Its legs span up to 26cm, as big as a page of this book.
***Cyclosa* spiders** of South East Asia fool predators by disguising their own victims as spiders.
Great grey slugs of western Europe mate by circling for over an hour on a branch, then launching themselves into the air to hang from a long trail of mucus. They then mate for 7–24 hours.

Garden snails tend to emerge to feed only when it is damp. They are related to the thousands of species that live in water, but they have a lung to breathe with rather than gills.

The leaf litter on the soil surface is as teeming with life as the soil itself. Bacteria, fungi, worms, snails and hundreds of different arthropods all live on the rotting plants and help turn them into the rich humus that makes the soil fertile.

Earthworms wriggle through the soil by contracting some of the segments that make up their long, thin bodies. As they move, they take soil in through the front of their bodies and excrete it through the end.

Centipedes hunt at night among decaying leaves and twigs, killing victims with the poison from their strong claws.

SEA CREATURES

Along the seashore and in shallow seas there are many fascinating and beautiful creatures, from sea anemones and starfish to crabs and lobsters, many of them living in the rocky pools filled by the sea at high tide.

STARFISH
Starfish are easily recognizable by their five arms. Inside their bodies are tubes that they use to pump water in and out of hundreds of *tube feet* which poke out under each arm. The pumping flexes the arms and drives the starfish along. Starfish are all meat-eaters and prey on molluscs and crustaceans.

CORALS, ANEMONES AND JELLYFISH
Corals may look very different from jellyfish, but like anemones, they are all creatures called *cnidaria*.

Coral reefs are made up of tiny animals like sea anemones called *polyps*. They stay all their lives fixed in one place, attached to a rock or to dead polyps, and grow a cup-shaped skeleton. The skeleton becomes hard coral when they die. Coral reefs are colonies made up from millions of these polyps and their skeletons, and can stretch for thousands of kilometres. *Fringing* coral reefs grow near shores. *Barrier* reefs form a little way offshore. Coral *atolls* form around the edge of an old volcano. As the volcano sinks or the sea level rises, so the coral grows up and eventually just a ring of coral, the atoll, is left at the surface.

Anemones tend to stay in one place, but can slide along. Jellyfish float freely, drifting with the currents. Like both corals and anemones, jellyfish have tentacles with stinging cells called *nematocysts*. These are both for protection and for catching fish. Jellyfish, though, can be very poisonous.

ALONG THE SEASHORE
Every seashore has its own variety of plant and animal life, each specially adapted to the conditions. The seashore is a testing place for anything to live – battered by waves, submerged in salt water twice a day, then dried by wind and bright sunshine.

Sandy shores often look completely lifeless, but there are many creatures just below the surface – razor clams, lugworms, sea cucumbers, tiny crabs and burrowing sea anemones – burrowing into the sand to protect themselves from the drying wind and sun and from hungry predators. Some filter food from sea-water when the tide washes over them, others eat tiny particles from the sand.

Along the highest tide line, you often see sandhoppers feeding on rotting seaweed. They are small crustaceans that look a little like yellow woodlice – except they have strong back legs for hopping out of danger.

Rocky shores The best shores for marine life are usually those protected from the worst of the pounding waves, perhaps by rocks

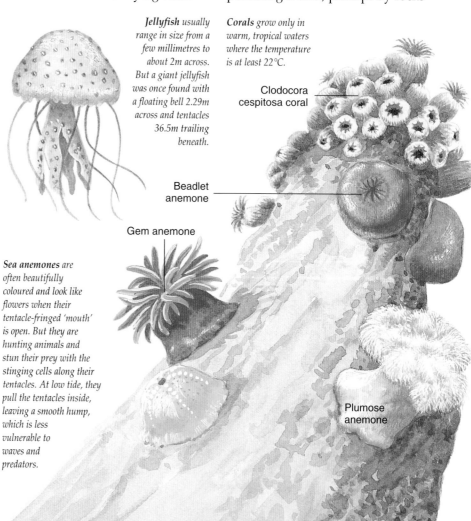

Jellyfish usually range in size from a few millimetres to about 2m across. But a giant jellyfish was once found with a floating bell 2.29m across and tentacles 36.5m trailing beneath.

Corals grow only in warm, tropical waters where the temperature is at least 22°C.

Clodocora cespitosa coral

Beadlet anemone

Gem anemone

Plumose anemone

Sea anemones are often beautifully coloured and look like flowers when their tentacle-fringed 'mouth' is open. But they are hunting animals and stun their prey with the stinging cells along their tentacles. At low tide, they pull the tentacles inside, leaving a smooth hump, which is less vulnerable to waves and predators.

and sea weeds. Here shellfish can clamp themselves to rocks and hide inside their shells from the drying wind and Sun while the tide is out.

High up the shore on many rocky coasts, along the high tide line, there are often hundreds of tiny snails called periwinkles, which feed on microscopic plants. Lower down, often hiding in cracks, are barnacles and limpets. Each limpet tends to return to exactly the same spot after feeding, slowly wearing an oval scar on the rock. There are often dense clusters of mussels, too, waiting for the tide to come in so they can open up and pump in water through their gills to feed.

Under rocks, there may be tiny brightly coloured sponges, colonies of sea squirts looking like jelly, and sea slugs which pick up the stinging cells from sea anemones and carry them on their backs for protection. And then there are predators such as crabs, starfish and ragworms, which prey on mussels and other shellfish.

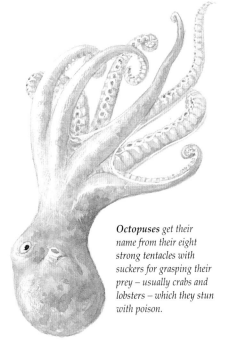

Octopuses get their name from their eight strong tentacles with suckers for grasping their prey – usually crabs and lobsters – which they stun with poison.

MOLLUSCS

After arthropods, such as insects, molluscs are the largest of all groups in the animal kingdom. Most tend to have hard shells and soft bodies, and most live in water, especially the sea.

There are seven main kinds including: *gastropods*, such as snails, limpets and winkles; *bivalves*, such as mussels, cockles, oysters and razor shells; and *cephalopods*, such as octopuses and cuttlefish.

The cephalopods are the most complex of all animals without backbones. They are also the biggest. Giant squids can have bodies up to 6 metres long, with tentacles adding another 10m.

Common cuttlefish have no shell but an internal skeleton of chalky material. When threatened, they eject a dark ink to hide them from predators, as do all cephalopods.

Sea urchins have long stinging spines that can grow up to 40cm long in some Pacific species.

Sea cucumbers often eject their gut when threatened. They grow a new one, abandoning the old twisted tubes.

Sea urchins and sea cucumbers *are, like starfish, echinoderms. Sea urchins live near the shore, and fragments of their shells are often found on beaches. When alive, they bristle with spines. These protect them and help them move, rather like stilts. The spines also have suckers that enable them to cling to rocks. The mouth is a hole in the underside, with five large teeth. Sea cucumbers have no shell, but they have a leathery skin and a covering of chalky plates called* spicules.

CRUSTACEANS

There are an enormous number of different crustaceans, ranging from tiny water-fleas or *Daphnia* and common woodlice to barnacles, shrimps, crabs and lobsters, but most of them live in water. They are all *decapods*, which means they have 10 legs, though the first pair are often strong pincers.

Crabs and lobsters are usually protected by their own tough shell, but hermit crabs live inside the discarded shells of some molluscs. They have two antennae on their heads, and a pair of eyes on stalks which they use for detecting prey. They use their large, strong pincers to hold and tear food. With lobsters, one of the claws usually has blunt knobs for crushing victims and the other claw has sharp teeth for cutting. Male fiddler crabs have one giant pincer which they waggle to attract a mate.

Spiny spider crab Giant Japanese spider crabs can grow carapaces (body covering) up to 30cm across and legs 120cm long.

Common lobsters can live up to 50 years – unless they are caught by humans and eaten. They are dark green when alive but turn red when cooked.

55

PLANTS

There are over 275,000 different kinds of plant, ranging from tiny plankton visible only under a microscope to giant trees over a hundred metres tall. Plants grow almost anywhere – on land and in the sea, on plains and mountain tops, even in deserts and snowy wastes – and 40% of the world's land surface is covered by forests and grassland.

STEM

The stem supports the leaves and flowers of a plant. It also carries water, minerals and food up and down between the plant's leaves and roots. Water and minerals run up through the stem from the roots in thin tubes called *xylem*. Food made in the leaves is carried down to the rest of the plant in tubes called *phloem*.

Many plants have stems that are green and bendy. Plants like this are called *herbaceous* plants, because many are herbs, such as mint and basil. Woody plants such as trees and shrubs have stiff stems or trunks covered in bark. Woody plants tend to have more xylem than herbaceous plants.

A *terminal bud* grows at the tip of each stem, making the plant grow taller. *Lateral buds* grow farther back along the stem, at places called *nodes*. Some lateral buds grow into new branches. Some grow into leaves or flowers.

SPORES AND SEEDS

The first plants ever to grow on land were plants such as fungi, lichen, mosses, liverworts, ferns and horsetails. Plants like these are usually quite simple in structure and grow from tiny cells called spores (see page 65). 300 million years ago, primitive plants like these dominated the earth.

Today, however, most plants grow from seeds not spores. Unlike the more primitive plants, seed-making plants have stems, leaves and often roots and flowers as well. There are over 250,000 *species* (kinds) of seed-making plants. 700 of them are plants called *gymnosperms* – that is, conifers and cycads (see page 64). All the rest are flowering plants or *angiosperms* (see pages 60–61).

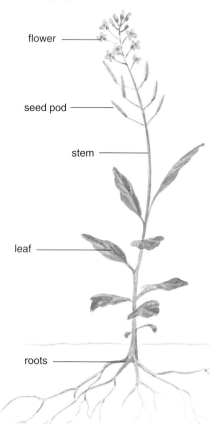

The parts of a plant.

flower ——

seed pod ——

stem ——

leaf ——

roots ——

Honeysuckle is a climbing plant that uses other plants or walls of buildings for support, as its own stem will not support it.

ROOTS

Roots are the parts of a plant that grow down into soil or water. They anchor the plant in the ground and absorb all the water and minerals it needs to grow. In some plants, such as beetroot, the roots also act as a food store.

When a plant begins to grow, the seed sends out a single primary root, which quickly branches out into secondary roots, protected by loose cells called *root-caps* as they probe through the soil.

With some plants, such as grasses, there are dozens of fine roots spreading out in all directions. These are called *fibrous* roots. With others, such as carrots, there is one large root, with just a few fine roots branching off it. The large root is called a *taproot*. On every root, there are tiny root hairs, which increase the root's ability to take up water and minerals from the soil.

Some plants are unable to make their own food, and they use their roots to draw food from other plants. Plants that do this are known as *parasites*. Mistletoe is a parasite that grows on apple trees.

A few climbing plants, such as ivy, have roots that grow high on the stem, as well as down into the ground. They use these roots to fix themselves to trees, walls and fences.

LEAVES AND FLOWERS

Leaves catch sunlight to make the food a plant needs to grow. They are usually broad and flat to catch as much sunlight as possible (see right). Each leaf is usually attached to the stem by a small stalk called a *petiole*. The flat part of the leaf is called the *blade*.

Flowers are the parts of a flowering plant that make the seeds from which new plants will eventually grow (page 60).

Oak tree leaves are called simple *leaves, because they have only one blade.*

Silver birch tree leaves, like all leaves, have a network of veins, which not only acts as a framework to hold the leaf up to the Sun but also carries water into the leaf and the food it makes out.

Walnut tree leaves are known as compound *leaves because they have a number of blades on the same stalk or petiole.*

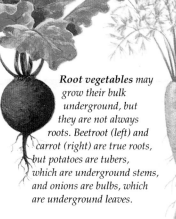

Root vegetables may grow their bulk underground, but they are not always roots. Beetroot (left) and carrot (right) are true roots, but potatoes are tubers, which are underground stems, and onions are bulbs, which are underground leaves.

FOOD FOR PLANTS

Unlike animals, plants make their own food by absorbing sunlight in a process called *photosynthesis*. The Sun gives the plant energy to convert carbon dioxide from the air and water into food.

Photosynthesis occurs mainly in the leaves, which contain two special kinds of cell: *palisade* and *spongy* cells. Inside each are tiny packages called *chloroplasts* that contain a green substance called *chlorophyll*, which makes leaves green.

Carbon dioxide is drawn from the air through tiny holes called *stomata*, on the underside of each leaf. Water is drawn up from the ground through the stem. When the Sun shines, the chlorophyll soaks up energy and changes water into hydrogen and oxygen. The hydrogen joins with the carbon in carbon dioxide to make sugar. The oxygen goes out through the stomata.

The newly made sugar is carried away through the veins to where it is needed. There it is converted into fats and starches for storage or is burned up at once, leaving carbon dioxide and water. This is called *respiration*.

PLANTS AND WATER

Plants cannot survive without water. Deprived of water, they soon wilt. Nearly all plants are at least two-thirds water, and some algae are 98 per cent water. Water fills up the tiny cells that make up each plant (page 8) and keeps them rigid, like air in a balloon.

For a plant, water is also like the blood in your body, carrying dissolved gases, minerals and nutrients where needed. Sometimes it oozes from cell to cell through the cell walls, a process called *osmosis*. Sometimes it streams up the long tubes or xylem; it is then called *sap*. The fine branching veins you can often see on leaves are xylem.

Plants lose water continually by *transpiration*. This is the evaporation of water through the stomata. As water is lost through the stomata, more water is sucked up through the xylem to replace it, like drink through a straw. In every plant, water is drawn in continually through the roots, up through the xylem and into the leaves.

Photosynthesis, the food-making process of green plants.

sunlight

carbon dioxide

oxygen

sugars

water and minerals

DID YOU KNOW?

The oldest plant in the world is a hawthorn bush in New England that is at least 10,000 years old.

The longest plant in the world is the rattan vine, which can snake through tree tops for over 150m.

The window plant survives in the intense heat of the South African desert by growing underground, with only a small window of transparent leaf exposed to the sun.

Pollen is so tiny you can see it only under a microscope. This is yew pollen.

SEEDS & FRUITS

Not only garden flowers and wild flowers, but every herb, grain, fruit, shrub, tree and vegetable is an *angiosperm*, or flowering plant. Many flowers are beautiful, but they are never just for show. The flowers of a flowering plant contain the parts that create the seeds and fruit from which new plants will eventually grow.

POLLINATION

For a seed to develop, pollen from the male anther has to get to the female stigma. Some flowers are *self-pollinating*. This means the pollen moves from the anther to the stigma on the same plant. Others are *cross-pollinating*. This means the pollen from the anther must be carried to the stigma of a different plant of the same kind.

Sometimes the wind will carry the pollen. Sometimes it is carried by insects such as bees, or even by birds or bats. In tropical forests, hummingbirds often carry pollen. Bees are attracted by the flower's colour and sweet-smelling nectar. As they sip the nectar, they may brush pollen on to the stigma or take some on their bodies to the stigma of other flowers.

MALE AND FEMALE

Just as there are male and female animals, so a flower has male and female parts. Seeds for new plants are made when *germ cells* from the male and female parts meet.

The short stalk in the middle of the flower is called the *pistil* and is the female part of the flower. Arranged around it are the spindly stalks of the male parts or *stamens*. The head of the pistil is the *stigma*; the head of a stamen is an *anther* and it makes grains of *pollen* (male germ cells) in pollen *sacs*.

For a flower to make a new seed, pollen from an anther must be put on the stigma. This is called *pollination*. The pollen then moves down inside the pistil to the eggs (female germ cells) in the *ovary*, in the heart of the flower. When the pollen meets the eggs, it fertilizes them and turns them into seeds. The ovary then gradually swells and hardens to become a fruit.

SEED LEAVES

When a flowering plant grows from a seed, it sprouts either one or two leaves at first (see GROWING FROM SEED). Seeds that sprout one leaf are called *monocotyledons*; seeds that sprout two leaves are called *dicotyledons*. Grasses, cereals, date palms, tulips, daffodils and lilies are all monocotyledons. Many other flowers, together with trees, vegetables and fruits, are dicotyledons.

Each of these two kinds of plant develops in its own way. The stems of dicotyledons, for instance, get thicker and often tough and woody (see page 56); those of monocotyledons grow quickly but stay soft and pliable. Dicotyledon leaves tend to be broad and net-veined, whereas those of mono-cotyledons are narrow and grass-like with parallel veins. In mono-cotyledons, however, the flower parts tend to be set in threes.

DID YOU KNOW?
The largest flower is that of the stinking corpse lily of Indonesia, which can grow up to 1m across and weigh up to 7kg.
The largest seeds are those of the double coconut or coco-de-mer of the Seychelles, which weigh up to 20kg.
The smallest seeds are those of orchids – one million of them weigh only 0.3g.
The smallest flowering plant may be the Wolffia duckweed – the entire plant is only 0.5mm across.
Orchids can make more than 2,000,000 seeds in a single capsule.

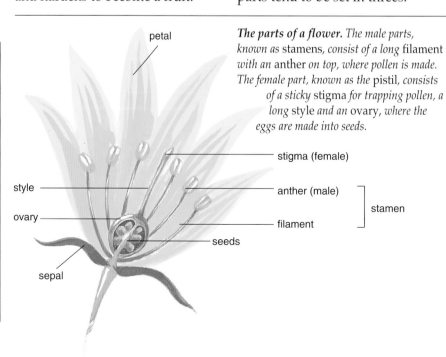

petal

The parts of a flower. The male parts, known as stamens, *consist of a long* filament *with an* anther *on top, where pollen is made. The female part, known as the* pistil, *consists of a sticky* stigma *for trapping pollen, a long* style *and an* ovary, *where the eggs are made into seeds.*

style

ovary

sepal

stigma (female)

anther (male)

filament

stamen

seeds

FRUITS AND SEEDS

Fruits come in many shapes and sizes. Some, such as oranges, bananas and tomatoes, are soft and juicy. The hard pips are the seeds. Others, such as acorns and hazelnuts, have a hard, dry shell. Peas, beans and other *legumes* are soft, dry fruits held in a case called a pod. Juicy fruits such as berries (including grapes) and citrus fruits are sometimes called *true fruits* because they are made from the ovary of the flower alone. Apples and pears are *false fruits* because they include other parts. In an apple, only the core is the ovary. Plums and cherries are called *drupes* because there are no pips, just a hard stone holding the seed. Walnuts are also *drupes*.

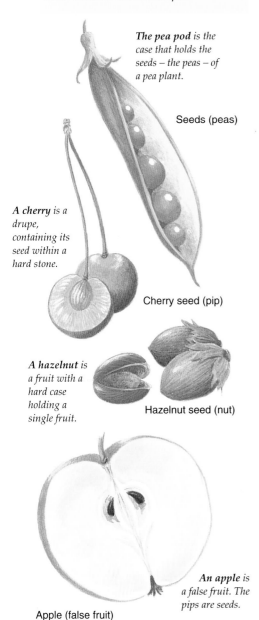

The pea pod is the case that holds the seeds – the peas – of a pea plant.

Seeds (peas)

A cherry is a drupe, containing its seed within a hard stone.

Cherry seed (pip)

A hazelnut is a fruit with a hard case holding a single fruit.

Hazelnut seed (nut)

Apple (false fruit)

An apple is a false fruit. The pips are seeds.

SEED DISPERSAL

If plants are to spread from one place to another, seeds must be scattered or dispersed. Different seeds are dispersed in different ways. Some seeds are light enough to be blown away. The feathery seed cases of many grasses can be borne on the wind for several kilometres. Some seeds, such as coconuts, are carried by water. Coconuts can float thousands of kilometres across the ocean before being washed up upon the shore.

Many fruits and seeds are dispersed by insects, birds and other animals – either because the animal eats the fruit or because the seed clings to the animal's body. Some fruits simply burst, showering seeds in all directions.

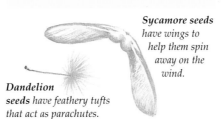

Sycamore seeds have wings to help them spin away on the wind.

Dandelion seeds have feathery tufts that act as parachutes.

GROWING FROM SEED

By the time the seeds leave the parent plant, each has the *germ* (start) of a new plant and the food to help it grow. But the seed will not *germinate* – grow into a plant – unless the conditions are right. It needs water, and the right amount of warmth. Poppy seeds can lie buried deep in the soil for many years until ploughing brings them to the surface and they start to grow.

When a seed germinates, a root and a green shoot sprout from it. The root or *radicle* grows down into the soil and the shoot or *plumule* grows up towards the Sun. The first leaves to break through to the daylight are the seed leaves or *cotyledons*. Soon after, the main stem begins to grow and true leaves appear.

Only certain parts of the plant, called *meristems*, can grow. These are usually at tips of shoots and roots, so when a young plant begins to grow, its shoots and roots grow mainly longer rather than fatter. This is called *primary growth*. Later on, however, some plants tend to thicken or branch out in different directions.

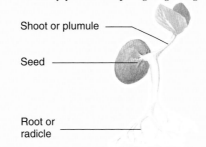

Shoot or plumule

Seed

Root or radicle

Cat-carried Some fruits are carried by sticking to animals. Burrs and some other seeds have tiny barbs that hook on to cat fur.

Bird-borne Birds feed on fleshy fruit, drawn by its bright colour. The hard seeds pass through the bird and emerge ready for germination.

True leaves

Cotyledons

59

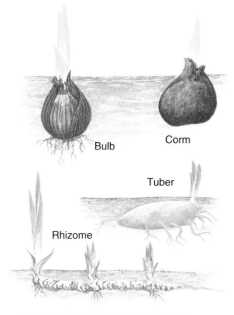

Bulb

Corm

Tuber

Rhizome

GARDEN & WILD FLOWERS

All flowers grew wild originally, but over the centuries gardeners have adapted flowers for the garden – selecting seeds and grafting plants together to bring out chosen qualities, such as red blooms or straight stems. There are now over a million kinds of garden flower. But many wild flowers are becoming rare as human activity restricts their habitats.

BULBS, CORMS, RHIZOMES AND TUBERS

Many perennials sprout not only from seed but also from parts of the root or stem. This is called *vegetative propagation*.

Plants such as lupins grow on the base of an old stem. As the plant ages, the stem widens and the centre dies, leaving a ring of separate plants around the outside. Plants such as irises sprout from thick stems called *rhizomes* that grow sideways beneath the ground. Sometimes, the rhizome ends swell into lumps called *tubers*. Potatoes are tubers. Crocuses have a bulbous base to their stems called a *corm*. Tulips have *bulbs*. Bulbs look like corms but are made of leaves, like the layers of an onion, rather than a stem. In winter, rhizomes, corms, bulbs and tubers all act as *storage organs* (food stores) for the plant. In spring, they send up new shoots.

Plants can also *propagate* (grow new plants) from long stems that creep over the ground (*runners*) or under it (*suckers*).

LIFE CYCLE

Garden and wild flowers and other herbaceous plants are divided into four basic types according to their life cycle: perennials, biennials, annuals and ephemerals.

Ephemerals are very short-lived, growing from seed, blooming and dying within a few weeks. However, since this may happen several times in the same season, ephemerals can spread quite rapidly. Many desert plants and weeds such as groundsel are ephemerals.

Annuals The word 'annual' means yearly, and annuals are plants that grow from seed, flower, disperse their seeds and die in a single growing season. Sometimes the seeds may lie in the ground for several years before conditions are right for germination (page 59). Most delphiniums are annuals, so are some herbs, and peas and cereals.

Biennials live for two years. In the first summer, the young plant grows a ring of leaves on an underground food store such as a bulb or taproot. The food store sustains it through the winter and in the spring sends up a stem that flowers in the summer. Foxgloves are biennials, as are many vegetables.

Perennials live for a number of years, surviving through the winters, like biennials, on food from an underground food store such as a bulb. Wallflowers, chrysanthemums, Michaelmas daisies and many other garden flowers are perennials.

Rhododendrons are among the most successful of all shrubs. They originate from Asia.

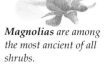

Magnolias are among the most ancient of all shrubs.

Clematis are climbing shrubs that have weak stems but stay up by wrapping their stems around a support.

SHRUBS

Shrubs are smaller than trees, and rather than having a single trunk, they often branch out just above the ground. In very cold or dry places, shrubs may simply be small, spindly versions of trees. Like deciduous trees, deciduous shrubs lose their leaves in winter. Evergreen shrubs, such as holly and rhododendron, keep their leaves all year round.

DID YOU KNOW?

The slowest flowering plant is the rare Puya raimondii of the Andes. It takes 150 years to grow its first flower – then dies.

The mirror orchid has flowers that look like female wasps – so male wasps are drawn to the flowers and help pollinate it.

The stapelia flower attracts flies by smelling – and looking – like rotting flesh.

GARDEN FLOWERS

People have cultivated garden flowers for their scent and colour for thousands of years, and there are now countless different varieties. Long and careful breeding by *horticulturists* (gardening specialists) means most have much larger, more colourful petals or stronger scents than their wild ancestors.

While wild dog roses have tiny, delicate pink or white blooms with just a few petals, garden roses tend to have large, many-petalled blooms in bright colours ranging from deep reds to purples and even blues. Wild roses also tend to have far fewer flowers and many more leaves than garden roses.

Lupins are large and colourful garden flowers very popular in the western USA.

The Canterbury bell is one of many bellflowers grown in gardens.

Clary is a biennial with scented leaves grown for use in perfumes and to brighten garden borders.

Carnations are popular as cut flowers because they last a long time once cut.

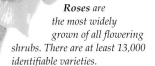

Roses are the most widely grown of all flowering shrubs. There are at least 13,000 identifiable varieties.

WILD FLOWERS

As farms and buildings take over more land, there are fewer places for wild flowers to grow and some have become very rare. A few are so rare that they must be protected by law, such as the lady's slipper orchid which now grows in only one place in Yorkshire.

Every kind of place has its own range of wild flowers. On heathlands, for instance, you may see purple blooms of bell-heather, yellow gorse and scarlet pimpernel. In meadows, you may see in the grass tiny flowers such as buttercups, daisies, clover, forget-me-nots and ragged robin. Woodlands are the home of bluebells, primroses and celandines. By the sea, sea campion and thrift bloom among the rocks and birdsfoot trefoil flowers in the grass on the cliffs.

The lady's slipper orchid is just one of the many kinds of orchids that have become very rare.

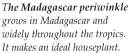

The Madagascar periwinkle grows in Madagascar and widely throughout the tropics. It makes an ideal houseplant.

The giant sequoia tree of California is the world's largest living thing. One called General Sherman is 83 metres tall and over 11m thick – as wide as four trucks side by side. It contains enough wood to build 40 houses – or 5000 million matches!

TREES

Trees range widely in size, from dwarf willows a few centimetres high to vast redwoods towering tall as a skyscraper. But they are generally the biggest of all flowering plants, and forests cover almost 40 million square kilometres of the world's land. They may be either coniferous (page 64) or broad-leaved, such as oaks and beeches, so called because they have broad, flat leaves.

TIMBER

Huge numbers of trees are cut down each year to provide timber for everything from cricket bats to buildings. Timbers are divided into softwoods and hardwoods.

Softwood is wood from coniferous trees, such as pine, larch, fir and spruce. 75–80% of the natural forests of northern Asia, Europe, and the United States is softwood, and vast areas are now covered by plantations, where fast-growing conifers are set in ranks for easy harvesting.

Hardwood is the wood from broad-leaved trees, such as oak, and most hardwood forests are in the tropics. There are many kinds of hardwood tree, but all grow very slowly. When hardwood trees are cut down, it is over a century before new trees grow in their place. So as more hardwood is used, the forests are becoming depleted.

DID YOU KNOW?
The roots of a wild fig tree in South Africa extend 120m into the ground.
Whistling thorn trees in Australia have seed balls with holes made by ants and whistle eerily in the wind.
The fastest-growing tree is a tropical pea tree, Albizia falcata. One grew over 10m in 13 months.
Willows and alders may warn other trees of caterpillar attack by releasing airborne chemicals.

LEAVES

You can identify broad-leaved trees by their leaves. Sycamore trees, for instance, have leaves shaped like three-pointed stars, horse-chestnuts have clusters of tongue-shaped leaves.

Deciduous trees Many broad-leaved trees are *deciduous*. This means that they shed their leaves at certain times of the year. In the tropics, deciduous trees shed their leaves at the start of the dry season. In temperate regions (between the tropics and polar regions), deciduous trees shed their leaves in autumn.

In temperate regions, as days grow shorter and colder, the chlorophyll (page 57), which makes leaves green, breaks down. This allows other colours – yellows, reds, purples and browns – to shine through, giving woodlands their glorious autumn hues. Scar tissue and sometimes a material called *wound gum* grows across the base of each leaf stalk, and eventually the leaf drops off.

Evergreen trees keep many of their leaves all year round. Each leaf lasts up to four years and often has a dark, waxy skin.

FLOWERS

Some trees, such as horse chestnuts, have big, showy flowers, but the flower of oaks and ashes are so tiny you would hardly notice them. Trees pollinated (page 58) by animals tend to have large flowers to attract the animals. Most trees pollinated by the wind have much smaller flowers.

TREE TRUNKS

Look at the trunk of a tree that has been cut down and you will see a series of rings. These are called *growth rings*, and show how the tree has grown each year. The edge of each ring marks where growth ceased in winter. By counting the rings, you can tell how old a tree is.

The dark, dense centre of the tree is dead *heartwood*. Around this is paler, living *sapwood*, run through with thin pipes (*xylem*) that carry sap up from the roots to the leaves. Further out is the thin *cambium* layer where the sapwood grows and then the *phloem* (food-conducting) layer. On the outside is a protective skin of *bark* made mainly of cork. Just underneath is another *cambium* layer where the bark grows.

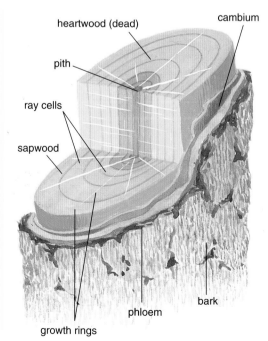

heartwood (dead)
cambium
pith
ray cells
sapwood
phloem
bark
growth rings

Many wind-pollinated trees have long clusters of flowers called *catkins*. Catkins have almost no petals, so the pollen sacs on the anthers (page 58) are exposed to the wind. So too are the sticky stigmas, ready to catch pollen carried to them from the anthers by the slightest breeze.

SEEDS AND FRUITS

Once the flowers are pollinated, the seed grows inside a fruit, which can be soft like a plum or hard like a nut.

Because trees are tall, the wind is often enough to carry seeds and fruits some way – which is why the seeds of many trees are wind-dispersed. Elms have seeds like flying saucers, maples have seeds with wings and willows have seeds like parachutes.

Inside soft fruits there is usually a hard seed. When a bird eats the fruit, the seed inside will pass right through the bird unharmed, ready to grow wherever it is dropped. Hard, dry fruits such as nuts and acorns are often buried by animals such as squirrels to provide a food store for the winter. In the spring, they may germinate where they are buried.

TROPICAL FORESTS

The forests of the tropics are the world's richest plant habitat. Temperate forests rarely have more than a dozen different trees. In tropical forests, 100 separate species are often found in one hectare.

Most tropical forests have several distinct layers. Towering above the main bulk of the forest are isolated *emergent* trees, growing up to about 60m tall. Below them, 30–50m above the ground, is a dense, unbroken *canopy* of leaves and branches at the top of tall, straight trees. In the gloom beneath is the *understorey*, where young emergents, small conical trees and shrubs grow. Clinging lianas wind their way up through the trees and *epiphytes* – a group including orchids and ferns – grow high on the trees where they can reach the daylight.

TREES LARGE AND SMALL

You can often identify a tree just from its shape. The wide dome of an English oak, or the spire-like shape of the Lombardy poplar may be obvious even at a distance. But tree-shapes may be distorted by, for instance, exposure to the wind on cliff tops and mountains. In such cases, a tree may be identified by the shape of its leaves, buds and twigs, by the colour and texture of its bark, or by its flowers and fruit.

Maple trees grow throughout the cooler regions of the northern half of the world and are especially common in Asia. Many are deciduous, with leaves that turn a brilliant red-gold in autumn. New England, USA, is famous for its autumn display of maples. The Norway maple shown here is one of the tallest maples, reaching 30m.

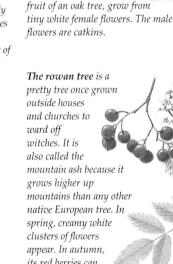

Oak trees grow all over the northern half of the world. There are hundreds of kinds. Oaks from cooler countries are usually deciduous; those from warm places tend to be evergreen. Acorns, the fruit of an oak tree, grow from tiny white female flowers. The male flowers are catkins.

The rowan tree is a pretty tree once grown outside houses and churches to ward off witches. It is also called the mountain ash because it grows higher up mountains than any other native European tree. In spring, creamy white clusters of flowers appear. In autumn, its red berries can be made into a jelly for eating with game.

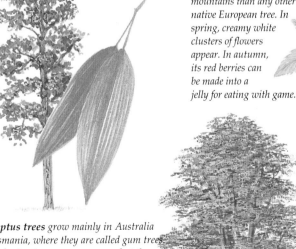

Eucalyptus trees grow mainly in Australia and Tasmania, where they are called gum trees. All eucalyptus trees are evergreens, but there are many kinds. Some reach barely 1m in height. The swamp gum grows about 90m tall. Among the gum trees widely used for timber are the jarrah, the messmate, and the blackbutt. The leaves of the Tasmanian blue gum provide an oil used as a medicine and to help refine petroleum.

Beech trees are part of the large beech family of trees, which includes oak trees and chestnuts as well as beech trees themselves. Beeches are often the dominant species in temperate forests.

Silver fir *resin is used to make turpentine.*

Larches *are the only deciduous conifers.*

Sitka spruce *provides good wood for paper.*

Cedar of Lebanon *gives a hard, scented wood.*

Western hemlock *is grown for box wood.*

Douglas firs *can grow to over 75m tall.*

Austrian pines *are often used as windbreaks.*

Cones *look very different from flowers but serve the same purpose. There are male cones and female cones, usually on the same tree. Small male cones make pollen. Wind wafts pollen through the air in yellow clouds to the larger, harder female cones, where it fertilizes the egg. After a year or so the fertilized egg becomes a winged seed, ready to be carried away by the wind.*

CONIFERS AND CYCADS

Conifers and their close relatives the cycads and ginkgos are among the oldest of all plants, first appearing over 275 million years ago. They are called gymnosperms and all make seeds in cones. Conifers are usually tall, ever-green (except for larches), and often grow in cool and mountainous regions. Cycads are tropical plants that look a little like palm trees. Ginkgos are tall Chinese trees.

Corsican pine *Pines are the largest family of conifers. They all grow fast and are full grown in less than 20 years – which is why they provide 75 per cent of the world's timber. Typically, they have needle-like leaves.*

FOREST AND WOODLANDS

In the colder parts of the world there are vast areas of coniferous forest – especially in Canada and Siberia, where the Boreal forests or *taiga* extend for thousands of kilometres. Forests like these contain a mixture of trees, and include spruce, pine, fir and larch. Coniferous forests tend to be dense and dark, with few other plants growing beneath the trees.

In slightly warmer areas, there used to be huge areas of broad-leaved temperate woodland, but much has been cut down.

Where they do survive, broad-leaved woodlands are usually more varied than coniferous forests, containing oak, ash, chestnut, beech, maple, sycamore, elm, alder and hickory. Most, though, are dominated by either beech or oak. Broad-leaved woods are not so dense as coniferous forests, and many plants can be found growing beneath the trees.

Coniferous forests *tend to be dense and dark, especially where dominated by spruce, allowing few other plants to grow. Fungi and bacteria are found feeding on the thick layer of decaying needles and mosses, while ferns and lichens grow on the trees themselves. If fire creates a gap in the forest, birch trees are the first to grow back. But after 60 years or so, the young pines, that grow slowly in between, take over.*

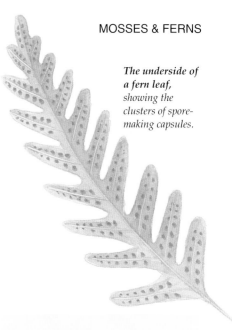

The underside of a fern leaf, showing the clusters of spore-making capsules.

MOSSES & FERNS

Not all plants grow from seeds. Mosses, liverworts, club mosses, horsetails and ferns are among the many that begin life as special cells called *spores*. These plants were among the first to grow on land, first appearing some 400 million years ago.

PRIMITIVE PLANTS

Mosses and ferns love damp, shady places and they are often seen carpeting rocks and growing on trees in moist woodlands and steamy tropical rainforests.

Mosses and liverworts make up a group of plants of their own, called *bryophytes*. Most form green cushions barely a few millimetres thick on walls, rocks and old logs. Unlike most plants, they have no true roots. Instead, they take in moisture from the air through their stems and tiny root-like threads called *rhizoids*.

Club mosses and horsetails make another group, called *pteridophytes* or featherplants. 300 million years ago plants like this grew up to 40m tall. Today, they are very much smaller and look a little like mosses. But unlike mosses, they have roots and primitive leaves, and veins to carry food and water up and down inside the stem.

Ferns are also pteridophytes, but their leaves look little different from those of seed plants. Some ferns are tiny, with mossy fronds less than 1cm long. Tropical giant tree ferns, though, can grow up to 25m tall and look like palm trees with their tall stem and crown of leaves.

FERNS

Ferns prefer damp, shady places. Most live on the ground, but some grow on the leaves or stems of other plants.

Like mosses, ferns grow new plants in two stages. First of all spores are made in knobbly clusters of *sporangia* (spore-making sacs) on the underside of the leaves. Then, providing the spore lands in a suitable place, it grows into a tiny heart-shaped plant called a *prothallus*, which makes male and female cells. This is the second stage. When the prothallus gets covered in a film of rainwater, the male cells swim to the female cell. A new root and stem then grow to become the new fern frond and the prothallus dies.

MOSSES AND LIVERWORTS

Mosses and liverworts are the amphibians of the plant world. Not only do they need plenty of moisture in the air to survive, they also need to be partly underwater to grow new plants successfully. This is why mosses and liverworts often live beside rivers and streams. Even so, mosses can survive for weeks at a time without water.

Mosses and liverworts grow new plants in two stages. In the first stage, male and female sex cells are made. The male cells are made on bag-like stems called *antheridae*. When ready, the male cells, which look like tadpoles, swim to the cup-like female stems, the *archegonia*.

Once the male and female cells have joined, the second stage begins. First a stalk called a *sporophyte* grows up from the ova. On top of the sporophyte is a little capsule containing thousands of tiny spores. Then, when the time is right, the capsule bursts, ejecting the spores. If these spores land in a suitable place, new male and female stems will grow from them, and the cycle can begin again.

Polytrichum moss (above) The yellow spore capsules have holes at one end. When wind shakes the capsules, spores are shaken out like pepper from a pepper pot.

Sphagnum moss (below) lives in bogs. It can soak up 25 times its own dry weight in water. It is the main constituent in peat, which is used as fuel in Ireland and Scotland.

Fern fronds

Fern leaves are called fronds. A new fern frond begins curled up like a shepherd's crook. As it grows, however, it gradually uncurls and spreads out to form feathery or broad, flat leaves. When it is mature, brown dots of sporangia called sori appear on the underside of the leaves.

Puffball (above) Some fungi reproduce by spreading spores. These can clearly be seen in this photograph, looking like whisps of smoke.

MORE FUNGI

Some fungi grow by spreading their hyphae in a mat or mycelium. Others reproduce with the aid of *spores*, minute cells that grow into new fungi. In a mushroom, the spores are inside the cap.

Like mosses, most fungi that reproduce by means of spores go through alternating generations (page 65). The first generation gives the male and female sex cells (the *gametophytes*); the second generation gives the spores from which the new fungi will grow.

POISONOUS FUNGI

Only ten of the 10,000 fungi found in Britain are really poisonous, though many more are bad to eat. But those that are poisonous can kill – which is why it is important not to eat any fungus or mushroom unless you are absolutely sure it is edible. Some poisonous ones, such as fly agaric, provide a warning in their bright colours. Others, like the harmless-looking destroying angel and death cap, look similar to mushrooms – but they are deadly.

Fly agaric is deadly. Eating even small amounts can knock you out.

FUNGI

Mushrooms, toadstools, yeast, the mould that grows on bread and mildew all belong to a special group of organisms called fungi. Some, such as mushrooms, are good to eat, but others are deadly poisonous. Some grow on plants and animals, making them ill; others provide antibiotic drugs. Yeast helps bread rise and beer ferment.

LIVING OFF OTHERS

Although they grow in the ground like plants, fungi are not really plants because they have no chlorophyll and so cannot make their own food. Because they cannot make their own food, fungi must live off other plants and animals.

Fungi are the *biodegraders* of the living world. *Parasites* live off living organisms; *saprophytes* live off plant and animal remains. Both feed by releasing special chemicals called enzymes which rot away whatever they are feeding on. The fungi absorb the nutrients and minerals from the rotting organism. The chemicals released by some mould fungi give blue cheeses their flavour, others can make mouldy bread deadly.

WHAT FUNGI ARE MADE OF

Fungi are made of hundreds of cotton-like threads called *hyphae*, which can digest and absorb the materials they live on. Hyphae usually spread out in a tangled mass through the soil – or within the tissues of the plant or animal they are living on.

Sometimes, the hyphae can bundle together in fruiting bodies such as toadstools and mushrooms; sometimes they may form pinheads, like the mould on rotting fruit.

cap ——————

gills ——————

—————— ring

Ordinary field mushroom. This is the edible one.

This 'field' mushroom is actually cultivated in caves for eating.

A mushroom (left) grows into the air from a mass of fine white threads underground called the mycelium. *The top has a protective layer or cap, under which there are lots of thin sheets called gills. The gills are covered in spores and a mature mushroom can produce some 16,000 million spores in its brief lifetime.*

Ring The fringing ring around the stalk is left when the cap opens.

Shaggy ink cap Black spores in the cap drip 'ink'. Other ink-caps are poisonous.

ALGAE

A kind of algae was among the first living organisms to appear on the Earth, some 3000 million years ago. There are now many kinds and despite their generally small size they are one of the most important of all forms of life, providing a food source for creatures such as shrimps and whales and providing oxygen for water life.

PLANT OR ANIMAL?

There are many kinds of algae, from single-celled micro-organisms to huge fronds of seaweed 60m long. Some live in fresh water, some sea water, some on wet mud, some on damp trees and wooden fences and some even inside small, transparent animals. The smallest float freely like animals, but others need a place to grow like a plant.

In fact, algae are such a varied group, and can live so differently from other plants, that many scientists include them not in the plant kingdom but with slime moulds in a separate kingdom called *Protoctista*. The oldest, simplest kind of algae, called blue-green algae, are classified as bacteria, called *cyanobacteria*.

Coloured algae One of the reasons algae are so important is that they have chlorophyll (page 57) so they can get energy from sunlight alone. Chlorophyll is green, but algae are not always green. In the bigger seaweeds, in particular, the green may be masked by other pigments, like brown or red. Green algae are found mostly in freshwater, forming long threads, such as *Spirogyra*, or flat leaf-like layers. Red algae are found mostly in warm seas.

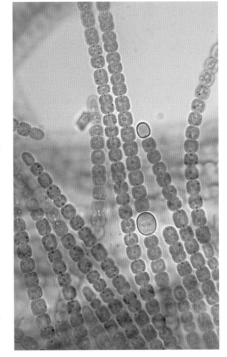

Diatoms (above) are tiny single-celled creatures containing yellow-pigmented chlorophyll. Some live in sea water, floating in countless billions; others are found in farmyard puddles and on wet mud. They are too small to be seen singly, but colonies sometimes form a brownish 'tidemark'. Over millions of years, their silica-based skeletons have formed deposits on the sea floor up to 300m thick. This is dug up as fuller's earth, once used to clean wool and now to decolourize oil and gas.

Seaweeds usually live in shallow water, because they need sunlight for energy. The biggest seaweeds – the brown algae such as kelp – grow at depths of 15–20m. Fern-like red algae grow slightly deeper at 30–60m. Those in shallower waters may be battered by the waves, and the survivors tend to have tough 'stems' and strong holdfasts fixed on rocks, such as those of oarweed.

Bladder wrack

Caragheen

Knotted wrack

Sea lettuce

Lichens (above) are a remarkable partnership between algae and fungi. The algae are tiny green balls, which make the food to feed the fungi. The fungi make a protective layer above and beneath, and hold water. Some lichens provide food for reindeer in the Arctic. The orange lichen here is Xanthoria parietina, which grows on roofs in the country. Lichens are very sensitive to air-pollution and will not grow where the air is dirty.

PLANTS FOR FOOD

Plants provide most of the world's people with their basic 'staple' food, whether it is bread or soya beans, and around the world an area almost one and a half times as big as the United States is devoted to growing crops.

IN THE GRAIN

Cereals such as wheat, rice, maize, barley, oats and rye are the world's major source of food. They are grasses, and we usually eat their seeds, or grain, leaving the stalks and leaves to rot into animal feed called *silage*. Wheat grain is usually ground into flour to make bread, pasta and other foodstuffs and is the basic food for 35% of the world's population. There are more than 30 kinds altogether. *Spring wheat* is planted in spring and harvested in early autumn. *Winter wheat* is planted in autumn and harvested the next summer. In Asia, most people live on rice grown in flooded fields called *paddies*, where they can grow up to three crops a year (above). Maize is an important food for animals as well as humans.

THE FARMING YEAR

For crops to grow well, they must be planted and harvested at the right time of year. Crops planted too early can be ruined as late frosts nip young shoots in the bud; crops planted too late may not have time to ripen. So the farmers follow seasons closely. To grow spring wheat, for instance, the farmer ploughs early in spring to break the soil into furrows ready for the seed. A *seed drill* plants a measured amount of seed and covers it with soil to protect it from the birds. Through the summer, the farmer tends the growing wheat, watering it if necessary and spraying it with chemicals to kill off pests and diseases. Then, when the wheat is ripe in late summer, the farmer harvests it – perhaps with a big machine called a *combine harvester* (right), which both cuts the wheat and separates the grain from the stalks.

FARMS ANCIENT & MODERN

Farmers first started planting crops in the Middle East at least 10,000 years ago. But there are signs that crops were grown almost as long ago in many parts of the world, including the Far East, India and Latin America.

The crops grown then were much the same as those grown now – wheat and barley, rice, oats and beans. But although the crops are the same, they are now farmed in a very different way in many places. Traditional crop farming involved ploughing small fields with muscle power alone, and allowing long *fallow periods* (rest years) for the soil to recover. Crops are still grown this way in much of Africa and Asia.

But in North America and Europe, crop farmers today use more and more machines to plough and reap huge, open grain fields. They also use every inch of soil, greenhouses and orchards for vegetables and fruit. They apply chemical fertilizers in huge quantities to keep the soil fertile rather than leaving it fallow. This is called *intensive* agriculture.

THE GREEN REVOLUTION

About 40 years ago, farmers in North America and Western Europe began to abandon traditional crops and plant special *high-yield* varieties of rice, wheat and maize instead. These high-yield kinds grow so fast and so big that farmers at once got bumper harvests. They could even plant crops two or three times in a year.

Farm machinery Once farmers used to work with muscle power alone – humans, horses and oxen. Nowadays farms in Europe and North America are highly mechanized. So a few people can run a large farm. Not only are there tractors to pull ploughs, but machines for seeding, machines for baling straw and machines for packaging silage and grain.

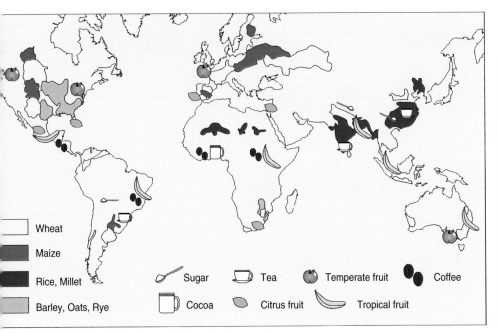

Wheat

Maize

Rice, Millet

Barley, Oats, Rye

Sugar | Tea | Temperate fruit | Coffee

Cocoa | Citrus fruit | Tropical fruit

THE WORLD'S CROPLANDS

The crops that farmers grow depend on the climate and soil, and also on the style of farming. Of the basic staple foods, cassava, for instance, is unsuitable for large-scale mechanized farming, but grows well in dry places, which is why it is grown widely in parts of Africa. Wheat is grown all over the world, especially in temperate regions. But Europe is the leading producer of potatoes, barley and rye, while Asia grows 90% of the world's rice and sweet potatoes, as well as huge quantities of wheat, sorghum and beans. North America grows almost half the world's maize crop.

Soon, impressed farmers were trying these grains out in other countries – and they grew so much more food that people called it the *Green Revolution*. In India, harvests doubled between 1960 and 1970. In Asia, harvests doubled between 1971 and 1976. Using these techniques, Western farmers now feed up to ten people from land that once fed only one.

Indeed, the Green Revolution seems to have been so successful that some people think we might solve the world's food problems just by pushing it further. This view has been helped by biochemists who have exploited genetic engineering techniques (page 13) to make millions of identical plants grow conveniently to the same height, in the same shape and at the same rate.

Limits to the revolution The success is an illusion: high-yield crops give big harvests only if the land is well irrigated and the farmer uses a lot of fertilizer, pesticides and machines. As farmers demand more from the soil, they have to put more back in to sustain yields. Farmers now need to use ten times as much nitrogen fertilizer as they did 40 years ago. Often only big businesses can afford to pay for all this – which is why, in the USA at least, just a few big agribusinesses farm so much land.

DID YOU KNOW?

Of the world's thousands of edible plant species, less than 100 are usually grown as crops.

Farms in Japan and England get grain yields from each hectare seven times the size of those in Nigeria.

Japanese farmers get their high grain yields only by applying 372kg of fertilizer to each hectare – 65 times the level in Nigeria.

The world grows each year over: 500 million tonnes of wheat; 470 rice; 450 maize; 300 potatoes; 172 barley; 110 beans; 120 cassava; 100 sweet potatoes; 75 oats and rye.

The highest ever wheat yield is over 13 tonnes per hectare.

CASH CROPS

Many farmers in the Third World are subsistence farmers, growing food mainly for themselves and their families to eat. But much of the best land is often owned by rich farmers who, rather than growing food for local people, grow crops to sell abroad for money. These crops, called *cash crops*, include everything from sugar and bananas, coffee and tea to cotton and jute. Many people in the Third World – in South America, in particular – work on big plantations growing cash crops. Some poor countries, such as Nicaragua, rely on cash crops to bring in desperately needed foreign income.

Grape picking in the Bourgogne region of France (left).

Coffee picking in Arusha, Tanzania (above).

HERBS & SPICES

For centuries, herbs and spices have been used to treat medical ailments and to add extra flavour to foods. In ancient times, many people believed that herbs and spices had mystical powers and they were often used for ceremonial purposes.

HERBALISM

Many herbs used to be grown for their medicinal properties, and even as late as the 18th century physicians often relied on herbal medicines to treat diseases. Scholars published huge volumes listing the healing qualities of thousands of plants. But these were usually written in Latin, so the herbal remedies were not easily available to ordinary people. Nicholas Culpeper (1616–1654) wrote *The Complete Herbal* in English, making all the remedies available to everyone for the first time.

THE SPICE TRADE

Throughout history people have used herbs and spices for food and medicine. They were prized by the early Chinese, Egyptian, Greek and Roman civilizations and the search for new spices was the reason behind much of the early exploration.

Spices were used to add variety to otherwise monotonous diets, and to conceal the flavour of foods that had gone bad. The aromatic properties of herbs and spices were also much appreciated. They could be added to oils and used to disguise body odours.

Trade in spices was a valuable source of income for many nations.

The Phoenicians were among the earliest specialist traders in herbs, spices and perfumes. Later, many European cities prospered under the spice trade, in particular Venice. The Venetians already had ships collecting silk from Damascus, and they also brought back spices, including pepper, ginger, nutmeg and cloves, to grace the tables of the wealthy. Spice prices soared. Pepper was regarded as black gold in the Mediterranean, and it became a universal currency. In some countries people had to pay their taxes in pepper.

During the 15th century, the great voyages of exploration

CULINARY HERBS

Herbs add flavour and interest to food. They also play an important part in the diet, despite the fact that they are usually eaten only in small quantities. Many raw herbs contain valuable nutrients. Fresh parsley, for example, contains large amounts of vitamin C, while others are rich in vitamin B, carotene (which the body converts to vitamin A), potassium, calcium and iron, all of which aid digestion and are needed for the proper functioning of the body.

Oregano, also called wild marjoram, has been used to flavour food, soothe sore throats and dye cloth.

Fennel is used extensively in the cooking of fish. Like many herbs, it also relieves stomach upsets.

Bay leaves were used as garlands to crown athletes, heroes and poets in Rome. The bay is a member of the laurel family of trees and shrubs.

Basil is often used in tomato dishes and is popular in the Mediterranean. In ancient Greece it was known as the `King of Herbs'.

Rosemary is a coastal plant and takes its name from the Latin ros marinus, *meaning sea dew. It was thought to improve memory.*

Sage, like many herbs, is thought to have healing qualities. Its scientific name, Salvia, *means healthy.*

Chives are used in many dishes where a mild, oniony flavour is needed.

Garlic is one of the oldest cultivated herbs. Egyptian pyramid builders thought that it gave them strength.

Thyme, along with parsley and bay leaves, is a vital ingredient in the versatile herb mixture called bouquet garni.

Parsley is one of the most commonly used herbs. It can be used either as a flavouring or as a garnish.

Mint adds a fresh taste to food and drinks. It is also used with cinnamon to keep clothes moths away.

opened direct sea routes for the spice trade. Vast profits could be made by trading in these lucrative products – in 1504, Vasco da Gama (1469–1524) brought 5000 tons of pepper and 35,000 hundredweight of other spices to Europe which he sold for a 400 per cent profit.

During the 16th and 17th centuries, wars were fought to gain a foothold in Asia and a share in the lucrative spice trade.

Spices were always considered a luxury in Europe, but in the Middle East and Asia they were used lavishly to add flavour to the staple diet of rice and pulses, and to disguise the taste of meat that had gone off. Markets offered a colourful array of herbs and spices that could be blended together for different dishes. Some curries, for example, contained up to thirty different spices.

MEDICINAL QUALITIES
Many herbs and spices are known to have antiseptic properties and throughout history, aromatic plants

Early Traders
Marco Polo (1254-1324) was one of the first Europeans to travel to the court of the Mongolian emperor Kublai Khan. Marco Polo spent 17 years travelling in China and helped to open the trade routes between Europe and the Orient.

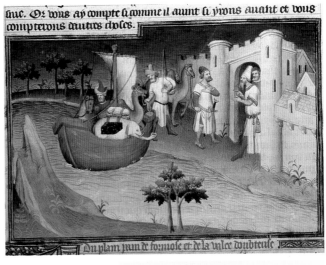

have been used, as they were believed to ward off disease. Monks began to grow and preserve these plants, and monasteries became centres for medical practice.

Many herbs were also believed to have magical properties. In the Middle Ages, superstition held that hyssop and garlic could repel witches and other evil spirits. In eastern Europe, people believed that garlic would keep vampires away, so they wore garlands of the pungent flowers around their neck for protection.

ANCIENT EGYPTIANS
Spices have always been sought after, and people have traded in them for centuries. The Ancient Egyptians imported many spices, herbs and aromatic oils from Babylon and India. Star anise, fenugreek, caraway, opium and saffron were used for cooking, medicines, and for the manufacture of perfumes and cosmetics. Aromatic oils were particularly important to the Ancient Egyptians. They believed that they could use these to conquer death through the process of embalming.

Chillies add spicy heat to many dishes. They cause sweating, which cools down the body, and are often eaten in hot countries.

Saffron is expensive because it takes 400,000 hand-picked crocus flower stamens to make a single kilogram.

Cloves are the dried flower buds of a large Asian tree. They are used for cooking and to help ease toothache.

Coriander plants have a very unpleasant smell before their seeds ripen.

Ginger comes from the root system of a tall grass-like plant. It is harvested after flowering and boiled if it is not to be used within a few days.

Peppercorns come in two main types: black pepper, which is the unripe fruit, and white pepper, which is the ripe fruit with the outer skin removed.

Nutmeg is the aromatic seed of a tree. When fresh, it is covered with fleshy pink tendrils called *mace*. Mace is used to flavour some beers and to season foods.

Cumin is used in a powerful stomach settler drunk in India.

Cardamom in coffee was a sign of hospitality in the Middle East because it was very rare and expensive.

Cinnamon comes from the bark of a tree. It is stripped when wet, scraped clean and left to dry. It is then tightly rolled.

Star anise comes from an oriental tree that takes over 15 years to produce its distinctive aniseed-like aromatic fruits.

FLOWERING HERBS
Edible flowers can be used to add flavour and colour to many dishes. Early herb gardens included lilies, briar roses, marigolds and mallows. The petals and flower-heads were used to bring colour to salad dishes. Borage was another important flowering herb. The young leaves and small purple flowers could be added to summer drinks.

ASTRONOMY

Astronomy is the study of all space outside the Earth's atmosphere – not just the thousands of stars you can see twinkling in the sky on a clear night, but the countless billions of stars you cannot see, the planets, comets, dust clouds, galaxies, invisible radiation waves and everything else in the universe.

WATCHING THE STARS

A major problem for astronomy is that we normally only see stars through the fog of the Earth's atmosphere. It is because air moves in the atmosphere that stars twinkle. So observatories are set high on mountains where the air is clear and dry. The photograph of the observatory above was taken by leaving the camera shutter open for several hours. The bright rings trace the paths of the stars across the sky during the time the shutter was open.

WHAT CAN WE SEE?

By far the brightest thing in the night sky is the Moon. Five planets are also bright enough to be seen – Venus, Mars, Jupiter, Saturn and Mercury. Most other points of light in the night sky are stars. About 6000 stars shine brightly enough to be seen by the naked eye – 3000 from the southern half of the world and 3000 from the north. The brightest is Sirius. Canopus and Vega are very bright too.

Star brightness As long ago as 150 BC, the Greek astronomer Hipparchus divided stars into six groups, according to brightness. A 1st magnitude star is 100 times as bright as a 6th magnitude star. Astronomers still use this system, but because we can now see many more stars with telescopes, there are more orders of magnitude. Indeed, the brightest star, Sirius is given a magnitude of minus 1.46; Canopus has a magnitude of minus 0.72. Good binoculars will show 9th magnitude stars; a small telescope shows 10th magnitude stars. The faintest objects detected so far have a magnitude of 26.

Distances in space Of course, some stars appear to be bright simply because they are fairly

THE CELESTIAL SPHERE

If you watch for long enough, the stars seem to sweep across the sky in a big circle. The stars are moving very fast, but they are so far away they are effectively fixed in one place. The movement we see is due to that of the Earth. As it spins from west to east, we see the stars revolve from east to west.

It is as if we were in a vast, spinning ball with the stars painted on the inside. This ball is called the *celestial sphere*. The whole star pattern seems to rotate once every 23 hours 56 minutes about the *celestial poles*, directly over the Earth's poles. So we see the same groups of stars come up over the horizon 4 minutes earlier each night. Each day, the Sun is in a slightly different place relative to the stars, as a result of the Earth's movement around the Sun. The Sun appears to move backwards relative to the stars, along a path called the *ecliptic*. It makes a complete circuit of the celestial sphere in a year.

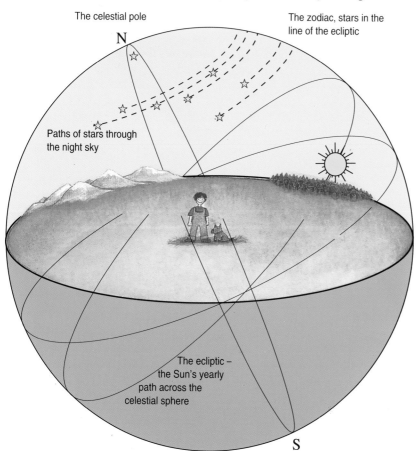

The celestial pole

The zodiac, stars in the line of the ecliptic

N

Paths of stars through the night sky

The ecliptic – the Sun's yearly path across the celestial sphere

S

close. To work out how bright a star really is, you have to find out how far away it is (right).

The distances involved are immense. Alpha Centauri, the nearest star to the Sun, is 41 million million km away – if our solar system were a grain of sugar, Alpha Centauri would be 5m away. So astronomers measure distances by how long light takes to cover the distance.

Light takes just 1.28 seconds to reach us from the Moon, 1.2 hours to reach us from Saturn, and over 4 years from Alpha Centauri. So Alpha Centauri is 4.3 *light-years* away. Yet Alpha Centauri is just one star in our galaxy, the Milky Way Galaxy, and although the Milky Way Galaxy is vast – 100,000 light-years across – it is just one of billions of galaxies in space. The most distant galaxy yet detected is 10 billion light-years away. This means we are not seeing this galaxy as it is now, but as it was 10 billion years ago, more than 5 billion years before the Earth formed!

MEASURING DISTANCE

As the Earth circles the Sun, nearby stars seem to move slightly compared to stars further away – the nearer a star, the more it moves. By measuring how much a star moves against background stars, we can work out how far away it is. This is called *parallax*. But it works only for nearby stars. For distant stars, we compare colour and brightness. We expect stars of a certain colour to be a certain brightness (page 77). If a star is dimmer than expected, it must be very far away.

With distant galaxies, we look at *red shift* – the way their light gets redder as they move away, just as the roar of a car deepens as it speeds past. From what we know of the universe (page 80), the redder they are, the faster they are moving – and the further away they must be.

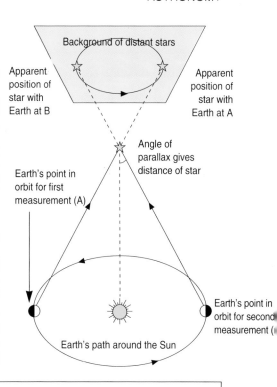

Background of distant stars

Apparent position of star with Earth at B

Apparent position of star with Earth at A

Angle of parallax gives distance of star

Earth's point in orbit for first measurement (A)

Earth's point in orbit for second measurement (

Earth's path around the Sun

DID YOU KNOW?
There is an observatory 1600m down a mine in the USA with a huge tank of cleaning fluid acting as a 'telescope'. This can detect neutrinos – sub-atomic particles so small they pass right through the Earth, but which react with chlorine atoms in the cleaning fluid to produce tiny but detectable flashes of light.
A light-year is 9,460,000,000,000 km.
Parallax distances are given in parsecs. One parsec equals 3.26 light-years.

SPACE TELESCOPES

Early astronomers had their eyes alone with which to scan the heavens. Today, astronomers have an array of telescopes and detection equipment. *Optical* telescopes use lenses and mirrors to magnify distant objects for the astronomer to see or, more commonly now, for recording on photographs or computer. Most observatory telescopes are *reflecting* telescopes, which magnify with curved mirrors. To see further or more clearly, observatories are building bigger mirrors, or linking small ones together. Optical telescopes show us only light, the visible radiation from the stars, but there is also invisible radiation. *Infrared* (heat) and *radio* telescopes pick up radiation with wavelengths longer than visible light. *Ultraviolet, X-ray* and *gamma ray* telescopes pick up radiation with wavelengths shorter than visible light. Each tells astronomers something slightly different about distant objects in space.

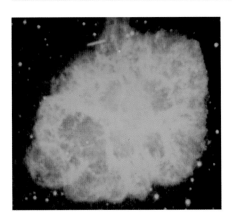

Optical image. *This photograph shows the Crab Nebula, the debris left when a giant star exploded as a supernova. The explosion was witnessed by Chinese and Japanese astronomers in 1054 AD.*

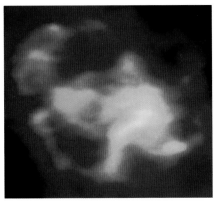

Radio image *of the Crab Nebula. Radio telescopes have shown that some galaxies (page 79), called* radio galaxies, *are far bigger than they appear to be in optical telescopes.*

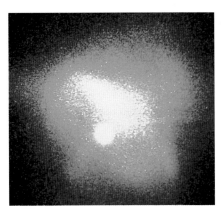

X-ray image *of the Crab Nebula. X-rays do not penetrate the atmosphere, so X-ray telescopes are mounted on orbiting satellites. This picture is from the Einstein satellite.*

SPACE EXPLORATION

The age of space exploration began in 1957 when the first spacecraft, *Sputnik 1*, was launched by the then Soviet Union. This was the start of a new series of adventures for mankind, which has taken astronauts to the Moon and probes to other planets.

THE FIRST MAN ON THE MOON

On 21 July 1969, astronaut Neil Armstrong stepped down from the lunar module of the *Apollo 11* spacecraft, which only hours earlier had landed on the surface of the Moon. Millions of people all over the world heard his comment: 'That's one small step for man, one giant leap for mankind.' He was followed soon afterwards by Buzz Aldrin. It was one of the great moments in the history of space exploration. For the first time, human beings had set foot on a different world.

THE FIRST SPACEMAN

Sputnik 1 was an unmanned satellite. The first person to travel in space was a Russian, Yuri Gagarin. In April 1961 he made one orbit round the Earth in his spacecraft *Vostok 1*. The early Russian successes inspired the United States to step up its space exploration programme, and during the 1960s there was one space 'first' after another. In 1965 an American space probe, *Mariner 4*, sent back the first close-up photographs of Mars. In 1966 came another milestone in space exploration when a Russian probe, *Luna 9*, made a soft-landing on the Moon and sent back the first pictures from the Moon's surface.

Three years later, on 21 July 1969, the American astronauts Neil Armstrong and Edwin 'Buzz' Aldrin became the first people to set foot on the Moon. Their first steps were seen by television viewers all over the world.

ROCKETS & COMPUTERS

This sudden burst of activity in space became possible because of new technology. Rocket engines had been developed years before, but it was only in the late 1950s that they were made powerful enough to escape from the Earth's gravity and travel to other parts of

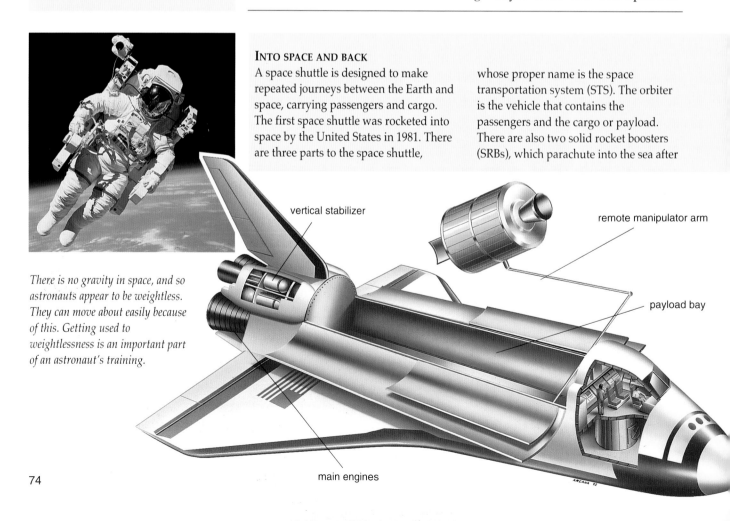

There is no gravity in space, and so astronauts appear to be weightless. They can move about easily because of this. Getting used to weightlessness is an important part of an astronaut's training.

INTO SPACE AND BACK

A space shuttle is designed to make repeated journeys between the Earth and space, carrying passengers and cargo. The first space shuttle was rocketed into space by the United States in 1981. There are three parts to the space shuttle, whose proper name is the space transportation system (STS). The orbiter is the vehicle that contains the passengers and the cargo or payload. There are also two solid rocket boosters (SRBs), which parachute into the sea after

vertical stabilizer

remote manipulator arm

payload bay

main engines

the solar system. The second invention that enabled space exploration to go ahead was the computer. Placing a spacecraft into orbit, guiding its progress, and bringing it back to Earth involves complex calculations which may have to be re-worked as the space flight progresses. Only a computer could make calculations of that complexity at the necessary speed.

SPACE PROBES

Hundreds of men and women have now travelled in space, some for a few days and others for several months. But manned space flight is only one side of space exploration. Many of the most important flights have been by unmanned craft equipped with instruments to send television pictures and scientific information back to Earth. Gradually, these space probes have extended farther out into the solar system. In 1974 the *Mariner 10* probe flew past Mercury, the nearest planet to

the Sun, close enough to send back clear, detailed pictures. Two years later two unmanned American *Viking* probes landed on Mars. All the planets in the solar system except the most distant, Pluto, have now been approached and photographed. Other unmanned probes have ventured out beyond the solar system into outer space and will never return.

LABORATORIES IN SPACE

Other aspects of space exploration have taken place closer to the Earth. These include the placing into orbit of space stations, where scientific work is carried out. These space stations, such as the American *Skylab* and the Russian *Mir*, stay in space and can be visited by astronauts as if they were 'space hotels'. Another exciting development is the *space shuttle* (see below), which is the first step towards regular passenger flights into space, and eventually the first human settlements beyond the Earth.

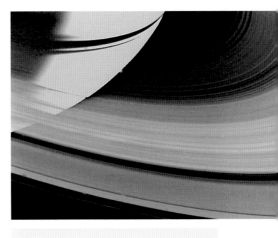

VOYAGER

The *Voyager* space probe programme was launched by the United States in 1977. Its aim was to fly past and photograph four of the outer planets of the solar system: Jupiter, Saturn (above), Uranus and Neptune. Among the surprises sprung by *Voyagers 1* and *2* was the existence of 'moons', or satellites, of Jupiter and Saturn that had not been seen before. Another was that Jupiter has a ring of gas round it . *Voyager 2* also flew past Uranus and Neptune and is now travelling out of the solar system.

the launch to be recovered and used again. The third part is the external fuel tank, which is released after the launch and burns up in the atmosphere. The orbiter, which travels on into orbit under its own power, is similar to a passenger aircraft. It has its own air supply so that the passengers and crew need not wear space suits. There are three decks in the orbiter, one above the other. At the top is the flight deck, from which the orbiter is controlled. Below this is a small galley, or kitchen, and sleeping quarters. The lowest deck contains equipment. Crew members can go outside the orbiter to carry out various tasks. They wear a manned manoeuvring unit (MMU), which has its own oxygen supply and gas jets which enable the astronauts to move around in space. When the orbiter re-enters the Earth's atmosphere, the resistance of the air brings its speed down sufficiently for it to make a safe landing on a special runway.

THE HUBBLE TELESCOPE

The Hubble Space Telescope (below), named after American astronomer Edwin Hubble, was the centre of an ambitious plan to launch a telescope into space. The idea was that a telescope in orbit would be able to take superb pictures without interference from the Earth's atmosphere. Unfortunately, a fault in its manufacture meant that at first it could not produce perfect pictures, but it has since been repaired.

DID YOU KNOW?

The first living creature to orbit the Earth was a Russian dog, Laika. She was launched in Sputnik 2 in November 1957 and lived in space for a week. Unfortunately, there was no way of bringing her back.

The first American to orbit the Earth was astronaut John Glenn. He made three trips round the Earth in his space capsule Friendship 7 in February 1962.

The largest group of people to have been sent into space at the same time was the eight-man crew of a space shuttle flight in October 1985. They remained in space for seven days.

The worst accident in the history of space exploration took place in January 1986. Seven crew members, including two women, were killed when the space shuttle Challenger exploded 73 seconds after takeoff.

THE STARS

The few thousand stars you can see twinkling in the night sky are just a tiny fraction of those scattered throughout the universe. Astronomers estimate there are 200 billion billion or so altogether. Like the Sun, they are huge fiery balls of hot gas.

CONSTELLATIONS
Ancient astronomers noticed that some stars seem to form patterns in the sky and gave each pattern a name, such as the Great Bear and Orion the Hunter (left and above). Astronomers now recognize 88 of these *constellations*, and give the brighter stars within each one a Greek letter such as alpha or beta. So the brightest star in the constellation of the Centaur is Alpha Centauri.

WHY STARS SHINE
Stars shine because they are burning. Deep inside, hydrogen atoms *fuse* together to form helium. This nuclear reaction creates so much energy that the temperature at the heart of a star may reach millions of degrees, making the surface glow brightly. It will go on glowing, and sending out light, heat, radio waves and other kinds of radiation, until nearly all the hydrogen is used up.

GIANTS AND DWARFS
Most stars are much the same size as our Sun, which is 1.4 million km across. But some *giant stars*, such as Aldebaran, are 20 to 100 times as big. *Supergiants* are vast. Antares is 330 times as big as the Sun, and there may be a star in the Epsilon Aurigae double-star system 3000 million km across. If this star were a football, the Sun would be a grain of salt. There are also tiny stars. Some *dwarf stars* are smaller than the Earth. *Neutron stars* may be only 15km across – yet contain as much matter as the Sun. They are so dense, a spoonful of their matter would weigh several tons.

STARLIGHT
Stars are so far away that they look like points of light even through the most powerful telescopes. But we can find out more about them by studying their colour.

If the light from a star is passed through a prism (page 161), it splits into a rainbow of colours called a *spectrum*. Different materials emit different spectra as

NORTHERN HEMISPHERE

SOUTHERN HEMISPHERE

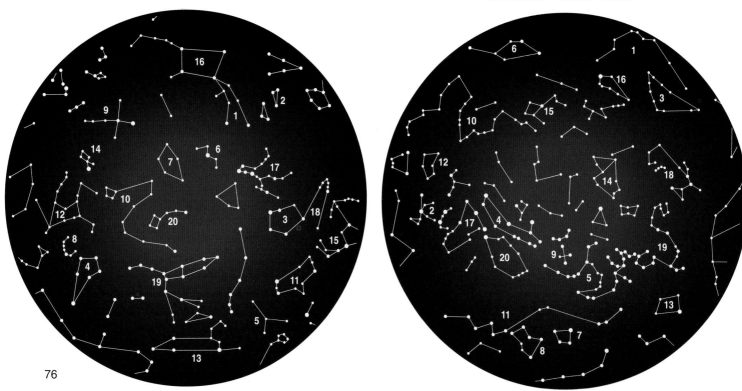

they burn. Very dense gases, like those deep inside a star, give an unbroken sequence of colours, called a *continuous spectrum*. Low-density gases, like those near a star's surface, give narrow bands of colours, called an *emission spectrum*. The pattern of bands tells us which gases are being emitted.

Spectra also show how hot a star is. Just as steel in a furnace glows red then white as it gets hotter, so hot stars with a temperature of over 35,000°C are white or blue-white; cooler stars (3000°C) are reddish.

Hot and bright, cool and dim In the early 1900s, astronomers Henry Russell and Ejnar Hertzsprung plotted a graph comparing stars' colour with their brightness (in absolute magnitude, page 73). They realized that the whiter and hotter medium-sized stars are, the brighter they glow; the redder and cooler they are, the dimmer they glow. Stars like this are called *Main Sequence stars* because they form a neat band across the graph. With giants, supergiants, dwarfs and neutron stars, the situation is a little more complex.

NORTHERN HEMISPHERE

1 Andromeda	11 Gemini
2 Aries	12 Hercules
3 Auriga	13 Leo
4 Boötes	14 Lyra
5 Cancer	15 Orion
6 Cassiopeia	16 Pegasus
7 Cepheus	17 Perseus
8 Corona Borealis	18 Taurus
9 Cygnus	19 Ursa Major
10 Draco	20 Ursa Minor

SOUTHERN HEMISPHERE

1 Aquarius	11 Hydra
2 Canis Major	12 Lepus
3 Capricornus	13 Libra
4 Carina	14 Pavo
5 Centaurus	15 Phoenix
6 Cetus	16 Piscis Austrinus
7 Corvus	17 Puppis
8 Crater	18 Sagittarius
9 Crux	19 Scorpius
10 Eridanus	20 Vela

Stars begin life as clouds of dust and gas called nebulae. *Clumps of dust and gas are pulled together by their own gravity.*

As the clumps form into dark blobs (dark nebulae), gravity pulls them together ever tighter and the pressure makes gas at the centre very hot.

Once the core reaches 10 million °C, nuclear fusion begins as hydrogen atoms fuse together to make helium. The star begins to shine.

With most stars, because the heat in the core pushes gas out as hard as gravity pulls it in, the star becomes stable.

THE LIFE OF A STAR

Stars are being born and dying all over the universe. The most massive stars shine brightly but live only ten million years or so. Stars like our Sun live for about ten billion years – so the Sun is about halfway through its lifespan. By looking at all the stars in the heavens, each at a different point in its history, astronomers have worked out how a star evolves. The sequence varies with the size of the star. When they are dying, the smallest stars become black dwarfs, not red giants or supergiants. The biggest stars end up as black holes. Mid-range stars become white or black dwarfs, or supernovae and neutron stars.

Eventually, hydrogen in the core is almost used up, but surrounding gas burns on and the star swells into a cool red giant. Big stars go on growing into supergiants; smaller stars lose their surface gas and shrink to white dwarfs.

In the core of a supergiant, the pressure may fuse even heavy elements, making iron. At this point, the star collapses in a second, then rebounds in a huge explosion as a supernova.

A supernova may collapse into a pulsar, a neutron star that sends out pulses of radiation like a lighthouse as it spins perhaps 30 times a second.

The Dumbbell Nebula is a planetary nebula – a vast cloud of gas that balloons away from the surface of a dying red giant. This nebula has been expanding at 27km per second for the past 50,000 years, and is already more than three light-years across.

A very big star can collapse with such force that nothing can stop it. The pull of gravity becomes so strong that even light is sucked in, creating a black hole.

HOW THE UNIVERSE BEGAN

Scientists believe that the universe began with a bang about 15 billion years ago. One moment there was just an unimaginably small, incredibly hot ball; a moment later the universe existed, after the biggest explosion of all time – the Big Bang. This explosion was so gigantic that material is still hurtling away from it in all directions at astonishing speeds.

1 The Big Bang The universe was born in a gigantic explosion, beginning with a split second's fantastic swelling (inflation).

IN THE BEGINNING

No-one knows why the Big Bang occurred, but scientists think this is what happened afterwards.

At the moment the universe was born, it was just a minute hot ball, many times smaller than an atom. Inside was all that was needed to make the universe, though the matter and forces were unlike anything we know today. Suddenly, it began to swell like a balloon.

A split second later, when it was still smaller than a football and as hot as ten billion billion billion °C, gravity went mad. Instead of pulling things together as it does now, gravity blew the tiny universe apart, flinging it out at a fantastic rate and swelling it a thousand billion billion billion times in less than a second! Scientists call this astonishing expansion *inflation*. Inflation provided the space for matter and energy to form.

Making matter As it mushroomed out, the universe began to cool, and matter and basic forces like electricity were created. There were no atoms, but there were quarks and electrons (page 150). There was also *anti-matter* – the mirror image of matter. When matter and anti-matter meet, they destroy each other and, for a moment, the fate of the universe was in the balance as they battled it out. Nearly all matter and anti-matter was destroyed in this battle, but there was just a little more matter. This is what survives today, a mere fraction of what was.

Inflation stopped after this titanic battle, but its momentum has kept the universe hurtling apart ever

since – and the afterglow of the giant explosion can still be traced today in the form of microwave radiation (page 161) coming from all over space. Most scientists agree that this *microwave background radiation* is good evidence that the Big Bang really happened.

Once inflation was over, gravity began acting normally, and soon the simplest atom, hydrogen, condensed from the chaotic stew. Within three minutes, hydrogen atoms fused to form helium. Before long, the universe was filled with swirling clouds of hydrogen and helium gas.

The formation of galaxies After a million years or so, the gases in the universe had curdled like sour milk into long thin strands, with vast dark holes in between. These strands themselves gradually clumped together into galaxies and stars.

It was gravity that gathered the gas clouds into strands – and yet scientists are puzzled how this happened. According to their sums, gravity could not have worked fast enough. Indeed, their sums only work if the universe holds up to 100 times more matter than it seems to. So some scientists think that the universe is really made mostly of *cold dark matter* that we cannot see.

But even dark matter does not explain why the gases clumped together in the first place. So some scientists believe the universe must have been slightly lumpy to begin with. In 1992, the satellite Cosmic Background Explorer detected faint ripples in the microwave background, which may indicate this was true.

BIG BANG TO BIG CRUNCH

As astronomers gaze into distant space, they see galaxies hurtling away from us in all directions at astonishing speeds. The further galaxies are away, the faster they seem to be moving. Most astronomers are sure this means that the universe is expanding.

But if it is expanding, will it go on expanding forever? Some scientists think so. This is called the *open universe* idea. Others argue that gravity is already

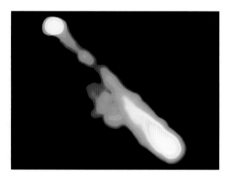

THE BLACK HEART OF A GALAXY

Quasars are the universe's most intense energy sources – as bright as 100 galaxies, yet no larger than our solar system. They are billions of light-years away yet emit radio signals that are easy to pick up. Because they are so far away, scientists think that they burst on the universe when it was young. As galaxies formed, huge amounts of gas were sucked together at their centre, forming a black hole (page 77). Quasars are the energy of the gas spiralling in.

3 Gas swirls *After a million years or so, the hydrogen and helium began to clump together in swirling clouds and strands.*

2 Matter forms *Once inflation ended, the universe kept on growing, but first very basic matter formed, then the first atoms – hydrogen and helium gas.*

4 & 5 Galaxies form *Eventually, the gas clouds condensed into galaxies of countless stars.*

beginning to put a brake on the expansion. If there is, indeed, a lot of dark matter (see left) out there, its combined gravity may eventually slow the expansion to a standstill. Once all the momentum has gone, gravity may finally begin to pull the galaxies back together again.

If and when this happens, the gravity of the galaxies will draw them closer at ever faster speeds and the universe will shrink almost as if the Big Bang were happening in reverse. Eventually all the billions of galaxies will fall together, and the universe will come to an end in a Big Crunch, just as it began with a Big Bang.

No-one can imagine what could follow a Big Crunch. Some people believe that if all the energy in the universe were squeezed into the size of a tennis ball in the Big Crunch, the universe would bounce back in a second Big Bang, and would go on alternately expanding and contracting forever.

Not all astronomers agree with the idea of either a Big Bang or a Big Crunch. Some say the universe has always looked the same and is not really getting any bigger. They argue that new galaxies are continually being born to replace those shooting away from us. A universe like this is forever in balance and has no beginning or end.

SPACE AND TIME

In 1676 Ole Roemer showed how an eclipse of Jupiter's moons was seen 10 minutes later because light from them took that time to reach us. This shows that we may not see events at the same time they happen. If we look at a star 5 billion light-years away, we see it as it was 5 billion years ago. From somewhere else, it is seen at a different time. So the timing of events depends on where you are. In 1905, Albert Einstein showed in his *special theory of relativity* that time can even pass faster or slower, depending where you are. If a car overtakes, the slower you're going, the faster the car seems to go past. But Einstein saw that if nothing can travel faster than light, then light would always move at the same speed, no matter where you were or how fast you were moving. So something overtaking you at the speed of light would seem to stretch; something coming towards you would seem to shrink. In the same way, time would stretch and shrink.

GALAXIES

Throughout the universe are countless systems of stars called *galaxies*. Our Sun is just one of 200 billion stars in our galaxy, the Milky Way Galaxy (right). The biggest galaxies were probably born within a billion years of the Big Bang. Smaller galaxies, though, may still be being born.

One idea is that galaxies formed as the strands of gas in the early universe condensed into billions of tiny blobs. Each blob became a star and their gravity

drew them together into galaxies.

The biggest galaxies are the ball-shaped *giant ellipticals*, with over 1000 billion stars. All galaxies formed from spinning gas clouds – but giant clouds spinning very rapidly formed beautiful *spiral galaxies* as stars and gas were dragged spinning towards their centre. The Sombrero Galaxy (left) is a spiral galaxy, though we see it only from side-on.

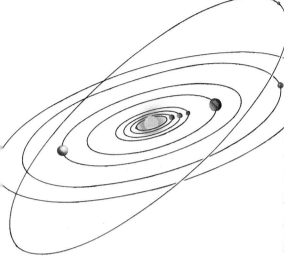

THE SOLAR SYSTEM

The Earth is just one of nine large bodies called planets that circle continually around the Sun. Other objects circle the Sun too, besides the planets and their moons – meteors, comets and other debris. Together, they all make up the Solar System.

THE PLANETS

Circling close to the Sun are four small rocky planets – Mercury, Venus, Earth and Mars. Further out are four giants made largely of gas – Jupiter, Saturn, Uranus and Neptune. Pluto is further out still.

Mercury is so close to the Sun it is hard to see. The cameras of the *Mariner 10* spacecraft showed a barren planet, with craters, mountains, ridges and valleys, rather like the Moon. With no atmosphere, temperatures can soar to 400°C or plummet to –180°C.

Venus is nearest to Earth and very bright because it is covered in clouds that reflect the Sun's light. These clouds hide the surface, but visiting spacecraft have revealed a great deal about it.

Mars is known as the 'Red Planet' because of the reddish dust scattered over vast areas of its surface, which is broken by craters, chasms and huge volcanoes up to 25km high. There may be water on Mars besides the ice locked in the polar ice caps. *Mariner 9* and *Vikings 1* and *2* showed vast areas worn away by floods.

Jupiter is so big that if it were hollow, 1300 Earths would fit inside. It spins so rapidly (about once every ten hours) that it bulges out at the equator. It has a faint ring of dust and its surface is covered by belts of swirling gas clouds. One distinct feature is its Great Red Spot, which is a whirling storm in the atmosphere over 24,000km long. Jupiter has 16 moons altogether.

CIRCLING PLANETS

All the planets except for Pluto *orbit* (travel round) the Sun the same way and in the same plane. Pluto's orbit cuts across at an angle, and at times it comes closer to the Sun than Neptune. The further out a planet is, the longer is its journey round the Sun: Mercury takes about 88 days; Earth takes 365.256 days; Pluto takes almost 250 years. As the astronomer Johannes Kepler worked out in the seventeenth century, the orbits are not quite perfect circles, but *ellipses*, a kind of oval.

HOW THE SOLAR SYSTEM BEGAN

Five billion years ago, the Solar System was probably just a spinning cloud of gas and dust. Gradually, the centre of the cloud condensed into a protostar that shrank to become the Sun. Further out, gas clumped together in the same way to form the outer planets – Jupiter, Saturn, Uranus and Neptune – each with a small hard core surrounded by gas. The rocky inner planets – Mercury, Venus, Earth and Mars – may have formed like this,

too, clumping into a hard lump from which most gases were driven off. But they could also be debris from the protostar Sun that condensed into small rocky lumps called *plantesimals*.

This description of how the Solar System formed is a modified version of a theory called the *nebular hypothesis*, first thought of by Pierre Laplace in 1796.

Jupiter is the biggest planet of all, 142,800km in diameter. It takes almost 12 years to orbit the Sun at a distance of 778 million km, but turns round once every 9.8 hours – which means the planet's surface is moving at over 45,000km/h. It is barely a quarter as dense as the Earth, since it is made mostly of gas.

Mercury is just 4878km in diameter and orbits the Sun in 88 days at a distance of 60 million km, turning round once every 58.65 days.

Venus is 12,104km in diameter and orbits the Sun in 225 days at a distance of 108 million km, turning once every 243 days. It spins the opposite way to the other planets.

Earth is 12,756km in diameter and orbits the Sun in 365.25 days at a distance of 149.6 million km, turning once every 23.93 hours. The Moon turns once every 27. 3 days.

Mars is 6794km in diameter and orbits the Sun in 687 days at a distance of 228 million km, turning once every 24.62 hours. It is slightly less dense than Earth.

Saturn With its broad, coloured rings and banded surface, Saturn is the most spectacular of all the planets. The rings are made up of millions of tiny ice-coated rock fragments. If you could slice through Saturn, you would find a small rocky core, surrounded by a thin layer of liquid hydrogen, then a deep layer of hydrogen gas. Saturn has at least 20 moons, the biggest of which, Titan, is almost half as big as the Earth.

Uranus is a giant gas planet made largely of hydrogen and helium, with an ice-coated rocky core. Oddly enough it is tilted over almost on its side as it circles the Sun. For years at a time one of its poles points almost at the Sun. It has 15 moons and a system of rings.

Neptune has a pale bluish disc with broad cloud bands and a Great Dark Spot similar to Jupiter's Great Red Spot. It has 8 moons and a system of rings.

Pluto is a tiny, icy planet of rock and methane. It has a slightly smaller companion called Charon.

VENUS OBSERVED

The atmosphere of Venus is mainly carbon dioxide, with clouds of sulphuric acid floating in it. This thick atmosphere gives a surface pressure 90 times that of the Earth, and creates a runaway 'greenhouse effect' (page 99) which boosts surface temperatures to 470°C.

Space probes have sent images back to the Earth showing rolling plains, vast upland areas, and deep rift valleys on the surface of Venus. The one in the view below was generated by computer from radar-maps made by *Magellan*. This picture shows that the surface of Venus is affected by tectonic motion, just like on Earth (page 90).

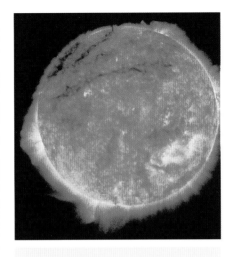

THE SUN

The Sun is a vast ball of gases – three-quarters hydrogen, and a quarter helium. The enormous pressure in the centre of the Sun fuses together hydrogen atoms in a nuclear reaction that boosts temperatures to 15 million °C. All this heat erupts on the Sun's surface in patches called *granules*. In places, there are dark spots on the surface called *sun-spots*, which reach a peak about every 11 years. At times, huge flame-like tongues of hot hydrogen may shoot 100,000km high. These are called *solar prominences*. *Solar flares* are explosions of energy on the Sun.

Saturn is 120,000km in diameter and orbits the Sun once about every 30 years at a distance of 1427 million km, turning once every 10.6 hours. It is 8 times less dense than the Earth – if you could find a big enough pond, it would float!

ASTEROIDS, METEOROIDS AND COMETS

Between Mars and Jupiter there is a belt of orbiting rocky lumps up to 1000km across called *asteroids*. Billions of tiny grains called *meteoroids* also orbit the Sun. Many hit the Earth's atmosphere and burn up; a few larger ones reach the ground. Sometimes *comets* made largely of ice head towards the Sun from a cloud at the edge of the Solar System. Some swing around the Sun and head back to the cloud, but others become trapped closer to the sun. Halley's Comet becomes visible this way once every 76 years.

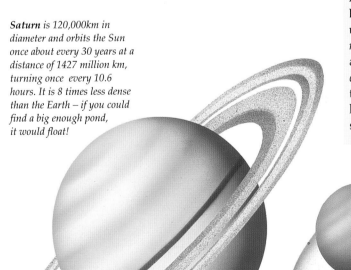

Uranus is 51,800km in diameter and orbits the Sun in 84 years at a distance of 2870 million km, turning once every 16.3 hours.

Neptune is 49,500km in diameter and orbits in 165 years at a distance of 4497 million km, turning once every 18.2 hours.

Pluto is the smallest planet, less than 2500km in diameter, and orbits in 250 years at an average distance of 5900 million km, turning once every 6.4 days.

PLANET EARTH

The Earth is just a tiny blue ball in the vastness of space – spinning round like a top at over 1600km/h, and hurtling through the darkness at over 100,000km/h as it makes its long yearly journey around the Sun.

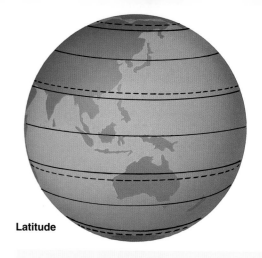

Latitude

ROUND EARTH

From the ground, the horizon looks straight and level, and it is easy to see why many people once thought the Earth was flat. Only if you go up in a plane, or look at pictures from space, can you see it really is curved. But the Ancient Greeks worked out it was round, 2400 years ago. They could see ships gradually disappeared as they sailed over the horizon. Travellers told them how stars dropped below the horizon behind them as they travelled north or south. And Aristotle (384-322 BC) noticed that the shadow of the Earth on the Moon in an eclipse was round.

THE MOON

As it journeys through space, the Earth is not entirely alone; spinning round with it is the Moon. Other planets have moons, but ours is very large compared to the Earth – about a quarter the diameter (3476km). It has no light of its own, but reflects the Sun's so well that it is bright enough at night to bathe the Earth in its pale white glow. As it circles round the Earth once every 27.3 days, it turns slowly on its axis to keep the same side facing towards us all the time. Pictures from spacecraft have shown the far side of the Moon is much the same as the side we see.

LATITUDE AND LONGITUDE

Any place in the world can be pinpointed very precisely with a simple grid system known as latitude and longitude. Lines of *latitude* are a series of lines running all the way round the globe parallel to the Equator (the line around the middle of the Earth). Latitude is given in degrees north or south of the Equator, up to 90°. Places near the Poles are called *high* latitude; places near the Equator are *low* latitude. Latitude is given in degrees because the position of each line is worked out by drawing a line from the centre of the Earth. Latitude is the angle between this

The crust is up to 40km deep under the continents and 6km deep under the oceans. With the topmost layer of the mantle, it forms a rigid skin around the Earth called the lithosphere, which is broken into giant fragments called tectonic plates (page 91).

The upper mantle is made of a different kind of rock from the crust. The topmost layer is the rigid lithosphere which extends down to about 100km. Below that is a layer of hot, slowly circulating molten rock or magma called the asthenosphere.

The solid lower mantle or mesosphere begins at about 200km and extends to a depth of 2900km. Temperatures rise from 2250°C at the top to 4500°C nearest the core.

The outer core is believed to be molten metal – largely iron and nickel. It extends to a depth of about 5150km.

The inner core is probably metal like the outer core, but pressure is so great here that it stays solid, even though the temperature may be as high as 7000°C.

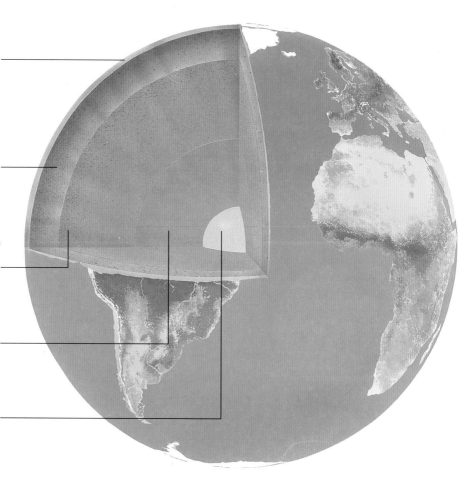

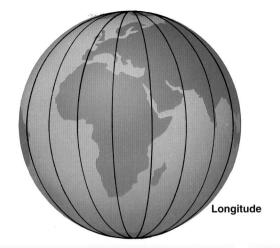

Longitude

Lines of latitude and longitude (left) drawn around the globe provide a a way of pinpointing anywhere on Earth very precisely.

The Earth's atmosphere (right) gets thinner and thinner higher up in a series of distinct layers until it eventually fades into empty space some 500-1000km above the ground.

line and a line drawn to the Equator.

Longitude divides the world into 360 segments, like the segments of an orange. Lines of longitude called *meridians* radiate from the North Pole out towards the Equator and converge again on the South Pole. A place's longitude is simply the angle at the Poles between the meridian on which it sits and the *prime meridian*, which runs through Greenwich, England. So longitude is given in *degrees east* or *west* of the prime meridian. For extra precision, degrees of longitude and latitude are subdivided into minutes and seconds.

THE ATMOSPHERE

The Earth is cocooned by a thin blanket of gases called the *atmosphere*, stretching 500 – 1000km above the surface. Without this blanket to protect us, we would be scorched by the Sun during the day and frozen solid at night. There are actually seven or more layers. Most are a thin mix of gases calm and unchanging as space beyond. But the lowest 11km – the layer in which we live – is thick with gases, water and dust. It is the churning of this layer, called the *troposphere*, in the heat of the Sun that gives us everything we call weather, from gentle summer showers to raging hurricanes.

satellite

Aurora Borealis

meteors

Thermosphere

Mesosphere

Stratosphere

Troposphere

INSIDE THE EARTH

The Earth is not just a solid ball; vibrations from earthquakes and explosions have revealed a complex structure. We stand on a thin rocky shell or *crust* of rock, just 40km thick on average beneath the continents and less than 6km thick beneath the oceans. Beneath the crust is a thick *mantle* of rock or *magma* so hot it flows like treacle (only very, very slowly). The metal (iron and nickel) *core* of the Earth begins nearly 3000km below the surface. The *outer core* is so hot that it is always molten; the *inner core* at the very centre of the Earth is solid because the pressure is so great it cannot melt, even though temperatures here may reach 7000°C.

The boundary between crust and mantle is called the *Mohorovicic discontinuity*. But the underside of the crust and upper mantle are in some ways so alike they blend into each other. This is why scientists sometimes talk instead of the *lithosphere*, extending 100km below the surface, and the *asthenosphere* going down a further 200km.

THE MOON AND TIDES

Every 12 hours, all the sea on opposite sides of the world rises a little, then falls back. This is called a tide. Tides occur because of the way the Moon and Earth circle round together. As the Earth spins, the sea nearest the Moon is raised by the pull of its gravity, creating a *high* tide. There is a high tide on the far side of the Earth too because the Moon and Earth

actually circle round each other like two spinning skaters. So the sea furthest away from the Moon is flung outwards by centrifugal force. The Sun affects tides too. Very high *spring* tides occur when the Sun and Moon line up to pull in the same direction. When Sun and Moon are at right angles to the Earth, their pulls conflict, causing small *neap* tides.

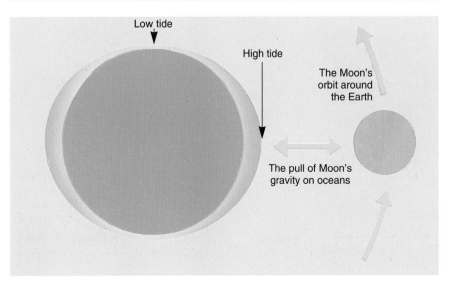

Low tide

High tide

The Moon's orbit around the Earth

The pull of Moon's gravity on oceans

TIME

Our years, months and days are calculated from the way the Earth and the Moon revolve in space and journey around the Sun. But all the divisions of the day – hours, minutes and seconds – come from the steady ticking of a clock.

HOURS OF THE DAY

Because the Sun moves steadily through the sky during the day, you can tell what time it is simply by looking where the Sun is. You must NEVER look at the Sun directly, but you can tell where it is from the direction of the shadows it casts. Sundials work like this. They have a special pointer called a *gnomon* to give a good shadow, and this shadow points out the time on a special dial.

Sundials were the earliest way of telling the time, and were first used at least 5000 years ago. But they do not work at night or if the Sun is clouded over. For a long time, the simplest way to measure time without the Sun was with steadily dripping water or sand. Then, in the Middle Ages, monks began using machines called clocks that sounded a bell to tell them when to say prayers. These prayer times were called *canonical hours*. Centuries before, the two halves of the day had been divided into 12 equal hours, giving 24 hours to each day, and clocks sounded out each hour. Now we use clocks to give us not only hours, but minutes, seconds and hundredths of seconds as well.

17th century lantern clock

DAY AND NIGHT

Shine a torch at a ball in a darkened room and you will see that one half is lit by the torch and the other is in shadow. It is the same with the Sun and the Earth. The half facing the Sun is brightly lit; the other half is in darkness. We get day and night simply because the Earth is forever turning us to face the Sun and turning us away again.

It may look as if the Sun is moving. You see the Sun rising in the east, climbing higher towards midday, then sinking out of sight again in the west at sunset. But it is the Earth moving, not the Sun; it just looks that way as we are carried round by the Earth.

The Earth spins eastward at the equator at 1600km/h – faster than a jet airliner – and spins once right round in 24 hours. This is why a day is 24 hours long. In fact, if you could fly west at 1600km/h, you could keep up with the Sun and stay in sunshine all the time.

Star and sun days There are two ways of measuring a day: by the Sun (*solar day*) and by the distant stars (*sidereal day*). A sidereal day is the time it takes for the Earth to turn once in relation to the stars, which is 23 hours 56 mins 4 secs. A solar day, at 24 hours exactly, is longer because the Earth moves a little way round the Sun during the course of a day. This means it has to turn 1° further before the Sun is back in the same place in the sky.

DIFFERENT DAYS

Each day is 24 hours long, but because the Earth is tilted towards the Sun, the amount of daylight varies throughout the year. It

THE MOON AND MONTHS

Just like the Earth, the Moon has a bright side and a dark side. We cannot see the dark side at all. So as the Moon travels around the Earth, it seems to change shape because we see different amounts of the bright side. A *full moon* is when we can see all the bright side. A *new moon* is when we can see just a thin crescent. A *gibbous moon* is when we can see two-thirds of the bright side.

Our calendar months come from the time it takes the Moon to go round the Earth once. It actually takes 27.3 days. It is also 29.53 days between each full moon because the Earth is moving as well as the Moon. The time between full moons is called a *lunar month*. But the number of days in a *calendar month* may be 28, 29, 30 or 31 so that we have exactly 12 months.

Phases of the Moon The new moon occurs when it is between us and the Sun (1), and we can just see a sliver of its bright side. We gradually see more and more as it moves around the Earth away from the Sun (2). This is called waxing. *Once the Moon is right round the far side of the Earth from the Sun, we see all its bright side (3). This is the full moon. As it moves on round, we see less and less again (4). This is called* waning.

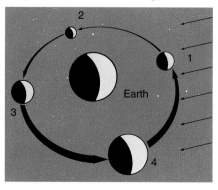

varies least at the equator, where it is daylight for about twelve hours all year round. It varies most at the North and South Poles, where it is never completely dark in the summer, and never completely light in the winter.

THE YEAR

Besides spinning round like a top once every day, the Earth travels right around the Sun, just as the Moon travels around the Earth. It is a very long way – almost 940 million km – but the Earth moves so fast that it takes just over 365 days to go round once. This is why a year is 365 days long.

In fact, it takes 365.256 days for the Earth to make its journey around the Sun. But it would be awkward to have 365.256 days in the year. Instead, we add an extra day every fourth year, called a leap year, but miss out leap years for century years that are not divisible by four. This way our calendar is always in step with the Earth, and every year the Earth is always in the same place on a particular day.

Not everyone uses this system. Muslims have a year of 354 or 355 days; the Jewish year varies from 353 to 385 days.

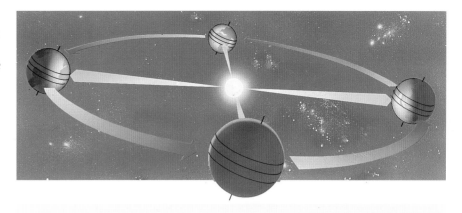

SEASONS

We get seasons because as the Earth goes round the Sun, different parts of it tilt towards the Sun or away from it. In summer, your part of the world is tilted towards the Sun. So days are longer, with the Sun staying in sight longer. At midday the Sun is directly overhead, making shadows short and the weather warm. In autumn, your part of the world is starting to tilt away from the Sun. Days get shorter and the Sun does not climb quite as high in the sky, so shadows are longer and the weather cooler. In winter, you are tilted right away from the Sun, and days are very short and cool. In spring, your part of the world tilts towards the Sun again, bringing longer, warmer days.

TIME ZONES

As the Earth spins round, the Sun is constantly coming up on a new part of the world – and setting in another. So the time of day varies all round the world. When it is dawn where you live, it is sunset on the other side of the world – and midday a quarter of the way round the world from you.

To make it easier to set clocks, the world is split into 24 *Time Zones*, one for each hour of the day. As you go west round the world, clocks are put back one hour for each zone – until you reach the *Date Line*. If you carry on past the Date Line, you go on putting the clock back, but put the calendar one day forward.

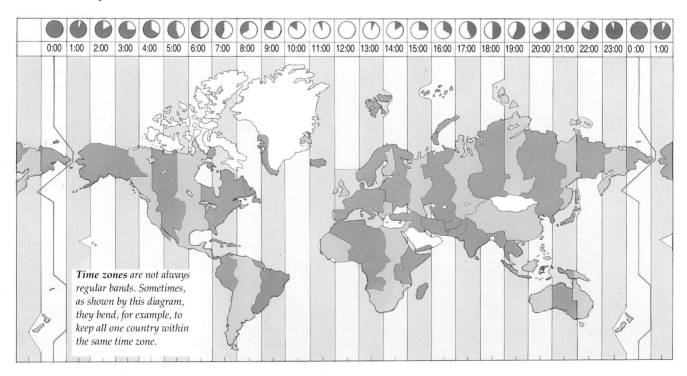

Time zones are not always regular bands. Sometimes, as shown by this diagram, they bend, for example, to keep all one country within the same time zone.

CLIMATE

Just as summer days can often be cool, so there are occasional cool days in the tropics. But the weather in the tropics is usually warm – just as the weather in the Arctic is usually cold. The typical weather in any place over a long time is called its *climate*.

CLIMATE ZONES

As a general rule, the nearer you are to the Equator, the warmer the climate is. This is because at the Equator, the Sun is high in the sky at midday and its rays are warm. Away from the Equator, it climbs less high and gives less warmth. At the North and South Poles, it gives hardly any warmth. The effect is to give three broad climate zones either side of the Equator: the warm tropics, the cold polar regions, and the *temperate* zone in between.

Tropical weather is hot. Manaus in Brazil, for instance, is warmer than 27°C on average all the year round, and never gets much cooler than 20°C. Some tropical areas are hot and wet; some are hot and dry (see Deserts); some have marked wet seasons and dry seasons (see Monsoon). In moist tropical areas, huge thunderclouds often build up in the heat of the morning and unleash torrents of rain in the afternoon. Steamy tropical forests flourish in this hot, damp climate.

The temperate zone Places like the USA, Europe, Japan and southern Australia all have temperate climates. Summers are usually warm and winters cool. Winds from the west bring rain all year round, especially to west coasts, but it is wettest in winter. Further north in the northern hemisphere, it may often snow in winter, especially far away from the sea. Nearer the tropics, summers are hot and dry and winters wet.

Polar regions Towards the North and South Poles, the Sun is always low in the sky and in winter hardly gets above the horizon at all. It is bitterly cold all the year round, and the ice and snow on the ground rarely melt. Antarctica stays below –50°C for over half the year.

SEA AND MOUNTAINS
Climate does not only depend on distance from the Equator. Both sea and mountains have a

MONSOON
For half the year in many tropical places, such as India, north-east Australia and East Africa, the weather is very dry, and the land is parched by winds blowing from the interior of the continent. Eventually, however, the air over the heart of the continent warms up enough to reverse the flow of air from land to sea. Then moist winds blow in from the sea bringing welcome rain for the rest of the year. This is called the *monsoon*.

Above 4300m
Above the snow-line, it is so cold that snow rarely melts, which is why the highest peaks are always snow-capped.

A sequence showing change in climate in the tropics.

3400-4300m *Above a certain height, called the* tree line, *winters are too cold and winds too strong for anything but grass, moss and lichen to grow. In Latin America, land above the tree-line is called* tierra helada *(frozen land).*

1800-3400m *Above about 1800m, it is too cold for tropical broad-leaved trees, and the slopes are covered in conifers. This is called* tierra fria *(cool land).*

600-1800m *Here it is wet enough for trees to grow, and the slopes are covered in moist tropical rainforests. This is called* tierra templada *(temperate land). Above 1200m, the trees are often in cloud and the forest is called* cloud forest.

MOUNTAIN CLIMATES
Air is heated mostly by the warmth of the ground, not directly by the Sun. So it usually gets colder the higher up you go. On average, it gets steadily colder by 6°C for every 1000m. This temperature drop is called the *lapse rate*. So just as climates get colder towards the poles, so they get colder higher up mountains, and as you climb a mountain you can often go through the same climate zones as you would if you were travelling towards either of the poles. Mountains are also much windier and wetter than lowland areas, and there is often a marked difference between slopes that face the Sun and those always in shade.

DESERTS

More than a fifth of all land on Earth is desert, where it hardly ever rains. Many of the biggest deserts lie in the subtropics, where the air is calm and clear. The vast Sahara desert and the Great Australian desert are here. Some deserts, like Chile's Atacama, occur in the lee of mountain ranges that shelter them from the rain. Some are near coasts where cool ocean currents dry the air.

Many subtropical deserts can be very hot, because there are no clouds to block out the Sun's rays. Summer temperatures in the Sudan desert can soar to 56°C. But it can get cold at night, because heat escapes through the clear skies.

significant effect too. The sea makes coastal areas wetter than places far inland. It also gives them cooler summers and warmer winters – because the water stops the air getting too hot or too cold. Northwest Europe is kept especially warm in winter by warm ocean currents flowing right across the Atlantic from the Caribbean.

GLOBAL WINDS

Some winds are local or blow only for a while, but there are certain winds, called *prevailing wind*s, that blow for much of the year. Each of the main climate zones has its own prevailing winds.

Tropical trade winds Over the Equator, the strong Sun makes warm air rise, drawing in air beneath from north and south to create dry prevailing winds called *trade winds*. The trade winds blow steadily towards the Equator throughout the tropics from northeast and southeast – not from due north or south because the Earth's spinning bends them westwards.

The zone where northeast and southeast trades meet is called the *Inter Tropical Convergence* zone. This shifts with the seasons, moving steadily north to the Tropic of Cancer from December to July and then south to the Tropic of Capricorn from July to December. The air here is often dead calm, and sailors call it the *doldrums*.

Temperate westerly winds In the temperate zone, the prevailing winds are warm, moist westerlies, but they are much less reliable than the trade winds. These westerlies collide head on with the polar easterlies along a line called the *Polar Front*, and their collision creates storm after storm.

Polar easterly winds In the polar regions, the prevailing winds are bitter winds blowing away from the poles, where cold air is sinking. Just like the trade winds, these are bent into easterlies by the spinning of the Earth.

> **DID YOU KNOW?**
> **The wettest place** in the world is Tutunendo in Colombia. The average yearly rainfall is over 1170cm.
> **Cherrapunji** in India gets almost as much water, even though it is fairly dry for half the year. In 1957, it got over 26m of rain!
> **The hottest place** is Dallol, Ethiopia, where it averages 34.4°C in the shade.
> **The highest temperature** ever recorded is 58°C in Al Aziziya, Libya.
> **The coldest place** is Vostok in Antarctica, where it averages –57.8°C, and once dropped to –88°C.
> **One of the most extreme climates** must be Yakutsk, Siberia, where temperatures can drop in winter to –64°C, yet soar in summer to 39°C.
> **One of the most moderate climates** must be Quito, Ecuador. It never drops below 8°C at night nor rises above 22°C during the day. 100mm of rain falls every month. It is called the 'Land of eternal spring'.
> **Only 7 per cent** of the world has a truly temperate climate, yet half the world's population lives there.

0-600m Towards sea level, the climate is warm enough for tropical fruits and palm trees to grow. This is why it is called tierra caliente *(hot land). The foothills facing into the wind are moist and steamy; those on the sheltered side of the mountains are often parched and bare.*

WEATHER

There are many different kinds of weather – wind, rain, snow, fog, sunshine, calm. But they are all simply caused by the lowest layer of the atmosphere, called the troposphere, moving as it is heated by the warmth of the Sun.

WHY THE SKY IS BLUE

Every colour in the sky comes from the Sun. Sunlight is white, which means it is a mixture of all the colours in the rainbow. Clear skies are blue because the tiny molecules of gas in the atmosphere scatter mostly blue light towards our eyes, leaving the rest unaffected. The sky gets paler when extra dust or moisture reflect other colours.

Sunsets and sunrises tend to be red because the Sun is shining through the thick, lower layers of the atmosphere. The dust and moisture in the air tend to absorb all colours of light but red, which is why the Sun looks red. The dustier or damper the sky, the redder it is.

WIND, WET AND WARMTH

Forecasting the weather is such a complicated process that it demands the world's most powerful computers. Yet all weather is the continual variation of just three factors: the way the air moves, the moisture content of the air, and its temperature – wind, wet and warmth, in other words.

Wind All wind is simply air moving. Strong winds are air moving fast; gentle breezes are air moving slowly. They all begin with a difference in *air pressure*. Air pressure is the pushing force air molecules exert all the time, although you can barely feel it. It varies with the density of the air.

Where air is dense, pressure is high; where the air is less dense, pressure is low.

The Sun warms some places more than others. Warmth makes the air expand, so it is light here, making pressure low. But where the air is cold and heavy, pressure is high. Winds blow from areas where the pressure is high, called *anticyclones*, to areas where the pressure is low, called *depressions*. The greater the difference in pressure, the stronger the wind is.

Some pressure differences are on a global scale, creating the world wind patterns described on page 87. Some are just local, creating, for instance, the gentle breezes that blow in off the cool sea some days.

WEATHER SYSTEMS

In the temperate zone (page 86), the stormiest, wettest weather is often associated with vast spiralling weather systems called *depressions* or *lows*, because they are centred on a region of low pressure. These begin as a tiny kink in the Polar Front (page 87), then grow bigger and bigger as they sweep slowly eastwards, bringing rain or snow and blustery winds.

There is a wedge of warm air intruding right into the heart of these depressions. The worst weather occurs along the edges of the wedge, called *fronts*, where the warm air meets the cold air. As the depression passes over, during the course of 12 hours or so, these fronts bring a distinct sequence of weather.

At the leading edge of the wedge, called the *warm front*, the warm air slides up over the cold air. The coming of the warm front is heralded by feathery *cirrus* clouds of pure ice very high in the sky. Soon the clouds begins to thicken until

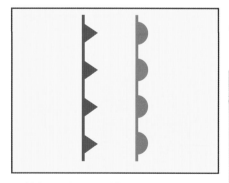

Symbols (left) On weather maps, cold and warm fronts are marked with different symbols.

Cold front Along a cold front (right), the air rises sharply as cold air undercuts warm air, and huge thunderclouds build up, bringing heavy rain and thunderstorms.

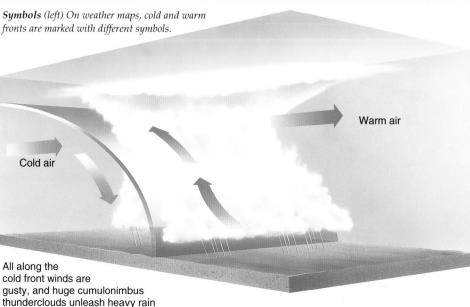

Warm air

Cold air

All along the cold front winds are gusty, and huge cumulonimbus thunderclouds unleash heavy rain

Wet Water evaporates into the air from oceans, rivers and lakes all the time. Some of this moisture stays in the air as invisible water vapour, giving air its *humidity*. If the air is cooled suddenly – by blowing over cold ground perhaps – the vapour condenses into water drops, leaving *dew* on the ground or *fog* in the air.

Some water vapour, though, is carried high up by rising air currents. Here it is so cold that the vapour condenses into *clouds* of water droplets. When the droplets become too big to be borne up by the air, they fall as rain. Air rising sharply creates tall clouds, such as thunderclouds, which give brief, heavy showers. Air rising gently, as at a warm front (see below), gives longer, steadier rain.

Warmth depends largely on the amount of sunshine and the cloud cover. Clear, anticyclonic weather gives the hottest days and the coldest nights because there are no clouds to keep the Sun's rays out or hold in any warmth at night.

HURRICANES

In the tropics, eastern coasts are often battered by cyclonic storms, known as hurricanes in the Atlantic. They begin a long way away as air rises over warm seas, building up huge thunderclouds. They then spin westwards across the ocean, growing ever bigger. In the centre is a small calm *eye*, but around it winds spiral at 120km/h or more, and rains are torrential. Even the calm eye can suck up a devastating *storm surge* of the sea.

THUNDERSTORM

Huge thunderclouds are formed by strong updraughts on a hot day or along a cold front. Eddies in the cloud throw water droplets and ice crystals together so hard they become charged with static electricity (page 152), with positive particles clustering high in the cloud, negative ones lower down. Soon the charge builds up so much that a lightning bolt leaps from positive to negative – either within the cloud (*sheet lightning*) or to the ground (*fork lightning*), heating up the air so much it bursts in a clap of *thunder*.

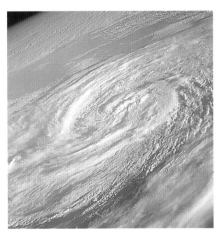

eventually the sky is full of slate-grey *nimbostratus* clouds, bringing steady rain. Once the warm front has passed, the weather becomes milder and the skies brighten for a while – but the respite is usually brief.

After a few hours, a build-up of vast *cumulonimbus* (thunderclouds) and increasingly gusty winds warn that the trailing edge of the wedge, called the *cold front*, is on its way. As the cold front passes over, the thunderclouds unleash short but heavy showers, and occasionally even thunderstorms.

Eventually, the cold front moves away, the air gets colder and the sky clears, leaving just a few fluffy cumulus clouds.

No-one knows quite what causes these depressions, but many meteorologists think that streams of air circling the Earth high in the atmosphere may play a part. The lows are linked with giant meanders (bends) in the air stream up to 2000km long, called *Rossby waves*.

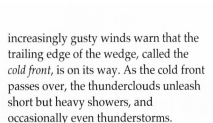

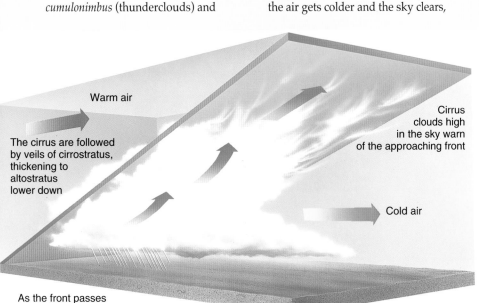

Warm air

Cirrus clouds high in the sky warn of the approaching front

The cirrus are followed by veils of cirrostratus, thickening to altostratus lower down

Cold air

As the front passes over, steady rain falls from dense grey nimbostratus clouds

The warm front (left) is the first to arrive, following an hour or so after feathery cirrus clouds are first seen high in the sky. When it comes it brings steady rain (above).

CONTINENTS & OCEANS

The ground beneath our feet is constantly shifting; as continents split apart and crunch together, new oceans open up and old ones are squeezed out of existence. Indeed, the whole of the Earth's surface is forever breaking up and moving – very, very slowly, but with enormous force.

VITAL CLUES

The first clues that the continents were once joined came in the 1800s, when naturalists found not only matching rocks in Brazil and the Congo, but identical species of turtles, snakes and lizards in South America and Africa. They found fossils of the long extinct reptile *Mesosaurus* in both continents too. Then, in the 1960s, scientists found in Antarctica a fossil of *Lystrosaurus* (above), a reptile known to have lived in Africa, India and China 200 million years ago. The only explanation was that the areas were all once joined. Now we can measure how fast they are moving apart with laser beams bounced off satellites.

DRIFTING CONTINENTS

Look at a map of the world and you will see how closely the west coast of Africa mirrors the east coast of South America. The English thinker Francis Bacon saw this as long ago as 1620, soon after the first maps of South America were made. But it was not until this century that scientists finally realized why.

In 1912, German scientist Alfred Wegener suggested that Africa and South America were once joined. Fit them together, he said, and '…it is just as if we were to refit the torn pieces of a newspaper by their matching edges.' Indeed, he argued, not just Africa and South America, but all the world's continents were once joined. Millions of years ago, they began to split apart and have been drifting to and fro ever since.

SPREADING OCEANS

Now we know that it is not just the continents that are moving but the oceans too. In fact, the continents move because they are carried along on top of the ocean crust (page 82) as it moves. The rocks that make up continents are much older than the rocks beneath the

CHANGING MAP

The map of the world has been steadily changing for millions of years. Once, the continents were all joined in one huge land mass scientists call *Pangaea*, set in one vast ocean, *Panthalassa*. Then around 200 million years ago, Pangaea began to break in two, with *Laurasia* to the north and *Gondwanaland* to the south. Gradually, these giant continents also began to split up, leaving the fragments to drift to where they are now. Scientists know much of this from the magnetic properties of rocks. When a rock forms, its magnetic particles line up pointing north just like a compass. As a continent twists and turns, so the magnetic particles in rocks formed at different times point different ways. So scientists can plot the wanderings of a continent over billions of years by looking at the direction of magnetic particles in rocks.

250 million years ago There was just one giant continent on Earth, called Pangaea, and a giant ocean, called Panthalassa. A long arm of sea, called the Tethys Sea, reached into the heart of the continent and would eventually split it apart.

200 million years ago Pangaea split either side of the Tethys Sea. To the north was Laurasia, including N America, Europe and most of Asia. To the south was Gondwanaland, including S America, Africa, Australia, Antarctica and India.

135 million years ago The South Atlantic opened up between Africa and S America. India broke off from Africa and drifted rapidly north towards Asia. Europe and N America began to separate only 40 million years ago.

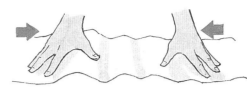

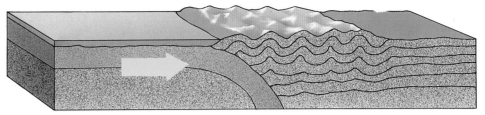

Rumple up a tablecloth and you will see how rocks are folded by colliding tectonic plates.

ocean. Indeed, there is a ridge down the middle of all the major oceans, like the seam of a football, where new rock is being made all the time. These *mid-ocean ridges* occur where hot rock from the Earth's interior bursts through the crust and spills on to the ocean bed. As this happens, the ridge gets wider and wider, driving the two halves of the ocean further and further apart. Even now the mid-Atlantic ridge is getting wider, forcing North America and Europe 7cm further apart every year.

Just as new ocean crust is made along the mid-ocean ridges, so old crust is swallowed up at the edges of the oceans. Here the crust is forced down into the Earth's interior as it is driven up against continents. This is called *subduction*.

TECTONIC PLATES

Scientists now believe it no longer makes sense to think of the world's surface as continents and oceans. The world's rigid outer shell, called the lithosphere (page 82) is actually split into 20 or so moving *tectonic plates* – nine huge plates and a dozen or so smaller ones. The continents are simply embedded in these plates like currents in a bun. The oceans are what lie between the continents.

Mountains are thrown up where two tectonic plates collide – the Alps and the Himalayas by the collision of two continents, the Andes and the Rockies where an ocean plate plunges beneath a continent, as shown in the diagram above.

BUILDING MOUNTAINS

Scientists had known for some time that the world's hills and mountains are made up of crumpled layers of rock. But until the discovery of tectonic plates, no-one knew quite how they came to be crumpled. Now it is thought that mountains are built as one continent crashes into another. The Himalayas, for instance, were thrown up where India ploughed into Asia's southern edge. In fact, India is still moving, so they are still getting taller. It is a bit like the bow wave of a boat, or pushing a block of wood through thick, sludgy mud. As long as the block is moving, the mud rumples up in front of it. But if you stop moving the block, the mud will soon flatten out, just as the Himalayas will when India finally comes to a stop.

Jagged peaks in the Alps Like most of the world's mountain ranges, the Alps have formed within the past 50 million years or so – and are still getting higher, as the African plate drives Italy into southern Europe. In the past 40 million years, Africa has moved 400km closer to Europe.

PLATES OF THE EARTH

The 20-odd plates of the Earth's surface are constantly on the move, slipping past each other and jostling this way and that. In some places, called *divergence zones*, they are pulling apart, as they are where the sea floor is spreading. In other places, called *convergence zones*, they are shoving up against each other, crumpling the edges or driving one down into the Earth's interior. In a few places, they are simply sliding past each other, as they are along the San Andreas Fault in California (page 92). The unimaginable power needed to move these plates creates earthquakes and volcanoes wherever they join.

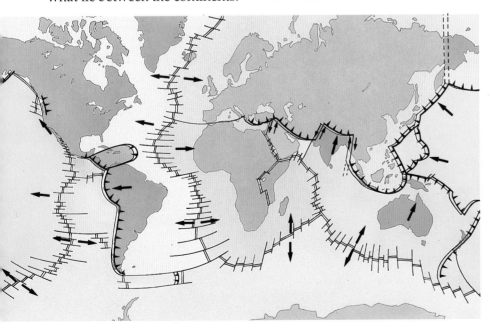

VOLCANOES & EARTHQUAKES

The Earth beneath our feet seems solid, but it is actually moving very, very slowly all the time, with incredible power. Every now and then, it moves suddenly and violently, causing earthquakes and volcanoes. An earthquake is when the ground shakes – sometimes gently, sometimes so violently that whole towns are destroyed. Volcanoes are places where *magma* – red-hot molten rock from inside the Earth – bursts up through the ground.

EARTHQUAKES

Earthquakes are the ground shuddering as the vast plates of the Earth's surface grind together (page 90). Plates slide past each other all the time, but sometimes they jam together. For years, the pressure builds up, then suddenly they lurch on again, sending shock waves in all directions. When these waves reach the surface, they create earthquakes.

Earthquakes generate two kinds of shock wave: *body waves* which vibrate through the rock and *surface waves* which ripple across the Earth's surface like waves in the sea. Body waves include *primary (P) waves* which pulse through the ground like train carriages banging into each other, and *secondary (S) waves*, which are like a snaking skipping rope.

Places near plate edges, such as south-east Europe and the Pacific coast, suffer major quakes repeatedly. The San Andreas fault in California (pictured above) marks the boundary between two giant plates. Movement along the fault has brought many devastating quakes to the region.

VOLCANOES

Some volcanoes, like those in Hawaii, are just cracks in the Earth's surface that ooze lava all the time. Many, like Mt Etna in Sicily, are cone-shaped mountains built up by a series of violent eruptions. In some eruptions, red-hot streams of *lava* (magma that has reached the Earth's surface) pour from the summit, and thick clouds of hot ash and cinders are thrown high in the air. In others, boiling mud roars down the mountain. A few eruptions are so violent they blow the mountain apart.

Active or sleeping If a volcano erupts frequently, it is said to be *active*. If it has not erupted for a long time, it is *dormant*. If it shows no signs of erupting again, it is *extinct*. At present there are some 800 active volcanoes, but many more that are extinct. Many hills and mountains are old volcanoes.

The strength and frequency of volcanic eruption depends on the magma. Where it is thin and runny, lava may ooze gently and often through the surface. Where it is thick and sticky, eruptions are fewer but more violent. This is because the magma clogs up the volcano's *vent* – until the pressure beneath builds up so much that it bursts through explosively.

Where volcanoes appear Nearly all volcanoes occur where the plates of the Earth's surface meet (page 91), especially in a ring around the Pacific Ocean called the 'Ring of Fire'. The most spectacular volcanoes occur where plates collide. Here, rock pushed far down into the Earth by the collision turns thick and sticky as it melts its way up to the surface, creating violent volcanoes like Mt Pinatubo in the Philippines.

There are volcanoes beneath the sea, too, where plates pull apart, continually releasing bubbles of magma. Some in the Pacific occur far away from the edges of plates over *hot spots* deep inside the Earth. Islands like the Hawaiian chain are the tips of volcanoes like this.

HOW BAD IS AN EARTHQUAKE?

Scientists measure the severity of an earthquake on the *Richter scale*. 1 on the Richter scale is an earthquake so mild you can detect it only on special instruments. The biggest ever recorded, reaching 8.9 on the scale, was in Chile in 1960. The *Mercalli scale* – illustrated right – is another scale, showing the severity of an earthquake by its effects.

1 Barely noticeable.

2 Water moves in glass and fish tanks.

3 Pictures may rattle on the wall.

4 Dishes, doors and windows rattle.

5 Unstable objec such as vases an stools fall over.

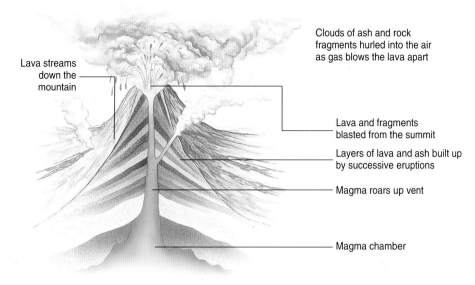

Lava streams
down the
mountain

Clouds of ash and rock
fragments hurled into the air
as gas blows the lava apart

Lava and fragments
blasted from the summit

Layers of lava and ash built up
by successive eruptions

Magma roars up vent

Magma chamber

INSIDE A VOLCANO

About 3 km beneath a volcano is a *magma chamber* where magma collects. As it fills, pressure builds up until the magma finally blasts or melts its way through to the surface. Then it is a bit like opening a fizzy drink – the magma froths up as gases previously dissolved in it form bubbles. With runny lava, the bubbles escape gently and the magma emerges as oozing lava; with sticky magma, the gas bursts out explosively and the magma roars up through the volcano's vent and out through the summit.

POMPEII

Pompeii was a Roman town near Naples in Italy. When nearby Vesuvius erupted in AD 79, the town was engulfed in a thick layer of volcanic ash, suffocating thousands of its citizens. But Pompeii was preserved through the centuries by this blanket of ash. Now it has been uncovered to reveal the Roman town almost intact, with even the remains of people and animals lying where they died nearly two thousand years ago.

TYPES OF VOLCANO

The shape of a volcano depends partly on the kind of material it spews out. Where the Earth's tectonic plates collide, magma is thick, eruptions are explosive, and the lava cools to form tall, cone-shaped mountains, like Japan's Mt Fuji. Ash falls on the lava after each eruption to create alternate layers of ash and lava, which is why this kind of volcano is called a *composite cone*. A *shield volcano*, like Mauna Loa in Hawaii, is where runny lava released by plates pulling apart spreads out into a wide, dome-shaped mountain. A *cinder cone* is built up from *tephra* (fragments of solid magma) and ash.

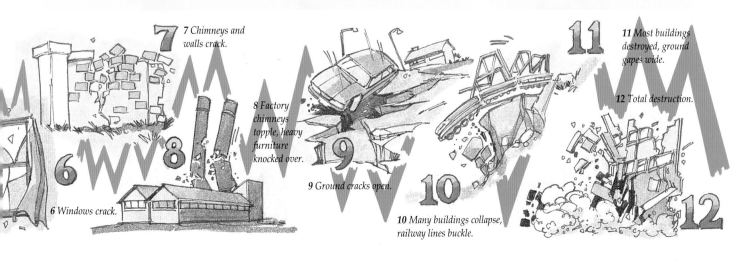

7 Chimneys and walls crack.

8 Factory chimneys topple, heavy furniture knocked over.

9 Ground cracks open.

6 Windows crack.

10 Many buildings collapse, railway lines buckle.

11 Most buildings destroyed, ground gapes wide.

12 Total destruction.

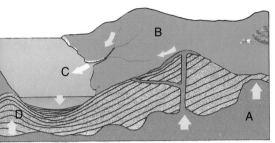

A Igneous rock forms from magma forced up from the Earth's interior. B Weather wears away the rock. C Fragments are washed into the sea and settle on the sea-bed. D Sediments are cemented into layers of rock, then lifted up above the sea to be worn away again.

ROCKS & MINERALS

Rocks and minerals are the raw materials of the Earth's surface, beneath every hill and valley, mountain and plain. Some are just a few million years old; others were formed at least 3.8 billion years ago when the Earth was still young.

THE ROCK CYCLE

All rocks are made from material that came originally from the Earth's hot interior as molten magma. Once the magma cools to form igneous rock, it is gradually worn away by the weather and the fragments are washed down into the sea. There they settle and form layers of sedimentary rock as they are squeezed and cemented together. When the movement of the Earth's crust thrusts these layers above the sea, they too can be worn away to form new sediments.

ROCK FORMATION

Rocks come in many shapes, textures and colours. But they are all formed in one of three ways.

Igneous ('fiery') rocks are formed from molten magma from the Earth's interior (page 92). Some is spewed out by volcanoes to form *extrusive* igneous rock. Some is forced up beneath the surface, forming *intrusive* igneous rock. Molten magma is incredibly hot as it nears the surface, but it soon starts to cool. As it cools, more and more crystals appear, until eventually all the magma becomes a solid mass of hard, crystalline rock.

Sedimentary rock forms in thin layers from debris that settles on the sea-bed and then is squeezed and cemented over millions of years into solid rock. Some, like limestone, are made largely from plant and animal remains, or from chemicals settling out of the water. Most, however, are *clastic* – made from fragments of rock worn away by the weather and washed down into the sea by rivers.

Metamorphic rock is made when rock is crushed by the huge forces that build mountains (page 91) or seared by the ferocious heat of magma. Scorched and squeezed this way, rock is changed so much it becomes a new kind of rock.

SEDIMENTARY ROCKS

Sedimentary rocks usually have clear horizontal layers, made as the sediments settled on the sea-bed. The top of each layer is called the *bedding plane*, and is often marked by a long crack. Bedding planes may be flat, or they may be tilted where the rock has been crumpled (above). Vertical cracks formed as the rock dried out are called *joints*.

ROCK SAMPLES

The photographs below show a selection of some of the more common rocks. Conglomerate, coal, sandstone and chalk are sedimentary; schist, quartzite and marble are metamorphic; and granite, dolerite and basalt are igneous. Igneous rocks have a hard, mottled, crystalline look. Sedimentary rocks are much duller and softer, and you can often rub off the grains. Metamorphic rocks are usually tough and shiny, with grains so small you can hardly see them.

Coal is made from the squashed remains of swampy forests that once covered large areas 300 million years ago.

Conglomerate is a solid mass of round pebbles cemented together. It was probably made from beach pebbles.

Sandstone is coarse grains of quartz sand, cemented together by silica or calcite.

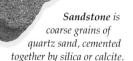

Chalk is a shelly limestone, made from the skeletons, called coccoliths, of microscopic sea creatures that lived in warm seas 65-144 million years ago.

94

MINERALS

Rocks are not smooth like plastic, but made up from grains and crystals, like a biscuit. All these grains and crystals are called *minerals*. A mineral is simply a chemical that forms naturally in the Earth, such as quartz or mica. Some rocks are made from just a single mineral; others contain half a dozen or more.

There are more than 1000 different kinds of mineral, but only 30 or so occur commonly. By far the most common are the *silicates*, made from a combination of oxygen and silicon. Silicates make up 98% of the Earth's crust, and minerals are usually divided into silicates and non-silicates.

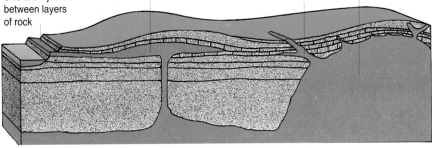

Types of igneous intrusion

Sills are injected between layers of rock

Laccoliths arch up between layers of rock

Dykes cut across layers of rock as it is split by the force of the intrusion

Batholiths are giant domes of igneous intrusion

METAMORPHIC ROCK

Metamorphism makes all rocks more tough and crystalline, but they are changed in two different ways.

Contact metamorphism is when rock is scorched by the heat of an igneous intrusion. This turns sandstone into quartzite, limestone into marble and mudstone and shale into hornfels.

Regional metamorphism is when rocks are crushed beneath mountains by the moving plates of the Earth's surface. This turns mudstone and shale to slate, then to schist and then to gneiss as it is squeezed harder and harder.

IGNEOUS ROCKS

Magma forms various kinds of igneous rock according to how quickly it cools and how acidic and sticky it is (page 93). When magma cools rapidly, the grains or crystals tend to be small; when it cools slowly, the grains grow much bigger. Extrusions cool quickly in the open air and so give fine-grained rocks, such as basalt, where the magma is *basic* (non-acid) and runny, and rhyolite where it is acidic and sticky. Large intrusions cool slowly underground to form large-grained rocks such as gabbro from basic magma and granite from acidic magma. Small intrusions such as dykes and sills cool a little quicker than large ones, so the rocks here tend to be medium-grained – typically dolerite where the magma is basic and micro-granite and porphyry where it is acidic.

PRECIOUS MINERALS

Most of our materials, from building bricks to diamonds, are minerals from the Earth's crust. Gems and crystals such as diamonds, rubies and quartz often form in *geodes*, gas pockets in cooling igneous rock. Metals, especially iron, copper, zinc and gold often form in *veins* – cracks in the rock once filled with hot, mineral-rich water.

Amethyst is a purple or violet transparent variety of quartz.

Schist is formed when slate made from shale is crushed even harder. It contains fine black grains of mica and, occasionally, gems like garnet.

Quartzite is a tough, crystalline rock formed by the metamorphism of sandstone.

Marble is a metamorphic rock formed by the re-crystallization of limestone.

Polished marble Like many igneous and metamorphic rocks, marble can be ground and polished smooth.

Granite Is a coarse-grained and fairly acid igneous rock found in batholiths and other large intrusions. It contains pink or pearly feldspar, black mica and glassy grey quartz.

Dolerite is a medium-grained, basic igneous rock found in small intrusions.

Basalt is a fine-grained, basic igneous rock often forming in thick sheets covering vast areas, like the Deccan of India.

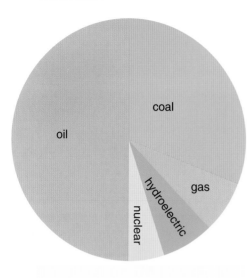

coal

oil

hydroelectric

nuclear

gas

ENERGY BUDGET

The diagram above shows the main energy sources used to generate electricity. We get our electricity from ten major sources. Over three-quarters comes from fossil fuels – coal, oil and natural gas. About 15% comes from *biomass* – that is, plant and animal matter that can be converted into fuel. Biomass (largely wood) is the main fuel for 80% of people in developing countries. 5% of our energy is *hydropower*, the power of running water. 3% is nuclear energy (page 174). Solar panels, windmills, geothermal power stations, and tidal and wave power stations provide less than 0.1% of our energy between them.

FUELS & ENERGY

The modern world demands vast amounts of energy not only to provide warmth and light and carry us about in cars, trains and planes, but also to power machinery and to sustain agriculture. But is there enough energy to go round?

WHERE ENERGY COMES FROM

Nearly all our energy comes from the Sun originally. The Sun delivers over 99% of the energy reaching the Earth's surface. The rest is heat from the Earth's hot interior (0.02%), called *geothermal energy*, and tidal energy created by the pull of the Moon and Sun (0.01%).

The amount of energy the Sun delivers each year is huge – equal to 178 million big power stations. But very little can be used. About 30% is reflected straight back into space. Nearly all the rest either warms the air and leaks back into space (47%), or is spent powering the water cycle (23%). Barely 0.06% is used by plants for photosynthesis (page 57).

We use very little of the Sun's energy directly. Solar cells gave less than 0.01% of the world's energy in the early 1990s. Most comes from *fossil fuels* – coal, oil and natural gas – created by plants long ago. Fossil fuels will take many million years to replace, so they are called *non-renewable*. Under 5% of our energy comes from *renewable* sources like trees, running water, and winds. They are called renewable because they are replenished fairly quickly. But even with renewable sources, some energy is lost forever every time it is used (page 158).

THE ENERGY CRISIS

The world now uses up 100 times as much energy as it did in 1860, and consumption is still rising. What's more, the industrialized world, including the USA and Europe, uses energy up at a much higher rate than other places. The average

COAL

In the 19th century, coal was the most important of all fuels, powering the steam engines of the Industrial Revolution, and keeping people's homes warm. Today it is still used in vast quantities, especially in countries like China where there are huge reserves. About half the coal mined each year is burned in power stations to generate electricity, a quarter is used for making steel and the rest is burned in home fires.

Coal is made from the plants that grew in huge, warm swamps in the Carboniferous Period, 300 million years ago. When the plants died, they fell into the swamps and became covered with mud. Over millions of years, they were buried deeper and deeper beneath layers of mud. Eventually the weight of layers above squeezed them solid, and the

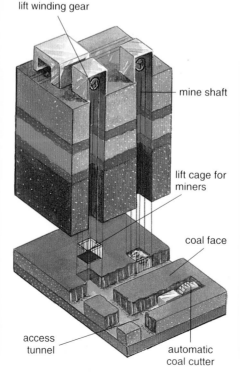

lift winding gear

mine shaft

lift cage for miners

coal face

access tunnel

automatic coal cutter

combined effect of heat and pressure turned them into coal.

There are actually three main kinds of coal. Lignite or brown coal is buried just below the surface, and can often be dug from shallow pits called strip mines. Because it formed quite recently, and contains less carbon and more water, it gives less heat. Bituminous coal and anthracite are both black and found in seams, often far below ground.

To get at the seams, mines (left) have deep shafts, often hundreds of metres deep, and tunnels along the seams from the shafts. In old mines, coal is prised away from the *coal face* (the exposed seam) by miners with picks and shovels. In newer pits, remote-controlled cutting machines are used. The newly won coal is then taken in trucks to the shaft and hauled to the surface.

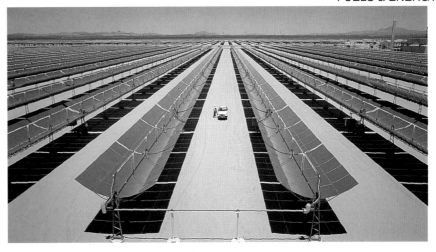

American, for instance, consumes 330 times as much energy as the average Ethiopian.

It is thought that the world's entire oil reserves will be gone within 30 years if we go on using it at the current rate. Even coal will last only 170 years. And it is likely that as Third World countries begin to develop their own industries, they will demand their fair share of energy too. Very soon then, there will not be enough fossil fuels to meet demand.

Moreover, the mounting use of energy is already harming the environment. Burning massive amounts of fossil fuels, for instance, pollutes the atmosphere badly, contributing to global warming (page 99), while large hydro-electric plants can not only drown farmland but devastate natural habitats by changing the flow of rivers.

Many people feel that the use of too much energy is the major problem facing the world. Some think the answer lies in alternative energy sources (see right); others think that we must rethink the way we use energy altogether.

ALTERNATIVE ENERGY

Because fossil fuels are irreplaceable and dirty, many people want to develop cleaner, renewable sources of energy. Of these, only running water (hydropower) is as yet widely used. Water power has been used in water mills for thousands of years. But today it is used mostly to generate electricity. Very few of the world's rivers have yet been developed, so the potential is huge. But the need to build big dams to control the flow is a real drawback. Tidal power – using the daily up and down movements of the sea – could also be developed but building tidal power stations may well upset the marine environment.

Solar energy (above) *Curved mirrors track the sun and focus the rays to heat oil in pipes. The heat is transferred to water, which boils. The steam drives turbines linked to electricity generators.*
Wind power (below) *A forest of wind turbines, which turn electricity generators.*

OIL

Oil is found all over the world, from the Middle East to Alaska. Some oil fields are in the sea – but onshore fields are in places covered by the sea millions of years ago.

Oil is made of tiny plants and animals that lived in warm seas. As they died, they were slowly buried beneath the mud of the sea-bed. The heat from deep underground and the increasing weight of mud above turned them into oil. The rock holding oil is porous – it has holes like a sponge. Pressure forces the oil up until it meets solid, non-porous rock, when it becomes trapped in a huge pocket underground.

Oil usually comes out of the ground as thick, black crude oil. It has to be refined (specially treated) by distillation to separate out fuels like petrol and diesel for cars and lorries and kerosene for aircraft.

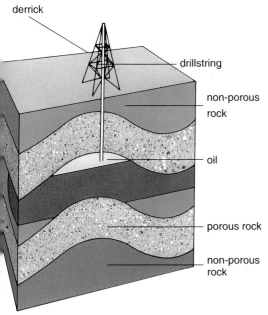

derrick
drillstring
non-porous rock
oil
porous rock
non-porous rock

Oil wells (left) *A well is sunk to a pocket of trapped oil. The well is bored using a drillstring lowered from a derrick.*
An oil refinery (right) *processes crude oil.*

THE EARTH IN CRISIS

We humans now dominate the Earth more than any other species has ever done – and the Earth is in grave danger of suffering irreparable harm from our activities. Our demands on its fragile resources are threatening everything from the atmosphere to plant and animal life.

The threat humans pose to the Earth is not new. Even 10,000 years ago, the arrival of hunting people in North America wiped out animal species like the mammoth. But since the Industrial Revolution began 200 years ago, the threat has grown much bigger, and as economic development gathers pace around the world, it is becoming more and more urgent to find a solution.

The Earth is being damaged in countless ways. Car exhausts and factory chimneys are choking the air. Gases from supersonic jets and refrigerator factories are punching a hole in the atmosphere's protective ozone layer. Rivers are poisoned by agricultural chemicals. Unique species of animals and plants are vanishing forever. Forests are being felled, vast areas of countryside are being buried under concrete and beautiful marine environments are being destroyed.

At the root of all these problems lies the raging consumption of energy and other resources that started in Europe and America – and is now spreading like a disease all around the world. Many people feel that unless we cure ourselves of this need to consume, we will kill the Earth – and ourselves.

Nuclear bomb testing fills the air with radioactive dust and leaves many areas uninhabitable for centuries

Huge spillages of oil from supertankers can do great damage to seabirds and other creatures

Wrecks may release dangerous chemicals as they gradually corrode

Danger points This illustration shows just some of the many places where the environment is threatened in modern industrial nations.

ENDANGERED LIFE

The mountain gorilla (right) is just one of millions of animal and plant species threatened with extinction by the loss of their natural habitats. Many species have become extinct naturally in the past, but they are now becoming extinct 400 times more quickly. Ecologists fear that the loss of variety leaves nature very vulnerable to any catastrophe.

DIRTY RIVERS

In the developing world, 25 million people die every year from diseases caught by drinking dirty water, and many more millions suffer from diseases such as malaria, elephantiasis and the eye disease, trachoma. But even in the industrialized world, where drinking water is relatively healthy, many rivers are badly polluted by chemicals and untreated raw sewage.

Vanishing Rainforest

One of the saddest and most worrying events of recent years has been the rapid destruction of huge areas of tropical rainforest. Rainforests cover less than 8% of the Earth's land surface, yet they make up half of the growing wood and provide a home for 40% of the world's plant and animal species. They protect the soil and act like a sponge, soaking up water and releasing it steadily through their leaves. They also help regulate climate, both locally and on a world scale, by affecting humidity and carbon dioxide levels in the air above.

In Brazil especially, vast areas are being burned, slashed and bulldozed – not to make use of the wood, but to clear the land for livestock rearing. Sadly, the unprotected soil is worn away quickly – and irreparably – in the tropical climate. So the stock farmers must soon move on and chop down more virgin forest.

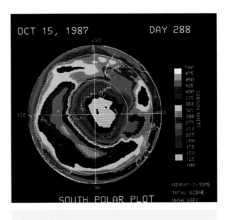

Poisoned Atmosphere

Carbon dioxide is one of the most important gases in the air because it helps trap the warmth of the Sun just like the panes of glass in a greenhouse. This greenhouse effect has, in the past, kept the world at a good temperature for life. But since we began to burn fossil fuels in huge quantities in the Industrial Revolution, the level of carbon dioxide in the air has gone up from 265 to 350 parts per million. The result is that the Earth is getting steadily warmer, rainfall patterns are becoming disrupted and the polar ice caps may be melting. Car exhaust is one of the major contributors to this global warming.

Burning fossil fuels, especially in coal-fired power stations, can cause rain to be highly acidic, damaging forests (below).

Meanwhile, the ozone layer in the upper air (page 83) is being damaged by chemicals like chlorofluorocarbons (CFCs) released by some aerosols, refrigerators and air conditioning systems – and by supersonic aircraft. Without the protection of ozone, the Sun may give us skin cancer and reduce the yield of many grain crops. Satellite pictures have revealed a large hole in the layer of ozone above Antarctica each spring (shown pink in the computer picture above).

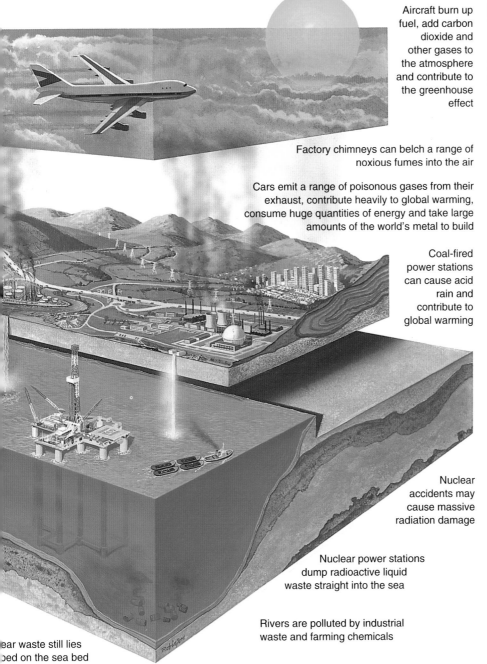

Aircraft burn up fuel, add carbon dioxide and other gases to the atmosphere and contribute to the greenhouse effect

Factory chimneys can belch a range of noxious fumes into the air

Cars emit a range of poisonous gases from their exhaust, contribute heavily to global warming, consume huge quantities of energy and take large amounts of the world's metal to build

Coal-fired power stations can cause acid rain and contribute to global warming

Nuclear accidents may cause massive radiation damage

Nuclear power stations dump radioactive liquid waste straight into the sea

Rivers are polluted by industrial waste and farming chemicals

...ear waste still lies ...ed on the sea bed

HOW THE EARTH BEGAN

Thousands of millions of years ago, there was probably just a vast cloud of gas and dust whirling around the newly formed Sun. Then, about 4600 million years ago, parts of the cloud began to clump together, forming the Earth and the other planets. The clump that was to be the Earth got smaller and hotter until it was a red-hot ball of molten rock. At last, it began to cool. A crust formed, like the skin on custard, and vast billows of gas and dust bubbled up to create a cloudy layer around the outside. This cloudy layer became the Earth's airy envelope, the atmosphere.

DID LIGHTNING MAKE LIFE POSSIBLE?
In 1953, a scientist sealed water and gases in a jar to mimic the oceans and atmosphere of the primeval Earth, and passed an electrical spark through it. A few days later, the jar was stained with a goo of amino acids – chemicals that link up to form proteins, the basic chemicals of life.

SPONGES AND JELLYFISH
Sponges and jellyfish are the oldest of all multi-celled creatures; faint imprints of their bodies are found in rocks 700 million years old. Sponges are made from various kinds of cell. Each performs a special task in the sponge – yet each can survive outside the sponge. It may be that multi-celled creatures evolved because single-celled creatures could survive better by cooperating.

EMERGING LIFE
For a long time, the Earth was a seething mass of erupting volcanoes and smoke. After a billion years or so, rain began to fall from clouds in the atmosphere, and the first oceans appeared.

About this time the first lifeforms appeared – perhaps in volcanic pools, perhaps in *hydrothermal vents* where hot water bubbles up under the ocean. These early lifeforms were tiny bacteria, made of a single cell, and fed on chemicals. Soon another kind of bacteria, called *blue-green algae*, appeared. They used photosynthesis (page 57) to obtain energy, and in doing so gave the air oxygen, the gas animals need to breathe.

All these primitive living cells have no central nucleus (page 8) and are called *prokaryotes*. But about 1.5 billion years ago, lifeforms called *protists*, including amoebas, appeared. Protists are made from a single cell. They are *eukaryotic*, which means they have a nucleus enclosed in a nuclear membrane, like the cells in all advanced lifeforms.

ANIMALS IN THE SEA
Fossils show that the first proper animals, like jellyfish and sponges, appeared in the sea about 700 million years ago. These creatures were entirely soft, but, for the first time, were made from many kinds of cell, each suited to a certain task. Over the next 100 million years, creatures with hard parts (shells and bones) appeared. Fish, the first creatures with backbones, emerged about 400 million years ago.

MOVING TO THE LAND
Until about 400 million years ago, life existed only in the sea. Then, the first small land plants, such as mosses and fungi, began to grow on the swampy shores.

330 mya: Giant ferns and club mosses

700 mya: Jellyfish and sponges

580 mya: Shellfish

400 mya: Fish

400 mya: Insects

350 mya: Amphibians

EVOLUTION

Today, there is an astonishing variety of life on Earth – yet every plant and animal has its own natural home or way of living. Some plants thrive in deserts, for instance; others prefer cold, wet places. Similarly, some animals eat only meat; others only grass. Every living thing, it seems, is perfectly suited to its surroundings.

In 1859, an English naturalist called Charles Darwin explained this with the Theory of Evolution. He suggested that over millions of years plant and animal species gradually change or *evolve*, adapting to suit their surroundings.

Evolution depends on the fact that no two living things are quite alike. So some plants or animals may start life with features that make them better able to survive. An animal, say, might have long legs that help it escape predators. A plant might have big leaves that help it grow better in shady places. Animals and

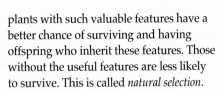

plants with such valuable features have a better chance of surviving and having offspring who inherit these features. Those without the useful features are less likely to survive. This is called *natural selection*.

Slowly, over many generations, better adapted animals and plants survive and flourish, while others die out or find a new home. In this way, Darwin believed, all the millions of different species of

plants and animals slowly evolved.

Fossils, though, show evolution is not quite so slow and steady as Darwin thought. Some scientists now believe change comes in rapid bursts, with long periods when little changes in between. This is called *punctuated equilibrium*. Others believe bursts of rapid change interrupt long periods of steady change. This is called *punctuated gradualism*.

Plants Gradually, over millions of years, plants began to colonize further inland, and tree-like plants began to grow. By about 300 million years ago, large areas were covered in thick forests. These forests were quite unlike those of today. They were often very swampy, and though they grew up to 30m high, the 'trees' were actually giant versions of plants that are quite small today, such as club mosses, horsetails and ferns. Proper trees, for example magnolias, began to appear only about 100 million years ago.

Animals The first land plants were soon followed by the first land animals, such as millipedes and insects, taking advantage of the food and shelter provided by the plants. Then about 350 million years ago, hot weather dried up lakes and rivers. Many fish died, but some were able to adapt to life on dry land. They grew lungs, legs, thick skins and strong skeletons for living on land – although they still returned to water to lay their eggs. These were the first amphibians (page 38), from which all land animals eventually evolved.

KEY DATES (million years ago)
4600	The Earth begins.
3800	First life-forms (bacteria).
3000	Blue-green algae appear.
1400	First eukaryotes, such as amoebas.
700	First multi-celled creatures.
570	First creatures with shells and bones.
400	First fish, land plants and insects.
350	First amphibians.

CHANGING LIFE

Since life began, many creatures have come and gone. Some survived for long periods; others died out rapidly as conditions changed. People used to see evolution as a steady progress towards complex, better-adapted creatures, culminating in humans. But many well-adapted species may have been killed off by catastrophes – and simple bacteria have been around for 3.8 billion years, 10,000 times as long as *Homo sapiens*.

220 mya: Dinosaurs

180 mya: Pterosaurs, flying reptiles

150 mya: Archaeopteryx, the first bird

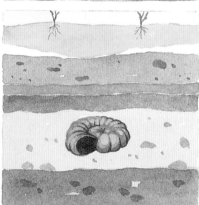

These three pictures show how an ammonite may have become a fossil. The series of events is described in detail below.

FOSSILS

How do scientists know that dinosaurs once roamed the Earth? Or that huge woolly elephants called mammoths were alive in Europe 12,000 years ago? The answer is fossils. Fossils are the relics of plants and animals that have been preserved for many thousands or millions of years, usually in stone. They may be the remains of living things – bones, shells, eggs, seeds and so on. Or they may just be signs, such as footprints they leave behind.

THE FOSSIL RECORD

When an animal dies, its soft parts rot away, but if its bones or shell are buried quickly in mud, they may eventually turn to stone, creating a fossil. As the next pages show, fossils give a remarkable picture of the history of life. We know from fossils when creatures first began to crawl ashore from the sea, what the dinosaurs were like, and much more besides.

Most fossils are either shells or just a few isolated bones. Complete skeletons are rare. Yet from their detailed knowledge of animal shapes, *palaeontologists* (people who study fossils) are often able to build up a picture of

what an animal looked like from just a few bones – even if the animal belongs to a species long since extinct. In fact, fossils show that animal species alive today are only a tiny fraction of those that have lived on the Earth. Over time, many millions of species have evolved and then died out, leaving only their fossils to prove they ever existed.

How old? You can work out how old a fossil is from the rocks in which it is found. Scientists know how old rocks are relative to each other because layers of rock form on top of each other, so the lowest layers are oldest. They measure

HOW A FOSSIL IS MADE

When a shellfish dies and falls to the sea-bed, its soft parts quickly rot away, to leave just the hard shell. This soon becomes buried under sand and mud. Over millions and millions of years, water trickles through the mud, dissolving the shell away, to leave a hole, called a *mould*. Minerals in the water may take the place of the shell, hardening to form a *cast* of the shell. So a fossil may be either a cast or a mould.

This series of events rarely happens on land, so fossils of sea creatures are more common than those of land animals.

Ammonite shells (above) are among the most common fossils. Like squids, ammonites had long tentacles. They are now extinct, but thrived in warm seas from 64 to 190 million years ago.

Fish (right) were the first creatures to have backbones, over 400 million years ago. The Devonian period from 408 to 360 million years ago is some-times called the Age of Fish.

Mammoths were common in Eurasia and North America until about 10,000 years ago. In 1977, a perfectly preserved baby mammoth was found in frozen soil in Siberia.

TRACE FOSSILS AND OTHER REMAINS

Trace fossils are fossils of signs left behind by animals or plants – dinosaur footprints may be fossilized (above). Remains may also survive in other ways. Frozen corpses of mammoths (left) have been found in Siberia and insects have been found in amber, solidified resin oozed by ancient coniferous trees (below).

radioactivity (page 149) to give a more definite date. Since dinosaur fossils are found only in rocks formed 65 – 220 million years ago, we know they lived at this time.

Limitations The picture given by fossils is very blurred. Only a fraction of the species that have ever lived are preserved in even one fossil. Of the fossils that do exist, most are of shellfish that lived in shallow seas. Animals with soft bodies such as worms and animals that live on land are very rarely found as fossils.

Another problem is that we usually have only the hard parts to tell us what the animal was like. So we can only guess what colour it was, whether it had fur or not and if it had large ears.

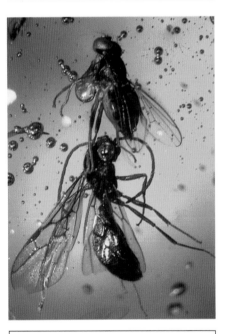

Fossil ferns

In a plant, there are no hard parts like shell and bone to be fossilized. But if buried quickly, plants too can make fossils, rotting away very slowly to leave just a thin black film of carbon, imprinted on the rock like a picture on a page. This is how we know that ferns (above) are among the oldest of all land plants, first appearing some 350 million years ago.

DID YOU KNOW?

The oldest fossils of all are stromatolites, fossil reefs formed by fossil blue-green algae and other bacteria 3.5 billion years ago.

The first fossils of creatures of more than one cell date from about 700 million years ago.

The Burgess shale of British Columbia, dating from about 550 million years ago, contains fossils of 20 to 30 major groups of arthropod (page 52). Only four exist today.

DINOSAURS

For 155 million years, from 220 million years ago, the Earth was ruled by giant reptiles called dinosaurs, including brachiosaurus, one of the largest creatures ever to have walked on land. Then suddenly and mysteriously, 65 million years ago, all the dinosaurs died out.

ANCIENT GIANTS

Dinosaurs were the biggest land animals that ever lived. The ferocious hunter *Tyrannosaurus rex* was over 15m long, weighed 7 tonnes and towered over 5m above the ground – taller than a double-decker bus. But even *Tyrannosaurus* was small compared with the sauropods – *Brachiosaurus* (above) was 23m long, weighed 80 tonnes and towered 12m in the air! *Brachiosaurus's* large size was a protection against predators and made it easier to keep a stable body temperature.

HARD EVIDENCE

Nearly all we know about dinosaurs is based on fossilized bones. Sometimes just a few bones are found, occasionally complete skeletons. So ideas about how dinosaurs behaved and what their skins looked like are little better than guesswork. However, a few rare finds, such as a mummified *Hadrosaurus* skin found in 1913, and dinosaur nests with eggs in Mongolia, have confirmed some of the guesses. Fossilized footprints, too, have helped build up a picture of how dinosaurs walked and ran, and how predators such as *Allosaurus* tracked sauropod prey.

DINOSAURS AND LIZARDS

The word dinosaur means 'terrible lizard', and it is apt, for dinosaurs were reptiles. Just like reptiles today, they had scaly skins and laid eggs with shells – although usually all that remains of a dinosaur is its fossilized bones. Similar creatures lived in the sea at the time (page 106), but dinosaurs were all land creatures.

However, dinosaurs were very different from modern reptiles in several ways. While modern reptiles all walk with bent legs splayed out, dinosaurs had straight legs under their bodies, as do mammals. This meant they could run fast, with long, agile strides, and also grow very heavy, for their legs acted like pillars to support their weight.

Dinosaurs may also have been warm-blooded, rather than cold-blooded like reptiles today (page 36). Some scientists argue that dinosaurs had to be warm-blooded to provide the energy they needed to run upright; the numerous blood vessels in their bones support this. They also argue that warm-blooded creatures need to eat a lot – which is why there are so many fewer predators (hunters) than prey, and why many plant-eating dinosaurs had hundreds of teeth.

In many ways, dinosaurs were more like mammals than reptiles. Some, especially the agile hunters, were as intelligent as modern mammals. Moreover, many plant-eating dinosaurs, such as the sauropods, lived in herds like modern *herbivorous* (plant-eating) mammals, such as antelope. Some may even have had fur.

KINDS OF DINOSAUR

Some dinosaurs ran on two legs, and were shaped like kangaroos. Others were bulky and stood on

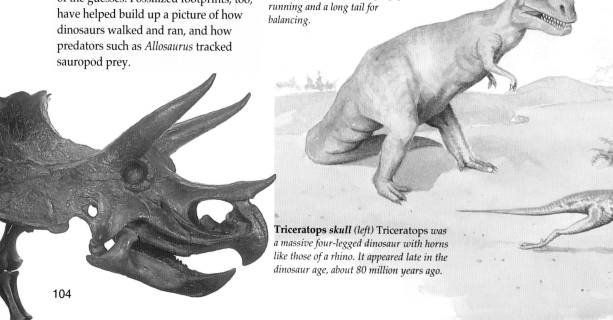

Theropods Tyrannosaurus *was the biggest of the meat-eating theropods.* Compsognathus *was the smallest. Both had long legs for running and a long tail for balancing.*

Triceratops skull *(left)* Triceratops *was a massive four-legged dinosaur with horns like those of a rhino. It appeared late in the dinosaur age, about 80 million years ago.*

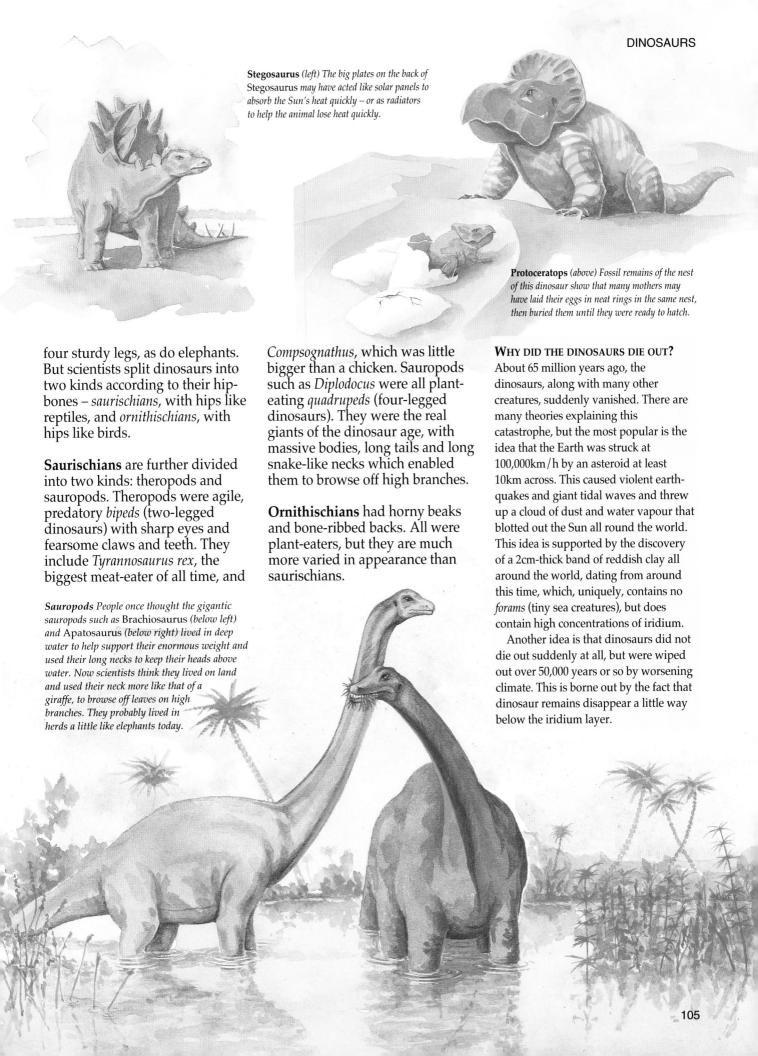

Stegosaurus (left) The big plates on the back of Stegosaurus *may have acted like solar panels to absorb the Sun's heat quickly – or as radiators to help the animal lose heat quickly.*

Protoceratops (above) Fossil remains of the nest of this dinosaur show that many mothers may have laid their eggs in neat rings in the same nest, then buried them until they were ready to hatch.

four sturdy legs, as do elephants. But scientists split dinosaurs into two kinds according to their hip-bones – *saurischians*, with hips like reptiles, and *ornithischians*, with hips like birds.

Saurischians are further divided into two kinds: theropods and sauropods. Theropods were agile, predatory *bipeds* (two-legged dinosaurs) with sharp eyes and fearsome claws and teeth. They include *Tyrannosaurus rex*, the biggest meat-eater of all time, and

Compsognathus, which was little bigger than a chicken. Sauropods such as *Diplodocus* were all plant-eating *quadrupeds* (four-legged dinosaurs). They were the real giants of the dinosaur age, with massive bodies, long tails and long snake-like necks which enabled them to browse off high branches.

Ornithischians had horny beaks and bone-ribbed backs. All were plant-eaters, but they are much more varied in appearance than saurischians.

WHY DID THE DINOSAURS DIE OUT?

About 65 million years ago, the dinosaurs, along with many other creatures, suddenly vanished. There are many theories explaining this catastrophe, but the most popular is the idea that the Earth was struck at 100,000km/h by an asteroid at least 10km across. This caused violent earth-quakes and giant tidal waves and threw up a cloud of dust and water vapour that blotted out the Sun all round the world. This idea is supported by the discovery of a 2cm-thick band of reddish clay all around the world, dating from around this time, which, uniquely, contains no *forams* (tiny sea creatures), but does contain high concentrations of iridium.

Another idea is that dinosaurs did not die out suddenly at all, but were wiped out over 50,000 years or so by worsening climate. This is borne out by the fact that dinosaur remains disappear a little way below the iridium layer.

Sauropods *People once thought the gigantic sauropods such as* Brachiosaurus *(below left) and* Apatosaurus *(below right) lived in deep water to help support their enormous weight and used their long necks to keep their heads above water. Now scientists think they lived on land and used their neck more like that of a giraffe, to browse off leaves on high branches. They probably lived in herds a little like elephants today.*

THE AGE OF THE DINOSAURS

Dinosaurs dominated the Earth from about 220 to 65 million years ago. But they were by no means the only living things on Earth during this time. There were other reptiles, insects, fish, birds and small mammals. There was plenty of plant life, too. Even the dinosaurs themselves changed, and scientists believe that some may have evolved into birds.

Archaeopteryx was a strange combination of bird and reptile, with a bird's wings and feathers and a reptile's teeth and claws. We know of it from six fossils found in an area of Germany that was a tropical lagoon in Jurassic times.

EARLY BIRD

While dinosaurs like *Tyrannosaurus rex* were still roaming the Earth, the first birds were seen in the sky. Indeed, the first bird-like creature, *Archaeopteryx*, dates from the Jurassic period, 150 million years ago. It looks so much like a small dinosaur called *Compsognathus* that scientists are convinced they had the same dinosaur ancestor. The only real difference is that *Archaeopteryx* had feathers and wings. It even had clawed hands on its wings. *Archaeopteryx* was not a good flier, and probably used its claws to haul itself up trees, to glide short distances and to find food and shelter.

LIFE IN THE WATER

The age of the dinosaurs was the age of reptiles. Just as the dinosaurs dominated the land, so large reptiles called *plesiosaurs* and *ichthyosaurs* ruled the ocean.

Ichthyosaurs or 'fish lizards' lived in shallow seas from about 220 to 90 million years ago. They looked a little like dolphins, with fins, flippers and a streamlined body, but their tail was held vertically like a fish's. They had long beaks with sharp teeth for grasping their prey – fishes and squid. Unusually for reptiles, they did not lay eggs but gave birth to their young.

Plesiosaurs were creatures with a barrel-shaped body, long neck and tiny head. They were powerful, agile swimmers and their four big flippers meant they could twist and turn to snap up passing fish.

There were turtle-like reptiles such as *Archelon* in the sea at this time too, along with vast numbers of squids and ammonites (page 102). In shallow seas, sea urchins and coral were abundant. Rivers and streams were terrorized by the gigantic crocodile-like *Deinosuchus*. *Deinosuchus* grew to over 15m – longer than a bus. Any dinosaur wading through the river, or taking a drink, could easily fall victim to its snapping 2m-long jaws.

Cretaceous ocean This picture shows some of the creatures that lived on or above the Tethys Sea (page 90)in the late Cretaceous period, 80 million years ago.

Pteranodon was one of the many fearsome flying reptiles called pterosaurs that darkened the sky during the Age of the Dinosaurs.

Archelon was a huge sea turtle, growing up to 3.5m long. It probably lived on jellyfish.

Long-necked plesiosaurs snapped up fish with a quick stab of their heads from above the surface.

Dimetrodon *was a mammal-like reptile that roamed Pangaea 260 million years ago. It had a huge 'sail' of skin on its back, which helped it soak up warmth from the Sun to build up energy for pursuing its prey.*

CHANGING WORLD

When the *Jurassic* period began, some 208 million years ago, there was just one giant continent in the world called Pangaea and one ocean, Panthalassa (page 90). The climate was warm and moist, and plants such as ferns and cycads flourished, creating vast forests. Everywhere, barely seen by dinosaurs, were billions of insects – ancestors of today's earwigs, ants, flies and caddis flies – along with tiny mammals active only by night. In the air, there were flying pterosaurs, huge reptiles with fearsome jaws, and the bird-like *Archaeopteryx*.

FLYING REPTILES

While the dinosaurs ruled the land, the air was dominated by huge creatures called *pterosaurs*, or 'winged lizards'. Most had vast leathery wings supported by arm and handbones and a very long fourth finger bone. Scientists once thought they flew mainly by gliding, but now some believe that they had shoulder muscles quite strong enough for them to flap their wings like birds.

Many pterosaurs were hunters with long pointed beaks. *Pteranodons* had no teeth and probably swept up fish to swallow them whole. *Pterodactyls* had teeth for snapping and chewing fish. *Pterodaustro* had comb-like teeth and probably skimmed over the water filtering small creatures through the comb.

THE FIRST MAMMALS

Even while the dinosaurs dominated the Earth, there were mammals like shrews scurrying about feeding on insects. They were descended from large mammal-like reptiles, which had dominated the Earth throughout the Permian and early Triassic periods (286-208 million years ago). These mammal-like reptiles walked on all fours, at first with their legs out to the side like lizards. By 190 million years ago, their legs were tucked in like today's mammals, allowing them to run faster. They were probably warm-blooded. *Cynognathus* may even have had fur and looked like a large dog.

By the *Cretaceous* period (144 to 66 million years ago), Pangaea had split in half. Sea flooded over the land, creating vast shallows where the sea-bed was carpeted with the skeletons of microscopic sea creatures – now fossilized as chalk (page 94). In huge swamps, filled with giant sequoia and cypress trees, frogs, salamanders, snakes, gulls and wading birds thrived. The climate grew cooler, and, on land, the first flowering plants appeared and spread rapidly, along with the butterflies and bees that pollinated them. High above soared the largest of all pterosaurs, *Quetzalcoatlus*.

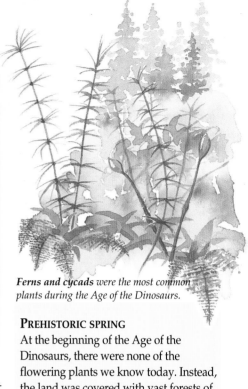

Ferns and cycads *were the most common plants during the Age of the Dinosaurs.*

PREHISTORIC SPRING

At the beginning of the Age of the Dinosaurs, there were none of the flowering plants we know today. Instead, the land was covered with vast forests of plants that were spread mainly by spores – giant tree ferns and horsetail ferns, cycads (page 64) and conifers, mosses and fungi. Then, about 100 million years ago, flowering plants began to appear. They spread rapidly – so rapidly that within 10 million years or so, 90% of all plants were flowering plants. There were trees, and shrubs, such as hickory, oak and magnolia, and *herbaceous* (herb-like) flowers, such as musk mallows.

Magnolias *are among the oldest of all flowering plants, first appearing 100 million years ago.*

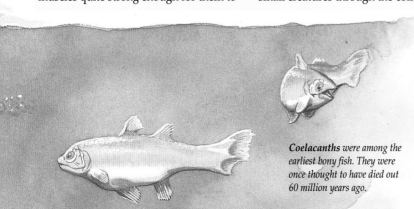

Coelacanths *were among the earliest bony fish. They were once thought to have died out 60 million years ago.*

> **DID YOU KNOW?**
> **Dinosaur names** are usually Latin descriptions of some feature of their appearance or behaviour.
> **Apatosaurus** means 'deceptive reptile'.
> **Stegosaurus** means 'roofed reptile'.
> **Triceratops** means 'three-horned face'.
> **Tyrannosaurus rex** means 'king tyrant reptile'.

Diatryma *may not have been able to fly, but it was a fearsome predator. It was over 2m high and would run after prey, snatch them with its huge clawed feet and rip them to shreds with its great parrot-like beak.*

AFTER THE DINOSAURS

When the dinosaurs vanished mysteriously about 65 million years ago, the way was clear for mammals and birds to become dominant. Many new species of mammal evolved, and each new era brought a new set of creatures – many of them ancestors of the mammals of today.

NEW BIRDS

Like mammals, birds too benefited from the death of the dinosaurs. Indeed, for a long while, giant flightless birds such as *Diatryma* and *Phorosrhacos* were the main predators. Flightless birds grew to huge sizes at this time. A New Zealand bird called *Dinornis* was over 3.5m tall – taller than an elephant – while *Aepyornis* weighed 440kg and laid eggs as big as a rugby ball. *Aepyornis* may have survived in Madagascar until the 17th century and was probably the great 'roc' of explorers' legend.

Flying birds too could reach gigantic sizes. *Argentavis* was a huge vulture-like bird that lived in Argentina 40 million years ago and hunted for mammals as big as modern sheep and horses. It weighed over 120kg and had wings up to 7.6m across. Pelican-like *Osteodornis* was also vast, with wings up to 5.2m across, and may have snapped up squid from the sea surface with its gigantic bill.

All kinds of smaller birds evolved as well. Vast flocks of duck-like *Presbyornis* fed on algae in salty lagoons 40 million years ago; early parrots called *Archaeopsittacus* perched in the tropical forests of France 30 million years ago; and the first known owl, *Ogygoptnyx*, dates from over 54 million years ago.

THE RISE OF MAMMALS

At the end of the Age of the Dinosaurs, the only mammals were tiny marsupials – that is, mammals that carry their young in a pouch. But with the dinosaurs out of the way, mammals began to grow much larger, and marsupials were steadily pushed aside by *placental* mammals, which gave birth to fully developed babies.

By this time, the remains of Pangaea had finally split into the continents we know today. On each continent, similar but unique species of mammals evolved to fill a particular role or *niche*. Each continent had its rodents, its insect-eaters, grass-eaters, meat-eaters and so on. In North America, for instance, there were: a squirrel-like rodent called *Sciuravus*; a leaf-eater like a snub-nosed, muscular rat called

Stylinodon; *Icaronycteris*, the earliest known bat; sheep-like *condylarths*; the first hooved grass-eaters; and many more besides.

Meat-eaters The first large carnivorous mammals appeared at this time. They are called *creodonts* and ranged in size from smaller than a rat to bigger than a polar bear. The smallest, such as *Deltatheridium*, were weasel-like and may have fed on insects; the biggest, *Megistotherium*, was the largest ever carnivorous mammal. Some big creodonts, such as *Hyaenodon* (a little like a modern hyena) were scavengers. Others hunted hooved animals such as condylarths and perhaps even elephant-like creatures. They were probably neither as fast-moving nor as clever as modern hunting mammals, but nor were their prey.

THE COMING OF THE WHALE

The catastrophe that killed the dinosaurs on land also wiped out the big reptiles in the oceans – the plesiosaurs and ichthyosaurs. Here too, large mammals – the whales – took their place. Fossils suggest that whales are descended from a meat-eating condylarth (early hooved mammal) called a *Mesonychid*. By about 52 million years ago, mesonychids had evolved into *Pakicetus*, which was like a

cross between a whale and a tapir. *Pakicetus* lived on land but could swim well. Gradually, these creatures became better and better adapted to life in the water, their limbs evolving into flippers and their bodies becoming longer and more streamlined. By about 50 million years ago, the first true whales appeared, dominating the oceans from Africa to North America.

Basilosarus was one of the first true whales, living around 50 million years ago. Its long snake-like body grew to over 20m. It fed on large fishes which it grabbed with its saw-edged teeth.

PLAINS OF GRASS

About 24 million years ago, early in the Miocene epoch, the world's climate got much drier and cooler, and tropical forests gave way to open grasslands much like the grasslands of East Africa today. As the grasslands spread, so too did grazing animals such as species of horse, camel, and rhinoceros. Creatures like these were sharp-eyed and long-legged and had hooves for running swiftly over the plains to escape predators. The creodonts could not catch them, but new, highly intelligent species of dogs and big, sabre-toothed cats often could.

THE ICE AGES

Two million years ago, early in the Pleistocene epoch, the world was gripped by the cold of the Ice Ages. Vast sheets of ice spread over much of North America, Europe and Asia, and the balance was tipped in favour of the mammals, which could survive cooler conditions. Creatures such as woolly rhinos and mammoths (page 103) were protected from the cold by their thick coats. Others, such as giant cave bears and lions, sought shelter in caves – as did the first humans.

THE BIG CARNIVORES

Gradually, about 25 million years ago, giant flightless birds and creodonts gave way to agile, intelligent, keen-eared creatures as the main hunters. There were runners that hunted in packs like dogs, cats that stalked and pounced and scavengers like hyenas. Among the most distinctive were the big sabre-toothed cats, with a pair of huge, curved fangs for slashing and stabbing their prey. It is because these fangs were so long (about 20cm), that scientists think they were used for stabbing victims – if the cat used them to hold on to a struggling victim, they would have been ripped out by the roots. Sabre-toothed cats died out less than 10,000 years ago.

Every now and then, it became warm for a while, and in these warm phases, monkeys, hyenas, hippos and elephants thrived in Europe. We live in a warm phase which began some 10,000 years ago, as the Pleistocene Epoch gave way to the Holocene. None of the big mammals of the Ice Ages – the woolly rhinos and mammoths, cave bears and lions – have survived. It may have been the change in climate that killed them off – or they may have been hunted to extinction by humans.

Smilodon
lived in the Americas from two million years ago to less than 10,000 years ago. It held down prey with its powerful front legs while slashing at blood vessels in the neck with its giant fangs.

KEY DATES (million years ago)

66–58 Palaeocene epoch: mammals and birds spread.

58–24 Eocene and Oligocene epochs: giant hunting birds and creodonts; condylarths and rodents.

24–2 Miocene and Pliocene epochs: spread of grassland; rise of long-legged ungulates, cats, dogs.

2 Pleistocene epoch and Ice Ages: woolly mammoths, cave lions and humans.

HOOVED ANIMALS

Among the most successful of all groups of mammals are the ungulates or hooved mammals. They are probably descended from the condylarths that thrived about 65–40 million years ago. From these evolved ungulates with odd numbers of toes, such as horses, rhinos and tapirs, and later ungulates with even numbers of toes, such as pigs, antelopes and cows. Of the odd-toed ungulates, the horse has continued most successfully since the Ice Ages began two million years ago.

Moropus was a big horse-like creature that browsed on leaves 18 million years ago.

Brontotheres were huge rhino-like plant-eaters that flourished 36–24 million years ago.

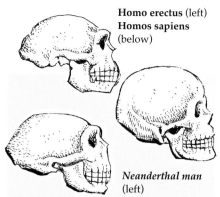

Homo erectus (left)
Homos sapiens (below)

Neanderthal man (left)

THE FIRST HUMANS

Compared with other animals, humans have been around for only a short time. We know from fossils that the first human-like creatures appeared barely six million years ago, and humans like ourselves arrived just 30,000 years ago.

CHANGING HEADS

Skulls have played an important part in working out the way humans have evolved. The shape of *Homo erectus's* mouth, for instance, shows he was physically unable to speak.

The skulls of the earliest hominids are similar to those of apes, but are smaller than those of modern humans', showing they had a smaller brain. Australopithecus had a 500cc brain, the same as a modern ape. This compares with 750cc for *Homo habilis*, 1000cc for *Homo erectus*, 1500cc for Neanderthal man and 1400cc for modern humans.

Early hominids' skulls have a very prominent jaw, large mouth and low forehead. As hominids evolved, the face became flatter, making the nose more prominent. The jaw receded, the mouth became smaller and the forehead grew taller as the brain expanded.

EARLY HUMANS

Humans have a great deal in common with apes – including their long arms and fingers and big brain – and it is clear we share the same ancestor. This ancestor was probably an orang-utan-like creature that lived in the grasslands of Africa.

Just when our ancestors became different from apes is not known, for there are few fossils to provide a clue. However, humans are so similar biochemically to gorillas and chimpanzees that most scientists think it is less than six million years ago.

Australopithecus The oldest fossil *hominids* (human-like creatures) date from around 3.5 million years ago. All are called *Australopithecus*, which means 'southern ape', because the first was discovered in South Africa. Among the earliest, and most famous, is a female known as 'Lucy', who was found at Hadar, in Ethiopia, in the 1970s. Australopithecines were much shorter than modern humans (barely 1m) and had a brain little bigger than apes. But they walked upright, and may well have used stones to help them obtain food.

Handy man About two million years ago, the first genuinely human creatures appeared. They were taller and had a bigger brain than Australopithecines. They also used stone tools to cut hides for clothes and meat for eating and built crude shelters. The best known is one called *Homo habilis*, which means 'handy man', from a fossil found at the Olduvai Gorge,

Hominid branches A few of the early hominids are shown below. The line begins with the oldest known Australopithecine, named 'Lucy'. Both 'Lucy' and Neanderthal man are from branches of the hominid family that died out, and are probably not direct ancestors of ours.

Australopithecus *'Lucy' fossils from Ethiopia are about 3 million years old.*

Homo habilis *(handy man), known from fossils from Olduvai Gorge, Africa.*

Homo erectus, *as tall as a human, from about 1.5 million years ago.*

Neanderthal man *lived in Europe and Asia about 100,000 to 30,000 years ago.*

Homo sapiens sapiens *(modern humans) evolved 30,000 years ago.*

EARLY HUNTERS

Crucial to the success of early hominids was their ability to hunt large mammals, using stone hand-axes and fire. Remains at Ambrona, in Spain, dating from 400,000 years ago show they hunted elephants and other large mammals by driving them into soft, marshy ground with fire – then smashing the trapped animals' heads with stones and spearing them with wooden spears. The carcass would be cut up with stone axes and cooked. Hunts involved many people working together and several major hunting trips like this were made each year.

The kill Here early men move in to finish off a sabre-toothed cat with stone spears. Deer, elephants, boars and ibexes were the most frequently hunted animals.

in Tanzania. But there may well have been others.

Upright man and wise man About one and a half million years ago, a hominid as tall as modern humans appeared, called *Homo erectus*. *Homo erectus* could light fires, and cook food, and hunted with long wooden spears with fire-hardened points. But these hominids had a smaller brain than ours. The first with a brain as big as ours, called *Homo sapiens*, appeared around 300,000 years ago.

Some scientists believe that the similarity of the DNA in our bodies (page 9) shows that all humans today are descended from a single woman, nicknamed 'Eve', who lived in Africa just 200,000 years ago. Others argue that because fossils of *Homo erectus* are found not only in Africa, but also in Asia and Europe, *Homo sapiens* evolved separately in different parts of the world.

The best known early *Homo sapiens* is *Homo sapiens neanderthalis* (Neanderthal man), who appeared about 100,000 years ago. He had a large face and rugged body. He also had a brain bigger than ours, wore clothes and knew how to paint. The first humans physically identical to us, called *Homo sapiens sapiens*, appeared about 30,000 years ago.

The search for our past Most of the earliest hominid remains have been found in Africa. The Olduvai Gorge, in Tanzania, has proved an especially rich source. Both Australopithecus and Homo habilis remains have been found here, along with footprints dating from three million years ago. This map also shows some of the other important sites in Africa, Europe and Asia where remains of Homo erectus or Homo sapiens have been found.

STONE TOOLS AND WEAPONS

Some scientists believe the earliest hominid tools may have been made from bone. But all early hominids used stone and wood, which is why the earliest period of human prehistory is called the Stone Age.

Three million years ago, Australopithecines chipped the edge off hand-sized round pebbles, perhaps to use as weapons. But the first proper tools were the two-sided hand-axes *Homo erectus* made by chipping flakes off flints with another stone to give a sharp edge. Axes like this were probably used for butchering large mammals, such as mammoths, for meat or hurling at them in the hunt.

Later, *Homo erectus* learned to fashion several fine blades from one flint, by hammering on a bone or wood punch with a stone. Careful shaping gave razor-sharp chips which could be tied to wooden shafts to make spears.

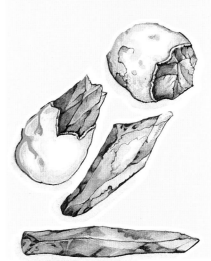

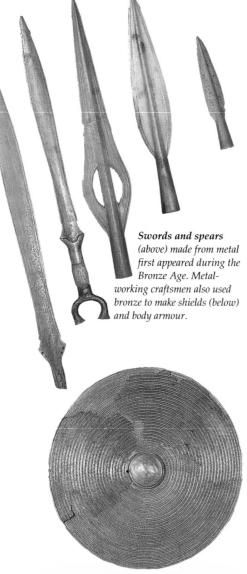

Swords and spears (above) made from metal first appeared during the Bronze Age. Metal-working craftsmen also used bronze to make shields (below) and body armour.

AGES OF BRONZE AND IRON

About 6000 years ago, people in South East Europe and the Near East made the first simple metal objects from copper. Soon after, they learned how to add tin to copper to make bronze, a much harder metal, which could be used for weapons. Metals were rare and costly, so possession of metal objects gave their owners power and status – as is clear from the hoards of metal objects in the graves of the Late Bronze Age. The use of iron spread from the Near East, from 1000 BC on, to the civilization of Ancient Greece and to northern Europe.

PREHISTORIC PEOPLE

The first written records date from about 5500 years ago. All the time before that – nearly all the time humans have existed – is prehistory. But archaeological evidence (remains and artefacts dug from the ground) has told us a great deal about the way people lived in prehistoric times.

THREE AGES

Archaeologists often divide prehistory into three ages, according to whether people used stone, bronze or iron to make tools and weapons: the Stone Age; the Bronze Age; and the Iron Age. They also split the Stone Age into three: the *Palaeolithic* (Old Stone Age), *Mesolithic* (Middle Stone Age) and *Neolithic* (New Stone Age). This system does not always work – especially outside Europe – for the change from one material to another occurred in different places at different times, but it provides a useful framework.

OLD STONE AGE

The Lower Palaeolithic began about two million years ago. It was during this period that *Homo erectus*, the first hominid to walk upright like us (page 111) first appeared. These beings left little behind to show how they lived – only the flint axes they used for hunting and the ashes of their fires for cooking and warmth.

The Middle Palaeolithic begins with the arrival of Neanderthal man 100,000 years ago. Europe and Asia were still often in the grip of the Ice Ages at this time, but

Neanderthals coped with the cold by living in caves and skin tents, and wearing clothes. Their flint tools, including spear heads, knives and scrapers, are much more sophisticated than those of *Homo erectus*. We also know that they buried their dead. At Shanidar cave in Iraq, one was laid to rest on a bed of flowers.

The Upper (late) Palaeolithic marks the arrival of modern humans about 30,000 years ago. The first modern humans are called *Cro-Magnon man*, from a cave in the Dordogne in France where remains were found. They probably emerged first in Asia, but spread rapidly across the world, and, about 12,000 years ago, were also living in the Americas and Australia.

Cro-Magnon people were deadly hunters, killing mammoths with flint-tipped spears, and possibly even bows and arrows – so deadly, in fact, that within a thousand years of their arrival in the Americas, they had wiped out nearly all the mammoths, horses, lions, and moose there. But they also left behind in Europe a rich collection of bone and ivory carvings and wonderful paintings

STONE AGE			BRONZE AGE	IRON AGE
PALAEOLITHIC	MESOLITHIC	NEOLITHIC		
2 million years ago	12,000 years ago	9000 years ago	6000 years ago	3000 years ago
Homo erectus to Cro-Magnon man gather plant food and hunt with flint weapons.	Use of bow and arrow in hunting; herding of sheep and goats.	Farming begins in Near East; first villages. Population grows and craft skills develop.	Bronze-making invented in SE Europe and Near East. Barrows and megaliths built.	Use of iron spreads from Near East. Rise of Classical Greek civilization.

Ages of prehistory The table on the left shows the sequence of the three ages of prehistory for Europe and the Near East. Elsewhere, the sequence is different. Bronze was not used in the Americas until the rise of the Incas barely 500 years ago. Even within Europe and the Near East, particular ages were reached at different times. In Britain, the Neolithic began 5000 years ago, and the Bronze Age came 2500 years ago.

Neolithic village Once people started to farm, they could build permanent villages where they could live all year round. Houses became much more substantial in construction. The extra food freed people to develop craft skills, such as weaving, spinning and baking, and also to begin trading with other people.

on cave walls showing such things as bison hunts.

NEW STONE AGE

About 12,000 years ago, the world was still peopled largely by small bands who hunted animals and gathered food from wild plants. But some people were already herding animals such as sheep and goats to provide a ready supply of food. Then, at the start of the Neolithic, people began to farm for the first time, growing crops such as barley and wheat, and rearing sheep, cattle and pigs.

This happened at different times in different places, starting perhaps around 10,000 years ago in the Near East and 4000 years later in northwest Europe, but its effect was dramatic. For the first time, people could settle in one place and build villages. At Jarmo, in

Iraq, there are the remains of 24 mud huts where about 150 people lived around 9000 years ago.

To begin with, farming was mixed with hunting, but the extra food meant people were free to do other tasks. Soon some people became skilled in things such as building houses and food stores, weaving cloth and making pots. They also learned how to use metals, first bronze in the Bronze Age and then iron in the Iron Age. Populations began to grow and, in time, villages grew into towns, leading to the first civilizations.

NEOLITHIC INVENTIONS
The change from hunting and gathering to a farming way of life during the New Stone Age brought many new and important inventions and discoveries.

New Stone Age people discovered how to make pottery from clay around 7000 BC. The vessels they made could be used for storing water and food. They also made cooking easier.

At about the same time, people were learning to grind grain into flour by using shallow stone bowls called *mortars* and club-like stone *pestles*.

Wooden ploughs that could be drawn by oxen were first used in the Near East around 4000 BC, about the same time as one of the most important inventions of all – the wheel.

Barrows and megaliths are relics of the Neolithic and Bronze Age in NW Europe. Barrows are burial mounds. Megaliths are made from huge slabs of stone. Sometimes they are tombs too. The most impressive megaliths are giant circles of standing stones such as Stonehenge (below). No one is sure what they were used for.

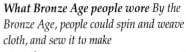
What Bronze Age people wore By the Bronze Age, people could spin and weave cloth, and sew it to make attractive clothes.

THE FIRST CIVILIZATIONS

The earliest civilizations grew up in the Near East, where people first learned to farm. Here, between the Tigris and Euphrates rivers in Iraq, the ancient Sumerians and other peoples lived in the world's first real cities, built great temples and learned how to write, as long as 6500 years ago.

Head-dress of Queen Shub-ad II This beautiful Sumerian royal head-dress found in the royal tombs of Ur is over 4500 years old.

SUMERIAN GODS AND MYTHS

The Sumerians were a very religious people and had gods and goddesses for every aspect of life. There was Enlil, god of the air, who first separated the sky from the ground and created all living creatures. There was Enki, the god of crafts, who organized the universe and gave the world fresh water. There was Ninhursag, the mother goddess, Inanna, the goddess of love, and many others.

Among the most famous of the Sumerian myths is the tale of Gilgamesh, King of Uruk. Handsome and strong, Gilgamesh had many adventures with his friend Enkidu. Once, Gilgamesh dived deep into the ocean to pluck a thorn that would bring everlasting life – only for it to be stolen by a snake as he slept, exhausted by his efforts.

THE FIRST CITIES

In 5000 BC, farming was flourishing along the banks of the Tigris and Euphrates rivers and around the marshes nearby. Each spring, the rivers flooded over the land, making it very fertile. But there was so little rain that by summer the soil was baked hard. In time, however, farmers learned to water their crops by diverting water from rivers through *irrigation* canals.

Irrigation opened up new land for crop growing and gave extra food, which allowed the population to grow rapidly. Soon a few villages in the triangle between the two rivers – an area called Sumer – grew into cities, such as Ur and Eridu. These cities grew as wars drove people to seek shelter behind the thick walls.

At the heart of each city was a temple, the first large buildings, where the Sumerians worshipped their many gods and goddesses. The Sumerians were not only great astronomers and mathematicians, but also created the first proper legal system and invented writing.

THE RISE OF BABYLON

For about 2000 years, Sumerian cities prospered. Then, around 2300 BC, they were conquered by King Sargon and the Akkadian people, their neighbours to the northwest. Over the next three centuries, Sumer was invaded again and again, until finally the Sumerians regained power under Ur-Nammu – but for barely 100 years, because peoples such as the Amorites attacked them.

Eventually, in 1792 BC, an Amorite king called Hammurabi

The first merchants Sumerian merchants travelled far and wide trading food, cloth, pottery and metal goods for basic raw materials such as timber and metals. Much of the cargo was carried in the high-prowed boats that travelled up and down the Euphrates.

Goat in a thicket This Sumerian statue dates from around 2500 BC, and shows the extraordinary skill of the Sumerian craftsmen.

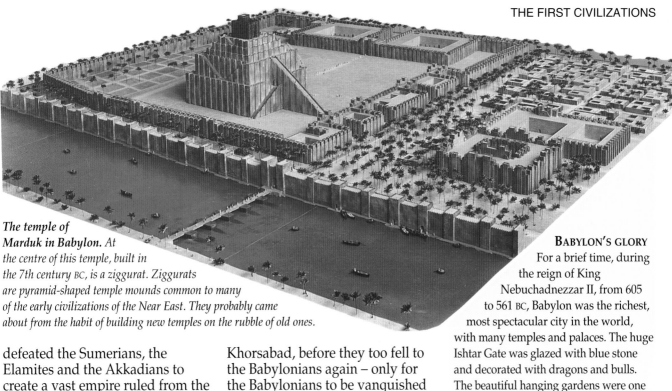

The temple of Marduk in Babylon. At the centre of this temple, built in the 7th century BC, is a ziggurat. Ziggurats are pyramid-shaped temple mounds common to many of the early civilizations of the Near East. They probably came about from the habit of building new temples on the rubble of old ones.

defeated the Sumerians, the Elamites and the Akkadians to create a vast empire ruled from the great city of Babylon. Hammurabi is famous for devising a strict legal code and systems of punishment.

In time, Babylon itself was taken over as various other peoples – Kassites, Hittites, Mittanians and Assyrians – vied for control of the area. The most successful (and ruthless) of these were the Assyrians. Their disciplined armies and two-wheeled chariots conquered almost all the Near and Middle East in the 7th century BC. The Assyrians built magnificent cities at Nineveh, Nimrud and Khorsabad, before they too fell to the Babylonians again – only for the Babylonians to be vanquished by Persians.

CITIES IN INDIA

Early civilizations appeared in the Indus valley in Pakistan soon after they began in the Near East, and the ruins of the ancient cities of Mohenjo-daro and Harappa date back to 2500 BC. These cities, too, had their own system of writing, which survives in many carved seals and other objects, but no one has yet been able to decipher it. From about 1800 BC, the Indus civilization went into decline too.

BABYLON'S GLORY

For a brief time, during the reign of King Nebuchadnezzar II, from 605 to 561 BC, Babylon was the richest, most spectacular city in the world, with many temples and palaces. The huge Ishtar Gate was glazed with blue stone and decorated with dragons and bulls. The beautiful hanging gardens were one of the seven wonders of the world. They were planted high on a ziggurat (see above) to remind Nebuchadnezzar's queen of her mountain home.

THE PERSIANS

In 550 BC, King Cyrus II of Persia (now Iran) conquered the neighbouring Medes to begin the world's first great empire. By 500 BC, the Persian empire stretched 4000km from India to Egypt, and had a population of over 10 million. A system of fast roads linked the capital Susa with all the outlying provinces. But the empire was weakened by frequent revolts and in 331 BC it was defeated by Alexander the Great.

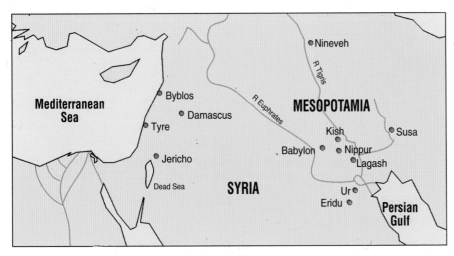

The Cradle of Civilization The world's first cities and civilizations developed in the fertile crescent of land between the Euphrates and Tigris rivers as they flow to the Persian Gulf.

This map shows some of the main cities of the region between 2500 and 6500 years ago. Mesopotamia was the Greek name for the land between the two rivers.

KEY DATES (BC)

c5000	Sumerian civilization begins.
c3500	Invention of writing, the wheel and the ox-drawn plough.
c2500	Mohenjo-daro at its peak.
c2300	Akkadians conquer Sumer.
c1792	Hammurabi creates Babylonian empire.
c700	Assyrian empire at its peak.
c570	The hanging gardens built in Babylon.
c500	City of Persepolis built by Persian king Darius I.

ANCIENT EGYPT

Over 5000 years ago, long before most of the world emerged from the Stone Age, the Ancient Egyptian civilization was born on the banks of the River Nile. The pharaohs (kings) of Egypt ruled for nearly 3000 years and left behind an astonishing series of monuments to their power and wealth – not only the great pyramids and statues visible for miles across the desert, but also the treasures of their tombs, including their mummified remains, written texts and beautiful objects made of gold and jewels.

PHARAOHS, VIZIERS AND NOMARCHS

The pharaohs wielded immense power – as the huge pyramids built to commemorate them show. They were thought to be descended from the Sun god Re and regarded as so holy that they could only be spoken of as the 'pharaoh', meaning 'Great House'. Pharaohs married within the family to keep their blood pure.

Although the pharaoh had the last word, the country was governed by officials, headed by two *viziers*, one for Upper (southern) Egypt, based at Thebes, the other for Lower Egypt, based at Memphis. The country was also divided into regions or *nomes*, headed by a *nomarch* or governor, whose power varied with the power of the pharaohs.

EARLY EGYPT

The River Nile was the life-blood of Ancient Egypt. Every spring, when the snows melted in the Ethiopian mountains, the Nile rose high in flood and spilled across the fields – not only watering them but leaving a fertile coat of mud too. Egyptians had farmed this rich soil for thousands of years when the first towns grew up and the art of writing was discovered c3500 BC.

Six centuries later, the pharaohs came to power when King Menes united north and south Egypt to create a single kingdom with a new capital at Memphis. From the time of Menes on, the pharaohs' rule is divided into three main periods – the Old, Middle and New Kingdoms – with an Intermediate Period when their power was weak and Egypt was wracked by conflict.

The Old Kingdom was one of the greatest periods of Egyptian history. Egypt prospered and its merchants travelled far and wide. Egyptian craftsmen made beautiful furniture and jewellery and mastered stone-masonry, copper smelting and many other skills. Egyptian scholars studied astronomy and mathematics and made great advances in medicine. But the period is remembered, above all, for the building of the pyramids – from the Step Pyramid of Saqqara created by the brilliant Imhotep for King Zoser around 2620 BC to the Great Pyramid of Giza built for Khufu in 2540 BC.

LATER EGYPT

The New Kingdom was the age of the warrior pharaohs. For the first time, Egypt's stability was

KEY DATES (BC)	
2925	Pharaohs' rule begins
c2575–c2130	Old Kingdom
c2540	Great Pyramid of Giza
c2130–1938	1st Intermediate Period
1938–c1630	Middle Kingdom
c1630–1540	2nd Intermediate Period
1540–1075	New Kingdom
c1539–1514	Ahmose
c1472–1458	Hatshepsut
1353–1336	Akhenaten
1333–1323	Tutankhamun
1075–656	3rd Intermediate Period
664–332	Late Period; foreign kings
332	Conquest by Alexander
305–145	Reign of the Ptolemies

Last voyage Boats and the Nile were important even in death. When pharaohs died, their bodies were taken down the Nile by boat; the boat was buried with them.

Egypt's gods The Egyptians had hundreds of different gods. The most important was Re, the Sun god. In the New Kingdom, the King of the Gods was Amun, who was so closely linked with Re that he was often called Amun-Re. Here, Shu, the god of air, holds up his daughter Nut, the sky goddess arching over all. The green reclining figure is her brother and husband Geb, god of the Earth.

threatened, with the invasion of the Hyksos people from Asia. King Khamose and his brother Ahmose drove the Hyksos out of Egypt and went on to conquer Syria, using horse-drawn chariots and sophisticated bows. The New Kingdom was also a time when queens gained influence – notably Hatshepsut, who was crowned 'king' and wore men's clothes.

King Amenhotep IV, also known as Akhenaten, hated the toughness now expected of pharaohs and began to worship a single Sun god, in the form of Aten (the disc of the Sun). He had many of the temples to the old Egyptian gods torn down and built a new capital, Akhetaten, in honour of Aten. He also encouraged artists to paint unconventional objects such as flowers and birds. But his changes

shocked many Egyptians and when he died, they were all reversed by his successor Tutankhamun.

From about 1200 BC on, Egypt was ruled by kings from places such as Libya and Nubia. In 332 BC, it fell without a struggle to Alexander the Great.

EGYPTIANS AND DEATH

The Egyptians believed life was just a stage on the way to the Next World, but a person's three souls would survive only if the body stayed intact on its voyage after death. This is why they tried to preserve bodies by embalming with oils and salt, then wrapping them in bandages to create a mummy. Mummies were buried with amulets and a *Book of the Dead*, containing spells to help them survive in the Next World.

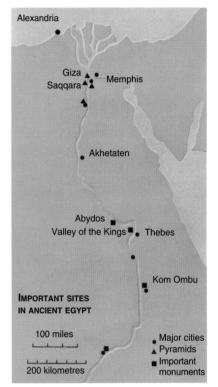

IMPORTANT SITES IN ANCIENT EGYPT

Alexandria
Giza
Saqqara
Memphis
Akhetaten
Abydos
Valley of the Kings
Thebes
Kom Ombu

100 miles
200 kilometres

● Major cities
▲ Pyramids
■ Important monuments

THE PYRAMIDS

The great pyramids built for the pharaohs are one of the great wonders of the world. There are three large pyramids at Giza, and the biggest, built for Khufu (Cheops to the Greeks), was originally 147m tall. It is made from 2.3 million blocks of stone, each weighing an average of 2.5 tonnes. In their heyday, the pyramids were covered in a smooth and dazzling casing of limestone.

The labour involved in building the great pyramids was huge and may have involved as many as 100,000 workers. To build Khufu's Great Pyramid, huge blocks of stone were quarried, transported and lifted into place by hand every day for 20 years. The pyramid was built up layer by layer, as the blocks were dragged on wooden sleds up long ramps that spiralled round the pyramid. The ramps were eventually dismantled.

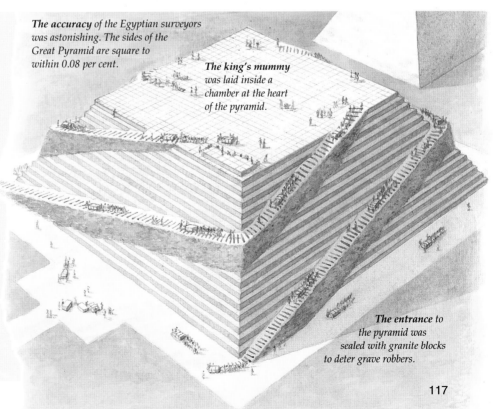

The accuracy of the Egyptian surveyors was astonishing. The sides of the Great Pyramid are square to within 0.08 per cent.

The king's mummy was laid inside a chamber at the heart of the pyramid.

The entrance to the pyramid was sealed with granite blocks to deter grave robbers.

ANCIENT GREECE

Pericles (c495-429 BC) was a powerful speaker and the most famous politician of democratic Athens.

No ancient civilization had such a lasting impact on our world as Ancient Greece. The style of Greek buildings is still widely copied today. Greek thinkers laid the basis of mathematics and science and posed questions about life that still occupy us. The idea of democracy (government by the people) had its roots in Grecian Athens. So too did modern theatre. Even many of our words were originally Greek.

DEMOCRATIC ATHENS

In Athens, democracy meant that all male citizens (but not women, slaves or foreigners) had a say in how the city was run. It was run on a day-to-day basis by a Council, made up of 500 citizens chosen by lottery for a year. Every ten days, citizens were summoned to attend an assembly on a hill called the Pnyx. At least 6000 citizens had to be present at the meeting – if not, police would round up a few more. At these meetings, people debated the Council's proposals and could approve or reject them. Once a year, the assembly could banish unpopular politicians by writing their names on pieces of broken pottery called *ostrakons*. This is called *ostracism*.

MYCENAE & THE DARK AGES

Civilization in the Aegean Sea first began on the island of Crete about 4000 years ago with the Minoan people. But the Minoan civilization was destroyed by a huge volcanic eruption which blew the island of Thera apart 3500 years ago. Soon after, people from the Greek mainland, called the Mycenaeans, invaded Crete. The Mycenaeans established cities all over the Aegean, but their world too broke up and Greece was plunged into the Dark Ages.

CLASSICAL GREECE

Slowly, however, new and thriving cities grew up in Greece, and by about 750 BC it had re-emerged into the Classical Age. Classical Greece was made up of many city states, each with a population of just a few thousand. The largest *polis* (city state) was Athens.

At first, the cities were ruled by a few powerful aristocrats, a system called an *oligarchy*. But riots resulting from their misuse of power persuaded people to let a single *tyrant* take control instead. In Athens, one of the better tyrants was Solon, who from 594 BC made reforms allowing middle class people – traders, craftsmen and so on – to hold power, as well as the aristocrats. But there was still unrest. Then around 500 BC, some Greek cities overthrew their tyrants to create *democracies*.

Odysseus, hero of the Odyssey, *is shown on this vase with bewitching seamaidens called sirens.*

GREEK GODS AND MYTHS

The Greeks had many gods and goddesses and told many stories about them. The 12 most important gods lived on top of Mount Olympus. Their constant squabbling always involved ordinary mortals in some way. Zeus was the ruler. He was married to his sister Hera, but had many affairs with mortal women – disguised as a bull, a swan or even a shower of gold. Aphrodite was the goddess of love and Ares the god of war.

Many tales were told about heroes of old, too. One famous Greek hero was Heracles (known as Hercules by the Romans). Heracles was the son of the god Zeus and a mortal woman called Alcmene. Hera was so angry about Zeus' affair with Alcmene that she made Heracles kill his family. To make amends, he was set twelve heroic 'labours'.

There were also tales about the Trojan wars, many of them told in Homer's famous poems, *The Iliad* and *The Odyssey*. In these poems, the Mycenaeans are great warriors who fought a long war against the people of Troy to take back Helen, the beautiful wife of Mycenaean King Agamemnon's brother, who had eloped with a Trojan prince called Paris. People once thought these tales were mythical, but in 1870, the site of the real city of Troy was uncovered in Turkey.

Life in Athens and other Greek cities focused on the *agora* or market place, where friends met in the shade of the colonnades, and traders sold their wares, often from platforms called *kykloi*. In one corner was the *Tholos*, where the leaders of the council met. There was also the *Bouleuterion*, where the council assembled. On a hill above the city was the *Acropolis*, a fortress enclosing various temples, including the Parthenon. Every four years, the *Great Panathenaea* festival would climax with a long singing, dancing procession up to the Erectheum temple on the Acropolis.

GOLDEN AGE OF ATHENS

At about this time the Greeks were attacked by the Persians. The first Persian attack was beaten off at the Battle of Marathon in 490 BC. But in 480 BC, Persian armies marched into Athens and destroyed all its temples.

Remarkably, Athens recovered from this blow with victories at sea and on land, and the city entered a golden age. Its most famous politician, Pericles, launched a huge programme to rebuild the city. The temples on the Acropolis, including the Parthenon, date from this time. Fine artists and sculptors, musicians, writers and thinkers flocked to Athens from east and west, and enjoyed considerable success.

Then Athens was conquered twice more, by the Spartans in 404 BC, and the Macedonians in 338 BC. From this time on, although it remained a centre of culture and learning, the city's influence steadily declined.

GREEK ART
Few ancient civilizations created such rich and varied works of art as the Greeks. Not only are there beautiful buildings such as the Parthenon, there are also many graceful statues. The most famous sculptor was Praxiteles, who made the first nude statue of a woman, portraying the goddess Aphrodite.

Ancient Greece was also famous for its theatre, and plays written by Sophocles, Euripides and Aristophanes are still

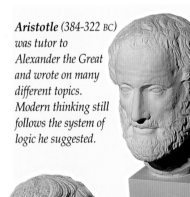

Aristotle (384-322 BC) was tutor to Alexander the Great and wrote on many different topics. Modern thinking still follows the system of logic he suggested.

Plato (427-348 BC) founded a famous Academy near Athens. His ideas on virtues form the basis of modern philosophy. He also tried to find the ideal way of governing a state in his book Republic.

GREEK SCIENCE AND PHILOSOPHY
By looking at the world and asking questions, Ancient Greek thinkers such as Thales and Aristotle made many important scientific discoveries. Pythagoras and Euclid, for instance, discovered basic mathematical rules which are still used today. Archimedes worked out why ships float. And Anaxagoras realized that eclipses occur when the Sun, Moon and Earth are all in a straight line. Indeed, many ideas we think of as new were first thought of by the Greeks. We only became sure all matter is made up of tiny atoms this century – yet the Greek scholar Democritus suggested it 2500 years ago. Greek thinkers such as Plato and Socrates also thought about how people should behave and what is the best political system. Their ideas laid the basis of modern philosophy.

KEY DATES (BC)

c1100	Dark Ages begin.
c800	Dark Ages end and Homer writes his great poems.
776	First Olympic Games held to test Greek athletes.
508	Democracy begins in Athens.
490	Battle of Marathon.
438	Parthenon built.
AD338	Greece conquered by Macedonians
393	Olympic Games end until revived in AD1896.

ANCIENT ROME

Two thousand years ago, the city of Rome presided over one of the greatest empires the world has seen. At its height in the 2nd century AD, it extended over 4000km from England to the Red Sea. With ruthless efficiency, the Romans introduced their own blend of advanced technology and civilized living to every corner of the Empire. Roman citizens could journey from Deva (Chester) to Damascus and still feel at home.

A legatus commanded a legion of about 5000 legionaries. All Roman soldiers had a short sword (60cm long) and carried two metal-tipped throwing spears. They also wore some form of armour – first, vests of chain-mail and a leather helmet; later, metal strips on a leather tunic and a metal helmet.

THE ROMAN MILITARY MACHINE

Rome owed its power to its disciplined army. It fought mainly on foot, advancing in tight squares bristling with spears, protected by large shields called *scutari*. Often they protected their heads from arrows with shields too, making a *testudo* (tortoise). Under the Republic, the army was divided into *legions* of around 5000 soldiers; legions were made up from 10 *cohorts*; cohorts were made up from *centuries* of 80-100 soldiers.

EARLY ROME & THE REPUBLIC

According to legend, Rome was founded in 753 BC by Romulus and Remus, who were said to have been brought up by a she-wolf. Whatever the truth, by the 6th century BC Rome was a large city ruled over by Etruscan kings. In 509 BC, the Romans drove out the Etruscans to set up a republic, governed not by a king but by an assembly called the *Senate*. In theory, all Roman citizens could vote in elections to the Senate and serve in the army. In practice, only a rich few, called *patricians*, had any real power; the *plebeians* (commoners) had very little. Slaves had no rights at all.

Over the next few centuries, Rome extended its power over all Italy by brute force and alliances. By 264 BC, it rivalled Carthage, the north African city that dominated the western Mediterranean. After a bitter struggle, called the Punic Wars, Rome utterly destroyed Carthage in 146 BC. But the cost at home was great.

The plebeians' efforts to gain a little power and the patricians' determination to stop them created constant trouble. When the end of the Punic Wars left thousands of people out of work, trouble increased. Many joined the army and became more loyal to their generals than to the Senate. In 60 BC, two popular generals, Pompey and Julius Caesar, used their armies to take over Rome.

When Pompey and Caesar fell out, Caesar became sole ruler. In 44 BC Caesar was assassinated by Brutus, who hoped to bring back the Republic – but Caesar's place was taken by another general, called Octavian. Octavian defeated Brutus and became so powerful that in 27 BC he was able to declare himself Emperor and take the name Augustus.

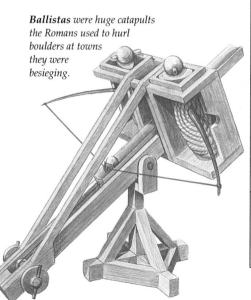

Ballistas were huge catapults the Romans used to hurl boulders at towns they were besieging.

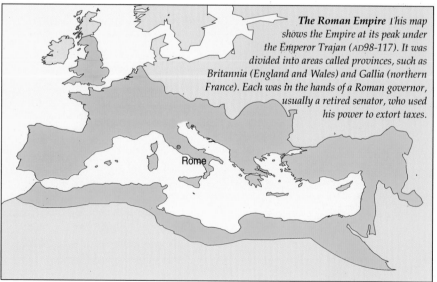

The Roman Empire This map shows the Empire at its peak under the Emperor Trajan (AD98-117). It was divided into areas called provinces, such as Britannia (England and Wales) and Gallia (northern France). Each was in the hands of a Roman governor, usually a retired senator, who used his power to extort taxes.

Rome

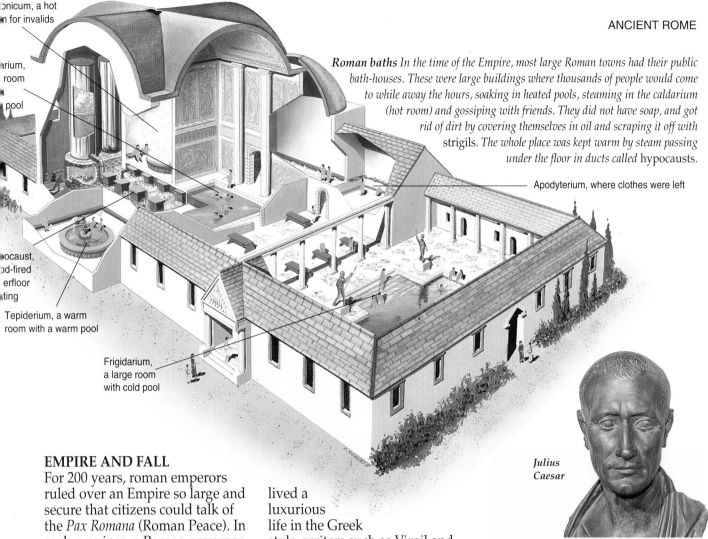

onicum, a hot
n for invalids

arium,
room

pool

ocaust,
od-fired
erfloor
ting

Tepiderium, a warm
room with a warm pool

Frigidarium,
a large room
with cold pool

Roman baths *In the time of the Empire, most large Roman towns had their public bath-houses. These were large buildings where thousands of people would come to while away the hours, soaking in heated pools, steaming in the caldarium (hot room) and gossiping with friends. They did not have soap, and got rid of dirt by covering themselves in oil and scraping it off with strigils. The whole place was kept warm by steam passing under the floor in ducts called* hypocausts.

 Apodyterium, where clothes were left

EMPIRE AND FALL

For 200 years, roman emperors ruled over an Empire so large and secure that citizens could talk of the *Pax Romana* (Roman Peace). In each province, a Roman governor kept control, backed by disciplined Roman troops. Fast roads were built everywhere and hundreds of towns were built in the Roman way – with a grid of streets, water brought in by *aqueducts*, a *forum* where citizens met, *stadiums* for games and comfortable *villas* (houses). Back in Rome, citizens lived a luxurious life in the Greek style, writers such as Virgil and Ovid wrote classic poems and huge new buildings testified to the city's wealth and skills. But political struggles within the empire, and constant attacks along its fringes slowly undermined Rome's might. In AD 410, a European tribe called Visigoths invaded Italy and sacked Rome.

Julius Caesar

JULIUS CAESAR

Caesar (100-44 BC) was the greatest of all Roman generals. He made his name in the Gallic Wars in France and conquered Britain in 54 BC. In 48 BC, he pursued his rival Pompey to Egypt, defeated him and fell in love with Egypt's beautiful queen Cleopatra. On his return to Rome, he became dictator, but his power was so resented that he was murdered in 44 BC.

ROMAN GAMES

Nearly every major town in the Empire had stadiums where thousands of people watched games (*ludi*) such as chariot races and bloody *gladiator* fights. Chariot races were held at a ring called a *circus* or *hippodrome*. At the Circus Maximus in Rome, 250,000 fanatical spectators would cheer their favourite team. Gladiators were prisoners, slaves or paid professionals who fought to the death, often with wild animals, in vast stadiums called *amphitheatres* like the Colosseum in Rome (left). One show involved 10,000 gladiators over 117 days.

KEY DATES

753 BC	Rome founded.
509	Etruscans expelled and Republic founded.
264-146	Punic Wars.
49	Caesar becomes dictator.
44	Caesar assassinated.
27	Octavian becomes Emperor Augustus.
AD **64**	Rome devastated by fire.
98-117	Empire at its height.
313	Emperor Constantine makes the Empire Christian.
410	Visigoths sack Rome.

ANCIENT CHINA

Isolated from the early civilizations of the Near East, China developed its own civilization. There were cities in China 4000 years ago, long before even Babylon was built, and the Chinese invented writing and many other things quite independently.

SHANG TO CH'IN

Farming began in China over 7000 years ago alongside the Huang Ho or Yellow River. Here the Yang-shao people hunted, fished and grew millet, fruit and nuts on the rich yellow soil. By 2500 BC, the Longshan people farmed here and lived in villages that gradually became towns and cities.

The Shang As cities grew, so a series of ruling families or *dynasties* came to rule China. The Xia dynasty is said to have begun in 2205 BC, but the first clear rulers to emerge were the Shang around 1600 BC. Writing was well-developed by this time, and the Shang's capitals at Cheng-chou and An-yang were large and highly organized, with streets laid out on a grid aligned with points of the compass.

Street in Ch'ang-an Early Chinese cities were large and vibrant places. Over 250,000 people lived in Ch'ang-an around 100 BC, and a brilliant culture flourished here, with many thinkers, writers and inventors. Ssu-ma Ch'ien (145-c85 BC) wrote an encyclopedic history of China.

The Chou By1000 BC, the Shang were ousted by the Chou dynasty. Under the Chou, China grew rich, partly by trading silk, spices, jade, and porcelain. But as Chou power waned after 770 BC, rival regions fought bitterly for control. The battles of the *Warring States* lasted centuries until the Ch'in emerged as victors. The Ch'in king Shih-Huang-ti was the first of a line of Emperors that lasted 2130 years.

Shih Huang-ti created a new legal system and had millions of men build China's Great Wall and a huge road network. But he was a harsh ruler, remembered for banning Confucius's books – and his vast tomb, filled with an army of 7000 lifesize clay soldiers.

The Ch'in empire collapsed with Shih Huang-ti's death in 210 BC, leaving the way open to the Han dynasty. Under the Han emperors, government officials followed the ideas of Confucius and Chinese cities such as Ch'ang-an were the most magnificent in the world.

The Great Wall of China, extending over 2400km right across the north of the country, is the largest single structure ever made by humans. It was completed in 214 BC in the reign of Emperor Shi Huang-ti to protect China from raids by Mongols and Huns.

Confucius (551-479 BC) believed that humanity was the highest virtue, and his thinking influenced Chinese culture for more than 2000 years.

Spinning silk According to legend, the Chinese discovered how to get silk from silk worms in 2640 BC.

CHINESE THINKERS AND SCIENCE

Paper and ink, gunpowder, canal gates, the camera obscura, the magnetic compass and printing were all early Chinese inventions.

Even while the Warring States were battling it out, philosophers travelled throughout China, spreading new ideas. They were so many that they were known as the Hundred Schools, and they included such profound thinkers as Confucius, Lao-tzu and Zhuang zi. Lao-tzu is said to have written the book on which the Taoist religion is based.

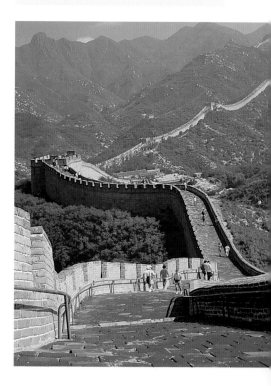

ANCIENT AMERICA

When Europeans arrived in the Americas in the early 16th century, they came face to face with two great civilizations – the Aztecs in Central America and the Incas in Peru. Spectacular though these cultures were, they were just the last in a long line of civilizations dating back almost 3000 years to the time of the Chavin and Olmec people.

Chasqui were messengers who relayed messages by word of mouth, running 1km before passing their message on to another.

EARLY CIVILIZATIONS

People began to farm in the Americas as long ago as 2500 BC, growing maize, beans, peppers, squashes and potatoes. Villages soon appeared, and huge temple mounds were erected – first of earth and then of stone. Religion had a central role in early America and temple-mounds spread all over Central America and Peru.

The first civilizations came around 1200 BC with the Olmec culture in Central America and the Chavins in Peru. Over the next 2500 years, a succession of cultures flowered then vanished, including the Moche, Tiahuanco, Nazca and Chimu in Peru and the Andes, and the Teotihuacan, Maya, Toltec and Mixtec in Central America. All of these cultures were dominated by a powerful ruling class who could organize large labour forces to build vast temple complexes, including huge stone pyramids, wide plazas, lavish palaces and

courts for ball games. They also used hieroglyphs (picture symbols) as did the Egyptians.

THE AZTECS

The Aztecs were a powerful people who ruled a vast empire in Mexico. In AD 1325, they created the magnificent lake city of Tenochtitlan which had canals, gardens and temples. The Aztec economy depended on farming, and people walked or rowed dug-out canoes for hours to the great markets in cities such as Tlatelolco to sell farm produce for cocoa beans, which they used as money.

Aztec society was tough and disciplined with a powerful priest-king and an elite few nobles and priests ruling over commoners, peasants and slaves with an iron hand. But the heavy taxes the Aztecs exacted made them many enemies, who eventually helped the Spanish destroy them.

Inca highway The Incas built a network of roads high up in the Andes, with rope bridges over ravines, which were continually inspected by the Guardian of Bridges. People went everywhere on foot, using llamas to carry bundles weighing up to 45kg.

Handle of a knife *probably used to make animal or human sacrifices.*

THE INCAS

The Inca empire lasted less than 100 years, from 1438 to the coming of the Spanish in 1532, but it was the biggest and richest in America. The Inca was actually the emperor, but the Spanish called all the people Incas. Incas were skilled engineers and their great buildings were built from massive cut stones. Taxes were heavy, but food was shared out among the people and there was never any theft.

Aztec pyramid The Aztecs built vast pyramids topped by temples where priests made bloody human sacrifices on a huge scale. Human sacrifice was believed to appease the gods and maintain the pattern of the seasons.

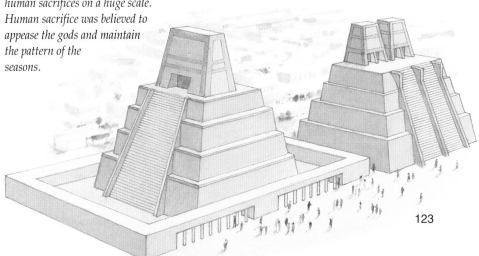

Page from the Book of Kells, a copy of the Gospels made by monks at Iona, Scotland, around AD 760-820.

THE DARK AGES

The Roman Emperor Trajan died in AD 117. During his reign, the Empire was at its height; he ruled most of Europe, North Africa and the Middle East. Millions of people paid Roman taxes and obeyed Roman laws. Yet within 50 years, these citizens of the Empire were fighting for their lives. Rome was under attack.

THE SPREAD OF CHRISTIANITY

The first Christians faced cruel persecution, in Judaea (Israel) and in Rome. But after AD 312, Christianity was tolerated within the Roman Empire and in 392 it became the Empire's official religion. Fine new churches and monasteries were built, and rich patrons paid for magnificent carvings, crosses, books, manuscripts and vestments to furnish them. Missionary priests travelled across Europe, preaching and baptizing new converts. By AD 600, there were Christian believers in many lands. Only the Saxons, the Scandinavians, the Poles and the Russians held fast to their pagan beliefs.

INVADERS

German tribesmen were the first to try to conquer Rome. They attacked in AD 167. From then on, Roman emperors fought a losing battle to maintain Roman power against hordes of barbarian invaders from many different lands. The last emperor in Rome was deposed by one group of invaders – the Ostrogoths – in 476. By 546, the city was almost deserted, and grass grew in the Roman streets.

THE END OF EMPIRE

To people living at the time, the collapse of Roman power seemed like the end of the world. Violence and uncertainty replaced strong Roman rule. Trade was disrupted and towns decayed, Roman roads and bridges crumbled, bandits lurked in the fields and forests. Even the mighty Roman army weakened as the soldiers guarding distant provinces deserted and went home. They realized they could not win against the powerful invaders.

DARK AND GLOOMY

Later historians call this period of lawlessness and disorder 'the Dark Ages'. In some ways this is a good description. Our picture of the 5th – 9th centuries is dark and confused. Without the careful records kept by Roman writers, it is almost impossible to discover exactly what happened. And, even though citizens of the Empire often complained about harsh Roman officials, they found that life was difficult and dangerous when government was removed. For many people, whose businesses and peaceful family life had been destroyed, prospects must have seemed very dark and gloomy indeed.

INVASIONS AND MIGRATIONS (AD)	
167	Germans invade Italy and Greece.
200	Visigoths and Ostrogoths move to Russia.
367	Picts and Scots invade England.
370	Huns invade Europe.
406	Vandals, Alans and Suevis invade Gaul (France).
410	Visigoths capture Rome, settle in Spain and southern France.
421	Angles and Saxons invade Britain.
429	Vandals invade north Africa. Burgundians and Franks invade France and Italy.
451	Huns invade France, but retreat.
455	Vandals conquer Rome.

Europe in chaos
As the Roman Empire grew weaker, it could no longer fight off attacks from barbarian invaders, who wanted to seize Roman riches. By AD 455, the old Roman lands in Europe were divided among many rival tribes.

BRILLIANT ART

In other ways, the 'Dark Ages' were not dark at all. They were a time of brilliant achievement in art, architecture and scholarship. Many beautiful weapons and carvings were produced by craftworkers for rich people to use and admire. Monks and nuns illustrated magnificent manuscripts. Scholars preserved ancient Roman texts and wrote prayers, plays and poems.

Eventually, strong new kingdoms emerged from the chaos and darkness of Europe, led by outstanding rulers like Emperor Charlemagne of France and Alfred, King of England.

RAIDERS FROM THE SEA

The Vikings were daring raiders, who lived in Norway, Denmark and Sweden. Between AD 800 and 1100, they terrorized the inhabitants of coastal towns and villages throughout Europe, searching for rich plunder to carry away. But not all Vikings were pirates. At home, they were farmers and fishermen, merchants and craftworkers. They were adventurous travellers, journeying eastwards overland through Russia, and sailing westwards across dangerous seas to settle in Iceland and Greenland, as well as in England, Ireland and France. Around AD 1000, Viking sailors crossed the Atlantic, reaching Newfoundland. They were possibly the first Europeans to set foot in America. In 1066, Norman soldiers, descendants of Vikings who had settled in France, invaded England. Their leader, William, became king.

Viking leather shoe with bone skate attached.

Comb made of polished bone.

Clues from the past Though there are few written records to tell us about life in the Dark Ages, many objects from everyday life have survived to the present day. Such things as the comb and shoe pictured left, together with jewellery, weapons and armour, are like clues which modern historians can use to recreate a picture of the past.

Viking raiders fought using swords, spears and sharp axes like this one, found in a Swedish warrior's grave. They protected themselves with metal helmets and strong wooden shields.

Vikings prided themselves on their bravery in battle. Tactics were simple – to kill as many men as possible. Most Vikings fought on foot, but rich men rode on horseback. Shock troops, known as berserkers, led the attack. They became fighting mad, through drink or drugs. They wore no armour ('berserk' means 'bear shirt'), because they trusted the god Odin to keep them safe.

The graceful wooden hull of a Viking ship.

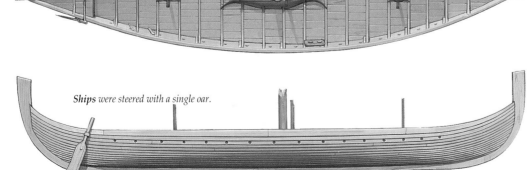

Bird's eye view shows position of mast.

Ships were steered with a single oar.

The Vikings were skillful sailors, navigating the stormy North Atlantic with only the stars and seabirds to guide them. Viking ships were fast and light, designed to skim over the waves. They were powered by wind trapped in their large square sails, or by men rowing.

ISLAM

Around AD 610, an Arab merchant named Muhammad left the busy city of Mecca to spend time in the mountains nearby. He wanted peace and quiet, to think and to pray. While he was there, he had a vision, or perhaps a dream. Before long, Muhammad's vision began to change the world.

A MESSAGE FROM GOD

Muhammad returned home, and told his family that he had received a message from God, explaining how to live a good life, and how to worship in the best way. Muhammad believed it was his duty to share God's message with everyone else. So he became a preacher and teacher. Many people admired and respected him, others ignored him. In 622, Muhammad and the people who listened to his preaching were driven out of Mecca. They settled in the city of Medina, and established a new community there, trying to live in the way God's message told them. Shortly before he died, in 632, Muhammad was welcomed back into Mecca. Many citizens decided to listen to his preaching and become Muslims – that is, people who have submitted to God. They prayed regularly and met to listen to Muhammad recite God's message. These recitations were later written down in a book called the Qur'an. It guided – and still guides – the Muslim community in every aspect of their lives. Because of Muhammad's vision, a new religion had been born.

FAITH AND CIVILIZATION

The first Muslims often had to fight to defend their faith. The Muslims won many battles, and became powerful. They believed that God gave them victory, and this encouraged them to extend their conquests to the lands nearby. Soon, Muslims ruled a vast empire. Wherever Muslims governed, they introduced laws and social customs based on the Qur'an. Many Muslim rulers also encouraged learning and the arts. Over the centuries, a distinctive new civilization grew up in Muslim lands, combining local styles and traditions with the Islamic faith.

MUSLIM STYLE
The Alhambra (Red Fort) Palace, Granada, was built between 1238 and 1354 as a home for the Muslim rulers of southern Spain. The Alhambra was sumptuously decorated, with rooms planned around shady courtyards, with statues, patterned tiles and cool fountains.

SCIENCE AND TECHNOLOGY
Muslim scientists were famous throughout the medieval world. They were especially knowledgeable about astronomy, mathematics, chemistry, medicine and engineering. This illustration shows two Muslim scientists performing an experiment. Muslim scholars made many important scientific discoveries.

World of Islam *After Muhammad's death in AD 632, the new faith of Islam spread rapidly, as Muslim rulers won control of a vast empire centred on Damascus and, later, Baghdad. Within 100 years, Muslim territory stretched from Spain to the borders of China.*

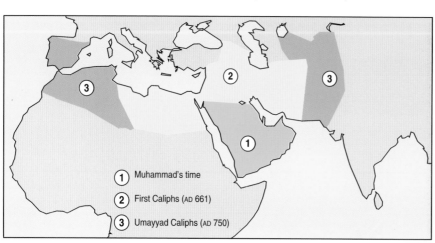

1. Muhammad's time
2. First Caliphs (AD 661)
3. Umayyad Caliphs (AD 750)

THE CRUSADES

Between 1096 and 1291 thousands of European knights travelled on a series of expeditions to the Middle East to fight against the Muslim peoples who lived there. These expeditions were called Crusades.

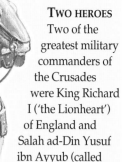

THE CALL TO ARMS

In 1095, Pope Urban II preached a sermon calling on Christian soldiers throughout Europe to fight against the Muslim people who were living in the 'Holy Land' (the countries of the Middle East where Jesus had lived). He feared that the Seljuks, a new Muslim power in Turkey and the lands nearby, would stop Christian pilgrims visiting the holy city of Jerusalem. His fears were probably exaggerated; Christians, Muslims and Jews had all lived fairly peacefully together there under Muslim rule since AD 638. The Pope also feared the Seljuks would soon attack the Christian inhabitants of the great Byzantine Empire.

A HOLY WAR?

Although Pope Urban II called for a 'Holy War' he had political as well as religious reasons for encouraging people to fight. For the next 200 years, Christian soldiers launched a series of invasions – the Crusades – which were designed to replace the existing governments of the Holy Land with new, Christian rulers. Many sincere believers on both sides fought bravely, and were killed. Christian troops were finally expelled from the Holy Land in 1291, but the legacy of bitterness and suspicion between Christian and Muslim communities lasted for many centuries.

TWO HEROES

Two of the greatest military commanders of the Crusades were King Richard I ('the Lionheart') of England and Salah ad-Din Yusuf ibn Ayyub (called 'Saladin' in Europe). They led the opposing armies during the Third Crusade (1189 – 1192). Crusader troops had achieved surprising successes during the First Crusade, including the capture of Jerusalem. But the Second Crusade had been a disaster and, after 1187, Muslim troops loyal to Saladin again held Jerusalem. King Richard aimed to regain Jerusalem, but his campaign failed. Saladin kept control of the Holy Land. He also founded a new ruling dynasty in Syria and Egypt.

Saladin (1138-1193)

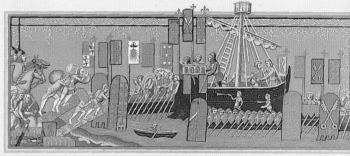

SIEGE WARFARE

Siege warfare (left) was used by both Christian and Muslim armies to starve out well-defended cities or castles. The only hope for the besieged city or castle was for a relief force from their own side to raise the siege by forcing the besieging army to move away.

JOURNEY TO JERUSALEM

The journey to Jerusalem (above) could take months or even years. Many travellers died on the way, in accidents or ambushes, or from disease. The first crusaders travelled over-land, through Greece and Turkey. By the 13th century, crusaders pre-ferred to travel by ship.

Norman warships, laden with well-armed soldiers (and their horses), sailing to invade England. A scene from the Bayeux Tapestry, a huge embroidered picture, probably made around 1100 by French craftswomen for Bishop Odo of Bayeux, northern France.

THE BATTLE OF HASTINGS

On 14 October 1066, Duke William's Norman invaders faced an English army, led by King Harold. The English soldiers had marched over 350km, after fighting the Vikings in Yorkshire. Their shield wall held firm, but King Harold was killed and the Norman army routed the English. William was Conqueror.

NORMANS

1066 is one of the best-known dates in British history. That year, the last native-born king of England was killed fighting to defend his kingdom, and a Norman-French adventurer ruled in his place. Many people said that England would never be the same again.

THE DOMESDAY BOOK

William relied on Norman noblemen to help him govern England, but he did not want them to become too powerful. He decided to check up on how much land and livestock they had, and the tax they ought to pay. In 1086, he sent out officials to compile a register recording this information. It still survives today.

THE CONQUEROR

Duke William of Normandy – known as 'William the Conqueror' – was descended from Viking settlers who had set up a state in northern France. He was brave, intelligent and ambitious. He was one of three men who claimed the throne after the death of the English King Edward the Confessor early in 1066. He ruled England for over 20 years, until 1087. During that time, he managed to gain control of the whole kingdom (although the English were rebellious and resentful at first), establishing a system of government that lasted for many years.

CONQUEST AND CONTINUITY

After the conquest, some things hardly changed at all. Ordinary men and women continued to work in the fields. Priests, monks and nuns continued to pray. Norman officials continued to collect taxes in the way the English kings had done. But there were important changes. Almost all the old English nobles were killed, and a new Norman aristocracy took their place. The old English language continued to be spoken, but with many new Norman words. New laws, designed to secure Norman rule, were made. And England became more closely involved in the politics of France and Europe.

The Normans built strong castles to defend their newly-won land. At first, these castles were made of wood – some were even shipped to England in sections, ready to be assembled. Later castles, like this one at Totnes in Devon, were built of stone. The central mound, or 'motte', was surrounded by a walled 'bailey', or yard. Castles of this type were called motte and bailey castles.

'Coats of arms', on shields. Originally, these identified men in battle. Later, they were used to show that the wearer belonged to a proud, noble family.

KNIGHTS

Who were the most important people in Europe at the time of the Norman Conquest? Kings, priests or peasants? Nobles or knights? Kings provided leadership, priests guided their people, and peasants grew food. Nobles helped to govern, and led armies into battle. But everyone depended on knights to defend their land. And the picture of a dashing knight on horseback, wearing splendid armour, is still one of our favourite images from medieval times.

A NOBLE CAREER

Knights originated as the armed followers of great noble families. When summoned by the king, nobles were meant to leave their estates and families and ride off to war, bringing all their knights with them. In that way, kings were sure of a well-trained fighting force. Knighthood was considered a great honour, usually restricted to the upper, wealthier, ranks of society. Knights were often the sons of nobles or of other knights, but a very brave soldier might be rewarded on the field of battle by being made a knight.

FIGHTING FOR MONEY

Over the centuries, the system of knighthood changed. Some nobles and knights preferred to pay money, rather than go to war. Kings used this to pay for professional ('mercenary') soldiers, or to equip a national army of volunteers. Fighting for profit was hardly noble or heroic, and the Church taught that it was wrong. And, although medieval poets made knights the heroes of their 'romances' – songs about love, bravery and death – it is perhaps not surprising that real-life knights could not always live up to their own glorious image.

THE HUNDRED YEARS' WAR 1337–1453

This war between England and France began when Edward III of England refused to submit to the French king, claiming to be rightful ruler of France instead. At first, the English conquered much land, but between 1360 and 1389 French troops won it back. There was peace from 1389 to 1414, then Henry V of England attacked again. He was successful, but died in 1422. Soon, French troops were inspired by Joan of Arc – a peasant who saw visions. By 1453, England had lost everything in France except Calais.

A DEADLY GAME

Knights took part in tournaments – mock battles designed to help them practise their fighting skills. Tournaments were also social occasions; ladies watched the competitions. Tournaments were exciting but dangerous; many men were killed as they fell from their horses, or were trampled underfoot.

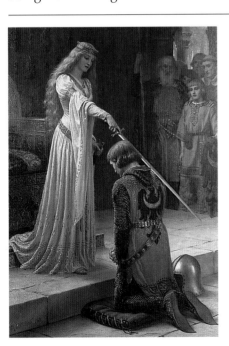

LOVE AND WAR

To poets, painters and songwriters, including those living in the Middle Ages, knights were romantic figures. The ideal knight – or 'the flower of chivalry' (an old French word for 'horsemen') – was meant to be bold and daring, but also good and gentle. He fought only to defend his lord, his lady-love, and the Church. Of course, reality was not like that. A few knights were noble, brave and kind, but others were just brutal fighting men. This painting shows how one artist looked back at the knights and ladies of the past.

THE MIDDLE AGES

Why 'Middle' Ages? Historians, looking back, use the word to describe the years (roughly, AD 1100–1453) between the last Viking invasions and the end of the Byzantine Empire. After that, Europe was no longer united by a single faith or a shared culture.

PRIESTS AND PEOPLE

In the Middle Ages, most people believed in God – or in magical and mysterious spirits who controlled the world. Modern, 'scientific', ways of thinking did not exist. In Britain and Europe, the Catholic Church was powerful. Priests taught that people should live good lives, and worship God. They encouraged people to give money to the Church, to show that they were sorry for their sins and to win life after death. Beautiful cathedrals – such as Canterbury Cathedral, shown here – were paid for in this way.

PROSPERITY AND PLAGUE

At first, the 'Middle' (or 'medieval') centuries saw rapid economic growth, as Europe recovered from centuries of raids. Farm profits rose and merchants grew rich through selling wool, cloth, and luxury goods imported from distant lands. Nobles built strong castles and stately manor houses. They enjoyed hunting, fine clothes, rich food and an extravagant 'courtly' lifestyle. But this prosperity was threatened by a terrifying epidemic of incurable disease. Population growth and climatic change led to famines. Incompetent governments provoked peasant revolts – such as the riots that shook England and The Netherlands at the end of

the 14th century. Weak kings struggled with powerful nobles; subjects resisted unjust laws. For over 100 years, England and France were at war.

A DIFFERENT WORLD?

The Middle Ages was also the time when the nations (and languages) of Europe began to take shape. Many modern government institutions, such as parliaments, originated in medieval times. Present-day towns and cities were first built then, along with churches, cathedrals, universities and hospitals. Strong kings made laws and collected taxes. In all these ways, the Middle Ages laid the foundations of modern Europe.

LIFE ON THE LAND

During the Middle Ages, most people lived in the countryside. They grew crops and raised animals for food. Men and women shared in this essential task, yet most villagers did not own the land on which they worked. It belonged to the king, or to great lords. They let villagers farm small amounts, in return for working on their own estates. Some lords 'owned' the villagers, too; they could not leave a lord's estate without his permission.

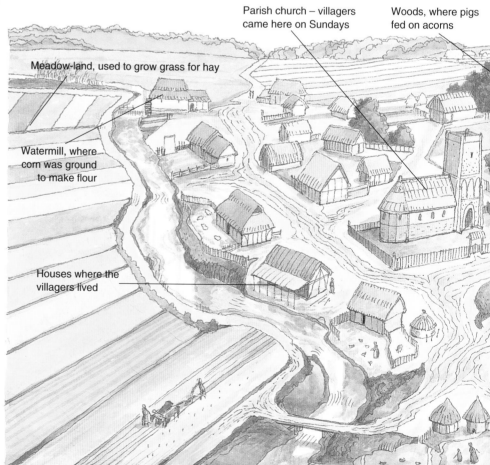

Parish church – villagers came here on Sundays

Woods, where pigs fed on acorns

Meadow-land, used to grow grass for hay

Watermill, where corn was ground to make flour

Houses where the villagers lived

THE BLACK DEATH

In the 14th century, Europe, Asia and the Middle East were devastated by bubonic plague. This was (and still is) a deadly disease, carried by fleas which live on rats. Victims die swiftly and suddenly. About one-third of the people in England died between 1348 and 1351. Many more perished in later outbreaks. Almost everyone knew somebody who had died. Medieval doctors did not understand how plague spread or how to cure it. To those people who had not caught it there was the fear that they might be next.

However, there were a great many differences between medieval times and today. There were far fewer people; even before the Black Death struck Europe in the mid–14th century, the total population was perhaps only ten per cent of what it is now. Most people worked on the land, rather than, as they do today, in offices, factories and shops.

There were enormous contrasts in living standards between rich and poor people. Almost all the land was owned by a few rich families, who also helped to run governments and lead armies in war. There were few machines. Medieval craftworkers achieved astonishing results – from massive castles to delicate manuscript illustrations – using the very simplest tools. But even if technology was simple, ideas were not. Medieval scholars wrote complicated books about religion, philosophy and law – as well as composing poems and songs.

COURTLY CULTURE

Wealthy men and women in the Middle Ages were great patrons of the arts. Kings and queens entertained poets, painters and musicians at their courts. Sometimes medieval art had a religious purpose, but often it simply celebrated the delights of courtly life. This picture – designed to illustrate a religious book, but showing richly-dressed lords and ladies enjoying a ride in the woods – was produced for a French nobleman in the early 15th century.

THRIVING TOWNS

In Italy and northern Europe, towns grew rich through the profits of trade. Craftworkers wove fine woollen cloth, and produced elegant glass, leatherwork, weapons and jewellery. Traders sold imported luxury goods. This painting shows a group of rich Italian merchants; you can see their city in the background.

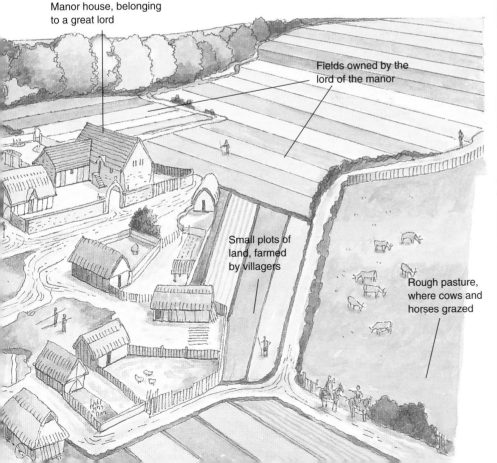

Manor house, belonging to a great lord

Fields owned by the lord of the manor

Small plots of land, farmed by villagers

Rough pasture, where cows and horses grazed

131

RENAISSANCE & REFORMATION

In the 200 years between AD 1350 and 1550, medieval Europe was transformed. Art, architecture, religion and philosophy all saw great changes. These were brought about by two great intellectual movements – the Renaissance ('re-birth') and the Reformation.

LEADER OF RENAISSANCE ITALY
Lorenzo de Medici – known as 'Lorenzo the Magnificent'– ruled the Italian city of Florence from 1469 to 1492. He asked leading artists, architects and sculptors to work for him, one of whom was Michelangelo. Other rich citizens followed his example, and Florence became known as 'the cradle of the Renaissance'.

RENAISSANCE MAN
Drawing of a human face by Leonardo da Vinci (1452–1519). Leonardo is often described as a 'Renaissance man', skilled in the sciences as well as the arts. He was an engineer, inventor, and student of medicine, animals and plants, as well as a painter of genius.

HUMANIST SCHOLAR
Erasmus of Rotterdam (1469–1536) was one of the most important Renaissance figures in northern Europe. He was famous for his Biblical scholarship, and his knowledge of Latin and Greek. He aimed to use his Renaissance learning to end religious quarrels. Like many Renaissance scholars, he worked as a tutor to noblemen and their sons. His ideas spread widely, because his books were among the first to be printed using the newly invented printing press.

THE GLORIOUS PAST
Great civilizations had flourished in Ancient Greece and Rome. By AD 1350, they had long since decayed, but evidence of their achievements still survived. In Italy and Greece, statues, temples and huge public buildings stood in many cities. Roman books had been preserved by monks in their libraries, and Greek scientific texts had been used by Muslim scholars in the Middle East to help with their own investigations. But these ancient remains were no longer valued. Statues and temples crumbled away, and books lay unread and forgotten. Since the coming of Christianity (around AD 300-600), Greek and Roman culture had been regarded as pagan, and wrong. A new, Christian civilization, equally splendid in its own way, had developed in medieval Europe.

THE RENAISSANCE BEGINS
By around 1300, scholars in Italy were eager for change. They began to investigate the ancient remains all around them, and were astonished and delighted by what they discovered. Artists, architects, poets and philosophers shared their enthusiasm, and began to incorporate subject-matter and techniques from ancient works into their own new designs. Ancient culture was 're-born' once more.

These new Renaissance creations were very different from existing medieval art. They aimed at

GOD AND MAN
Painting the ceiling of the Sistine Chapel, Rome. This huge project was designed by the Italian artist Michelangelo Buonarroti (1475–1564). It shows religious scenes, but also – in true Renaissance style – glorifies man.

celebrating the beauty and achievements of men and women, rather than praising God. Renaissance writers also preferred human, rather than holy, topics. In style, Renaissance artists and architects copied Greek and Roman designs, rather than continuing medieval (or 'Gothic') traditions. They also looked closely at the world around them, and recorded it as accurately as they could in their works. They were helped by Renaissance scientists, and by new, printed scientific books.

All these great achievements were possible only because rich men and women, at first in Italy, and then elsewhere in Europe, were willing to act as patrons and support artists and scholars.

THE REFORMATION

Renaissance discoveries gave a great boost to learning. New books, and new skills at reading Greek and Latin, led to criticism of many medieval texts, including Latin translations of the Bible itself. Like Renaissance scholars, many priests and monks were eager for change. They felt Church leaders were corrupt. They wanted to be able to discuss religious ideas freely, to worship in the way they chose, and to read the Bible in their own languages. These critics became known as 'Protestants'. They wanted to reform the Church from within, but soon their differences of opinion became so great that they left the Church entirely, and formed new congregations of their own.

WARS OF RELIGION

In the 16th century, European states were almost constantly at war. They fought for many reasons – jealousy, fear, greed and religion. Often, these motives were mixed together. In the Netherlands, Protestants wanted independence from Catholic Spain. England and Spain were enemies, too. They feared each other's power, and hated each other's religion. In 1588, a Spanish fleet – or Armada – was sent to invade England, but it was wrecked by storms at sea.

FAITH AND FREEDOM

Martin Luther (right) was born in 1483. He was a priest, a scholar and the leader of the Protestant movement in Germany. He aimed to reform the Church, to have the Bible translated from Latin and to worship in a new way.

Tintern Abbey, on the borders of England and Wales, was closed – or 'dissolved' – in 1537, along with all other English monasteries, after King Henry VIII's break with Rome. Monks fled abroad, or found other work. Monastery land was sold to raise money for the king.

THE REFORMATION IN ENGLAND

For centuries, English kings had wanted priests to obey English laws, but the popes – leaders of the Catholic Church in Rome – claimed that Church law was supreme. The final clash came in 1531 after Henry VIII of England demanded a divorce from his first wife, because she had not produced any sons. The pope refused, and so King Henry – who was, anyway, sympathetic to the Protestant reformers – declared himself head of the Church in England. New English Church leaders taught the Protestant faith.

THE ENGLISH CIVIL WAR

King Charles I of England was an elegant man, fond of his wife and devoted to his children. He was a generous patron of the arts, with exquisite taste in painting, clothes and jewels. Yet in 1649, his subjects cut off his head.

GUNPOWDER PLOT

On 4 November 1605, barrels of gunpowder were discovered hidden in the cellars at Westminster, just before the King and Members of Parliament were due to arrive. A Catholic soldier, Guido Fawkes, was arrested. English Catholics were blamed for this plot to destroy the government, and Fawkes was executed. King James I and his parliament, who had been quarrelling, now became friends, united by anti-Catholic feelings. Some people suspected that the plot had been arranged by the government.

THE BUILD-UP TO WAR

King Charles I was stubborn and sentimental. He quarrelled with Members of Parliament, trying to force them to accept his religious policies. He insisted on a form of church organization that gave bishops and priests considerable power. He also sympathized with Roman Catholics, in England and abroad. Many members of the House of Commons wanted a simpler, 'Puritan' form of worship.

Charles also had favourites, whom he appointed to important government posts. And, when MPs refused to vote to give him money to pay for his government policies, Charles dismissed Parliament and ruled for 11 years on his own. During that time, England was peaceful and well run, on the whole, but there was discontent beneath the surface, especially over taxation.

Then, in 1639, the Scots invaded and in 1641, the Irish rebelled. Charles found he could not manage without Parliament. He needed money to pay for these wars. The MPs who came to London were highly critical of

King Charles I was beheaded in public, in the centre of London, in 1649. Although Charles was unpopular, and his troops had lost the war, his execution caused an outcry – no king had ever been treated like this before. Vast crowds watched the execution. Some people fainted, while others saw him as a martyr, and rushed to touch his 'holy' blood.

ROUNDHEADS AND CAVALIERS

The opposing sides in the war gave each other nicknames. Parliament's followers were called 'Roundheads', because they wore plain clothes and had close cropped hair. Supporters of the king got their nickname, 'Cavaliers', from the way they fought – on horseback, if they could afford it. 'Cavalier' came from a French word, meaning 'horseman'. It was not a compliment to be compared with the French. Rather, it suggested that the Cavaliers were 'foreign' and disloyal.

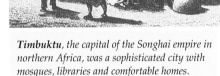

Timbuktu, the capital of the Songhai empire in northern Africa, was a sophisticated city with mosques, libraries and comfortable homes.

Charles' 11 years' rule. They drew up a long series of demands for reform, and executed his leading ministers. The nation was at war.

REVOLUTION AND REPUBLIC
Fighting lasted from 1642 to 1646. At first, the king's army was successful, but Parliament's troops, led by Sir Thomas Fairfax and Oliver Cromwell, eventually won. Charles was captured by the Scots and put in prison. In 1649 he was tried for treason, and beheaded.

After this revolutionary event, Parliament invited Cromwell to become Lord Protector. He governed England as a republic until his death in 1658. In 1660, King Charles' son, Charles II was invited to be King. But his royal powers were limited: King and Parliament would rule together.

A SCIENTIFIC REVOLUTION
At the time of the English civil war there were revolutionary changes in Europe, as well. Scientists were formulating a whole new way of looking at the world, based on observation and measurement, rather than faith or belief.

Exploration brought European thinkers into contact with new peoples, animals and plants, and made them re-examine some of their old ideas. There was a sense of opportunity. Some historians call this scientific revolution the 'beginning of our modern world'.

EUROPE EXPLORES THE WORLD
At the same time as European scientists were making great discoveries in their libraries and observatories, European travellers were setting out to explore the world. Many journeys were made by sea. Other travellers ventured overland. Everywhere, European adventurers were finding rich and fascinating civilizations. For example, elaborate cities such as Timbuktu, capital of the Songhai empire in northern Africa, were built with mosques, libraries and comfortable homes, all designed to make best use of the local desert environment. Sadly, contact with Europeans often led to the destruction of these civilizations, through ignorance, disease and war.

THE WORLD TURNED UPSIDE DOWN
That is what many people feared, when they listened to radical preachers, who were allowed openly to criticize society and to put forward new ideas during the Commonwealth years in England. Many of these preachers – including some women – called for a return to a pure, simple lifestyle, based on what they read in the Bible. The 'Levellers' asked rich people to share their goods with the poor, and demanded the abolition of kings, governments and priests. They wanted religious toleration, and freedom of speech for all people. The 'Diggers' even set up a new ideal community, to put their beliefs into practice.

TRAVELLERS AND EXPLORERS

1487-88	Dias sails round Cape of Good Hope in southern Africa.
1492	Columbus crosses Atlantic.
1497	Cabot sights Newfoundland.
1497-99	Da Gama sails across Indian Ocean to India.
1499	Vespucci reaches the Amazon.
1514	Portuguese ships sail to China.
1519-22	Magellan and Elcano make the first voyage right round the world.
1534	Cartier explores the St Lawrence.
1610	Hudson explores Hudson Bay.
1616	Schouten rounds Cape Horn.
1642	Tasman sights Australia and New Zealand.
1728	Bering sails to Siberia.
1768-75	Cook explores Pacific; lands in Tahiti, Australia, New Zealand.

THE FRENCH REVOLUTION

'Man is born free, but everywhere he is in chains.' Ideas like this were discussed by thinkers in Europe throughout the 18th century. It was interesting – and safe – to talk about reforming society. But the French Revolution of 1789 showed what might happen when radical ideas were put into practice.

REASONS FOR REVOLUTION

French kings and queens ruled over a glittering court in the palace of Versailles. But outside, there was distress and discontent. King Louis XVI had failed in his aim of making France the leading European nation. His government faced bankruptcy after years of war. In the cities and the country, people were starving. There was also a dangerous gap between royalty and ordinary people. When Queen Marie Antoinette heard that citizens had no bread, she joked, 'Let them eat cake'. But to mothers of hungry children, the shortage of food was no laughing matter. King Louis asked the Church and the nobles for help. But, in return, they wanted to control the government. So Louis summoned an old French assembly – the Estates-General – which had not met for over 200 years. After six weeks of angry debate, one section of the Estates claimed to be the true National Assembly – in other words, a new government.

King Louis tried to dismiss the Assembly, but this provoked riots. The Assembly passed laws guaranteeing liberty, equality and freedom of speech to all citizens. A crowd of women marched to Versailles, and captured the royal family. The king was a prisoner. Soon he was executed; a new Republic was declared.

EMPEROR OF EUROPE

Napoleon Bonaparte was born in Corsica in 1769. He became a successful soldier. In 1799 he seized control of the French government, and in 1804 was crowned emperor. He aimed to restore peace and prosperity after the Revolution. He reformed the law, education and administration. Abroad, he led armies against England, Austria, Prussia and Russia. By 1810, France controlled most of Europe. But Napoleon had over-reached himself. He tried to invade Russia, and his soldiers died in the bitter cold. In 1815 he was defeated by the English and Prussian armies at Waterloo. He was exiled from France, and died in 1821.

OFF WITH THEIR HEADS

The guillotine was designed by a Scottish doctor as a humane method of executing convicted criminals. During the French Revolution, it was used to exterminate 'enemies of the state'.

Left: Georges Danton (1759–1794) leader of the 'Jacobins' (extremist revolutionary group) in the French Revolution.

Below: Maximilien Robespierre (1758–1794), lawyer and member of the radical Committee of Public Safety which seized control of the Revolutionary government in 1793.

THE 'TERROR'

The Committee of Public Safety tried to reform the economy and the voting system. But its methods were brutal. All opponents were executed: 40,000 people died during its one-year 'Reign of Terror', including Robespierre and Danton in 1794.

THE INDUSTRIAL REVOLUTION

In 1750, most people worked in the countryside. They lived in small village communities, raising crops and animals. By 1900, most people worked in towns. Even in the countryside, the traditional way of life was gone for ever.

TRAVEL BY TRAIN

The first passenger steam railway began to operate in 1825. Railway travel revolutionized life in Britain, Europe and America. Trains were faster than canal boats and cheaper than horse-drawn coaches. They also carried heavy raw materials and manufactured goods. By the late 19th century, they were carrying regular passengers, or 'commuters', to work in towns, and on holiday excursions to seaside resorts.

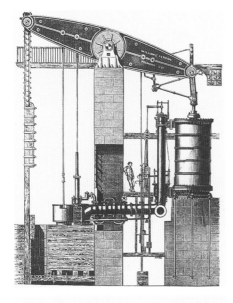

STEAM POWER

A steam-powered beam engine (above). Rapid industrial growth became possible only after the invention of new machines such as this. They provided enormous power to lift loads, pump out water, hammer tough materials or perform boring, repetitive tasks more quickly and easily than ever before. These new machines could also be used as precision tools – they were more accurate and (on the whole) more reliable than human craftworkers.

REASONS FOR REVOLUTION

The French Revolution was not the only major change taking place in Europe at the end of the 18th century. A slower, but no less important revolution was transforming the way in which people worked. What caused this change?

Machines All through the 18th century, engineers had been perfecting inventions designed to perform tasks that men and women had done before. One of the earliest industrial machines was the 'flying shuttle', made by John Kay in 1733. To begin with, it used hand-spun thread to weave cloth, but spinning machines – like the 'spinning jenny' – were developed within 30 years.

The Human Cost In some ways, these machines were a great advance; they were quicker, cheaper and more efficient than people could ever be. They helped British factory owners grow rich, producing more goods than overseas competitors who still relied on hand power. But their human costs were great. At first, they caused unemployment among people who had only traditional skills. Later, when workers moved to the factory towns, machines caused pollution, and the need to work long hours for low wages ruined many people's lives.

INDUSTRIAL CITIES

Machines needed people to operate them, and these industrial workers needed homes. Large cities grew up in the new manufacturing areas, close to essential raw materials – coal, iron ore and water. At first, people flocked eagerly to the cities from the countryside, in hope of a better life and higher wages. But industrial towns were unhealthy places to live. Homes were badly built, dirty and crowded. Air and water were polluted. Food was stale, or mixed with dangerous additives. Factory hours were long, and accidents were common.

LAWS FOR A NEW LAND

After Independence, the United States no longer paid British taxes, or obeyed British laws. American politicians drew up a Constitution – a list of principles designed to ensure a fair and democratic system of government. It still rules America today.

AMERICA

For over 200 years, European colonists fought for control of American territory and for independence. Sadly, while fighting for their own freedom, they also destroyed the ancient American civilizations that had flourished before they arrived.

NEW COMMUNITIES

The earliest colonists in America were undoubtedly brave and daring. They risked their lives out of a sense of greed or adventure, or because, like the Pilgrim Fathers, they wanted to build a new community based on their religious beliefs.

The first European colonies in America, in the late 16th century, were dismal failures. To this day, we do not know what happened to the colonists who settled in Roanoke in 1587. Successful colonization really started with Jamestown (British, founded 1607) and Quebec (French, founded 1608). By 1700, there were around 250,000 European settlers in North America, with numbers rising fast.

These settlers fought against one another, as European wars 'spilled over' on to American soil. They also fought – and killed – many Native American people (whom they called Red Indians, because the men painted their faces with red and yellow earth for war, or on festival days). Europeans had guns and horses, and could easily drive the Native Americans from their ancient tribal lands.

THE REBEL THIRTEEN

By the mid-18th century, there were thirteen British colonies in North America. They joined with Britain to defeat the French, but then (as Britain saw it) turned on their natural rulers, and demanded the right to govern themselves.

NATIVE AMERICANS

People had been living in America for over 10,000 years before the first European colonists arrived. Around 100 different tribes – or nations – of Native Americans were scattered across America's vast lands. They spoke many different languages and followed different ways of life – hunting, fishing, or farming – depending on local climate, plants and soils. But they all shared similar religious beliefs, including a profound respect for the environment and a wish to live in harmony with the natural world.

THE WILD WEST

United States' territory doubled in size in 1803, after the 'Louisiana Purchase', when the American government purchased former colonies from France. Before long, millions of European settlers moved westwards, in search of farmland, gold and freedom. To them, the western territories seemed empty, and ripe for exploitation. Land was cheap, and they set up townships, houses and farms.

But the 'Wild West' was not 'empty' land. Native Americans lived there, and

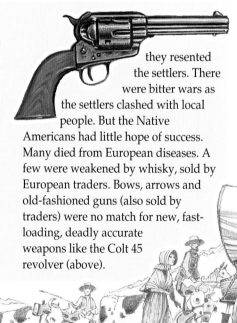

they resented the settlers. There were bitter wars as the settlers clashed with local people. But the Native Americans had little hope of success. Many died from European diseases. A few were weakened by whisky, sold by European traders. Bows, arrows and old-fashioned guns (also sold by traders) were no match for new, fast-loading, deadly accurate weapons like the Colt 45 revolver (above).

CIVIL WAR

The economies of northern and southern states in America developed differently. Northern states were farmed by free settlers; there were also rapidly growing industrial towns. Southern states depended on black slave labour to work great estates. By the 1860s, northern politicians, led by President Abraham Lincoln (above), were determined to abolish slavery – it had no place in the 'land of the free'. After a bloody Civil War (1861-1865), in which a million men died, they finally succeeded.

The Confederate and Union Flags (left and right above).

A group of Union generals before the battle of Gettysburg (1863). The American Civil War was one of the first to be recorded on film.

The colonies particularly disliked having to pay English taxes, as they received no benefit from them, and had no say in how they were spent. Eventually they decided to declare an 'economic war'. They stopped paying taxes and banned all British goods except tea. In 1775, American demonstrators clashed with British troops. This was real war.

The following year, 1776, the colonies signed a Declaration of Independence. Fighting continued until 1781, when the colonies won. America was free. In 1787, a new Constitution established a republican system of government, led by a president, Congress, and a supreme court. The former colonies joined together in a United States of America.

THE AMERICAN WAY OF LIFE

The new republic grew rapidly. Millions of European settlers came seeking their fortunes and hoping to be free. Towns, trade, industry and farms all prospered. Education flourished. For many people, living standards were high. New states continued to join the Union, and a 'pioneer' spirit encouraged inventions and discoveries. Great railway systems crossed America from coast to coast. But the problem of slavery still needed to be solved, and this led to a bitter and costly Civil War.

KEY DATES

1607	British colony of Virginia founded.
1619	First black slaves sold in Virginia.
1765-75	Growing tension between colonists and home government.
1775-83	War of Independence.
1787	United States Constitution.
1789	George Washington becomes first President.
1861-65	American Civil War.
1876	Native Americans win battle of Little Bighorn.
1890	Final defeat of Native Americans at battle of Wounded Knee.

SOUTH AMERICAN NATIONS

In 1494, at the Treaty of Tordesillas, Spain and Portugal agreed to divide the 'New World' of Central and South America between them. These colonial overlords ruthlessly exploited their new possessions – and the people who lived there – in order to secure precious supplies of gold and silver, sugar and jewels.

The French Revolution of 1789 encouraged all downtrodden peoples to rebel. Between 1810 and 1831, led by freedom fighters like Simon Bolivar (right), who gave his name to the country of Bolivia, almost all Spanish and Portuguese colonies in South America achieved independence.

THE VICTORIAN AGE

Victoria was born in 1819. She became Queen of England in 1837, aged only 18. At a time when women were considered incapable of ruling, she became a symbol of Britain's dignity and (some would say) self-righteousness. She gave her name to an age.

WALTZ
ON OFFENBACH'S POPULAR OPERA,
BY
CARLO ZOTTI.

HOW TO BE QUEEN?

Victoria faced problems when she became queen. Although she was leader of the nation, Parliament had the real power to make laws, raise taxes and declare war. All these decisions needed Victoria's approval, but if she opposed Parliament, she knew she would not stay queen for long. How could she stop herself being pushed out of politics?

Victoria solved her difficulties in a number of ways. She held discussions with senior ministers, and took advice from her husband, Prince Albert, an intelligent and sensible man. She also decided to rule by example. Her own behaviour revealed the moral standards she valued. She became a devoted wife, and was a caring mother. She worked hard, and had a strong sense of duty, but could be bossy, obstinate and proud.

After she was widowed, she retired from public life – and was severely criticized for doing so.

Victorian Britain was powerful and prosperous. People believed in hard work and progress. Scientists made great discoveries, technology raced ahead. Slowly, Parliament passed laws to improve conditions for working people and to provide education for all.

'CITIES OF LIGHT'

Paris and Vienna were the most elegant cities in Europe in 1880. Both saw major rebuilding programmes; there were wide new streets, lined with comfortable apartments and luxurious shops. There were parks and gardens, restaurants, ballrooms, theatres and concert halls. Vienna was famous for music and dancing, Paris for fashion and art.

SHOP WINDOW FOR THE WORLD

In 1851, the 'Great Exhibition' opened in London. It was planned by Prince Albert as a celebration of Victorian achievement. Albert hoped it would improve standards of manufacture and display British skills to the world. There was also space for foreigners to show their own products. The exhibition hall was made of glass and iron. It was 563 metres long and 139 metres wide.

WHAT ABOUT THE WORKERS?

Victorian prosperity was based on hard work by everyone involved in industry, from the engineers, owners and managers who planned new factories, to the men, women and children who worked in them. But this work was not equally well rewarded, and conditions in factories could be terrible. Social reformers and trade union leaders campaigned for new laws to increase wages and to protect working people from injury and disease.

Powerful print
Novelists and journalists with a 'social conscience' also campaigned for reform. Popular books by Charles Dickens made people aware of the dark side of Victorian life.

THE ADVENTURES OF OLIVER TWIST BY CHARLES DICKENS
ILLUSTRATED BY GEORGE CRUIKSHANK
A NEW EDITION
Revised & Corrected
To be completed
IN TEN NUMBERS.

COLONIAL TIMES

In 1901, at the end of Queen Victoria's reign, the British Empire covered a large part of the world including Canada, Australia and New Zealand, India, Burma (now Myanmar), southern and western Africa, Malaya (now Malaysia) and many Pacific islands.

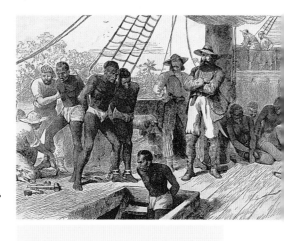

THE NEED FOR AN EMPIRE

This mighty empire grew for two reasons, neither of them political: the need to reach new markets, and the need to find new raw materials. During the 19th century, many countries (such as China and Japan) that had banned European merchants now welcomed them. The Industrial Revolution had given British traders many new goods to sell. This created wealth which could be invested in new machines. But machines needed raw materials, such as some metals and rubber, that were found only overseas. Consumers at home had more money to spend on imported goods such as tea, ivory, diamonds and silk. For Britain to remain prosperous, it had to control these supplies. It had also to stop other European nations taking them for themselves.

Victorian values The British Empire was established by a strong army and maintained by well-trained colonial staff. Queen Victoria's personal qualities were mirrored in the way the British treated their colonies. Politicians used the image of the queen to inspire devotion. And British administrators treated conquered nations like Victorian children – to be praised for obedient behaviour and punished when they were bad.

CRUEL TRADE

European slave traders shipped about nine million slaves from the west coast of Africa to the Caribbean between 1648 and 1815. They were taken to work on sugar plantations. Some people thought that this 'trade in human misery' was wrong, but others preferred to think about its profits. In 1791, slaves in Haiti rioted. This rebellion was put down, but the slaves' plight could no longer be ignored. Reformers in Europe campaigned against slavery and the slave trade. Britain banned slave trading in 1807; but slavery was not abolished in the British Empire until 1833. America finally abolished slavery on 14 April 1865.

BRITISH INDIA

By 1757, British troops had defeated rival French colonists in India and had conquered Indian opponents in many states. Legally, Mughal emperors still ruled, but they were powerless puppets in British hands. In 1857, after Indian soldiers mutinied, Britain dismissed the Mughals and made India part of its empire. Government, law, education, trade and the armed forces were all British-run. Even British styles shaped India; this is Bombay Railway Station.

ZULU WARS

The Zulus were a fierce and warlike tribe from southern Africa. Their armies, called impis, carried spears and shields. Their chief, Chaka, was killed in 1828, but the armies he had trained fought on against Dutch and British colonists in southern Africa. They were finally defeated in 1879.

NEW NATIONS

What makes a nation? Is it a common language? A shared ethnic background? Centuries of history, or obedience to a single, national government? Is it the excitement of founding a new state, or a heroic determination to defend one's ancient land?

Central Europe, around 1871
The peoples of Europe belonged to many different ethnic, religious and language groups. This explosive mixture was controlled by great empires, but by 1871 Germany and Italy existed as independent nations, forged by nationalists such as Bismarck and Garibaldi.

THE RISE OF NATIONALISM

Throughout the 19th century, nationalism was a powerful force in Europe. After the fall of Napoleon in 1815, the continent was divided between the great powers: Britain, France, Austria, Prussia and Russia, with Turkey in the east. The great powers ruled lands inhabited by many different peoples. Encouraged by nationalist leaders, European patriots began to seek independence from great power rule. In 1848, the 'year of revolutions', there were revolts in Austria and Hungary, riots in Germany and a revolution in France. Britain, too, faced demands for freedom from its Irish subjects. None of these protest movements created new nations, although many were inspired by nationalist feelings, and they all threatened – if only briefly – government power.

Elsewhere, new nations were being formed in Europe. In Germany and Italy, politicians such as Bismarck and Cavour used a combination of military power and careful negotiation to unite separate political 'fragments' into strong, independent new states. In other parts of the world, European settlers struggled to establish new nations in 'unknown' lands. ('Unknown' only to them, since all of them were inhabited long before European settlers arrived.) They took European farm animals and equipment with them. They built houses and farms in European styles. They also copied European ways of government to help them rule their new lands.

THE IRON CHANCELLOR

For hundreds of years, Germany was divided into many small states. After the French Revolution, and again in 1848, there were calls for a united Germany. Nationalists hoped that this new Germany would be powerful and free, ruled by the people, not by dictatorial kings. Full German unity was created largely by one man, Otto von Bismarck (1815–1898), chief minister of the north German state of Prussia (right). Bismarck wanted Prussia to be the leader of a strong, united Germany, and was prepared to use diplomacy and harsh tactics ('blood and iron') to achieve this. Prussian troops won wars against Denmark, Austria and France. Germany finally became united in 1871. King Wilhelm I of Prussia was chosen as emperor ('Kaiser'), with Bismarck as his Chancellor. Bismarck introduced social welfare schemes, encouraged industry and strengthened the army. There was even a new parliament, elected by all the German people, but Bismarck could ignore it. Germany was strong, rich and ambitious (page 144).

GIUSEPPE GARIBALDI

Garibaldi (1807–1882) was a dashing, romantic figure. He inspired great loyalty among his men, and admiration from nationalists throughout Europe. He began his career as a sailor, travelling to South America, where he commanded revolutionary armies. He returned to Italy in 1848 to fight for independence. In the north, he battled against the Austrians. Further south, he led Roman troops against French invaders. He was defeated both times, but vowed to continue. In 1860, Garibaldi again joined in the fight for Italian independence. With 1000 volunteers, he conquered Sicily and Naples, recently claimed by France. He became a national hero, but also an embarrassment to Cavour, who now planned to use diplomacy, rather than banditry, to set the rest of Italy free.

INDEPENDENT ITALY

In 1849, the Austrian Prince Metternich scornfully described Italy as just 'a geographical expression', and not a proper nation. It was divided into rival states, and most of these were ruled by Austria. There had been unsuccessful Italian riots against Austria in 1848, but after 1852, opposition to foreign rule was more carefully planned.

Count Cavour, chief minister of the state of Piedmont, led the campaign for independence. In 1858, he asked the French to help him. Rebels in many states demonstrated to show their support. Cavour was successful, but France claimed stretches of Italian territory as a 'reward'. Garibaldi (see below) was not prepared to accept this, and, in 1860, fought successfully against France. Most of Italy was now free from foreign control. It was united, too, under the rule of the Piedmontese or their allies. In 1861 Victor Emmanuel of Piedmont was crowned first king of independent Italy. Garibaldi's next aim was to free the city of Rome from foreign control. French troops were finally driven out in 1870.

A NEW LIFE 'DOWN UNDER'

The first foreigners to make their homes in Australia were mostly British convicts, transported to New South Wales. But soon, willing European settlers began to colonize Australia and New Zealand. They were eager to set up sheep farms (like the bush ranch shown above, dating from 1899) or to mine for gold, iron, coal and other valuable resources. Refrigerated ships carried vast amounts of meat and butter back to Europe. But settlers were often cruel and greedy. Local peoples were driven from their land, herded into reservations, or shot.

AUSTRALIA AND NEW ZEALAND

1778 First British convicts arrive. They included a boy of 11, guilty only of stealing a ribbon; and a woman of 82, guilty only of lying in court.
1829 Britain claims Australia.
1840 Britain claims New Zealand.
1851 Gold discovered in Australia.
1860 Maori Wars (until 1871). New Zealand people fight to defend their land against settlers.
1879 Australia exports almost 150 million kilos of wool to Britain.

Garibaldi and his volunteers ('redshirts') spent hard times living like bandits in exile. Here he is shown resting on campaign.

IRELAND'S SORROWS

In 1800, the British government passed the Act of Union, which made Ireland part of the United Kingdom. The Irish Parliament was abolished, and, until 1829, Roman Catholics were not allowed to be elected as British MPs. These actions provoked fierce opposition, as Irish campaigners demanded 'Home Rule'. Protesters also resented the gap between rich 'Anglo-Irish' landowners and poor peasant farmers. These tensions worsened after the potato famine. British laws kept corn prices high (to protect farmers). Irish people could not afford bread, and so when their potato crop was ruined by blight, they starved. Ireland was unhappily divided along religious lines as well. In the north, the majority of people were Protestants; in the south, they were Roman Catholics.

Searching for potatoes (2nd December 1849) In the great potato famine of 1845–1851, one million Irish people died.

WORLD WAR I

On 28 June 1914, a middle-aged Austrian nobleman was shot at Sarajevo in Bosnia by a Bosnian Serb. At first glance, this might seem a tragic, but minor incident. But it sparked off the worst war the world had ever seen.

British troops going 'over the top' Weighed down with equipment, attacking troops faced murderous machine-gun fire and barbed wire.

The nobleman was Archduke Franz Ferdinand, heir to the Austrian and Hungarian thrones. He was killed because Serbian extremists wanted to free the people living just north of Serbia from Austrian rule.

War broke out because other European nations joined in this complicated local dispute. They tried to solve, through fighting, the political problems in Europe at that time. France wanted revenge on Germany, after being defeated in 1870. Britain feared Germany as a commercial and colonial rival. Russia was also nervous of growing German power. By August 1914, Britain, France and Russia were fighting Austria-Hungary and Germany. Later, Turkey supported Germany, while Italy, Japan and America helped Britain and France. Everyone expected it would be a short war, but it lasted for four terrible years, involving over 65 million soldiers. New weapons, such as tanks, poison gas, submarines and light aircraft were used, but most of the fighting was concentrated in muddy trenches, dug along the 'front line' separating Allied and German lands, which ran from the Channel coast to the Swiss frontier.

'NEVER AGAIN'

Millions of men died trying to push the front line forward a few hundred metres into enemy territory. Conditions were so bad that troops on both sides came close to mutiny. There were bloody battles in Russia and on the Turkish beaches at Gallipoli.

But it was stalemate; neither side

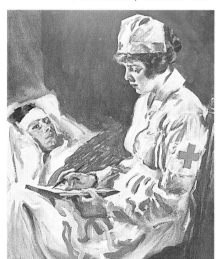

Woman Red Cross worker writing a letter for an injured soldier. Letters (which were censored) comforted soldiers and families.

could win. The end of the war came only after the Allies received troops from Canada and the USA, and after Germany's allies, Austria and Turkey, were crushingly defeated. On hearing this news, demoralized civilians rioted in the German streets and the German Emperor gave up his throne.

TRENCH WARFARE

Armies on both sides fought in trenches – deep ditches dug to provide shelter for troops. Conditions were appalling; there was floodwater, mud, rats and dead bodies. Front-line trenches were targets for heavy gunfire; men climbed 'over the top' to attack enemy troops. Over 8.5 million men died and 20 million were injured, mostly in trench warfare.

WOMEN AND WAR

Women played an important part at home, doing jobs that had previously been labelled 'unfeminine', or reserved for men. They drove lorries, assembled guns and packed dangerous munitions – bullets, bombs and shells. Women also travelled to Belgium and France to nurse injured soldiers in army hospitals there.

World War I saw the first use of planes in warfare

KEY DATES
1914 Archduke Ferdinand murdered. War begins. Germany invades Belgium. Russia attacks Germany. Austria attacks Serbia.
1915 In east Europe, Germany crushes Russia. Britain fights Turkey. Italy joins Britain and France.
1916 Appalling slaughter in France.
1917 USA allies with Britain. Russian Revolution; truce with Germany. Britain fights Turkey in Mid East.
1918 Final German attack in west fails. Italy defeats Austria, France defeats Turkey. Armistice 11 November; war ends.

THE RUSSIAN REVOLUTION

'The people need peace; the people need bread; the people need land.' Lenin, the exiled communist leader, was cheered by the crowds when he made rousing speeches, voicing their demands, during the Russian Revolution of 1917.

Russian peasants were miserably poor, many little better than slaves.

THE ROAD TO REVOLUTION

The Russian people no longer supported the Tsar and his government and welcomed Lenin back from exile. In March 1917, workers in St Petersburg went on strike, and the army joined them. When the Tsar tried to restore order, he was arrested and decided to abdicate. Soon, he was a prisoner. For a while, the Tsar's administration tried to rule, but it was taken over by members of the Soviet, or workers' council, who formed a Provisional Government. Lenin joined them, together with a group of communist exiles known as the Bolsheviks. He demanded an end to Russia's participation in World War I, and for nobles' land to be given to the peasants. At first, people were cautious, but after the Provisional Government lost an important battle against the Germans and failed to supply enough food and fuel for the workers, they supported Lenin's demands for revolutionary change.

The 'October Revolution' (which began on 7 November by the modern calendar) brought sweeping reforms. Members of the Provisional Government were arrested, estates and private bank accounts were seized, factories were given to workers, and church property was taken away. Russia made peace with Germany.

Lenin was trying to build a new, communist society, but not everyone supported his aims. There were revolts by Cossacks and demands for independence from former provinces in the Tsar's empire. 'White' Russians, from Europe, remained loyal to the Tsar. Russia's enemies – Japan and Poland – decided to attack. But Lenin survived.

In 1921, Lenin planned a 'New Economic Policy', and a communist state, the USSR, was formally declared in 1922. The Russian Revolutionaries had won.

PEASANTS AND THE REVOLUTION

In 1861, Russian serfs (unfree peasants, almost slaves) had been set free. Government reforms aimed to improve peasant life, though most Russians remained poor. Socialist campaigners encouraged peasants to revolt. This happened in 1905 and again in 1917, when peasant soldiers rioted for food.

'FATHER OF THE USSR'

Vladimir Ilyich Lenin (1870-1924), a lawyer by training, was leader of the Bolshevik ('majority') communist group in the Russian Revolution of 1917. He became the first leader of the new Soviet state.

THE END OF THE TSARS

The elegant Winter Palace at St Petersburg was built for the Russian royal family in 1754–62 by the Italian architect Rastrelli. In 1917, it was bombarded from a ship by communist rebels, who saw it as a symbol of royal extravagance and a reminder of the huge gap between rich and poor Russians. The supporters of the Revolution hoped it would end this inequality, once and for all.

Tsar Nicholas II (1868-1918), the last ruler of the Russian empire, with his family. After the Revolution, they were all murdered by Bolshevik guards.

In America, the Depression led to many families, like the one above, losing their homes.

THE RISE OF FASCISM & WORLD WAR II

In 1918, people were calling World War I 'the war to end all wars'. They agreed there must never again be slaughter on such a massive scale. A new League of Nations was set up in 1920, to work for peace. For a short time, hopes were high.

THE GREAT DEPRESSION

In October 1929, the New York stock market 'crashed'; banks, businesses and private investors lost their money. This financial disaster led to economic depression. Farms and factories failed; people went hungry. By 1932, there were 13 million people out of work in the United States of America.

MADMAN OR 'GREAT LEADER'?

Adolf Hitler (1889–1945) became leader of the German National Socialist (Nazi) Party in 1921. After Germany's defeat in World War I, he wanted to rebuild a mighty German nation which would control Europe for the next 1000 years. These wild – perhaps mad – ambitions appealed to Germany's wounded pride.

Hitler also attracted followers by his extraordinary skills as a public speaker, and by the power and ruthlessness of his personality. The picture below shows Hitler and other Nazi leaders at a rally in Germany, designed to win popular support.

THE BUILD-UP TO WAR

America and the new USSR both refused to join the League of Nations, weakening it from the start. By the 1930s, people paid little attention to its demands. The peace settlements made at the end of World War I proved largely unworkable. They relied too much on American willingness to support anti-German states in Europe, and left unresolved certain areas of possible future conflict – such as who should rule the Sudetenland, between Germany and Czechoslovakia. America soon became involved in its own problems, including a catastrophic economic depression, and was unwilling to play a leading part in European affairs. The 1917 Revolution in Russia and the years of unrest that followed also threatened to spill over into

Europe. There were strikes in Britain and Italy and communist-inspired revolts in Hungary and Spain. There was also a right-wing reaction to the 'communist threat' in several countries; military regimes took control of Bulgaria, Poland, Yugoslavia and Greece.

A new, right-wing political theory, known as 'Fascism', became powerful. In Italy, Benito Mussolini set up a Fascist government in 1922. He passed strict laws, and used gangster-style violence to stay in power. In Spain, between 1936 and 1939, there was a bloody civil war between communists and fascists led by General Franco.

HITLER AND GERMANY

At the same time as the Fascists were gaining power in Italy and Spain, the German National Socialist (Nazi) Party, led by an

Jewish children, fenced in like animals at a Nazi concentration camp somewhere in Germany. Hitler wanted to remove what he called all 'non-Aryan' people from his new German state, to ensure racial purity. He aimed to exterminate all gypsies and Jews. In this Holocaust, 5.7 million Jewish men, women and children died.

THE HOME FRONT
Life was hard for civilians in British towns during World War II. Food, clothes and petrol were rationed, lights were blacked out, public transport was slow and crowded. Much worse, there was the threat of night bombing. During the 1940 'Blitz' (an intense German air attack), important buildings were destroyed in London and in many other cities. Children were *evacuated* (sent away) to safe homes in the country; adults spent the nights underground in bomb shelters. But Churchill defiantly declared Britain would continue 'business as usual'.

KEY DATES
1939 Germany invades Poland.
1941 Germany invades Russia. Japan attacks US fleet in Hawaii.
1942 Japan captures British Empire lands in Far East; Germany defeated by British at El Alamein.
1943 Germany defeated by Russia at Stalingrad. American victories in the Pacific. Italy surrenders.
1944 Germans retreat from France.
1945 Allies invade Germany.

Austrian soldier named Adolf Hitler, won considerable support in the 1932 parliamentary elections. Like many other countries, Germany faced an economic crisis. There were 6 million unemployed out of a total workforce of 10 million. German money was almost worthless, and people faced shortages of food. Rightly or wrongly, they believed Hitler's Nazis offered the hope of better things. Hitler seized complete control of the German government in 1933. He quickly introduced a programme designed to reshape the German state. He blamed communists and Jews for Germany's problems, and they were persecuted or sent to concentration camps. The Nazi Party controlled everything, and punished anyone who dared disobey it. In 1938, Hitler took control of Austria, then demanded the Sudetenland as well. In Munich, the British and French prime ministers tried to negotiate a peaceful settlement, but, six months later, Hitler invaded Czechoslovakia, and, soon afterwards, Poland. Other nations could no longer stand by and watch. Two days later, Britain and its allies declared war.

BEGINNING OF THE END
On 'D-Day' (6 June 1944) Allied troops launched an invasion of German-occupied France. They sailed across the Channel, defeated the German defenders, and marched towards Paris. They reached the city and recaptured it on 25 August. The Germans had lost control of France, but fighting continued until 1945.

British troops landing on the beaches of Normandy (France) during the D-Day invasion.

The war in the Far East was ended by the first-ever use of nuclear weapons, dropped by American planes. United States scientists had worked secretly to develop them, at top speed. In August 1945, atomic bombs flattened the Japanese cities of Hiroshima and Nagasaki. Injuries to civilians, and damage to property, were far worse than anything seen before. Japan had no choice but to surrender; no one could hope to win unless they had these terrible new weapons themselves.

THE MIDDLE EASTERN CONFLICT

The Middle East is often called the 'cradle of civilization'. It was the home of some of the earliest, most magnificent empires. Its cities are holy places for three of the world's great religions. Yet it has often been torn apart by war.

ISLAMIC GOVERNMENT

Muslims can discover God's laws – which govern public and private life – in the holy book known as the Qur'an. Muslim religious leaders (above) have traditionally devoted years to studying the Qur'an. From a Muslim perspective, this makes them well qualified to rule.

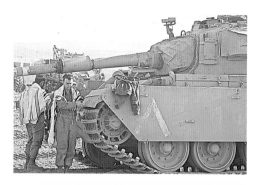

ARAB–ISRAELI CONFLICT

Israeli soldiers find time to pray during the Six-Day War (1967), when Israel, backed by the USA, defeated Egypt, Jordan and Syria in six days. In 1979, Egypt recognized Israel's right to exist, and Israel withdrew from some of the territory it had captured in the Six-Day War.

WAR IN THE GULF

In the 1980s, millions were killed in a war between Iran and Iraq. This was partly a religious war between Iran's Shi'ite Muslims and Iraq's Sunni Muslims, and partly about territory. The war ended in 1988, but in 1990 Iraq invaded Kuwait, a small but wealthy neighbour. A UN force led by the USA went to defend Kuwait and ensure vital oil supplies were not disrupted. Iraq was defeated in 1991, but not before many Iraqis had died and much of Kuwait and Iraq lay in ruins.

Much of the Middle East was part of Turkey's Ottoman Empire 100 years ago. But the Empire collapsed after World War I, leaving Britain and France to carve up the region into countries. The borders they set often showed little regard for ethnic differences, and many peoples were thrown together in new nations like Iraq and Lebanon. This sowed the seeds for conflict.

Borders are still bitterly disputed. They are one reason why Iran and Iraq went to war in 1980. Disputes are fuelled by religion too, for Jews, Muslims and Christians live close together here. And because the Middle East has the world's biggest oilfields, foreign powers, such as the USA and Britain, take a keen interest, further confusing the situation. Moreover, Israel and the USA have strong ethnic links.

Israel is at the centre of many disputes. Up until the 1920s, the Jewish people were scattered around the world. Then in the 1920s, the British encouraged Jews to make their home in Palestine. But Arabs felt the Jews were stealing their land. So, in 1948, the UN split Palestine between Arabs and Jews. The Jewish part became Israel. At once, Arab armies invaded Israel, but were defeated, and Israel took over all of Palestine.

Since then, Israel has been in constant conflict with its Arab neighbours, especially over Palestine. The Palestinian Arabs want a homeland of their own, and are fighting a struggle they call *intifada* to gain it.

THE COLD WAR & COMMUNISM

During World War II, American and Russian troops were united in their determination to defeat Hitler. Yet within just a few years, the USA and the USSR were bitter opponents in a 'cold war'. Why did these former allies become enemies?

In 1945, the 'big three' allied leaders – Winston Churchill of Britain, Franklin D. Roosevelt of the USA and Joseph Stalin of the USSR – met at Yalta, in the Ukraine. Fighting had not yet ended, but they felt confident of victory. Now they needed to work out how their three countries could live side-by-side in a post-war world. This would not be easy. The allies held differing political views. Britain and the USA had capitalist economies. Both saw themselves as champions of the free world. The USSR was a communist society, where everything was organized and provided by the state. Criticism of state policies was not allowed. At Yalta, it was confirmed that Britain, France, the USA and the USSR would jointly occupy Germany, as had been agreed in 1944. The future of Germany itself was left for a later peace conference.

Unintentionally, these decisions led to trouble. The USA and the USSR stood face-to-face, as rival guardians of a divided Europe.

There were quarrels over refugees, borders and, most important of all, the city of Berlin.

By 1948, the former allies were almost at war. But it was a 'cold' war of words, not weapons. Only once or twice did a real war look likely – once, in 1962, when the USSR wanted to set up missile bases in Cuba. But the struggle was fought in all kinds of secret ways, often using spies and secret agents. The USA and the USSR also entered an 'arms race' to build up nuclear bombs and missiles and keep one step ahead of their rival. The superpowers also found themselves fighting conventional (non-nuclear) wars in distant lands. As each side sought to win more power, they made global alliances, backing rival groups or supporting spies and rebels.

The cold war 'thawed' after 1985, when Mikhail Gorbachev introduced reforms in the USSR and started a policy of cooperation with the West. But its effects are still felt in many parts of the world.

REVOLUTIONARY CHINA

Mao Zedong (above, 1893–1976) was leader of the Chinese Communist party and ruler of the Chinese state. He lived through a period of great change, from the Long March (1934–1935), when he led communist rebels to safety in the

mountains, through the Japanese invasion to the 'Cultural Revolution' (a brutal mass education movement 1965–1968). Mao's 'Thoughts' were published in a famous 'Little Red Book' (above).

After Mao's death, there was renewed contact with the western world, and steps taken towards freedom. But these were halted after the army intervened.

The Vietnam War (1955–1975) was a tragic conflict between opposing local groups, backed by the superpowers. Many soldiers and civilians died, and the countryside was wrecked by chemical sprays and mines. Protesters in the USA called for an end to the war after horrific scenes appeared on TV.

KEY DATES

1949	NATO & COMECON (communist economic union) formed.
1955	Vietnam War begins.
1955	Warsaw Pact: defence treaty among communist nations.
1960	US spy plane shot down over Russia.
1961	Berlin Wall built.
1962	Russian missiles found in Cuba.
1968	Soviet troops invade Czechoslovakia.
1987	USA–USSR ban some nuclear weapons.
1989	Berlin Wall taken down.

Hydrogen, with one electron in the first shell, is very reactive.

Carbon is the basic chemical of life. With four electrons in its outer shell, it has four vacancies to form a huge variety of compounds.

Oxygen is in the air we breathe. With six out of a possible eight electrons in its outer shell, it will combine with two hydrogen atoms to form water.

ELECTRON SHELLS

Electrons spin round the nucleus in different layers or shells. There is a limit to the number of electrons that can fit in each shell. In the first, nearest the nucleus, there is room for only two; in the second, eight, and so on. Just how easily the atom interacts with others depends on how full or empty the outer shells are.

MATTER

Matter is every substance in the universe, from the tiniest speck of dust to the biggest star – everything that is not simply empty space. Some matter is solid and can be seen and picked up, but invisible gases and liquids are matter too.

ATOMS AND MOLECULES

Ancient Greek thinkers had two ideas about matter. Aristotle (384-322 BC) thought it is one continuous substance – so you can go on chopping it up into ever smaller lumps. But Democritus (460-400 BC) believed matter is really billions of tiny *atoms* – the smallest pieces matter can be cut into ('atom' is Greek for uncuttable). For centuries, most scientists agreed with Aristotle. But Democritus was at least partly right.

This book may look solid enough but, like every substance in the universe, it is mostly empty space dotted with atoms. Atoms are so small you see them only with very high-powered specialist microscopes. You could fit two billion atoms on the full stop at the end of this sentence.

Scientists once thought atoms were like tiny hard balls that could never be split up, destroyed or created. In fact they are more like clouds of energy than hard balls. Indeed, they are mostly empty space dotted with a few even tinier particles, called *sub-atomic particles*.

Right in the centre of every atom is a dense nucleus containing two kinds of particle, *protons* and *neutrons*. Protons have a positive electrical charge while neutrons have none. Around the nucleus are tinier, negatively-charged particles called *electrons*, travelling as fast as the speed of light. Most atoms have identical numbers of protons and electrons, so the charges balance each other.

Atoms can be split up, but they are usually held firmly together by three forces – the strong electrical

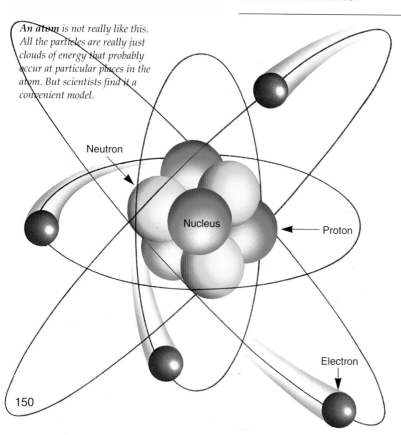

An atom is not really like this. All the particles are really just clouds of energy that probably occur at particular places in the atom. But scientists find it a convenient model.

Neutron

Nucleus

Proton

Electron

INSIDE AN ATOM

During the 1920s, most scientists accepted that there were just three different types of sub-atomic particle – and they called them electrons, protons and neutrons.

Since then, however, scientists have discovered many more types as a result of experiments involving smashing atoms to pieces. In addition to this it has been established that every particle has an *anti-particle* associated with it, which is essentially its mirror image, though every bit as real.

Nowadays, scientists believe all particles are made from just two types of particle, known as *quarks* and *leptons*. Protons and neutrons are made from different *flavours* (kinds) of quark; while electrons are leptons.

attraction between the negative electrons and the positive protons, and the *strong* and *weak nuclear forces* that bind the particles of the nucleus together. These forces, with *gravity*, are the basic forces that hold the universe together.

ELEMENTS AND COMPOUNDS

The character of an atom depends on how many protons it has. The most yet found in an atom is 105 – so there are 105 kinds of atom. Substances made from identical atoms are called *elements* and they are the basic building blocks of the universe. Just as there are 105 different kinds of atom, so there are 105 elements, each made from atoms with a certain number of protons and its own unique character. For example, iron atoms have 26 protons, gold atoms have 79.

All the millions of known substances are combinations of these elements. Some are *compounds*, made when the atoms of two or more elements join together. Table salt, for instance, is a compound of sodium and chlorine. A compound is usually very different from the elements it contains. Sodium (a

SOLIDS, LIQUIDS AND GASES

Just as ice melts to water and water turns to steam when it gets hot, so too does every substance change from solid to liquid to gas at certain temperatures. The temperature at which a substance melts from solid to liquid is called its *melting point*; the highest temperature a liquid can reach before turning to gas is called its *boiling point*. Boiling point and melting point vary for different substances

In a solid, molecules are held together tightly by bonds, and simply vibrate. Heat makes them vibrate faster, turning the substance liquid. Increasing the heat makes the particles move all over the place so fast that the bonds between molecules break and the substance becomes a gas. In a gas, particles are far apart, which is why gases are less dense.

metal) fizzes and gets hot when dropped in water; chlorine is a thick, green gas. Pure elements or compounds are rare, however, and most substances are *mixtures* of two or more. Pure water is a compound made from hydrogen and oxygen, but tap water is a mixture, for there are always various substances dissolved in it.

Liquid and gas Liquids evaporate *to gas as more and more fast-moving particles break away from the surface. A gas condenses to a liquid, as particles slow down and bonds begin to hold them together. Water begins to evaporate well below its boiling point, 100°C. But steam is actually droplets of water; the gas made from water is invisible and called water vapour.*

Solid In ice, like many solids (except glass), particles are arranged in rigid patterns called lattices. Heat makes the particles move enough to break the pattern. Ice normally melts to water or freezes from water to ice at 0°C.

MOLECULES

Atoms join together to form *molecules*. Hydrogen atoms, for instance, usually exist only in pairs, or joined with atoms of other elements. A molecule of hydrogen gas is a pair of hydrogen atoms; a molecule of water is a combination of two hydrogen atoms and one oxygen atom. Compounds are made of identical molecules, each with the same combination of atoms.

The atoms in a molecule are held together by *bonds*. Bonds are the forces that exist between atoms and are generated by electrons. In a water molecule (above left), the negatively-charged electrons of the hydrogen atom are drawn to the positively-charged nucleus of the oxygen atom, and vice versa. The strength and form of these

bonds varies. In diamond, which is pure carbon, five carbon atoms are linked together in a pyramid or *tetrahedron* shape so strong that diamond is one of the hardest substances in the world (below). Carbon joins up with other atoms so well that a single molecule of some carbon compounds such as DNA (page 9) can be made from millions of atoms. There are so many kinds of molecules containing carbon that an entire area of chemistry is devoted to studying them. It is called *organic chemistry*, because molecules containing carbon are the basis of life.

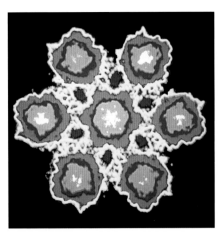

Atoms This photo of a uranium atom was taken with a scanning tunnelling microscope.

ELECTRICITY & MAGNETISM

Electricity is one of the most versatile of all forms of energy, providing everything from heat to make light bulbs glow, to the tiny impulses that make computers work. But it is also, with magnetism, one of the basic forces that holds all matter together.

A dry cell battery converts chemical energy to electrical energy, as the potential energy it contains is used up.

Lead-acid battery This is sometimes called an accumulator because it can be recharged. The electrodes are big plates, often of lead, while the electrolyte is weak sulphuric acid.

BATTERIES

Batteries use chemical reactions to create electricity. Each *cell* (part) of a battery has a positive and a negative *electrode*. In a simple *wet cell*, the electrodes are metal plates dipped in a salt or acid solution called the *electrolyte* and connected by a circuit of wire. *Positive ions* (atoms that have lost electrons) dissolve in the electrolyte from one electrode, leaving it negatively charged and freeing electrons to set up a current in the circuit.

STATIC ELECTRICITY

The way dry hair stands on end when combed and the flashes of lightning in a thunderstorm are both *static electricity*. What they have in common is rubbing. With your hair, the comb rubs on strands of hair; with lightning, ice crystals and drops of rain in the thunder-cloud crash into each other.

The effect of rubbing is to create a *charge*, a force that either attracts or repels. It depends on electrons, tiny particles with a negative charge (page 150). As two surfaces brush together, electrons are knocked off one and stick to the other. The surface losing electrons is positively charged; the surface gaining them is negatively charged. Unlike charges attract, so the surfaces are drawn together.

ELECTRIC CURRENT

Stationary electric charges are called *static electricity*. An electric charge can move through certain materials. This is called *current electricity* and can be used to power anything from light bulbs to computers.

For a *current* to flow, there must be a *circuit*, an unbroken loop for the charge to follow, and a driving force (called an *electro-motive force* or *emf*) to push the charge along. The emf can be either a battery (above left) or a generator (below). The material must also be a good *conductor* like copper – that is, it must transmit a charge easily.

Current electricity gets its name because people once thought it flowed like water. In fact, it is more like a row of marbles – flicking one end jolts the marble at the far end.

SUPPLYING ELECTRICITY

Electricity is generated at power stations in the form of an alternating current (AC) – a current which regularly reverses direction. The voltage of this AC current is boosted dramatically by *transformers* – up to 400,000 volts – for sending long distances across the country through a network of cables known as a *grid*. Near its destination, more transformers in a *substation* reduce the voltage to 110 or 240 volts. This low voltage is then fed to houses and shops. Big factories usually have their own transformers because they prefer a high voltage.

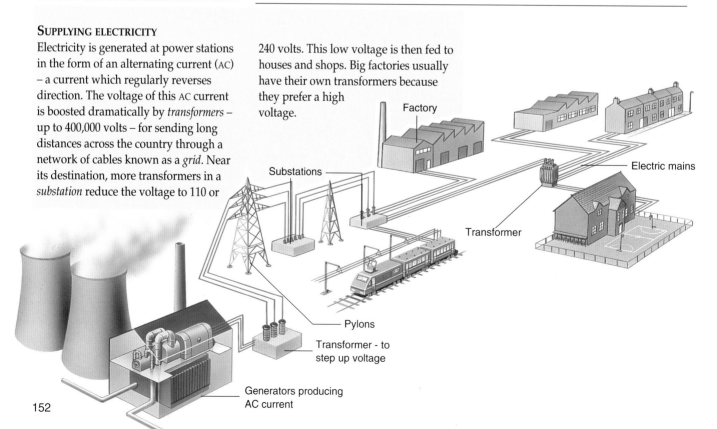

Factory

Substations

Electric mains

Transformer

Pylons

Transformer - to step up voltage

Generators producing AC current

MAGNETS

Magnetism is the invisible force between magnetic materials such as iron and nickel that either attracts or repels. This force affects a certain area around each magnet called its *field*. The pattern created in filings of iron by the fields around two magnets is shown here. The field is especially strong at the magnet's two poles. The same poles of two magnets repel each other; different poles attract.

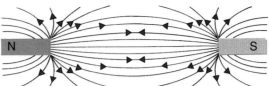

Unlike poles attract (left)With unlike poles together, the field between the two is strong. The two poles of the magnets are drawn towards each other.

Like poles repel (right) With like poles facing each other, the magnets push each other apart and the field between is weakened so much that a neutral spot appears. Lines of magnetic force curve away from this.

In any good conductor, some electrons drift freely. When the circuit is switched on, these *free electrons* all move the same way a short distance, knocking into each other and passing on the charge.

For the current to flow, there must be more electrons at one *terminal* (end) of a circuit than the other. This difference, called the *potential difference*, is created by the battery or generator and is measured in *volts*. The rate at which the current flows (measured in *amps*) depends on not only the voltage but the circuit's *resistance* – that is, how much it obstructs the flow of electricity. Resistance is measured in *ohms*.

ELECTROMAGNETISM

In 1819, Danish scientist Hans Oersted noticed that an electric current creates a magnetic field just like a magnet. This discovery paved the way for the invention of generators and electric motors (below). Since then, it has become clear that the link between electricity and magnetism, called *electromagnetism*, is among the most important in science.

Electromagnetism is not only one of the four basic forces that hold the universe together (page 151); it is also every kind of known radiation, including radio waves, television waves, visible light, X-rays and cosmic rays.

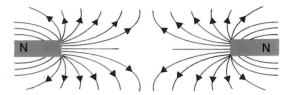

POLES

The Earth itself is a giant magnet, and all magnets are influenced by its field. If a magnet can swivel freely, it always points the same way, with one end aimed at the North Pole and the other at the South. This is why the two ends of a magnet are called the North (or North-seeking) pole and the South (or South-seeking) pole. All magnets have these two poles, whatever shape. Legend has it that it was the Ancient Chinese who first used magnets to make a compass to help them find their way at sea.

MOTORS AND GENERATORS

An electric current creates its own magnetic field similar to an ordinary magnet, except the lines of force run round the wire. Electricity can be used to create strong *electromagnets*. Just as electric currents create their own magnetic fields, so a magnet can create a current. If a magnet is moved near a coil of wire, or a coil of wire is moved near a magnet, a current is set up in the coil. The magnetic field is said to induce a current and the effect is called electromagnetic induction. Generators use this effect to create nearly all of our electricity. Most work by spinning magnets within coils of wire. Direct current generators give a *direct current* (DC) that always flows in the same direction. Alternating current generators (alternators) give an *alternating current* (AC) that continually switches direction.

Simple AC generator or alternator Here, the coil of wire is a single loop, driven round between two big magnets, As the commutator at the end of the coil turns, it makes contact first with the positive end of the circuit through the carbon brushes, then the negative, continually reversing the current.

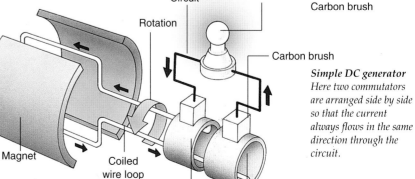

Simple DC generator Here two commutators are arranged side by side so that the current always flows in the same direction through the circuit.

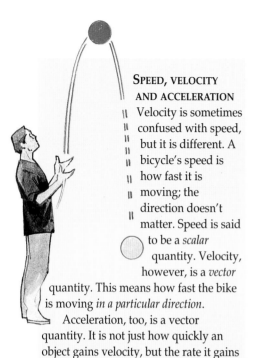

SPEED, VELOCITY
AND ACCELERATION

Velocity is sometimes confused with speed, but it is different. A bicycle's speed is how fast it is moving; the direction doesn't matter. Speed is said to be a *scalar* quantity. Velocity, however, is a *vector* quantity. This means how fast the bike is moving *in a particular direction*.

Acceleration, too, is a vector quantity. It is not just how quickly an object gains velocity, but the rate it gains velocity in a particular direction.

When you throw a ball up in the air, the force of your throw gives it enough *acceleration* to move up against the force of gravity. But the pull of gravity steadily slows it down from the moment it leaves your hand. Eventually, it stops climbing altogether and the force of gravity accelerates it back to the ground.

The ball accelerates while falling at just the same rate as it decelerates while climbing, and its curved path through the air is always a *parabola*, in which the downward curve always mirroring the upward path exactly. A parabola is a shape you can make by slicing across one side of a cone.

FORCE AND MOTION IN ACTION

With enough information, you can work out the *dynamics* (force and motion) involved in everything.

You could work out the force used to hit a tennis ball, for instance, by multiplying how fast it accelerates by its mass, or how fast a car can accelerate by dividing the force generated by the engine by the car's mass.

If you know the size and direction of all the forces acting on an object, you can also work out in exactly which direction it will move.

FORCE & MOTION

A force is any action, for example a push or pull, that causes a change in a body's shape or movement – from the twitch of an eyebrow to the spiralling of a giant galaxy. It is also what it takes to slow things down or hold them together or split them apart.

INERTIA AND MOMENTUM

Back in the 17th century, Italian scientist Galileo made an important discovery. He realized that everything in the universe has *inertia* – that is, it will not move unless something forces it to. A ball only rolls downhill because it is pulled down by the force of gravity; you lift your hand with the force of your muscles. If anything starts to move, you can be sure some force is pushing or pulling on it.

Similarly, all moving objects have *momentum*. This means they go on moving at exactly the same speed and in the same direction unless some force makes them slow down or speed up. Momentum is what keeps you going on a bicycle some time after you stop pedalling and what crumples a car in a crash.

Just how much force is needed to overcome inertia and start something moving depends on its *mass* (how heavy it is or, more precisely, how much matter it contains). Once it is moving, just how much force is needed to slow it down or speed it up depends not only on its mass but also on its *velocity* – that is, how fast it is moving (see left).

A force makes an object *accelerate* (gain velocity) or *decelerate* (lose velocity). How quickly depends on the size of the force and the mass of the object. The larger the force and the lighter the object, the quicker it accelerates or decelerates.

Friction Once you have accelerated your bicycle to 20km/h you could stop pedalling and maintain that velocity for ever… so long as you or your bicycle is not acted on by a force. Unfortunately there is a force called friction which acts on moving things, tending to reduce their velocity. Friction force is made when two surfaces rub together. The smoother the surfaces, and the slower they pass one another, the weaker the force of friction. Sometimes friction force is very useful, for example on shoe soles and brake blocks, where grip

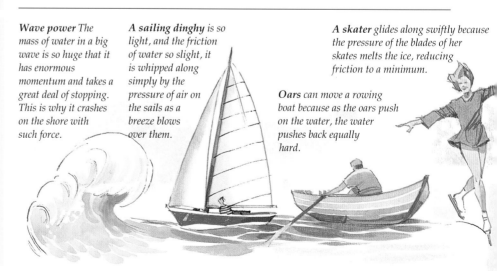

Wave power The mass of water in a big wave is so huge that it has enormous momentum and takes a great deal of stopping. This is why it crashes on the shore with such force.

A sailing dinghy is so light, and the friction of water so slight, it is whipped along simply by the pressure of air on the sails as a breeze blows over them.

A skater glides along swiftly because the pressure of the blades of her skates melts the ice, reducing friction to a minimum.

Oars can move a rowing boat because as the oars push on the water, the water pushes back equally hard.

between two surfaces is needed.

Friction makes things hot because the energy of momentum (kinetic energy, page 158) is changed into heat. This is why bicycle brakes get a little warm when you brake sharply.

Action and Reaction Forces work in not one direction but two. When you walk, the ground pushes your feet as hard as your feet push on the ground. If your feet pushed harder than the ground, they would push the ground away; you might even sink in. If the ground pushed harder, it would lift you up.

Similarly, when you hit a tennis ball, the ball hits the racquet just as hard as the racquet hits the ball. Indeed, whenever something moves, there is always this balance of forces pushing or pulling in opposite directions – one acting, the other reacting. This is Newton's Third Law of Motion.

FORCE AND DIRECTION

There are many different kinds of force. Some are *contact* forces – forces which directly push or pull an object, like someone hitting a ball. Some forces act *at a distance*. Gravity, electro-magnetism and the nuclear forces (page 174) all act at a distance. Forces like these depend inversely on the distance between the two affected objects – that is, they get weaker the further apart they are.

NEWTON'S LAWS

In 1665, Isaac Newton (1642-1727) summed up the link between force and motion with three famous laws. The First Law is about how an object accelerates (or decelerates) only when a force is applied. The Second Law is that the acceleration depends on the size of the force and the object's mass. The Third Law is that when a force pushes or acts one way, an equal force pushes in the opposite direction.

Calculations based on these laws enable engineers to build bridges and scientists to guide spacecraft through billions of kilometres of space. Theoretically, if you knew where everything was in the universe, you could use them to work out everything that has ever happened and everything that ever will. But in the 1920s, as scientists delved inside the atom, they found that particles moved and interacted in different ways, and had to develop the idea of *quantum mechanics* to describe how they move and to predict how they will move in the future.

LIQUID FUEL ROCKETS

Oxygen (a) and the *propellant* (b), usually liquid hydrogen or kerosene, mix and burn in the combustion chamber (c), producing the exhaust (d) which gives the rocket its thrust.

Rocket power Rockets can move through space, where there is no air to push against, because of the action and reaction between the burning rocket fuel and the rocket's body. As the rocket fuel burns, it expands, pushing on the rocket nozzle, so the rocket is pushed one way and the burning fuel equally the other.

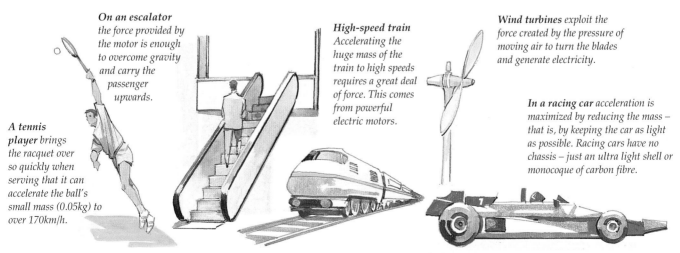

On an escalator the force provided by the motor is enough to overcome gravity and carry the passenger upwards.

A tennis player brings the racquet over so quickly when serving that it can accelerate the ball's small mass (0.05kg) to over 170km/h.

High-speed train Accelerating the huge mass of the train to high speeds requires a great deal of force. This comes from powerful electric motors.

Wind turbines exploit the force created by the pressure of moving air to turn the blades and generate electricity.

In a racing car acceleration is maximized by reducing the mass – that is, by keeping the car as light as possible. Racing cars have no chassis – just an ultra light shell or monocoque of carbon fibre.

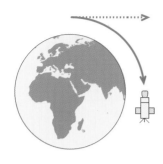

GRAVITY

Gravity is the force that keeps you on the ground, makes rivers run downhill, stones fall to the ground and determines the movements of the stars and planets. It is the most important force in the universe.

ORBITS

For month after month, artificial satellites circle high above the Earth, beaming messages and information around the globe. They are not defying gravity by staying in orbit so long. Rather, they are moving around the world so fast and so far from the ground that the force of gravity is balanced by the satellite's momentum (page 154) which would carry it off into space.

Space scientists calculate a satellite's speed and *trajectory* (path) so they can be sure of placing it in the right orbit. The lower the orbit is, the higher the satellite's speed must be to avoid it being pulled down by gravity. An orbit 35,800km above the ground takes exactly 24 hours to complete – the same time that it takes for the Earth to spin round once. Satellites placed in this orbit remain above the same place on the Earth. This type of orbit is called a *geostationary* orbit.

PULLING TOGETHER

Gravity is the force of attraction that pulls all matter together. Every bit of matter in the universe exerts its own *gravitational pull* on other matter. The strength of the pull depends on mass. Massive objects exert a strong pull; small, light objects exert a weak pull. Compared to the pull of the Earth, the gravitational pull of an orange is undetectable. The pull also depends on how far things are apart. The further things are apart, the more weakly they pull.

Gravity is actually a weak force, too weak to pull two bricks together even if they are sitting right next to each other. Yet gravity is the force that holds the Moon in orbit around the Earth (see below).

WEIGHT AND MASS

We often use the word *weight* when talking of how heavy an object is. But scientists use the word *mass*. Mass is how much matter something contains. Scientists use the word weight to refer only to force – that is, how strongly a massive object like a planet pulls on another object.

FALLING DOWN

Like all forces, gravity makes things accelerate. So if you drop a stone, it falls faster and faster towards the ground. But everything gets faster at 9.8m per second – no matter how heavy they are. A lead ball accelerates downwards at the same rate as a rubber ball. This steady rate is called the *acceleration of free fall*.

As objects fall faster, however, the resistance of the air has more and more effect. Eventually air resistance balances the pull of gravity and the object can fall no faster – which is why skydivers can free fall (below). The object then falls at a steady speed, called the *terminal velocity*. Terminal velocity depends on the weight of an object and its shape, because this alters the effect of air-resistance.

A huge or very dense planet pulls strongly

The small planet pulls back, less strongly

A small or light planet pulls less strongly

The gravitational pull of a planet depends on its mass.

PLANETS AND GRAVITY

In the 1600s, Isaac Newton realized that the gravitational attraction between two objects such as planets is constant throughout the universe and depends on their mass and the distance between them. A big, dense planet pulls far more than a smaller one. In fact, gravity is relatively insignificant unless the mass is very big. This is why planets have a gravitational pull, but the pull of smaller objects is negligible. Since the pull varies with mass, things weigh far more on massive planets than smaller ones. This is why things weigh six times as much on Earth as they do on the Moon.

MACHINES

A machine is a device which makes a task easier. It provides a way of reducing the effort or time needed to move something. It can be as simple as a screwdriver or lever, or as complex as a submarine or spacecraft.

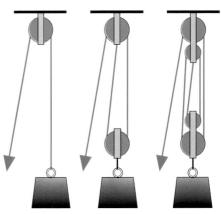

LOAD AND EFFORT

In every machine there are two main forces involved. The *load* is the force to be overcome – that is, the force resisting movement. If you are trying to lift a box of bricks, the weight of the box and bricks is the load. If you are trying to slide it along the ground, the friction between the box and the ground is the load. The other force is the effort, which is the force applied to move the load.

The amount a machine reduces the effort needed to move a particular load is called the mechanical advantage (MA). To calculate the MA of a machine, you divide the load by the effort.

WORK AND EFFICIENCY

Machines do not give you anything for nothing, because the amount of energy needed to shift a particular load is always the same. What machines do is alter the effort needed to a more convenient form. It might make the load ten times easier to move, for instance, by allowing you to apply the effort over ten times the distance. The distance moved by the effort divided by the distance moved by the load is called the *velocity ratio*. If the velocity ratio is greater than 1, the effort moves further than the load.

Moving anything requires *work*. Work is the force applied times the distance moved. In a perfect machine, the work put in at one end would match the work coming out at the other to shift the load. So applying an effort of 1kg over 10m might move a load of 10kg 1m. In practice, no machine is perfect, for friction and other forces reduce *efficiency*. In a machine that was 50% efficient, an effort of 1kg over 10m would only move a 1kg load 5m. Another way of assessing efficiency is simply to divide the MA by the velocity ratio, and multiply by 100 to give a percentage.

PULLEYS

Cranes can lift things not only because they have powerful motors but because they make use of pulleys. Pulleys reduce the effort by running cables around wheels and allowing the crane to lift heavier loads for the same effort simply by winding in more cable. There are many different pulley arrangements, some with *fixed pulleys*, some with *moving pulleys* that move up and down with the load. Some of the more common arrangements are shown in the diagrams above.

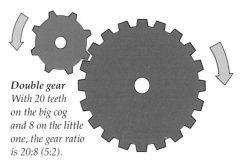

Double gear
With 20 teeth on the big cog and 8 on the little one, the gear ratio is 20:8 (5:2).

LEVERS

A lever is a simple machine that makes it easier to move a load. If an object, like a plank of wood, is fixed at one point, called the *fulcrum*, then an effort applied on one side of the fulcrum can cause the load to move on the other side. This is called a *turning effect*. Whenever you swing open a door, you are exploiting a turning effect – the hinge is the fulcrum. The size of a turning force is called a *moment. Levers* are devices that multiply your efforts by using moments. The further away from the fulcrum the effort is applied compared to the load, the less force needed to move the load.

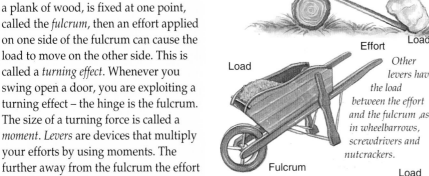

Some levers have the fulcrum between the effort and the load, as in crowbars and scissors.

Effort

Fulcrum

Load

Effort

Load

Other levers have the load between the effort and the fulcrum, as in wheelbarrows, screwdrivers and nutcrackers.

Fulcrum

Load

Effort

Fulcrum

Another sort of lever has the effort between the load and the fulcrum as in tweezers.

GEARS

Gears make it easier to cycle uphill, or for a car to accelerate from a standstill, by spreading the effort over a greater distance. They are basically pairs of wheels of different sizes that turn together, making one shaft turn another. The number of times the driving wheel turns for each turn of the wheel being driven by the engine is called the gear ratio. With a ratio of 4:1, the driving wheel turns 4 times for every time the driven wheel turns. Gear wheels usually have interlocking teeth; another way to assess gear ratio is to compare the number of teeth on each gear wheel.

ENERGY & HEAT

Without energy, nothing can move or change or even exist. Indeed, everything that ever happens from the blink of an eyelid to the creation of a galaxy depends on energy.

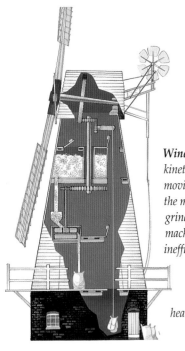

Windmills use the kinetic energy of moving air to turn the millstones and grind corn. Like all machines, they are inefficient, and turn most of the wind's energy into unwanted heat and sound.

THE JOULE

In the mid 19th century, the English physicist James Joule (1818-89) found by stirring water with paddles that just as a steam engine turns heat into work, so work can be turned into heat. The basic unit used to measure energy is now called the *joule*. One joule is roughly the energy needed to lift an apple one metre off the ground.

Energy chains Energy can neither be created nor destroyed, so all the energy in the universe has been around since the dawn of time. This means that when you turn on an electric fire you are using energy that has always existed and always will. Energy can change form again and again. The heat energy of the fire can be traced back through a series of conversions to light from the Sun (below). There are similar chains of conversions for every bit of energy in the universe, stretching right back in time.

WHAT IS ENERGY?

Energy is really the power to make something happen. When scientists define it as 'the capacity to do work', they mean the same thing. Energy is not just the heat that comes from burning coal or wood, or electricity from power stations; it is the source of every change in the universe. Whenever anything happens – when grass grows, rockets fly, or stars explode – energy makes it happen.

Energy comes in many forms, from the chemical energy locked in sugar to the mechanical energy in a moving bicycle. But it always works in two ways – energy transfer and energy conversion. *Energy transfer* simply means it moves from one place to another, as it does when you throw a ball or smoke rises. *Energy conversion* means changing from one form of energy to another. A runner's muscles, for instance, turn chemical energy into movement; power station generators turn the heat energy in steam into electricity.

Stored and moving energy Energy is sometimes divided into two kinds.

Potential energy is energy stored up ready for action. There is potential energy in a wound-up rubber band, in a squeezed spring and in food, coal, wood, oil and other fuels. There is potential energy too in things far above the ground, because gravity could make them fall.

Kinetic energy is energy something has because it is moving; the word comes from the Greek *kine*, meaning movement. A rolling ball has kinetic energy. So too does a moving car, a wave or a falling stone.

ENERGY CHANGES

If you are exhausted after a long walk, you may say that you've run out of energy. But your energy has not disappeared; it was converted into heat as you walked, and left behind in the air and the ground, making them slightly warmer. Indeed, it is impossible to destroy or create energy; it can only be moved or changed from one form to another. This is the *Law of Conservation of Energy*. What this means is that the total amount of energy after any change is always exactly the same as the total before. Energy is never really lost; it is just converted to another form.

Heat loss Energy is never lost, but it can be burned up. Indeed, every time energy is used, some is turned

1 *The Sun's energy is absorbed by the leaves of plants living millions of years ago. When they die, the plants are slowly buried deeper and deeper.*

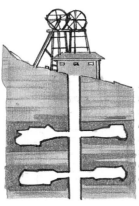

2 *The plants are squeezed into coal by the weight of rock above, concentrating the energy. Coal mines extract these concentrated blocks of energy.*

3 *The coal is burned in a power station to boil water to steam to drive turbines and generate electricity.*

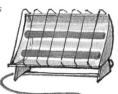

4 *So much electricity is sent through the thin coils of wire in the fire that they glow red hot.*

into heat. This is why you feel hot after running and why light bulbs get hot. This matters because heat spreads out thinly in all directions. So although energy is not lost, it is *dissipated* (gets less concentrated) and is much harder to use again.

When wood burns, for instance, its energy is scattered through the air and is hard to use again. A little more becomes unusable this way each time energy is used – so the energy available to make anything happen (called *free energy*) gets less and less. Scientists use the term *entropy* to describe how much energy has become unusable. The less free energy there is, the greater the entropy. Entropy is at a maximum when there is no free energy left at all.

Heat transfer The word entropy was coined by German physicist Rudolf Clausius in 1868, but the idea dates back to the 1820s and a young Frenchman called Sadi Carnot. Carnot was trying to find out why a steam engine works. He realized it is because it is hot in one place and cold in another. The flow of heat energy from hot to cold drives the engine.

Clausius showed this is true for all forms of energy. Work is done and things happen because energy moves from areas of high energy (or temperature) to areas of lower energy – just as water falling over a dam can turn a water wheel.

The movement is strictly one way, from high to low. Left standing, a cup of hot coffee gradually cools down as it loses heat to the air around, warming the air very slightly. Eventually, the coffee is as cool as the air and there is no longer any energy difference to make anything happen. In this *equilibrium* state, entropy is at a maximum.

Thermodynamics Clausius summed it all up in 1865 in two universal *thermodynamic* laws. The *First Law of Thermodynamics* is similar to the Conservation of Energy Law. It says that the total energy in the universe is fixed at the beginning of time and will remain so until the end. The *Second Law of Thermodynamics* is about the way energy is dissipated as heat every time it is used. This means that the total entropy of the universe must increase. Eventually, scientists once argued, the universe will end because all energy will be nothing but heat. Few scientists agree altogether with this idea of *Heat Death* for the universe, but the two laws of thermodynamics are considered the most important scientific laws of all.

Convection Heat makes molecules move further apart, so substances expand as they get hotter. Warm air is less dense than cold air and rises.

Conduction Hot coffee heats the mug and a spoon standing in it by conduction – that is, because fast-moving molecules collide with slow-moving molecules, passing on heat.

A candle flame, like all flames, radiates heat in all directions in the form of infra-red rays. The Sun's heat reaches the Earth in the same way, travelling through space at the speed of light. The heat of the flame also creates convection, drawing in cold air, warming it and making it rise.

HEAT TRANSFER

If something is hot, it always passes its heat to its surroundings, heating them up and cooling itself down in three main ways: conduction, convection and radiation. *Conduction* is like a relay race, with molecules passing on their energy by jostling their neighbours. *Convection* is when warm air (or water) rises, because it is less dense than cold air around it. *Radiation* is the heat rays you feel from an open fire. Heat rays are called *infrared*. Like light, they are electromagnetic (page 153) and can pass through empty space.

HEAT AND TEMPERATURE

Heat is molecules moving. The faster they move, the hotter it is. Temperature is a measure of how fast the molecules move, whereas heat is the combined energy of all the moving molecules.

Heating a substance raises its temperature by making the molecules move faster. Just how much the temperature goes up when heat is added varies with the substance. A certain amount of heat raises the temperature of the gas argon more than the gas oxygen, for instance. This is because oxygen molecules absorb some of the heat, not by moving faster, but by spinning, because they are a different shape from argon molecules.

When a hot substance meets a cold substance, some of its particles collide with those of the cold substance, making them move faster, while some of the cold ones collide with the hot ones, slowing them down. This transfer of energy goes on until both substances are at equal temperatures.

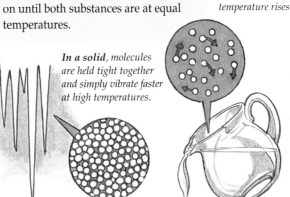

In a gas, molecules are free to move to fill the space available. They move faster as the temperature rises.

In a solid, molecules are held tight together and simply vibrate faster at high temperatures.

In a liquid, there are still strong attractive forces between the molecules, but they can begin to move about.

Shade in the desert
Shadows have a dark umbra and paler penumbra.

LIGHT

Light enables us to see and plants to grow, and provides us with nearly all our warmth and energy. Yet it is just one of the many forms of electromagnetic radiation, from radio waves to cosmic rays. Light is simply the one form of radiation our eyes can see.

SHADOWS

When light strikes an opaque object, it casts a shadow behind the object where the light cannot reach. Just how distinct the shadow is depends on how bright the light is and how far away the light is from the object. Big light sources – like the sky on a dull day – cast soft shadows. Small bright lights like spotlamps cast very sharp shadows.

There are actually two parts to every shadow. In the middle is a very dark shadow called the *umbra*, where the light rays are blocked off altogether. Around the edge is a narrow band of lighter shadow called the *penumbra*.

An eclipse of the Sun (*solar eclipse*) is when the Moon passes in front of the Sun and casts its shadow on the Earth. An eclipse of the Moon (*lunar eclipse*) is when the Earth's shadow falls on the Moon.

WHAT MAKES THINGS VISIBLE

Although we are surrounded by light during the day, few things give out light. The Sun and the stars, candles, electric lights, luminous watches and glow worms are all *light sources*. Most things you see only because they reflect light from light sources. If things do not emit or reflect light, they are invisible, like air.

Look at laser beams piercing the night (page 175) and you can see that light travels in straight lines. When light rays hit an object they bounce off, are absorbed, or pass through. Substances that let light through, like glass, are called *transparent*; those that let it through in a jumbled way, like frosted glass, are *translucent*; those that stop light or bounce it back are *opaque*.

BULLETS OR WAVES?

Scientists have argued about what light is for hundreds of years. In the 1670s, there were two conflicting ideas. Isaac Newton (1642-1727)

thought light was tiny fast-moving bullets called *corpuscles*; Dutch scientist Christiaan Huygens (1629-1695) believed it was waves, like ripples on a pond.

Most scientists preferred the idea of corpuscles. But in 1805, Thomas Young showed how shining light through two slits created a pattern of alternate dark and light bands on a screen beyond the slits. Young argued that they were made by the waves of light from each slit interfering with each other. Other experiments seemed to confirm the wave idea. In the 1860s, James Clerk Maxwell showed that light was just a part of a wide range of electromagnetic waves.

But doubts remained. If light really is waves, how can light from the stars reach us through space where there is nothing to transmit waves? In 1900, Max Planck found that the way heat radiated from a hot object could be explained only if it was emitted in tiny packets of energy that he called *quanta*, from

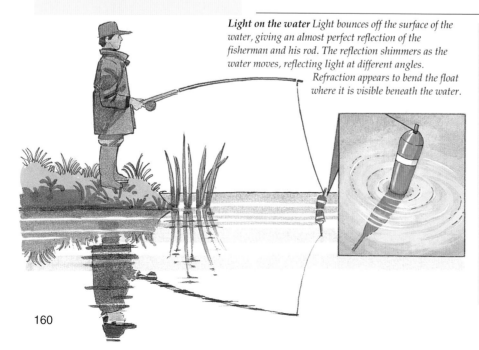

Light on the water Light bounces off the surface of the water, giving an almost perfect reflection of the fisherman and his rod. The reflection shimmers as the water moves, reflecting light at different angles.

Refraction appears to bend the float where it is visible beneath the water.

REFLECTION AND REFRACTION

When light strikes a surface, some or all of it is *reflected*. From most surfaces, it is *scattered* in all directions. With mirrors and other very shiny surfaces, every ray may bounce off in exactly the same pattern as it arrives, showing you a perfect mirror image. When light passes through something transparent like glass or water, the rays are bent or *refracted*. This is why swimming pools sometimes look shallower than they are, and spoons appear bent when standing in a glass of water. This happens because light is slowed down when it enters glass or water.

the Latin for 'how much'.

In 1902, Philipp Lenard discovered the *photo-electric effect* now exploited in solar cells. He found that when light strikes certain metals, electrons (page 150) are released. Later Albert Einstein suggested the photo-electric effect can be explained if light is tiny energy packets like quanta. Most scientists now accept light is indeed energy packets, which they call *photons*. Photons are neither bullets nor waves; sometimes they are one, sometimes the other, depending on how you look at them.

Light from electrons Light comes from atoms. When an atom is energized by, say, an electric spark, it becomes *excited* and an electron may be pushed further out from the nucleus. It's a bit like stretching a rubber band. Then, as if the rubber band is released, the electron slips back in again, firing off a photon as it goes.

The wavelength of the photon fired off depends on the size of the electron's jump as it returns to its original level. This depends, in turn, on the atom's structure. This is why every gas emits its own unique range of colours (called an *emission spectrum*). It also absorbs a unique range (*absorption spectrum*).

ELECTROMAGNETIC RADIATION

Light is just one of many forms of *electromagnetic radiation*, which is basically a form of energy, radiating out through space in tiny little packets, each with its own wavelength. The full range is called the *electromagnetic spectrum*. At one end are radio, television and other long waves. Slightly shorter are *microwaves* like those for cooking. Then come *infrared rays* which we cannot see but feel as heat. Shorter still is light, the short band of wavelengths which we can see. Just beyond the range we can see are *ultraviolet rays*, some of which give us a tan and others skin cancer. *X-rays* have short waves which pass clean through flesh but not bone, which is why they can be used for pictures of inside the body. The shortest, most energetic waves are *gamma rays* released by nuclear reactions and radioactive substances, and *cosmic rays* emitted by stars.

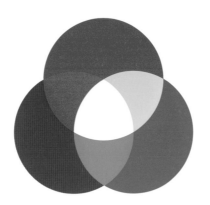

COLOURS

When we see different colours, we are seeing different wavelengths of light. Sunlight appears colourless but is actually *white light*, a mixture of all the colours of the rainbow. You can see these colours if you set a triangular glass *prism* in a dark room so it is caught by a thin shaft of sunlight. Short waves are refracted more by the prism, so the light fans out in a *spectrum* of colours from red to violet (above). Things look certain colours in sunlight because they reflect these colours and absorb the rest.

Every colour can be made by mixing just three colours called *primary colours*, in different proportions (left). When mixing light, the three primary colours are red, blue and green. Our eyes respond to only these three colours and we recognize other colours by how much red, blue and green they contain. Colours in a picture come from absorbing some colours and reflecting the rest. Where we see red in a picture, the ink absorbs blue and green light. So colours in a picture are made up from another three *subtractive* primaries: yellow, magenta (red-blue) and cyan (blue-green).

SPEED OF LIGHT

Light – and all electromagnetic radiation – travels at 299,792 kilometres per second in space, which means it could circle the Earth almost 450 times in a minute. It travels slower in air, and slower still in water, but still very fast.

Einstein showed that for everything slower than light, speed is only relative. If you walk at 5km/h, you only walk at 5km/h for someone on Earth. For someone in space, you are moving at 1205km/h (5km/h plus the speed of the Earth's rotation). But nothing can travel faster than the speed of light, so the speed of light is not relative, but constant throughout the universe.

SOUND

Everyday sounds, from the whisper of the wind in the grass to the roar of a jet, are made by air moving. When a dog barks or a guitar is strummed, it makes the air vibrate, and these vibrations carry the sound to your ears.

Sound waves ripple out in all directions from the sound source, gradually losing energy.

SOUND WAVES

The vibrations that carry sound through the air are called *sound waves*. Sound waves are not like waves in the sea, which ripple across the surface in lines. Sound waves travel by alternately squeezing and stretching the air. When a sound is made molecules in the air nearby are squeezed together. These molecules in turn squeeze those next to them, and then are pulled back in place by the molecules behind them.

Sound waves actually travel faster through solids and liquids than through air, because the molecules are more closely packed. In a vacuum there is complete silence because there are no molecules to carry the sound.

Frequency and pitch The boom of thunder sounds very different from the squeal of a car braking. The difference is basically in the frequency of the waves that produce the sound. If the waves follow each other in quick succession, they produce a high frequency, high-pitched sound. If they follow only slowly, the sound is low frequency or low-pitched.

Sound frequency is usually measured in *Hertz* (Hz) or cycles (waves) per second. Human beings are most sensitive to sounds around 5000Hz (human voice). But they can hear sounds down to about 20Hz (rumble of thunder) and up to about 20,000Hz (squeal of bats). Sounds too low for humans to hear are called *infrasound*; sounds too high are called *ultrasound*.

Overtones Most sounds contain a mixture of different frequencies – a basic or *fundamental* pitch and a range of *overtones*. Overtones help make sounds recognizable. A flute, for instance, has quite a pure sound with most overtones in harmony with the fundamental. A violin has a brighter sound with harsh overtones. Cymbals have so many discordant overtones there is no clear fundamental.

SPEED OF SOUND

Sound travels at different speeds in different substances, and travels faster in warm air than cold air. The speed of sound in air at 20°C is about 344m per second. In pure water, it reaches 1500m per second, and in solid steel it travels at 6000m per second. A *mach number* is a measure of an aircraft's speed relative to the speed of sound at the height it is flying, falling from 1124km/h at sea level to 1062km/h 11,000m up.

Vibrating string
If you look closely at a violin or guitar string, you can see the vibrations that send sound waves through the air. The shorter the string is, the more quickly it vibrates to and fro, making higher-pitched sound.

THE DECIBEL SCALE

Loud sounds are sounds with plenty of energy, making big waves; quiet sounds have much less energy, making smaller waves. The amount of energy in a sound can be measured, but loudness is usually measured in *bels*, or rather in tenths of bels called *decibels* (dB). The decibel scale is logarithmic, which means a 2dB sound is ten times as loud as a 1dB sound and a 20dB sound is 100 times as loud.

140dB Supersonic jet airliner taking off

10dB The sound of leaves rustling

20-50dB People whispering

60-90dB Home hi-fi system

70-100dB High-speed electric train

120dB Overhead thunder

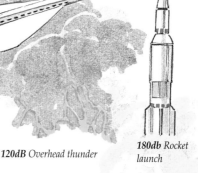

180db Rocket launch

WATER

Water is the most common compound on Earth. As ice and liquid, it covers 70% of the Earth's surface. It is vital to life, filling every living cell and making up almost three-quarters of your body. It plays an important part in a huge range of physical and chemical processes, from making tea to nuclear power production.

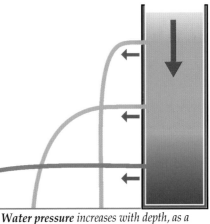

UNIQUE PROPERTIES

Water is a unique substance because it commonly occurs in all three states of matter – solid, liquid and gas. Normally, though, water is a liquid, and although some water evaporates at any temperature above its freezing point (0°C), it does not boil until 100°C. Equally strangely, water expands when it freezes, like no other substance. This is why frozen pipes burst. It is also why ice floats because expanding makes ice less dense.

Water behaves like this because of its chemical make up. In every molecule of water, there are two hydrogen atoms and one oxygen atom – hence its formula H_2O (page 151). But the arrangement of atoms means one end of the molecule is more negatively charged than the other. This difference is called *polarity*, and water is said to be a *polar molecule*.

One effect is that the negative end of one molecule is drawn to the positive end of another, forming a *hydrogen bond*. Water stays liquid because hydrogen bonds draw molecules together so tightly that it is hard for molecules to escape to become gas. When frozen, however, the molecules are arranged in a lattice, which is why ice is less dense than water.

Another effect of polarity is that water dissolves things well. In fact it dissolves things so well that pure water rarely occurs in nature. Sea water, for instance, is 3.5% salts (mostly sodium chloride like table salt). All living things use a*queous* (water-based) solutions, such as blood, digestive juices and inside cells, for vital biological processes.

Water pressure increases with depth, as a simple experiment with holes in a plastic bottle of water shows. Water shoots much further out of the lowest hole than the highest.

WAVES

Waves are created by wind blowing over the sea. Waves can travel long distances, but the water in them barely moves, rolling around a bit like rollers beneath a conveyor belt. Where the water is too shallow for the complete circle, the waves break.

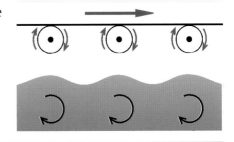

BUOYANCY

2200 years ago, the Ancient Greek mathematician Archimedes discovered that an object weighs less in water than in air – which is why you can lift someone who is quite heavy if they are in a swimming pool or the sea. The reason for this *buoyancy* is the upward push or *upthrust* of the water. When an object is immersed in water, the weight of the object pushes down. But the water around it pushes back with a force equal to the weight of the water *displaced* by the object (pushed out of the way). The object will sink until its weight is equalled by the upthrust of the water, at which point it begins to float. Objects that are less dense than water float, while those that are more dense than water will sink.

Finding a level If you drop a 100cm³ block of wood in water, it may sink at first but then bob up until it displaces a volume of water equal in weight. If the block weighs, say, 70g, it bobs up until it displaces exactly 70g of water. 70g of water takes up 70cc, so the wood bobs up until 70cc is submerged. A foam block the same size may weigh, perhaps, 30g. So the foam block floats higher, because it can be supported by 30cc of water.

Ships float because of the air in their hulls, but they may float at different heights because water density varies. Ships float higher in salt water than fresh water because salt water is denser, and higher in cold seas than warm seas. British ships are marked with a Plimsoll Line (below) to enable the ship to be loaded to the right level in the tropics (T), in freshwater (F), in summer (S) and winter (W).

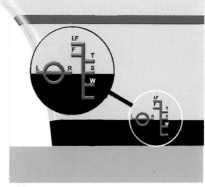

INVENTIONS & DISCOVERIES I

Over the centuries, countless numbers of machines have been invented, some simple, some incredibly complicated. Often it is the simplest inventions, like the clock and mass-production, which have had the most lasting effect on the way we live.

An early clock This is a drum clock made in Nuremberg around 1590. There is only an hour hand, but the clock also shows the position of the Sun and the Moon's phases.

WATERMILL

For more than 1500 years, the watermill was people's only real source of power, apart from muscle. The Greeks described a waterwheel as early as 100 BC. A jet of water from a stream turned a paddle wheel mounted on an upright shaft. As the shaft turned, it turned a millstone to grind corn against another stone.

By the 3rd century AD, the Romans were using vertical wheels. Gears transmitted the power from the horizontal waterwheel shaft to the vertical millstone shaft. With *undershot* wheels, the wheel just dipped into the flowing stream. With *overshot* wheels, water was channelled over the wheel and caught in buckets on the wheel. The weight of water turned the wheel.

The Domesday Book lists over 5000 mills in England in 1086. By 1800, there were more than half a million in Europe. They were the power houses of every village – not only for milling corn, but for powering bellows and hammers to make iron, for grinding rags to make paper, for crushing olives for oil, for drilling gun barrels, and many more tasks.

Indeed, the Industrial Revolution began not with steam power but water power. The first large factories were set up not in the coalfields, but by fast-flowing streams. When Richard Arkwright (1732-92) set up his cotton factory at Cromford in Derbyshire in 1771, it was powered by water.

PRINTING

The Chinese were printing on paper as long ago as the 2nd century AD. The writing was carved out of a block of wood so that the characters stood proud. They could then be dipped in ink and used to print the text on paper. By the 14th century, printers had blocks for each of the 80,000 or so Chinese characters, and could make up pages by assembling these blocks, rather than by carving each page individually – a system known as *movable type*. But it was still a slow laborious process.

The printing revolution began in Europe around 1450 with the German goldsmith Johannes Gutenberg (c.1398-1468). Gutenberg found a way of making any number of identical letters quickly and simply by casting them from metal. This is called *typecasting*. The letters for each page could then be locked in a frame, inked, and pressed on to the paper with a powerful screw press. In 1448, Gutenberg printed the Bible in Latin. 27 years later, William Caxton (c.1422-91) printed the first book in English. By the end of the 15th century, 240 printing presses all over Europe were turning out thousands of printed books a year from Aristotle's works to Boccaccio's love stories.

CLOCKS AND WATCHES

The first mechanical clocks appeared in English and Italian monasteries in the later 13th century to help call the monks to prayer at regular intervals. No-one knows who invented it, but the idea behind the mechanical clock was the *escapement*. The escapement was just a way of stopping a weight at regular intervals as it slid down a cord. The falling weight was used to drive a series of cogged wheels. Each time the weight fell, the wheels jerked round a

Woodcut of early book printing from around 1522. This shows how the pages of type were pressed on to the page using a powerful screw press. Presses like these were originally used for pressing grapes for wine, but Gutenberg adapted them for printing.

Steam engines Hero of Alexandria invented a steam engine during the 1st century AD but regarded it as a toy. The first working steam engine was invented by Thomas Savery in 1698 to pump water from mines. The first steam locomotive was built in 1801 by Richard Trevithick.

The spinning jenny was invented in about 1764 by James Hargreaves.

The assembly line was introduced by the Ford car factory in 1908 to make the Model T Ford in large enough numbers to be cheap. Henry Ford got the idea from moving carcasses in an abattoir. The system speeded up car assembly by moving it along a conveyor belt as bits were gradually added.

little further, moving the clock on. The earliest clocks had a horizontal bar called a *verge* with weights attached. When the weights were moved outwards, the clock ticked slower; when the weights were moved in, the clock ticked faster.

At first, clocks just rang a bell at regular intervals. But by the mid-14th century, they had dial faces and hands. Around 1410, clocks began to have spiral springs to drive the wheels. The spring was wound up, and then allowed to slowly unwind, stopped at regular intervals by the escapement. The spring made it possible to carry small clocks or watches, so called because they were used to mark the *watches* (duty hours) of the night.

SPINNING MACHINES
Natural fibres such as wool and cotton are only a few centimetres long. To use them for weaving cloth, they must be twisted together in a long yarn. For thousands of years, this was done simply by spinning

An early typewriter This is a Hammond typewriter from 1895. A variety of different arrangements for the keyboard were tried out before people finally settled on the pattern of letters and numbers most commonly used now.

them round a stick. By AD 1300, however, people were spinning the fibres with a foot-driven wheel, an idea that came originally from India.

In about 1764, Lancashire weaver James Hargreaves invented a device called a *spinning jenny* which spun yarn on eight hand-turned spindles at once. This dramatically increased the amount of yarn spinners could turn out. But it was still a device for people to use at home. The device which started the Industrial Revolution (page 137) was Richard Arkwright's water frame, invented two years later. The *water frame* was driven by a belt, powered by a water wheel. In 1771, Arkwright installed the frame in a mill in Cromford, Derbyshire, to create the world's first factory.

BICYCLE
The first bicycle to have pedals and brakes was invented by a Scottish blacksmith, Kirkpatrick Macmillan, in 1839. Unlike modern bicycles, it had no chain. Instead, the pedals turned the back wheel through connecting rods linked to cranks that turned exactly like the pedals.

Despite its name, however, the velocipede was very slow, for even rapid pedalling turned the wheel only slowly.

In 1870, James Starley (1830-81) designed the first Penny Farthing bicycle. The rider sat on a saddle on top of a huge wheel 1.5m or more across. The rear wheel was very small. Because the wheel was so big, pushing the pedals round just a little way carried the bicycle some way and cyclists could reach great speeds. Unfortunately, the Penny Farthing was hard to get on – and easy to fall off.

The breakthrough for cyclists came in the late 1870s, with the introduction of the *safety* bicycle by James Starley. This was

basically like the bike of today, with equal-sized wheels, a chain from the pedals to turn the rear wheel, and a diamond-shaped frame. Once the wheels were given soft *pneumatic* (air-filled) tyres – patented by John Dunlop in 1888 – the bicycle became very popular.

ELECTRIC MOTOR
Electric motors are used to drive everything from trains to toothbrushes. The basic principle (page 153) was demonstrated by Michael Faraday in 1821. But the first practical motor was made by Vermont blacksmith Thomas Davenport, and he used it to drill holes in steel. But while motors ran off batteries, they could not be a commercial success. Only when dynamos (that generated electric power continually) were invented in 1873, did electric motors really make an impact.

KEY DATES

1509	Watch invented by Peter Henle in Nuremberg.
1609	Telescope invented in Holland.
1698	Steam pump invented.
1709	Abraham Darby discovers how to make pig-iron by coke smelting.
1825	First steam passenger railway.
1838	Electric telegraph.
1860	Internal combustion engine invented.
1876	Telephone invented by Bell.
1878	Electric streetlights in London.
1903	First successful powered flight by Wright Brothers.
1936	First TV broadcast service.
1946	First electronic computer.
1948	Transistor invented.

INVENTIONS & DISCOVERIES II

By no means all important inventions are mechanical. Over the centuries, many new materials have been found to improve or replace natural substances, and many vital discoveries have been made in medicine and health care.

GLASS

Glass is one of the oldest and most useful of all man-made materials, and is used for everything from vases to bullet-proof screens. The Ancient Egyptians and Mesopotamians knew how to make glass 5000 years ago. But it was not until about 1500 BC that they made glass vases and bowls in any numbers. Bowls were shaped by carving from solid glass or by dipping a sandbag in a tray of molten glass.

By 300 BC, Alexandrian glass-makers had learned how to mould glass. Then in the 1st century BC the Syrians invented the idea of shaping glass by blowing through a pipe into a blob of molten glass. The technique spread rapidly. Bottles and bulbs are still made this way, but machines, not people, normally blow the glass.

A few wealthy Romans had glass windows, but it was not until the 12th century that glass was widely used in windows. Then glass-workers found how to make stained-glass – coloured glass used to assemble beautiful picture windows in churches and cathedrals.

By the late 15th century, Venetian glass craftsmen had learned how to make glass that was almost completely clear, and so were able to make lenses for spectacles, and later telescopes and microscopes.

In the 14th century, it was found that thin, flat glass for windows called *crown glass* could be made by spinning glass out from a large blob on the end of a rod.

All the same, glass windows remained expensive, and it was only in the 1800s that ordinary people had glass windows in their houses. Then glass was mass-produced for the first time, and windows in big houses became large and clear and gardeners built greenhouses. Joseph Paxton built the Crystal Palace in London, in 1851, with 300,000 sheets of glass held together in an iron frame.

Spectacles The idea of using glass lenses to improve eyesight was described by the English monk and scientist Roger Bacon in the 13th century. Some people in Venice and China may have worn convex spectacles for close work around this time. Concave lenses, used to help short-sighted people see long distances, appeared in the 15th century.

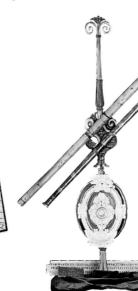

The telescope was probably invented by Dutch spectacle-maker Hans Lippershey in 1608. Italian scientist Galileo made his own (above) and, in 1609, used it to look at the sky. He was the first man to observe Saturn's rings and four of Jupiter's moons.

VACCINATION

Vaccines protect people from diseases caused by viruses and bacteria by using the body's own defence system. They work by giving a dose of the disease too small to do any harm, but big enough to spur the body into making special proteins called *antibodies* which attack the germs. These antibodies stay in the body ready to fight off the germs of a real infection.

The idea stems from a way of fighting smallpox called *variolation* long known in Turkey and brought to Britain in the early 18th century by Lady Mary Wortley Montagu. At the time, smallpox was a terrible disease and many died from it or were left scarred for life by the terrible blisters. Variolation involved deliberately scratching into the skin some fluid taken from the blisters of someone with a mild dose of smallpox. It worked, but all too often those treated this way caught smallpox for real and died.

Then English country doctor Edward Jenner made a vital discovery. He had noticed that milkmaids who had been infected with cowpox, a mild kind of pox caught by cows, were immune to small-pox. In 1796, he scratched some fluid from a cowpox blister into the skin of a boy called James Phipps. It was soon clear that James was immune to smallpox. In 1798, Jenner published his ideas on *vaccination* (the word comes from the Latin *vacca*, meaning cow), and within 20 years, millions of people were being vaccinated all over the world.

Later in the 19th century, Louis Pasteur found how to make vaccines against other diseases by growing germs on special *cultures* (mould beds) to weaken them. In this way, he made a vaccination against cholera in 1880, anthrax in 1881 and rabies in 1885. Now there are vaccines against most of the world's worst infectious diseases, including diphtheria, tuberculosis and polio.

ANTIBIOTICS

Antibiotics are substances that kill germs. Originally most were natural substances found in mould. Now many are made synthetically.

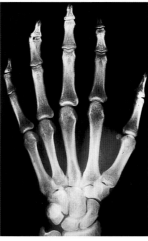

The idea of vaccination or inoculation against infectious disease was discovered in 1796 by Edward Jenner of Gloucestershire. Jenner had noticed that milkmaids who were exposed to the cow disease cowpox became immune to the much more terrible smallpox – which is why they were renowned for their beauty and fair complexions.

X-rays pass through paper, wood and flesh, but not metal or bone. Within months of their discovery in 1895 by Wilhelm Röntgen, they were being used by doctors to 'see' inside the body. They are still widely used, but they are now being superseded by scanners (page 197). X-rays are also used to treat cancer in radiotherapy.

(page 197)

The first antibiotic was *penicillin*, discovered in 1928 by Alexander Fleming at St Mary's Hospital, London. He noticed how penicillin mould killed off certain bacteria. By 1940, Florey and Chain at Oxford had made it a usable drug.

During World War II, both penicillin and another antibiotic, *streptomycin* (effective against tuberculosis), were mass-produced. Now there are many kinds, including *broad-spectrum* drugs like *tetracycline,* used against a wide range of germs, and more specific kinds such as *polymyxin,* effective against a certain class of bacteria. Unfortunately, many are less effective than they once were because resistant strains of germ have evolved.

PASTEURIZATION

Pasteurization is a way of treating food, especially milk, to kill off germs. The idea was developed by Louis Pasteur in the 1860s. At the time, the processes that made wine and vinegar ferment and milk turn sour were thought to be chemical. Pasteur found they only took place in air, because germs in the air were causing the changes. In 1862, he found that heating milk to exactly 63°C for 30 minutes, then cooling it rapidly, killed the germs without affecting the flavour of the milk much. Milk treated this way would keep longer. Nowadays, pasteurization helps kill off tuberculosis and brucellosis germs.

PLASTIC

Plastic is one of the most remarkable of all materials made by people, used in everything from spaceships and car parts to bottles and artificial body parts. What gives plastic its special quality is the shape of its molecules. With only a few exceptions, plastics are made from long organic molecules called *polymers*, made up from lots of smaller molecules called *monomers*. Polythene, for instance, is a chain of 50,000 tiny molecules of ethene.

A few polymers occur naturally, such as cellulose, the main woody substance in plants. In the mid-1800s, people already knew that cellulose could be made into a brittle substance cellulose nitrate. In 1862, British chemist Alexander Parkes discovered that by adding camphor, he could make cellulose nitrate tough but bendy, and possible to mould. But he was poor at marketing his *Parkesine*.

In 1869, however, an American called John Hyatt created a similar substance, which was used instead of ivory in manufacturing billiard balls. He called it *celluloid*. When celluloid was taken up to make photographic film by George Eastman and Kodak in 1889, its success was assured.

Now there are hundreds of different plastics, including Plexiglass, polythene, PVC and cellophane, each with its own special uses. One problem with plastics, though, is that it is very hard to dispose of them, since they do not naturally rot and they melt when burned, often emitting harmful fumes.

Bakelite was invented by Leo Baekeland in 1909 by treating phenol resin made from coal tar with formaldehyde. Bakelite was the first entirely synthetic plastic. Like earlier plastics, it could be moulded, but once moulded it set hard and was heatproof. Bakelite was a good electrical insulator, so was at once used for switches and plugs. It was also used to make radios, telephones, kitchenware and much more.

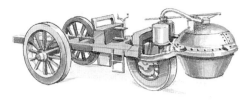

CARS

Cars are the main means of transport for billions of people around the world, and they dominate our cities in a way that no other machine does. There are now enough cars in the world to make a traffic jam stretching right round the world ten times.

THE FIRST CARS

Nicolas Cugnot built a steam-powered vehicle (above) as long ago as 1769. But Cugnot's steam engine was far too heavy and slow to be practical. A century later, in 1862, another Frenchman, Etienne Lenoir, created the light and powerful *internal combustion engine* – that is, an engine like those in modern cars. Lenoir set up his engine in an old horse cart so that it drove the wheels via a chain round the axles. The idea worked so well that soon the first experimental cars were being built – many, like Lenoir's based on horse carts, which is why early cars were called 'horseless carriages'. In 1885, the first cars to be sold to the public (below) came out of the workshop of Karl Benz in Mannheim, Germany.

PETROL POWER

Most cars are powered by a petrol engine. This works by burning *fuel* (a mix of petrol and air) inside tubes in the engine called *cylinders*. When the fuel is *ignited* (set on fire) by a big electric spark, it swells rapidly and forces a drum called the *piston* down the cylinder. The piston then turns a rod called the *crankshaft*, and this turns the wheels via a series of gears (page 157). On most cars, the engine only turns two wheels – usually at the front – called the driving wheels. On cars designed for going off roads, the engine drives all four wheels. This is called *four-wheel drive*.

To improve performance and reduce fuel consumption, many modern cars include electronics and computers to time the spark perfectly, and to deliver just the right mix of fuel.

The big problem with cars is the *exhaust* – that is, all the hot gases left over after the fuel is burned, blown out through the *exhaust pipe*. Car exhausts are by far the biggest source of air pollution in most cities, chucking out poisonous gas, dirt and gases that may help cause global warming (page 99). Many new cars have *catalytic converters* in the exhaust to filter out some of the poisonous gases.

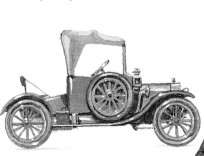

The 1885 **Benz,** *the first-ever production car, was actually a tricycle.*

HIGH-PERFORMANCE CAR

High-performance cars are recognizable from their sleek shape. The shape is *aerodynamic*, to help the car slice through the air with the minimum resistance. The powerful engine is not in the front as in ordinary cars, but in the middle or at the back to keep the car stable and deliver power straight to the back wheels. *Fuel injectors* squirt the right dose of fuel into the cylinders and *electronic ignition* ensures the spark is well-timed. Squat *low-profile* tyres keep plenty of rubber in contact with the road for maximum grip when accelerating or braking.

A high-performance car – the Ferrari 348tb.

Model T Ford *The age of popular motoring began in 1908 with the Model T Ford, the first mass-produced car.*

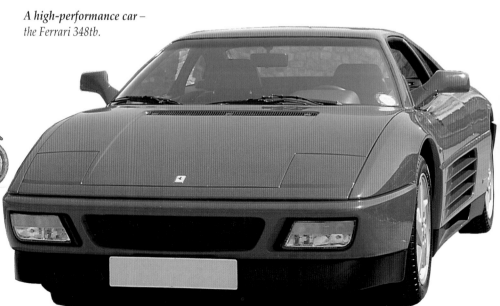

RAILWAYS

The coming of railways 150 years ago changed the world forever, enabling goods and passengers to be carried long distances in vast quantities, and allowing cities to grow as never before. Now many people believe they may be the best form of transport for the future, because of the harm cars do to the environment.

Replica of George Stephenson's **Rocket** *locomotive of 1829.*

TRACKS

Railway trains all run on steel rails that guide the wheels. Usually, the wheels have a lip or *flange* that sits inside each rail and keeps the train on the track. The wheels are made of steel so that trains can carry heavy weights at high speeds.

In the past, tracks were laid in short sections, and train passengers could often hear the click of the wheels as they ran from one section to another. Modern track-laying vehicles weld the track into one *continuous rail* to give a smooth ride. The tracks are usually supported on beams of wood or concrete called *sleepers*. Trains change track at *points*.

ENGINES AND CARRIAGES

Nearly all trains have a *locomotive* to provide the power and a series of carriages for carrying passengers or trucks for carrying goods. The first locomotives were steam-powered. These burned coal to boil water into steam to drive the wheels. Most now have electric or diesel motors (like lorries), except in places like China where coal is so plentiful that steam trains make sense. Diesel trains carry their fuel with them. Electric trains pick up power either from a live rail lying parallel to the track and called the third rail, or through an arm called a *pantograph* from overhead cables.

THE FIRST TRAINS

Railways date back 4000 years to the Babylonians, who used to push carts along grooved stones. But it was not until 1804, when Englishman Richard Trevithick ran a steam locomotive on rails for the first time that the railway age really began.

The earliest steam railways were built to carry coal from mines. In 1825, though, railway pioneers George Stephenson and his son Robert opened the first passenger-carrying railway, the Stockton and Darlington. Five years later, a line opened between Liverpool and Manchester and launched a spectacular boom in railway building that by 1855 had created vast rail networks all over Europe and North America.

HIGH SPEED TRAINS

The future of railways has been transformed by the introduction of high-speed electric trains. High-speed trains run on specially-built tracks and can carry passengers at speeds of 350km/h or more. The first high-speed train was the Japanese Bullet Train or Shinkansen, built in 1964, which hurtles the 1176km from Tokyo to Fukuoka in under 6 hours. In Europe, France has its Train à Grand Vitesse (TGV). It is planned to build huge networks of these trains all over Europe to carry people from city to city at speeds which rival aeroplanes.

Further in the future, trains may not run on wheels at all but glide smoothly at incredible speeds just above a special track, held there by the force of magnetic repulsion (page 153). The force of magnetic repulsion also propels these *magnetic levitation* trains (*maglevs*) along. Experimental maglevs are already in operation.

Steam train in the heyday of steam in the 1930s.

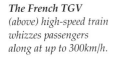

The French TGV (above) high-speed train whizzes passengers along at up to 300km/h.

Some maglevs (right) may be propelled by jet engines like those of aeroplanes.

BALLOONING

People flew first not in aeroplanes but in balloons filled with gas lighter than air. On 21 November 1783 in Paris, two men were lifted into the air by a huge paper balloon filled with hot air made by the French Montgolfier brothers. A fortnight later, two others had flown over Paris in a rubberized silk balloon filled with hydrogen gas. In the 1800s, flying in hydrogen balloons was a fashionable sport. When the idea of ballooning revived in the 1960s, however, people used a cheaper, safer hot-air system.

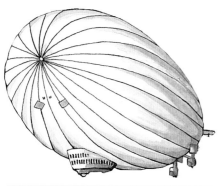

AIRSHIPS

The problem with balloons was that they floated where the wind took them. So in 1852, Frenchman Henri Giffard made a cigar-shaped balloon and fitted steam-powered propellers to make it *dirigible* (steerable). Powered with petrol engines and given a rigid frame, these 'airships' became the first large aircraft. By the 1920s, vast airships were floating people across the Atlantic in the style and comfort of an ocean liner. But airships were doomed by a series of disasters caused by the inflammable hydrogen gas.

AIRCRAFT

Aircraft are the fastest of all means of transport, able to reduce journeys that would take days by road or sea to just a few hours. 50 million or more people travel each year from the world's busiest airports, such as Chicago's O'Hare and London's Heathrow.

JET AIRLINERS

Jet airliners have transformed air travel since they were introduced in the 1950s. They are not only fast and quiet (on the inside), but carry passengers smoothly high above the weather in special *pressurized* cabins to protect them from the low air pressure at this height.

On the surface, the jet airliners of today look similar to those of the 1950s, but there are substantial changes. *Airframes* (aircraft bodies), for instance, are built using strong, light new materials, like titanium, plastics and carbon fibre. Computer-designed wings cut fuel costs and improve safety. And powerful jet engines mean airliners such as the Boeing 747 'jumbo jet' can carry 400 or more passengers at a time.

Control systems The jets of today have sophisticated electronic control and navigation systems to keep them flying safely on course. *Autopilots* were introduced as long ago as the 1930s to keep planes flying straight and level automatically. By the 1950s, they held a course between *radio beacons* on the ground. Now advanced electronic guidance systems continually monitor the plane's position and guide the pilot even during landing and take-off.

In the past, the wing flaps that control the plane's direction were altered directly by the pilot via levers and cables. Most jet airliners are now *fly-by-wire*. This means the flaps are moved by hydraulic motors activated electrically. Some planes are *fly-by-light*. This means the flaps are controlled by light signals sent along optical fibres.

The pilot and crew control the plane from the *flight deck*. In the airliners of the 1980s flight decks had a daunting array of dials and switches, most duplicated for the benefit of the co-pilot. Now, as computers take over more and more functions, most airliners have *glass cockpit*s. In these, all the dials and switches are being replaced by neat screens on which the pilot can change the display at the flick of a button.

Blériot Type XI The first controlled, powered flight with a winged aircraft was made by the American Wright brothers in December 1903. Within six years, Louis Blériot flew his Type XI 41km across the English Channel.

HOW WINGS WORK

An aircraft's wings are lifted by the air flowing above and beneath as they slice through the air. Because the top of the wing is curved, air pushed over the wing speeds up and stretches out. This stretching of the air reduces its pressure. Underneath the wing, the opposite happens and pressure here rises. The result is that the wing is sucked from above and pushed from below. Just how much lift this creates depends on the angle and shape of the wing and how fast it slips through the air. Aircraft get extra lift for climbing by increasing airspeed and dropping the tail so that the main wings cut through the air at a steeper angle.

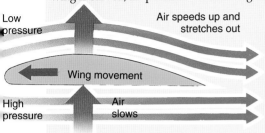

Low pressure

Air speeds up and stretches out

Wing movement

High pressure

Air slows

Small helicopters like this are ideal for everything from traffic-watching to crop-spraying.

CONTROL FLAPS

Aircraft are controlled in the air by hinged flaps on the trailing (rear) edges of the wings and tail. On the simplest planes, there are *elevator* flaps on the *tailplane* (rear wings) to *pitch* the plane nose-up or down to climb or dive. There are *ailerons* on the trailing edge of main wings to *roll* it to either side, dipping one wing or the other. And there is an upright *rudder* on the *tailfin* to *yaw* it to port (left) or starboard (right).

To climb, the pilot pulls back on a *control column* in the cockpit; to dive, the pilot pushes it forward; to roll, the pilot tilts the column. Swivelling a foot bar controls the rudder. Like a bicycle, planes bank into turns, so the pilot uses control column and rudder together.

On jet airliners, there are many other flaps besides the basic aileron, elevator and rudder. Most, for instance, have *spoilers* like big doors on top of the main wings to slow the plane down as it lands. The spoilers also help control roll. Most jet airliners also have *high-lift* flaps on the front of the wing that swing down to give extra lift for take-off.

HELICOPTERS

Able to fly straight up and down, hover for minutes in one place and land in a space just a few metres across, helicopters are the most versatile of all aircraft. The key to their success is in the whirling rotor blades on top. The rotor blades cut through the air just like the wing of an ordinary plane to lift the helicopter in the air. They also haul it along like the propeller on piston-engined planes. The tail rotor makes sure the rotors spin and not the helicopter.

Helicopters take great skill to fly, for they have three main controls, not two as conventional aircraft have – a rudder, *collective pitch* and *cyclic pitch*. To go up or down, the pilot uses the collective pitch control to alter the angle or *pitch* of the blades. To fly forwards or backwards, or bank into a turn, the pilot uses the cyclic pitch control to tilt the whole rotor in the direction the pilot wants to go.

JET ENGINES

In the early days of flight, aircraft were driven by spinning propellers turned by piston engines little different from those in cars. Nowadays, all but the smallest aircraft are powered by jet engines which can propel even big airliners along at speeds of up to 2200km/h, – twice the speed of sound.

The simplest jets, called *turbojets*, work by pushing a jet of hot air out the back to thrust the plane forward. Engines like these are used on the supersonic airliner Concorde and fast military planes. But most airliners use quieter, cheaper-to-run *turbofans*, which combine the hot air jet with the draught from a whirling, multi-bladed fan to give extra thrust at low speeds.

Military jets like these F18 Hornets travel so fast that the pilot cannot afford to glance down, so information is projected on glass before his or her eyes.

Concorde is the world's only supersonic airliner – that is, the only airliner that can fly faster than sound. In fact, it can fly at Mach 2.25, which is 2.25 times the speed of sound. But its turbojet engines are very noisy and burn up a great deal of fuel. It also has to fly so high that it may well be disturbing the world's ozone layer (page 99).

SHIPS

People have travelled on rivers and oceans in ships for over 40,000 years, and ships have played a crucial role in history. Ships still carry most of the world's trade, and, all the over the world, they ferry thousands of people across water every day.

EARLY BOATS

Some early boats were made by burning the heart of a log then hollowing it out. Lighter, easier to handle but less robust canoes were made by stretching animal skins over a wooden frame, like the coracles still seen on Welsh rivers, or by sealing basketwork with bitumen, as they still do today in the Iraqi *gufa*. In Mesopotamia, where there were vast reed beds in the swamps, boats were made from bundles of reeds.

4000 years ago, the shipbuilders of Ancient Egypt were making ships over 40m long by interlocking 1000 or more small planks of wood, lashed together with tough grass rope. By 1000 BC, Phoenician traders were braving the Atlantic Ocean in stout sea-going ships from long planks of cedar of Lebanon, held together with wooden ribs.

DUG-OUTS TO DIESELS

No-one really knows when boats were first used, but we know that the Aborigines arrived in Australia at least 50,000 years ago and other people spread through the Pacific Islands about the same time. So they must have had quite sophisticated, ocean-going boats as long ago as this.

The oldest remains of boats, however, are around 10,000 years old, like the 4m long canoe dug out of pine found at Pese in Holland. These boats were driven along with paddles. Sails may have been used on the reed trading boats of Mesopotamia by 5000 BC; wooden sailing ships were plying up and down the Nile in Egypt at least

5500 years ago. 2500-3000 years ago, the Egyptians, Phoenicians, Greeks and Chinese had large fleets for trading and for war.

For a long while, merchant vessels, such as the Mediterranean round ship, used sails, while military ships used banks of rowers to help them move fast in any direction. Only in the 17th century did these oared *galleys* finally give way to sail. In 1787, the first iron boat was built. Six years later, the Marquis d'Abbans built the first steam boat. By 1900, nearly all new ships were iron-hulled and steam powered. Now steam, in turn, has given way to diesel engines.

The lateen sail (left) The earliest sailing boats had square sails and depended on a following wind. By AD 200, boats like the Arab dhow of today had triangular lateen sails. By changing its angle, sailors could use winds from the side as well as behind.

Medieval trader (right) For 1000 years or more, merchants' ships changed little. They were steered by an oar over the side, and rarely had more than two sails. But around 1200, the steering oar was replaced by a hinged rudder at the stern (the rear end) making the boat much more manoeuvrable. At the same time, more sails and up to three masts were added. A mixture of square and lateen sails meant they could sail with winds from many directions. By the 15th century, Spanish, Portuguese and Italian explorers like Vasco da Gama and Columbus were using light, fast boats called caravels to make epic voyages of discovery across the oceans.

POWERED SHIPS

The first commercially successful steamship was William Symington's 17m canal steamer, the *Charlotte Dundas*, launched on the Forth and Clyde Canal in Scotland in 1801. Like all early steamships, the *Charlotte Dundas* was driven by paddle wheels. Then, in 1836, Francis Smith and John Ericsson each invented the *screw propeller* and this proved crucial to the steamship's success. Iron hulls and steam power meant there was practically no limit to the size of ships, and for the next 100 years, they got steadily bigger and bigger. From 1900 on, the Parsons steam turbine engine drove them even faster. Passenger liners of the 1930s and 40s, like the *Queen Mary* and the *Queen Elizabeth*, were gigantic floating palaces. The *Queen Mary* was over 80,000 tonnes and could carry over 2000 passengers. Nowadays ships are powered mainly by diesel engines, and have become increasingly automated, with giant 300,000 tonne oil-carrying supertankers being sailed by a crew of less than 20.

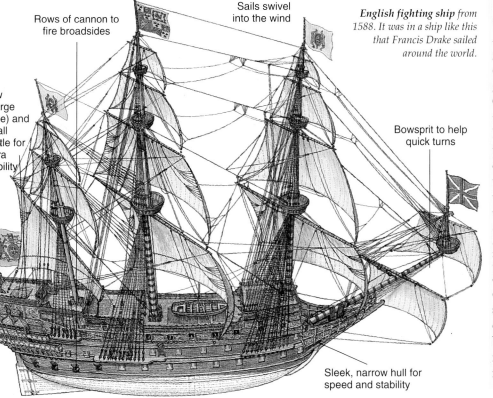

Rows of cannon to fire broadsides

Sails swivel into the wind

English fighting ship from 1588. It was in a ship like this that Francis Drake sailed around the world.

Bowsprit to help quick turns

Sleek, narrow hull for speed and stability

GALLEONS

As Spanish colonies in the New World grew in the 1500s, huge sailing ships called *galleons* sailed the Atlantic, carrying gold and other treasures to Spain. Galleons were magnificent sights, with their colourful flags and ornate carvings. Dozens of sails flew from three tall masts, tall *castles* towered at either end and they could weigh over 1000 tonnes. Galleons were also heavily armed with cannon to ward off attacks from English pirates. Yet when the Spanish sent a vast *armada* (fleet) to invade England in 1588, they proved no match for the English ships. English ships were much faster, lighter and sleeker. They had rows of cannons down each side. In battle, the ship turned side-on to aim all these cannon at the enemy to fire *broadsides*. For 300 years, broadsides remained the standard battle method, and later ships had row upon row of cannon to fire at once.

CLIPPERS

Perhaps the most spectacular of all sailing ships were the *clippers* of the 1800s (right). They got their name because they tried to clip time off as they raced to get their cargoes of Indian and China tea first on the market in England and America. Clippers had small hulls and huge areas of sail to make the most of the wind. Some could sail at 30 knots (60km/h) or more. In 1866, the clippers *Taeping*, *Serica* and *Ariel* raced 25,700km in 99 days with the new tea crop from Foochow in China to London.

INTO THE WIND

Sailing ships can sail into the wind because the wind does not push the sail so much as suck it. The sail is a bit like an aircraft's wing (page 171). As the wind blows around the curve of the sail, it speeds up and its pressure drops, creating suction – just as above an aircraft wing – as long as the sail is kept at the right angle. The effect is to suck the boat forward.

NUCLEAR ENERGY

Locked within the nucleus of every atom are enormous amounts of energy. Nuclear reactors in power stations release this energy by splitting atoms of uranium or plutonium.

NUCLEAR WASTE

Every stage of the nuclear process creates dangerous radioactive waste. Exposure to this waste can cause cancer, mutations and even sudden death. The deadly radioactivity eventually fades to nothing, but this may take 80,000 years. All but the most radioactive liquid waste is pumped out to sea; gaseous waste is vented into the air. A stockpile of solid waste is now building up while scientists throughout the world debate what to do with it. Some advocate sealing it underground; others say it is safer to store it above ground where it can be watched.

NUCLEAR FISSION

Like coal-fired and oil-fired power stations, nuclear power stations use steam to drive turbines that generate electricity. The difference is that nuclear power stations get the heat to make steam by splitting atoms of uranium rather than by burning coal or oil. The process is called *nuclear fission*, because it is the atomic nucleus that is split. Scientists hope one day to release energy by *nuclear fusion* – that is, by fusing nuclei together, which is what happens in the Sun.

When an atom is split, it shoots out gamma rays, neutrons and intense heat. In an atom bomb, all this energy is released in a tiny fraction of a second. In a nuclear reactor, *control rods* ensure energy is released gradually over several months. The control rods absorb some of the neutrons before they split other nuclei apart.

Most reactors use *isotopes* of uranium-235. These are special atoms of uranium with 235 protons and neutrons in their nucleus, rather than the basic 238. But the fuel elements in the reactor are usually small pellets of uranium dioxide in thin tubes separated by *spacers*. 3kg of uranium fuel provides enough energy to supply electricity to a city of 1 million people for a day.

Chain reaction Nuclear fission depends on a chain reaction. When the nucleus of a uranium fuel atom is hit by a neutron, it splits, releasing energy in the form of heat. It also sets free two or three neutrons which shoot away and collide with other uranium nuclei. The collision splits these nuclei too, unlocking more energy and fast-moving neutrons. And so the process goes on. Breeder reactors work by encouraging the released neutrons to join certain uranium nuclei to create plutonium.

Control rods slow the process by absorbing neutrons

Steam drives turbines to generate electricity

Water or gas may be used to draw heat from the fuel, and create steam

Uranium fuel rods give heat

A moderator such as graphite slows down the neutrons so they hit more nuclei

REACTOR TYPES

There are various kinds of nuclear reactor. The first reactors, *N-reactors*, were designed to make plutonium for bombs. *Magnox* reactors make plutonium and electricity. *Pressurized Water Reactors* (PWRs) came originally from nuclear submarines and are now the most widely used kind. Unlike *Advanced Gas Reactors* (AGRs), PWRs can be built in factories. *Breeder reactors* create more fuel than they burn, but in a much more radioactive form.

Spent fuel (above) is sent for reprocessing in special containers. Reprocessing does not cut waste, but makes new fuel and plutonium for nuclear bombs, leaving highly radioactive liquid waste.

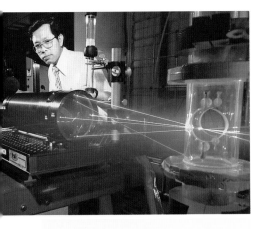

LASERS & HOLOGRAMS

Laser light is the brightest light known, brighter even than the Sun. Lasers create a pencil-thin beam so intense it will punch a hole through steel, and so straight and narrow it can be aimed precisely at a mirror on the moon, 384,401km away.

HOW LASERS ARE USED

Lasers are used in a huge number of ways, apart from spectacular light shows. Geologists, for instance, bounce them off satellites for a perfect measure of how the continents are moving. Doctors use them for delicate eye surgery and to cut bloodlessly into the body for surgery. Compact disc and video disc players rely on laser light to pick up the fine indentations on the disc that carry the recording. The military have X-ray lasers that can blow apart enemy missiles.

LASER LIGHT

Inside a laser there is a tube containing a mixture of gases such as helium and neon and a liquid or a solid crystal such as ruby. *Gas lasers*, such as argon lasers, give a low-powered beam for delicate work such as eye-surgery. *Chemical lasers* use liquid hydrogen fluoride to make intense beams for weapons.

Projecting into the tube are two electric terminals which create an electric spark. The spark gives extra energy to the atoms of the lasing material and excites them into firing off photons – little bursts of light (page 160). The photons shoot off through the lasing material in all directions,

hitting other atoms and making them fire off photons too. Soon there are billions of identical photons zooming around within the tube.

Mirrors at either end, however, reflect photons moving straight up and down the tube so that they zoom back and forth again and again, gathering more photons as they go. One of the mirrors is designed to let a fraction of the photons through and after a while they surge through. Immediately, the laser flashes out its intense beam. Some lasers send out a continuous beam. Powerful *pulsed lasers* shoot out a beam at regular intervals.

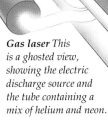

Gas laser This is a ghosted view, showing the electric discharge source and the tube containing a mix of helium and neon.

Lasing begins when a spark excites atoms in the lasing material.

The excited atom emits a photon – a little burst of light.

When photons hit other atoms, they fire off photons too.

Identical photons bounce backwards and forwards between the mirrors at each end.

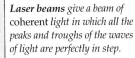

Laser beams give a beam of coherent light in which all the peaks and troughs of the waves of light are perfectly in step.

Most light, like that from an ordinary light bulb, is incoherent. It is a jumble of different wavelengths and spreads out in all directions.

PERFECT LIGHT

Remarkably, a laser beam is perfectly straight – so straight it is much better for making accurate measurements than any ruler. The light is also *coherent*, which means that the light is not only all the same wavelength (colour), but the waves are perfectly in step (page 160).

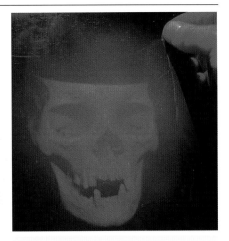

HOLOGRAMS

Holograms are special photographs made with laser light that give a 3D view. They are made by splitting a laser beam in two. One half, called the *reference beam*, goes straight to the film. The other bounces off the object first, breaking up its neat pattern of waves. The film records the way this broken pattern interferes with – differs from – the neat pattern of the reference beam.

ELECTRONICS & COMPUTERS

Electronics is one of the newest of all sciences, less than a century old, yet electronic devices have already become a seemingly indispensable part of our lives, involved in everything from aircraft safety to hi-fi systems.

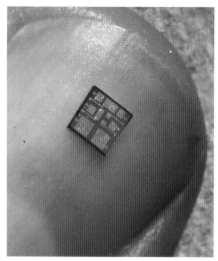

COMPUTER MEMORY
Since electronic circuits can only be on or off, computers work by using a *binary* system to handle data. This is a system that converts all numbers and letters into 1s and 0s, each represented by a binary digit or *bit* inside the computer. Bits are grouped into bytes, so a computer's memory is described in bytes, kilobytes or megabytes. Some of the memory, called the *ROM* (*read-only memory*), is built into the computer in microchips. The RAM (*random-access memory*) takes in new data and instructions as needed. Data can also be stored on magnetic discs, which may be either hard, storing vast amounts of data, or floppy, which store less but can be taken out of the computer and carried around.

ELECTRONIC SIGNALS
Electricity is not only a source of power; it can be used for sending signals as well, and this is the basis of electronics. Electronics is about switching on and off tiny electrical circuits to send a message or control a task.

Inside every electronic device, from televisions to air traffic control systems, there are small circuits continually switching on and off telling the device what to do. In a computer, for instance, combinations of switching circuits represent all the millions of numbers, and other data the computer handles.

Switching devices Electronic systems use a variety of devices for switching the flow of electricity on and off, including resistors and capacitors. But the most important switching devices are transistors.

Transistors are made using *semiconductors*, such as germanium and silicon, whose ability to conduct electricity rises with temperature. Transistors can control current in several ways, including amplifying it (making it bigger), and switching it on and off.

Most transistors are kinds of *triodes*. Triodes and *diodes* were devices originally developed to amplify radio signals. Diodes were valves with two electrodes that allowed current to pass only one way. This meant they could be used to *rectify* (convert) the alternating current (page 152) created by the radio signal into a simple direct current.

A triode has a third electrode which can be used to switch in a much bigger current, so amplifying a faint signal dramatically. This means very low-powered circuits

COMPUTERS AT WORK
It is only recently that computers have become common at work and at home, but they are now an indispensable part of everyday life, and there are few industries or businesses that do not use them in some capacity.

Computers help us run our businesses more economically and safely. They perform complex calculations in a fraction of the time that would have been needed in the past. Aircraft, cars, and ships use computers to monitor things like geographical position, fuel consumption and engine temperature.

Many industries use computers, including book publishing. Computers were used in every stage of the creation of this book.

Modern aircraft cockpit
Today's aircraft use computers in many ways.

FRACTALS

In trying to make computers work better, people have learned a great deal about numbers and systems. One surprising development was the discovery that computers can generate beautiful patterns from simple repeated mathematical calculations. These patterns, called *fractals*, seemed to mimic some of the wonderfully irregular shapes we see in nature such as trees and coastlines. Since these patterns were generated randomly, some people believe we may have underestimated the role of chance in forming natural shapes.

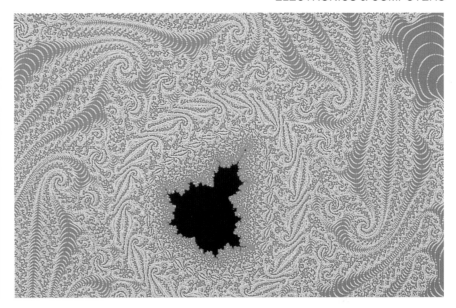

can be used to switch on and off anything from a television screen to a high-powered electric motor.

Chips and circuits Most transistors are now incorporated into *integrated circuits*. This means that all the circuitry is packed inside a single tiny sliver or *chip* of silicon. Since they were first invented in 1971, microchips have become smaller and smaller and incorporate more and more complex circuits. Chips may now be anything from simple circuits to control a clock to complex micro-processors for computers containing a million or more transistors.

ROBOTS

Electronic systems have made robots a reality, and many factories now have robots that paint and weld. Most are simply devices to perform boring or dangerous tasks reliably or safely. A few sophisticated versions have 'senses' such as cameras to guide them in their tasks. But the idea of thinking robots is still far off. Research into Artificial Intelligence (AI) has brought such things as *expert systems*. These are computer programs that help solve a problem such as diagnosing disease that would otherwise need an expert. But they are far from being able to think.

INTERACTIVE SYSTEMS

The earliest computers were little more than calculators; numbers were fed in one end and numbers came out the other. But computers and related devices are now becoming more and more *interactive*. This means the user is able to feed instructions continually into the computer. Interactive video systems, for instance, can store huge amounts of information on CDs. The user decides exactly which route to take into this store of information. Interactive systems include books with sound and animation which the user can delve into at will. Virtual reality systems use touch sensitive gloves to feed hand movements into the computer and to create an illusion in special eye and earpieces.

Virtual reality may one day give us the illusion of reality with scenes projected in front of our eyes that seem to respond to our every movement.

Computer-aided design (CAD) systems help engineers design anything from skyscrapers to microchips by 'building' a trial design on screen.

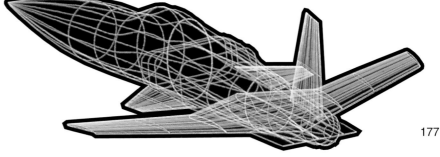

PHOTOGRAPHY

Whether you want an identity picture for a passport or just a happy snapshot for the memory, there is no quicker or simpler way of making an accurate record of a scene than with a photograph taken with a camera.

THE FIRST PHOTOGRAPHS

Cameras are very old, but photography was invented in the 1820s. The first known photograph was taken by Frenchman Joseph Niepce in 1826, but it was very fuzzy and the exposure took eight hours. In 1839, another Frenchman, Louis Daguerre, introduced a way of making sharp photographs in just a few minutes on a copper plate coated with silver. *Daguerreotypes* soon became very popular for portraits – but it was impossible to make a copy of a photograph. The *negative-positive* process used for making repeat prints today (see below right) was invented by Englishman William Henry Fox Talbot in 1839.

CAMERAS

Nearly all photographs are taken with a camera. A camera is essentially a lightproof box with a hole at the front holding a glass lens to project into the camera a bright, sharp image of the world. This image is recorded either on film (see below) or, in video cameras, electronically by light sensitive cells.

The simplest cameras have just a *shutter* to snap the lens open and shut to expose the film briefly to light, and a *winding mechanism* to wind the film into place behind the lens for each picture. But most modern cameras have various electronic circuits to ensure each picture gets just the right amount of light (*autoexposure*) and is perfectly sharp (*autofocus*).

Types of camera There are different cameras to suit different *formats* (sizes) and types of film. Medium-format cameras take 68mm-wide film. Far more popular is 35mm format, which is widely used in *compact* cameras for taking snapshots, and *single-lens reflex* cameras. A new type of film gaining popularity is APS (Advanced Photo System). It enables photographers to take three different shapes of photo, from standard portrait shots to long, narrow landscape pictures.

A single-lens reflex camera has a viewfinder that shows the user exactly the same view that will appear on film. The lens can also be swapped for another to give a wide view (*wide-angle lens*) or magnify the subject (*telephoto lens*).

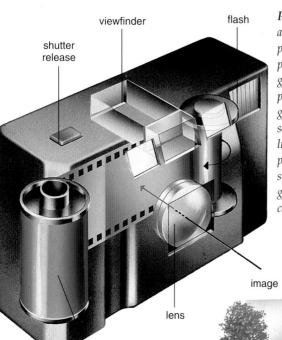

viewfinder

flash

shutter release

image

lens

film

Photographs on film Photos for prints are usually made by a negative-positive process. In a black and white photo, the picture is made up from millions of tiny grains of blackened silver salts. The picture is darkest where there are most grains. In a negative, light areas in the scene are dark on film. In a positive, light areas in the scene are light in the picture. Colour photos use three layers of silver salts, sensitive to red, blue or green light. These layers are converted to coloured dyes during processing.

1 Exposure When the picture is taken, light subtly alters some of the film grains.

2 Processing To reveal the negatives, the film is developed in chemicals in a lightproof tank to change the altered film grains into silver. More chemicals dissolve away the unaltered grains to fix the image.

3 Enlarging To make a positive print, each negative is placed in an enlarger. This has a lens to project a magnified version of the picture on to white print paper coated with light sensitive grains like film.

4 The print A light in the enlarger is switched on briefly to expose the print paper. The print is then developed and fixed like the film to give the final print.

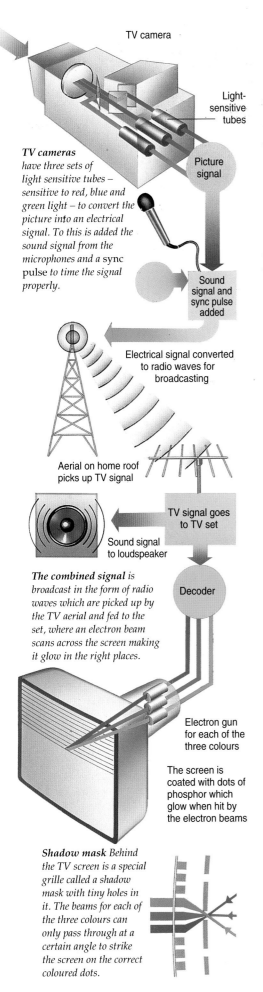

TV camera

Light-sensitive tubes

TV cameras have three sets of light sensitive tubes – sensitive to red, blue and green light – to convert the picture into an electrical signal. To this is added the sound signal from the microphones and a sync pulse to time the signal properly.

Picture signal

Sound signal and sync pulse added

Electrical signal converted to radio waves for broadcasting

Aerial on home roof picks up TV signal

TV signal goes to TV set

Sound signal to loudspeaker

The combined signal is broadcast in the form of radio waves which are picked up by the TV aerial and fed to the set, where an electron beam scans across the screen making it glow in the right places.

Decoder

Electron gun for each of the three colours

The screen is coated with dots of phosphor which glow when hit by the electron beams

Shadow mask Behind the TV screen is a special grille called a shadow mask with tiny holes in it. The beams for each of the three colours can only pass through at a certain angle to strike the screen on the correct coloured dots.

TELEVISION

Television brings the world into our homes every day. All types of programmes, from situation comedies to news as it happens across the world, are shown with such clarity that viewers can almost imagine they are on location.

BROADCASTING

The idea of broadcasting dates back to the 1880s and to the German physicist Heinrich Hertz. Hertz found that a big electric spark sends out waves of electro-magnetic radiation (page 161) called *radio waves*. He then found that radio waves can create a current in another electrical circuit, the *receiver*. Soon Italian inventor Guglielmo Marconi realized that by switching the sending circuit on and off you could send a coded message in radio waves to the receiver. In 1901, he sent a message right across the Atlantic this way.

Later, people learned how to tune receivers to respond only to certain wavelengths. By the 1920s, scientists found a way to vary the waves to mimic sound waves by adding a second, smaller wave

pattern on to the main (*carrier*) wave. This way, speech and music could be transmitted.

In 1926 Scottish inventor John Logie Baird demonstrated a way of changing a picture into a coded electric signal by scanning it in lines into dots of light. In 1929 Vladimir Zworykin demonstrated a camera with a series of tiny cells that responded to light by sending out an electric signal (basically the same as modern TV cameras). This electrical signal could then be broadcast as radio waves, picked up in a receiver, decoded and used to recreate the picture in a TV set.

TV is now usually transmitted by networks of transmitters across the country. The signal can also be bounced off satellites in space to give *satellite TV* or sent down electric cables to give *cable TV*.

A TELEVISION SET

A TV set is basically a *cathode ray tube*. A cathode ray tube is an empty glass tube a bit like a giant light bulb, with a *cathode* (a negative electrical terminal) at the narrow end, and the TV screen at the wide end. The cathode fires out a constant beam of negative particles (*electrons*) towards the TV screen. Wherever it hits, the stream makes the screen's phosphor coating glow.

To build up the picture, the electron beam scans rapidly back and forth across the screen making it glow in certain places – so rapidly that to us it looks as if all the screen glows at once. The picture we see is a pattern of glowing phosphor. In colour TVs, there are three electron guns, one to make red phosphor stripes in the screen glow, one for blue and one for green.

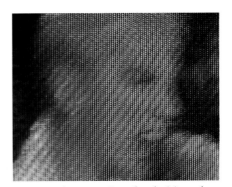

Lines on the screen In early televisions, the electron guns scanned back and forth across the screen just 405 times, giving a fairly fuzzy image. The picture became much sharper when the 625-line system was introduced in the 1960s. Although the lines form too quickly to see with the naked eye, they show up in a photo (above). In future, high definition TV may use 2000 or more lines, giving a picture that looks almost as sharp as film or photographs.

SOUND RECORDING

Years ago, a king would send for the finest musicians in the land and order them to play for him at his court. Today, thanks to sound recording, we can all listen to world-famous artists and orchestras in our own homes.

An engineer (above) *controls the recording, which is made on a multitrack machine.*

WAVES INTO SIGNALS

Sound is produced when objects vibrate in the air. When you press one of the keys of a piano, a hammer strikes a wire, called a string, inside the piano and sets it vibrating. The vibrations make sound waves, which travel to your ear. Sound recording 'captures' sound waves by turning them into magnetic patterns on a tape. When you play back the tape, the magnetic patterns are changed back into sounds, just like those made during the recording.

RECORDING ON TAPE

In a recording studio, sound is recorded on plastic tape, which has a coating of magnetic particles. This is similar to the tape in a cassette, but it is wider and moves at a faster speed. Microphones in the studio pick up each instrument and turn the sounds into electrical signals. An engineer at a control desk adjusts these to the right level for recording. A tape machine records the signals on separate tracks along the tape. If one musician plays a wrong note, he can re-record his part, leaving the others as they are. The multitrack recording is later replayed through the control desk and 'mixed down' to two tracks. These are copied onto a stereo tape recorder. Various mixes may be tried until the effect is satisfactory. The resulting 'master' recording is copied to make the stereo discs and cassette tapes sold in the shops.

How a CD is produced (right)
After the initial recording session (see above) there is a 'mix-down' session. The multitrack tape is played back through the control desk. An engineer mixes the sounds and records the result on another recorder. The tape produced is called the master tape. To make a compact disc, this tape is played and the sound signals sent to a CD cutter, which converts them into pulses of laser light. These etch pits in a blank disc, which is then copied to make CDs for the shops. When played, laser light reflected from the disc is changed into electrical signals. Amplifiers strengthen these signals. Loudspeakers then turn the signals into sounds.

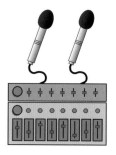

HOW CDS WORK

On a compact disc (CD), sound is recorded as patterns of tiny pits. These are originally etched on to a blank disc by a laser beam. The laser converts electrical signals from tape into light signals. When a compact disc is played, a laser beam is directed onto the disc. The reflected light patterns are converted back into electrical signals, which go through an amplifier to the loudspeakers.

SPIRAL TRACK

The pits on the underside of a CD are arranged in a spiral track, which starts at the centre of the disc and runs towards the outside edge. The track is only 1.6 millionths of a metre wide. It is etched on a disc of aluminium which is given a coating of plastic to protect it from damage.

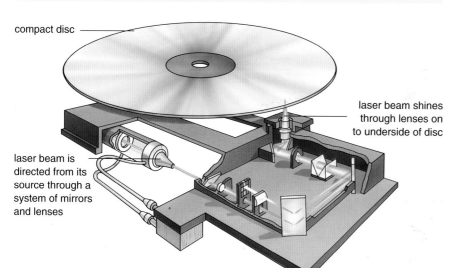

compact disc

laser beam shines through lenses on to underside of disc

laser beam is directed from its source through a system of mirrors and lenses

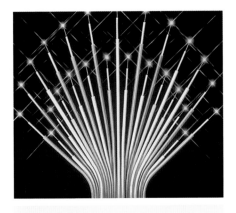

COMMUNICATIONS

Every second of every day, information is passing from one part of the world to another. Radio and television programmes, telephone calls, fax messages, weather and business information all rely on telecommunications.

OPTICAL FIBRES

These thin glass tubes with a plastic coating on the outside are optical fibres. They are taking the place of copper cables in modern telecommunications. They carry signals in the form of laser light.

VIDEOPHONES

The man below is using the kind of telephone we may all have in a few years' time. The videophone enables him to see the person he is talking to. Optical fibres carry more information than copper cables, and part of this can be in picture form.

SPECIAL SATELLITES

Some satellites receive and transmit many different kinds of information, but others have been launched to carry out special tasks. One of these is INMARSAT. Its name is short for INternational MARine SATellite. INMARSAT provides communications links which ships and offshore oil rigs can use to communicate with each other or with radio stations on land. Another special satellite is NAVSTAR, which helps ship and aircraft navigators by transmitting time and position signals. The LANDSAT series of satellites made detailed maps of the Earth's surface. Other satellites are launched to carry out experiments and observations in space.

BOUNCING SIGNALS

Not very many years ago, all this information had to be carried by cables under or over the ground, or be broadcast from terrestrial radio transmitters. Today, the world-wide network of telecommunications depends on satellites. These are placed in orbit above the Earth so that they can 'bounce' radio signals from one part of the world to another.

GEOSTATIONARY ORBIT

Many communications satellites are placed in an orbit called a geostationary orbit about 36,000km above the Earth's surface. At this particular height a satellite travels round the Earth in exactly the same time as it takes for the Earth to spin once. This means that the satellite is always over the same point on the Earth's surface.

RECEIVING & TRANSMITTING

Satellites carry radio receiving and transmitting dishes. A receiving dish is positioned precisely so that it points towards a dish transmitter on Earth. As a communications satellite is always in the same position relative to the Earth, the dishes can be fixed in position. The satellite's receiving dish receives signals from the Earth transmitter and passes them to its own. The satellite's transmitter then sends the signal back to a dish receiver which may be thousands of kilometres away on the Earth's surface. Thanks to satellites, we can see on television events that are happening on the other side of the world a fraction of a second after they take place.

Most satellites (right) *are intended to operate for many years without attention, so they have to have a reliable electricity supply, which they obtain by using solar power. The panels, which look like wings, collect radiation from the Sun and convert it into electricity, which is stored in batteries.*

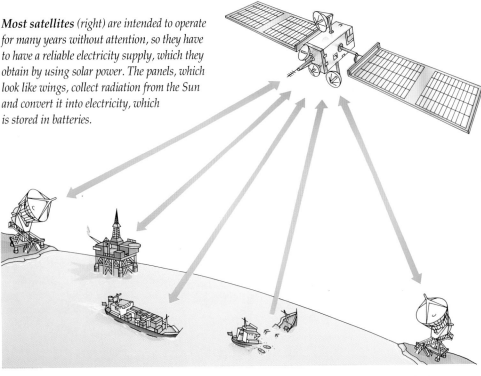

GOVERNMENT

For the last century or so, the world has been divided into countries, each ruled by a government. Governments vary from harsh dictatorships to liberal democracies, but they are all intended to control the particular way the country and its people run their affairs.

KINGS, QUEENS AND EMPERORS

In the past, most societies were ruled by kings, queens or emperors. Often kings were said to have gods as ancestors, and so had the right to rule, like the Pharaohs of Ancient Egypt. In the Middle Ages, Christian kings and queens were thought of as the agents of God, which is why they were crowned in church. In later centuries, powerful kings such as Henry VIII of England and Louis XIV of France were said to rule by divine right. This idea only ended with the English Civil War and the French Revolution.

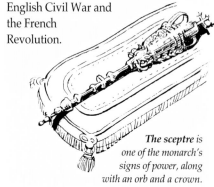

The sceptre is one of the monarch's signs of power, along with an orb and a crown.

IDEAS OF GOVERNMENT

People have been governed by kings and others since the first days of civilization. But modern ideas of government date back to the 1600s when, for the first time, people began to question a king's right to rule, once thought to be god-given.

The English thinker Thomas Hobbes (1588-1679) argued that without government, peoples' lives would be 'solitary, poor, nasty, brutish and short'. Hobbes said they should agree to obey a king who could keep peace between them. He called this agreement a *social contract*.

Later thinkers like Rousseau (1712-78) argued that people should only obey laws if they helped make them. This is the basis of *democracy*, which means rule by the people. The idea of democracy originated in Ancient Greece (page 118), but it was only in the 1800s that countries like Britain began to slowly move towards it.

MODERN DEMOCRACIES

Today, democracy usually means an elected government made up of politicians voted into power every few years by all adults. Most democracies have a written set of laws called a *constitution* setting out how the government should be run. Britain does not have one.

Some democracies, like France, are *republics*. This means the head of state is not a king but an elected *president*. In the USA, the president is very much in charge. In other republics, however, the president is just a figurehead and the country is run by a *chancellor* or *prime minister*.

Britain, Spain and many other democratic countries are still *monarchies* – that is, they have a king or queen. But the monarch's powers are limited and the country is run by a government led by a prime minister. The government is made up from the party with most elected members.

The capitol *The US Congress sits in the Capitol building in Washington DC with the House of Representatives at one end and the Senate at the other.*

SYSTEMS OF GOVERNMENT

Every country has its own system but the government is usually split into three sections: the legislature, the executive and the judiciary. The *legislature* amends laws and makes new ones; the executive puts them into effect; and the judiciary makes sure they are applied fairly. In the UK, the legislature is *Parliament*, with its two houses: the important *House of Commons* made up of members (MPs) elected by the public, and the less important *House of Lords* made up of peers. The executive is the prime minister, cabinet and other ministers.

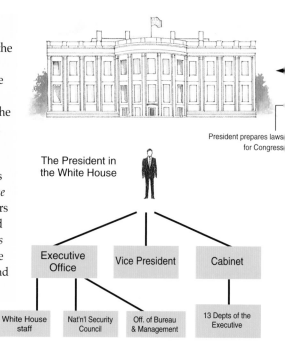

President prepares laws for Congress

The President in the White House

Executive Office — Vice President — Cabinet

White House staff — Nat'n'l Security Council — Off. of Bureau & Management — 13 Depts of the Executive

Autocracies In an autocracy, a single person or small group holds all the power. In Iran, Islamic religious leaders hold power; in others, it is the army. A *dictator* is someone whose word is law, like Hitler in Nazi Germany.

POLITICS

People who stand for election are called politicians. *Left-wing* politicians want to change things, perhaps to make government more democratic or to bring in *socialist* ideas. *Right-wing* politicians want to conserve or keep the system as it is, which is why they are called *conservatives*. Usually politicians with similar views join a group called a party. In most democratic countries, the party with the most votes forms the government.

Political systems Most countries are *capitalist*, which means most things, including industries and businesses, are owned by small groups or individuals. In *communist* countries like China, all property is owned by the community, or rather, the government. *Socialists* believe government should ensure everyone has equal rights, a fair share of money, and good health, education and housing. *Fascists* believe in army discipline and that they and their country are superior to others.

In democracies, governments are chosen by election. In a *general* election, all adults in the country can vote for *candidates* (politicians) who want to be elected. People usually vote by putting a mark next to a name on a list called a *ballot sheet*. Just who is elected depends on the system. In *first-past-the-post* systems like Britain's, only the candidate who receives the most votes in each *constituency* (area) is elected. So if a party loses by just a few votes in every area, it might get no candidates elected at all. With *proportional representation*, the number elected for each party depends on how many of the votes the party got across the whole country.

Campaign *Politicians and their supporters spend a great deal of effort and money to win over voters. This is Republican Bob Dole's 1996 campaign for the US presidency.*

EXTREME GOVERNMENTS

Many countries have oppressive governments – governments that allow a few people to force their will on the rest of the country. They do this in a number of ways. Some use soldiers and tanks. Some use the power of money. Some use secret police and spies to stamp out opposition. Some use television and newspapers to fool people into thinking the 'right' way. This is called *propaganda*. Most oppressive governments use a combination of all these tactics. Communist China is thought to have an oppressive government. So too are countries like Iraq.

South Africa *Black people are in the majority, yet whites ran the government for many years. The first multiracial elections were held in 1994, when Nelson Mandela became President.*

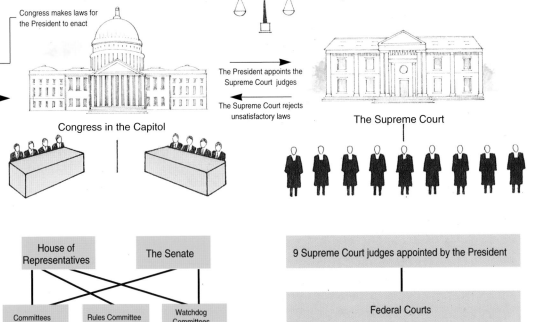

Congress makes laws for
the President to enact

Congress in the Capitol

The President appoints the
Supreme Court judges

The Supreme Court rejects
unsatisfactory laws

The Supreme Court

House of Representatives	The Senate

Committees   Rules Committee   Watchdog Committees

9 Supreme Court judges appointed by the President

Federal Courts

The government of the USA is divided into three arms: the President and the Executive; Congress (the legislature) and the Supreme Court (the judiciary). The Constitution of 1787 split them like this to prevent any part of government becoming too powerful. Each arm of government is provided with a range of checks and balances to keep the others under control. Although the President prepares laws, for instance, only Congress can make them legal. The President can also veto (prevent) Congress's laws unless two-thirds of Congress vote for them.

TRADE & MONEY

Trade dominates our lives. You are making a trade every time you buy a can of drink or a packet of crisps – exchanging something you have (money) for something you want. But trade is also the way industries sell their products, shops sell their goods, countries earn their incomes, and much more besides.

ADAM SMITH
Many ideas on how the market works are based on a book called *The Wealth of Nations*, written in 1776 by Adam Smith (1723-1790). Smith argued that people are naturally selfish. This is a good thing, he said, because everyone looks for the kind of work best for them, and this benefits everyone. So, he implied, if factories are free to make what they want, and people to buy what they want, the 'invisible hand' of the market place would bring wealth and the right goods to everyone.

Government finances The diagrams below show where a government, such as that of the USA, gets its money, and the areas in which it is spent.

THE MARKET
In most countries in the world, trade and money work through *markets*. By markets, economists don't just mean the stalls in the local street, they mean anywhere things are sold. A market could be just the people who buy cans of drink at your local shop, or it could be all the countries that might buy a particular kind of aircraft.

Supply and demand Economists argue that *market economies* – that is all but Communist countries – work by *supply and demand*. In theory, factories, shops and so on make and supply things only if there is a demand for them – that is, people want them. More people want to buy sunglasses, for instance, if it is sunny than if it is raining. So demand varies. The sunglasses factories, on the other hand, will vary how many they make – the supply – according to how many they can sell. If they think they can sell a lot, they take on more workers and make more; if they think they can sell only a few, they lay off workers.

But they must charge the right *price*. If they charge too much, fewer people will want to buy sunglasses. And other factories which can make sunglasses cheaper might succeed in selling them instead. So prices and supply vary all the time according to whether or not people want things.

The theory is the same for anyone who works for a living. Someone who is in great demand

BALANCE OF TRADE
Countries trade with each other to earn money to buy food and things they can't make themselves. Some people favour *free trade*, which means there are no restrictions at all on what goods and services are traded. Others believe that control – such as imposing taxes on foreign goods – is needed to protect home industries from foreign rivals. Most countries use a mixture of both ideas.

Countries measure the success of their trade by their *balance of payments*. This is the difference between the amount they sell abroad (*exports*) and the amount they buy in (*imports*). *Invisible earnings* are payments for services such as banks and hotels. *Visible earnings* are for goods you can pack up, such as coal or radios.

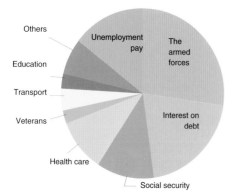

can earn a high income; someone who is not earns much less.

Limitations Although it works in theory, the market idea often fails in practice. Factories, for instance, might not find enough workers to make more products when demand rises. A fall in the market demand, on the other hand, can leave millions of people without a job. Furthermore, if there is just one company supplying the market, the company might keep prices higher than people can really afford simply because there is no-one to undercut it. This is called a *monopoly*.

So governments often 'interfere' with the market. They might give extra money to factories to help them through times of low demand. They might stop people charging too much. Or they might set up an *Office of Fair Trading* to make sure monopolies work fairly.

GOVERNMENTS & ECONOMIES

In most countries, governments play an important role in trade. Just how much varies from country to country. In *centrally*

RAISING MONEY

If someone wants to start a business, they may get money to start by selling *shares* in the business. Anyone who buys a share partly owns the business and gets some of the profits. The value of shares goes up and down according to how well the business is expected to do. People buy shares on the *stock market* in the hope that they may be able to sell them for more at a later date.

*planned economie*s, such as China's, the government owns most industries and decides what to make and sell. In a *private-enterprise econom*y, individuals and firms own industries and adjust how much they make according to the market. Economies such as those of Britain and the USA, however, are *mixed*. This means private firms make things and supply some services, while the government may run things such as trains and power stations. However, in the 1980s and 1990s, several government-run services in Britain were privatized.

Huge sums of money change hands on the world's financial markets, where people gamble by buying shares in the hope they will go up in value.

DID YOU KNOW?
The first coins were in use in Lydia, Turkey, over 2700 years ago.
The pound gets its name because the Anglo-Saxons used a pound (weight) of silver split into 240 coins as money. There were 240 pence in a pound until 1971.
Bank notes were first used by the Chinese in the 11th century.
Tariffs are taxes on imported goods.
In the European Union it is intended that there will be no tariffs on goods transferred between member countries.

MONEY

Money is usually just discs of metal and pieces of paper – and yet you can buy all kinds of things with it. This is because money is basically a promise to pay. If you use money to buy something from someone, they can use this promise to buy something from someone else, and so on. In the past, people used anything as money, from stones and shells to belts and furs. The important thing is that everyone agrees how much the money is worth when you exchange it for anything else.

The paper that banknotes are printed on is worthless; they are simply a promise to pay. Many banknotes have the words, 'I promise to pay the bearer on demand…'. When banknotes were first issued, the bank that issued them promised to swap them for gold. So, in theory, you could exchange the notes for gold. However, most governments will no longer give gold in exchange.

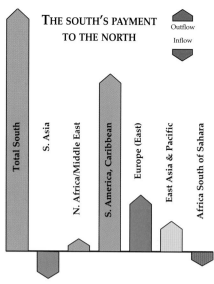

THE SOUTH'S PAYMENT
TO THE NORTH

Outflow
Inflow

Total South
S. Asia
N. Africa/Middle East
S. America, Caribbean
Europe (East)
East Asia & Pacific
Africa South of Sahara

Above the line: money going to the North
Below the line: money going to the South

RICH & POOR COUNTRIES

The world is divided into rich and poor. In Europe, North America, Japan and Australia, there are many poor people, but most people live fairly comfortable lives. But in the rest of the world, including all of Africa and Latin America, most people are desperately poor, and many are starving to death.

THE DEBT PROBLEM

In the 1970s, countries in the North encouraged those in the South to borrow money to build and develop new industries. Paying just the interest on these loans is now costing the South a huge amount of money. On average, poor countries pay 17% interest per year. Indeed, the South is now paying the North $50 billion more in interest payments than the North is giving the South in aid. Africa's debt is more than the continent's entire annual income.

NORTH AND SOUTH

Nearly all the richest countries of the world are in the northern hemisphere, so people talk of the North-South divide when they are talking about rich and poor. The North includes North America, Europe, Japan, and also Australia and New Zealand (which are actually in the southern hemisphere). The South is all the rest of the world.

Nearly everyone in the South is poor, but over one billion people, a fifth of the world's population, live in absolute poverty. It is hard to describe what 'absolute poverty' means, but these people all live in desperate circumstances. They

have no real homes. In cities, they sleep rough or crowd into dirty shacks with no water, no light or heat, and no drains. They never have enough to eat or drink. They suffer from disease. Children die young. In Zambia, for instance, children are 20 times more likely to die before the age of ten than in Germany. And all through their short lives – most adult people in Mali die before they are 50 – they are open to exploitation.

Some 450 million people are starving or badly nourished. Millions die every year from lack of food, or from disease brought on by lack of food in countries such as Ethiopia and Somalia.

INCOME PER PERSON

The widening gap between rich and poor is visible in all too many ways, but economists often look at it in terms of GNP per person – that is, what a person would get if the country's entire income was divided equally among the whole population. People in America earn over $27,700 each, while the people of Mali earn under $300. If you added up all the GNPs of the world, you would find that the North, with less than a quarter of the people, takes over three-quarters of the money, while the South, with over three-quarters of the people, takes less than a quarter of the money.

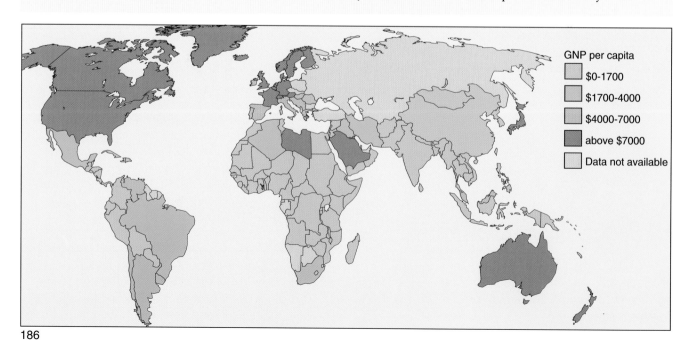

GNP per capita
$0-1700
$1700-4000
$4000-7000
above $7000
Data not available

FAMINE

In 1990, 100 million people were starving all around the world, but especially in countries in the Horn of Africa – Ethiopia, Somalia and Sudan – and in Bangladesh. Many things have been blamed for this. In Ethiopia, for instance, years of drought and war had a devastating effect on food production. Yet even in these countries, farmland is often devoted not to growing food for home consumption but crops for export to the richer countries of the world. Even when food is available, many people cannot afford to buy it.

Drying landscape
Scenes like these, with dying trees and animals scratching in the dust have become increasingly common in North Africa. Many experts feel the Sahara desert is gradually getting bigger. Either way drought spells disaster.

INDUSTRIAL PROGRESS?

Many economists insist the North is rich because of its industries. So countries in the South have been encouraged to borrow money to develop industries of their own. But there are many other reasons for the poverty gap – not least the North's history of exploiting and colonizing the South. So often the attempts to build industries have not lifted people out of poverty, but have done the reverse. In countries like Brazil and Mexico,

people have moved to swelling cities like São Paulo and Mexico City only to live in even more misery than poor country people. And the drive to industrialize quickly means factories are often dangerous to work in and pollute the environment terribly.

Sadly, the South borrowed so much money to pay for these new industries (see left) that the poor countries are actually repaying more in interest than they receive in aid.

DID YOU KNOW?

14 million children in the South die of malnutrition every year; 4.6 million children die of diarrhoea each year; 2 billion people never have enough water to drink; 3 billion people earn less than $500 a year.

The North consumes 80% of world energy, 85% of chemicals, 90% of cars, 25 times as much water, and 200 times as much energy per person.

500 big companies control 70% of world trade and take 30% of its income.

SOLUTIONS?

Many attempts to 'develop' the South have actually only made the problems worse. Large-scale projects such as big dams and power stations bring the Northern sponsors much prestige but can land countries in the South in debt, and also create other problems. The huge Aswan Dam in Egypt, for instance, upset the flood patterns of the River Nile that poor farmers relied on to keep their soil fertile.

Cutting bananas (left) in the Dominican Republic.

***In dry countries,** water is vital for growing crops (above). Here water from an oasis is used for crop irrigation.*

***A miner using a power drill** in a gold mine in Zimbabwe (above).*

***Rio de Janeiro,** Brazil (above),showing the modern city skyline with a shanty town in the foreground.*

LAW

Every society has rules and regulations to help people live together and to keep them in order. In every country in the world nowadays, these rules are written down as laws decided by the government or by religious leaders.

PUNISHMENT

The way in which anyone convicted of a crime is punished varies according to the severity of the crime. In the past, even those only guilty of minor theft could be hanged, and hangings were popular spectacles. For the last 200 years or so, a prison sentence has been usual for all crimes except murder, and there are now millions of people in prison around the world. Capital punishment (the death penalty) for murder is still retained in certain states of the USA, but it is rare now in Europe, where people convicted of murder are usually sent to prison.

SCHOOLS OF LAW

In English-speaking countries, many laws have their roots in *common law*. This is a group of laws passed down from medieval times, based on customs common everywhere rather than just locally. But these laws were often so unjust that in the 15th century the English chancellor issued the first of many decrees to restore *equity* or fairness.

In most European countries, however, the law has its roots in the system of laws created by the Ancient Romans. So these countries are said to have *Roman law* systems.

In socialist countries, the legal system is based on the ideas of Karl Marx and Lenin (page 145). In many Muslim countries, laws are based on the Qur'an.

CRIMINAL AND CIVIL LAW

The laws of most countries today are split into two kinds: criminal law and civil law.

Criminal law is directed against crimes like murder, theft and rape. Just what a crime is varies from country to country, but it is basically an act that either injures someone or someone's property, or offends the government. While the aim of civil law is to settle disputes, criminal law is designed to punish people for crimes.

Typically, anyone accused of a crime is taken to court to be tried. It is usually the government law agencies rather than individuals which bring them to court. This is called *prosecution*. In court, the law agencies who brought them to

IN COURT

People have long wondered how best to find out the true facts about whether the accused person is guilty. In the Middle Ages, people were often tried by *ordeal* – perhaps by burning, drowning or in a battle. The idea was that if they were innocent, God would save them. Now, in *jury trials*, lawyers argue it out with the aid of witnesses and evidence, one speaking for the accused (or the *defendant*) and the other speaking against (the *prosecution*). In theory, the *burden of proof* lies with the prosecution – that is, it is up to the prosecution to prove the defendant is guilty. The defence lawyer does not need to show that his or her *client*, the defendant, is innocent, only that the prosecution's *case* (argument) is weak. At the end of the trial, the jury decides if the prosecution's case has been proved beyond reasonable doubt.

Jury sitting on the Bench

Judge

Witness

Clerk of the Court

Defence

Prosecution

Defendant

EARLY LAWS

The earliest known written laws were created in Mesopotamia by King Ur-Nammu in about 2100 BC. They provided compensation for injuries and punishments for runaway slaves and witches. Much more detailed was the code of King Hammurabi of Babylon recorded in 1758 BC on a stone column found in Susa. They covered everything from punishments for crimes such as murder and theft to debt settlements, marriage contracts, taxes and the price of goods.

Tribal law In many societies, there is no written law. Everyone knows that they should not commit certain deeds. In case of disputes, or if a punishment is needed, a decision may be made by a leader, or a group of elders (older people).

court try to prove they committed the crime. If the proof is not strong enough, they are set free (*acquitted*); if they are found guilty, the judge or magistrate passes *sentence* (decides the punishment).

Civil law is about settling disputes between individuals, such as arguments over contracts (agreements) and injury while at work (called *tort* disputes). People who lose a civil law case are usually ordered to pay compensation.

THE TRIAL

In common-law countries, trials are *adversarial*. This means that there are lawyers on each side, who try to persuade the judge that they are right. The lawyer who is most persuasive wins the case. More serious crimes are tried by a *jury*, a group of 12 or so ordinary people who decide whether the accused is guilty. Then the judge passes sentence.

In Roman-law countries, trials are *inquisitorial*. Here the judge asks all the questions to get at the truth before coming to a decision.

APPEALS

If a person feels wrongly convicted of a crime, or that the sentence was too harsh, the law in many countries allows an appeal for the case to be heard again. But the principle that no-one should be placed in *double jeopardy* (twice accused of the same crime) means the prosecution cannot usually appeal against an acquittal. The appeal system

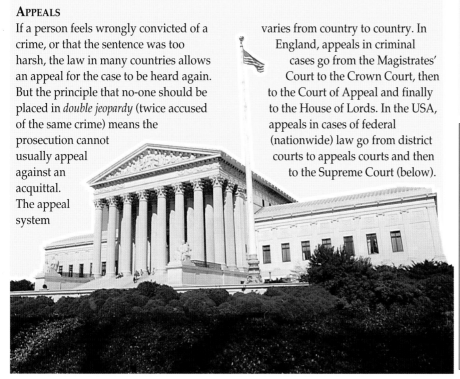

varies from country to country. In England, appeals in criminal cases go from the Magistrates' Court to the Crown Court, then to the Court of Appeal and finally to the House of Lords. In the USA, appeals in cases of federal (nationwide) law go from district courts to appeals courts and then to the Supreme Court (below).

INTERNATIONAL LAW

The countries of the United Nations have agreed a code of international laws to control how they behave to each other. Disputes may be settled by the 15 judges of the International Court of Justice in The Hague in the Netherlands.

DID YOU KNOW?
Under Hammurabi's laws (above left), a child who hit his father would lose the hand that struck.
In England in 1600, many criminals chose to be slowly pressed to death with heavy stones rather than admit guilt – for if they did, their family lost all their property.
In medieval Europe, some criminals were hung, drawn and quartered – that is, hung by the neck, disembowelled while still alive, beheaded and cut into four pieces.

RELIGION

Throughout world history religious beliefs have formed an important part of many people's lives, often to the extent of governing them completely. Today, there are scores of religions around the world, each with its own set of beliefs and values, from Christianity to Taoism.

BUDDHISM

Buddhism is the religion of 300 million people in S E Asia. It is based on the teachings of Prince Siddhartha Gautama, the Buddha, who lived in N E India from 563 to 483 BC. The Buddha was deeply saddened by people's suffering. After long meditation, he came to believe suffering came from desire and from too strong personal attachments. To be free of pain, we must rid ourselves of desire and reach a state of peace called *Nirvana* by following the *eightfold path*: perfect understanding, perfect aims, speech, action, way of life, effort, thinking and meditation. Buddhists believe that after death we are all reborn in a new body. But the course of our lives depends on our *Karma* – the way we behaved in both this and our previous lives.

EARLY RELIGIONS

Most major religions are devoted to a single God or a few gods, but it was not always so. Many early humans may have been *animists*, who believe there is a spirit or god in everything, from animals to rocks. Even today tribal societies in all parts of the world are often animists. They may believe that certain plants, animals or stones are especially important to the safety and happiness of the tribe. These things are called *totems*. They may also believe certain things are to be avoided at all costs. These are *taboos*.

Ancient civilizations like the Egyptians and Greeks had much more organized religious beliefs. They were *polytheistic*. This means that, like animists, they had many gods but the gods were all part of the same story. The Egyptians, for instance, had 2000 gods, but all the major gods were related to Re, the sun god and creator. The major Greek gods were all associated with Zeus and Mount Olympus (page 118). There were also temples devoted to their worship and trained priests who alone knew their secrets. Religion was an important part of the social order.

ISLAM

Islam is one of the world's largest religions with an estimated 1100-1300 million believers. It was founded in Arabia in the 7th century by the Prophet Muhammad, who Muslims believe was the greatest and the last of the prophets sent by God (*Allah* in Arabic).

The word Islam means submission, and Muslims believe they must obey God totally and base their lives on the *five pillars* set out in the holy book, the *Qur'an*. These are: the profession of faith, prayer, payment of a welfare tax, fasting and pilgrimage to the holy city of Mecca in Saudi Arabia.

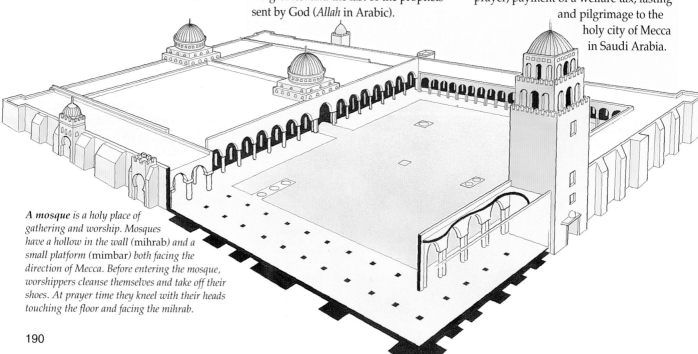

A mosque is a holy place of gathering and worship. Mosques have a hollow in the wall (mihrab) and a small platform (mimbar) both facing the direction of Mecca. Before entering the mosque, worshippers cleanse themselves and take off their shoes. At prayer time they kneel with their heads touching the floor and facing the mihrab.

The Star of David is one of the holy symbols of Judaism. King David (1012-972 BC) was a Jewish national hero. Amongst his many great feats, he is said to have written the holy verses, the Psalms.

JUDAISM

Jews were the first to believe in a single god, Yahweh, 4000 years ago. God made an agreement with their ancestor, Abraham, that he would be their god and they would be his people if they obeyed his 613 laws and spread his word. Generations later, God rescued the Jews from slavery and gave his laws to their leader, Moses. These laws are written in the *Torah* (the holy book) and they guide Jews in all aspects of life and prayer. Jews look forward to the coming of the Messiah (God's anointed one), who, they believe, will bring an age of peace and security.

CHRISTIANITY

Christianity is probably the world's biggest religion with more than 1500 million followers all over the world. Christians believe the Messiah was Jesus Christ, a Jew who lived in the Holy Land (Israel) 2000 years ago. Christ, they believe, was the Son of God. When he was *crucified* to death (nailed to a wooden cross) by his enemies, he rose from the dead to join God in heaven. Christ died, they say, to atone for our sins. After his death, his followers spread his teachings far and wide. There are now three main branches of Christianity: Roman Catholics whose leader is the Pope in Rome; Protestants; and the Eastern Orthodox Church.

RELIGIONS TODAY

Today many of the world's major religions, such as Christianity and Islam, are *monotheistic* – that is, they believe there is just one God. Hindus, however, worship many gods. In China, Confucianists base their lives on the teachings of Confucius (page 122), believing society is only happy and calm if people follow the Will of Heaven. Taoists believe there is a mystical power behind all events, and every person has their own special path. In Japan, Shintoists believe they find strength and wealth by worshipping *kami* (holy energy).

RELIGIOUS STRIFE

Over the centuries, many people have been persecuted for their religion. Early Christians such as St Sebastian were *martyred* (killed for their beliefs), while during the Reformation, Protestants and Catholics slaughtered and tortured each other – most notoriously on St Bartholomew's Day, 1572, when the French Protestant *Huguenots* were massacred.

Religion has also been at the heart of many bitter conflicts throughout history, including the Crusades (page 127) and the troubles in Ulster (page 205).

HINDUISM

Hinduism is one of the world's oldest religions, founded 5000 years ago. It is also one of the most complex. Hindus worship many different gods, but they all believe in *dharma*, which is the right way to live. Like Buddhists, they also believe

we all have past lives. If our lives were good, we are born again in a higher state; if they were bad, we are born as animals or insects. By following the dharma we may reach the perfect state of *Moksha* and so never need to be born again.

DID YOU KNOW?

There are over 11 million Jews living outside Israel and 3.5 million living in Israel.

The Hindu holy text, the Mahabharata is, with 200,000 verses, the longest poem ever written.

Islam forbids Muslims to portray plants or animals, so they decorate things with geometric and other shapes.

William Tyndale was burned in 1535 for translating the Bible into plain English.

Jains of India will not take any form of life. They don't eat meat or fish and most will not eat eggs. Jain priests sweep paths to avoid stepping on insects.

Three million Muslims visit the holy city of Mecca in Saudi Arabia every year on a pilgrimage.

Café was once only French for coffee; now it is also English for a cheap place to eat out.

LANGUAGES

There are over 5000 languages spoken in the world, each with its own words, sounds and grammar. Some, like English, are spoken by many millions of people all around the world. Others, like Trumai in Venezuela, are spoken by less than 100.

NEW WORDS

New words are being adopted all the time. Some are just new ways of using old words; young black New Yorkers shortened *definitive* to *def* to coin their own word for something good. Some new words are made up to describe a new invention. The word *laser*, for instance, comes from the initials of Light Amplification by Stimulated Emission of Radiation. Many scientific and technical words are based on Latin and Greek words – *television* is simply *vision*, with the Greek word *tele*, meaning *far*.

New words often come from foreign languages. In the early 1600s, English gained many new words as explorers ventured overseas. In 1977, the French were so worried about how many English words were being used in France that the government banned them from official documents.

FIRST WORDS

Some people say the first words were grunts of love between people. Some say they were imitations of animal sounds. But there is no real way of knowing. Nor is there any way of telling when people first began to speak. A close study of the skulls of early hominids (page 110) suggests that Australopithecus, who appeared around 4 million years ago, could not speak. Like apes, this hominid did not have a throat able to make the sounds of speech.

However, Neanderthal man, who appeared around 70,000 years ago, could probably make a few recognizable sounds. Scientists generally agree that people first learned to speak 50-30,000 years ago. But it may be that people could communicate by signs and in other ways a long time before this. They did not learn to write until about 5000 years ago.

FAMILIES OF LANGUAGES

In the 1700s, *philologists* (language historians) began to compare languages. They already knew that French, Spanish, Italian and other languages from the area once occupied by the Roman Empire are all descended from Latin, the language of the Romans. Their studies showed that there were striking similarities between these languages and many other languages throughout Europe and Asia, including Sanskrit, the oldest language of India.

They concluded that all these Indo-European languages were descended from a single language, which they called *Proto-Indo-European*. This is now thought to have been spoken by a group of semi-nomadic people called the Kurgans who lived in southern Russia 6000 years ago. They then worked out a complete family tree to show how it evolved. Latin,

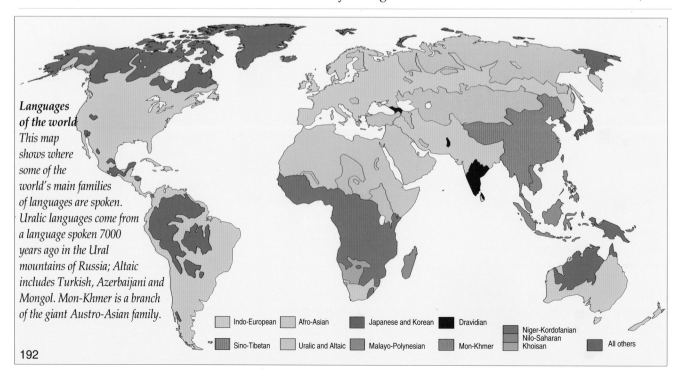

Languages of the world This map shows where some of the world's main families of languages are spoken. Uralic languages come from a language spoken 7000 years ago in the Ural mountains of Russia; Altaic includes Turkish, Azerbaijani and Mongol. Mon-Khmer is a branch of the giant Austro-Asian family.

	Indo-European		Afro-Asian		Japanese and Korean		Dravidian		Niger-Kordofanian Nilo-Saharan Khoisan
	Sino-Tibetan		Uralic and Altaic		Malayo-Polynesian		Mon-Khmer		All others

Works in Latin
The beautiful Book of Kells *was made by Irish monks in the 8th century. Like most books of the time it is in Latin. Indeed, until well into the 1600s, scholars and church people always wrote in Latin, not their native language. The formal grammar of Latin has influenced written English.*

GRAMMAR

Every language has its own set of rules or *grammar* about the way words are used and in what order. Language is broken into sentences or phrases. A sentence normally has a *subject* – that is, the thing the sentence is about – and a *verb*, describing what the subject does. It may also have an *object*, the thing affected. In the sentence, 'The girl kissed the boy', *The girl* is the subject (S), *kissed* is the verb (V) and *the boy* is the object (O). In 75% of the world's languages, the normal order is SVO (French, English) or SOV (Japanese). In Welsh and others, the verb comes first. In English, too, the order may be changed to create a particular effect. A poet, for instance, might say: 'Strange fits of passion have I known' (OSV), rather than 'I have known strange fits of passion' (SVO).

Greek, Sanskrit are all daughters of Proto-Indo-European; French and other Romance languages are all daughters of Latin.

World languages Most of the world's languages are grouped into families like Indo-European, although linguists often disagree about how they should be grouped.

Indo-European includes nearly all of the languages spoken in Europe. The Basque tongue of north east Spain is an exception, unrelated to any other known language. Gaelic and English, French and German, Russian and Bulgarian, Hindi and Bengali, and many others are all Indo-European.

In southern India, people speak *Dravidian* languages such as Telugu and Tamil. In China and Tibet, billions of people speak the many hundreds of *Sino-Tibetan* languages, including Chinese, Burmese and Tibetan. Africa is the home of more languages than any other continent – about 1300 altogether, spoken by 400 million people. 1000 of them belong to the *Niger-Congo* family, including 500 Bantu languages like Swahili, spoken in Kenya, and Zulu in South Africa. In the Americas, Indian languages belong to many different families.

DID YOU KNOW?
More than 2 billion people speak an Indo-European language.
More than 1 billion speak Chinese.
350 million speak English as their first language.
Over 600 languages are spoken in New Guinea alone.
Treacle once meant wild animal.
Taxation once meant fault finding.
Villain once meant farm labourer.
Cheat once meant rent collector.
Pretty once meant ingenious.
Banshee comes from Irish Gaelic.
Kiosk comes from Turkish.
Tomato came from Nuahatl (an American Indian language).
Yen is Chinese for desire.

CHANGING SOUNDS

Philologists long ago noticed similarities between words in many different languages that could not be simply coincidence. Notice, for instance, the similarities of the words for father, mother and brother shown right for languages as far apart as Irish and Sanskrit. In the early 1800s, Jacob Grimm (1785-1863), now best known for his fairy tales, realized that the words always differed in exactly the same way. The words *father* and *fish* in English are *pater* and *piscis* in Latin. In other words, the 'p' in the Latin word becomes a softer 'f' in English. Similarly, *pater*, *mater* and *tres* in Latin become *father*, *mother* and *three* in English, with the 't' softening to a 'th'. Grimm found nine sound shifts altogether, showing how languages evolved.

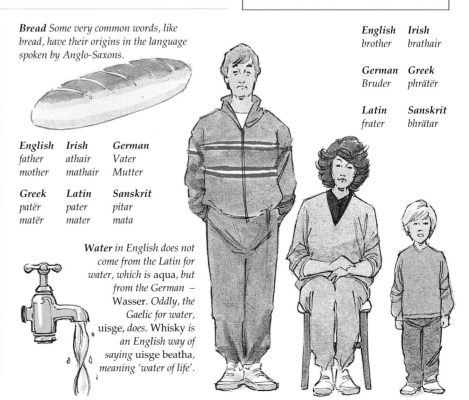

Bread Some very common words, like bread, have their origins in the language spoken by Anglo-Saxons.

English	Irish	German
father	athair	Vater
mother	mathair	Mutter

Greek	Latin	Sanskrit
patër	pater	pitar
matër	mater	mata

Water in English does not come from the Latin for water, which is aqua, *but from the German –* Wasser. *Oddly, the Gaelic for water,* uisge, *does. Whisky is an English way of saying* uisge beatha, *meaning 'water of life'.*

English	Irish
brother	brathair

German	Greek
Bruder	phrätër

Latin	Sanskrit
frater	bhrätar

WRITING

From a request for a bottle of milk to a history of the world, writing is a simple and effective way of communicating with people you can't talk to. It is also an ideal way to keep a permanent record, whether for legal purposes or just as a

CUNEIFORM

One of the earliest systems of writing is called cuneiform. It was used in Sumer, Babylon, Assyria and other areas in the Middle East between 3100 and 75 BC. Cuneiform used groups of marks that looked like tiny wedges. These marks were made by pressing a reed pen on to damp clay tablets. At first the groups were simplified pictures. But as cuneiform developed, the groups were used to show the sounds of words or even *syllables* (parts of words). The writing shown above describes a scene from courtly life in ancient Assyria.

EARLY WRITING

Writing did not begin in any one place, but in the Middle East, in China and in Central America independently. No one knows quite why people started to write, but the first written symbols were probably used by rulers to show their power, and by city officials to record and label food and other items. In Central America, for instance, writing was used only for royal monuments.

Scribes and clerks Even after writing systems were developed, very few people knew how to read and write. Usually, only a few specially trained *scribes* had the skill. In Mesopotamia in the Middle East, just a few boys were taught to write.

In Ancient Egypt, too, only scribes and a few officials could write. Some worked for the king recording things to be taxed. Others hired their services to anyone who wanted a letter read or written. Scribes learned to write on slates. But once trained, they wrote letters in ink on rolls of paper made by cutting the pith of papyrus reeds into thin strips and squeezing it together. They also jotted down notes on pieces of broken pottery called *ostraca*.

Parchment and manuscripts In the Dark Ages, monasteries kept the art of writing and reading alive.

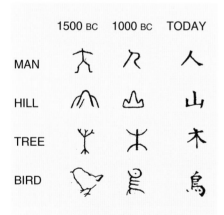

	1500 BC	1000 BC	TODAY
MAN			
HILL			
TREE			
BIRD			

Chinese writing changed gradually over thousands of years from pictures of objects to shapes representing words or the sound of words.

PICTURES AND SOUNDS

People made records with clay tokens shaped to represent different things over 10,000 years ago. But the oldest known writing is marks on clay tablets from the Sumerian city of Uruk dating from around 3500 BC. They record land sales, business deals and tax details.

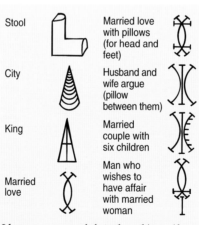

Stool · City · King · Married love — Married love with pillows (for head and feet) · Husband and wife argue (pillow between them) · Married couple with six children · Man who wishes to have affair with married woman

Ideograms use symbols to show things. Above left are Hittite ideograms from around 1500 BC. Above right are Nigerian ideograms from 1904.

Today writing uses letters to show the different sounds in a word. But the earliest writing used pictures (*pictographic*) or symbols (*ideographic*) to show things directly. The sea, for instance, might be shown by wavy lines and a man by a stick man. Some Egyptian hieroglyphs (facing page) are picture writing.

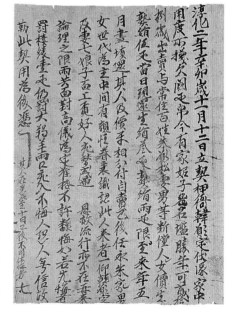

Later on, however, people began to use symbols to show different words. Chinese *characters* work like this, using one symbol for each word. There are nearly 50,000 different characters in Chinese.

From AD 100 on, monks wrote on *parchment*, paper made from untanned animal skins, like sheep or calf. Skins were soaked, scraped and stretched, then rubbed with chalk and pumice. Parchment was often leaved together into a *codex*.

Since writing and reading was a rare skill, monks put a lot of effort into the *manuscripts* (writings), and many are beautifully *illuminated* (illustrated) with decorations and pictures.

The age of print With the coming of printed books in the 1400s (page 164) more people learned to read and write. But for a time, lords still paid clerks to write letters – not just official letters but love letters too. By 1800, about 60% of men and 45% of women could read and write a little – that is, they could sign their names. Today, most people in Europe and America are taught to read and write at school and adult *literacy* rates are high. In countries like Cuba and Tanzania, literacy campaigns teach many more people to read and write.

The Greek alphabet has 24 letters.

Devanagari (46 letters) is used for writing Hindi.

The Cyrillic alphabet used in Russia has 33 letters.

ALPHABETS

Today, most writing uses alphabets. Words are made up from letters, each representing a sound. English is written in letters from the Roman alphabet. Like the Greek, Cyrillic (Russian), Hebrew and Arabic alphabets, it is descended from the earliest-known alphabet, invented in Syria some 3500 years ago. The Syrian alphabet was developed first by the Phoenicians, then the Ancient Greeks about 1000 BC and later the Etruscans of Ancient Italy who gave it to the Romans.

ANCIENT EGYPT

The writing of ancient Egypt is called *hieroglyphic*, and it is found in many of the temples and pyramids that still stand today. This system of writing is a very complicated one which uses over seven hundred different signs.

At first, every object was represented by its own picture, called a *pictogram*. As the writing developed, the pictograms came to represent words or sounds. Groups of these sounds, called *phonograms*, were used to build up new words.

HIEROGLYPHS

Hieroglyphs (above) from the temple of Rameses II (1290-1224 BC). Hieroglyphs are written from left to right, right to left or top to bottom. The pictures face the start, so these signs are read down each column from right to left. The eye-shaped sign at the top meant 'mouth'. But it is used here to represent the sound 'r'. The falcon represents the god Horus.

RE-HORUS

THE GREAT

GOD

LORD OF

HEAVEN

195

Amputation (above), where a whole limb or part of a limb was removed, was an extremely painful operation before the introduction of anaesthetics in the 1840s. Often the patient would die. This contemporary woodcut shows an amputation of the lower leg.

EARLY SURGERY

For thousands of years people have known about the healing properties of certain plants, but primitive surgery lost more lives than it saved. Until the 16th century, knowledge of human anatomy was inaccurate and there was a high risk of infection. The shock to the system during surgery could be fatal, until the introduction of pain-killing anaesthetics in the 1840s. Risks were further reduced when antiseptic surgery techniques were introduced by Lister in the 1860s.

HOSPITALS

Modern hospitals have areas to deal with each type of treatment. Accidents and emergencies are treated by the Casualty Department, which sends them to a ward or to the X-ray Department or the operating theatre, if necessary. The general wards are for patients undergoing treatment or recovering from an operation. In an intensive care unit the condition of critically ill patients is monitored by machines. The X-ray and scanning departments are used for diagnosis and treatment. The physiotherapy unit is specially equipped for patients to exercise injured or weakened limbs and muscles.

MEDICINE

Until the beginning of this century, most people died before the age of 50. Rapid developments in modern medicine have conquered many diseases and disorders. Now, people in developed countries expect to live an active life until they are over 70, but in the Third World, lack of health care is still a major problem.

Medicine is the science and art of healing, dedicated to saving lives and relieving suffering.

A person becomes ill when a part of their body does not function properly. They may have been injured, caught an infectious disease, or have inherited a weakness or defect in their genes. There are also psychiatric disorders of the mind.

The human body is a wonderful machine capable of building and repairing itself, provided it has a good supply of fresh air, water and food. But if an illness is serious, a person may need medical aid to help them get better.

Medical care begins with the diagnosis or identification of a disease or injury, followed by treatment to cure it.

PREVENTIVE MEDICINE

Modern medicine also concentrates on the prevention of disease, with worldwide programmes for immunization and health education.

Genetic engineering is being used to try and eliminate inherited disorders such as haemophilia.

DIAGNOSIS

Doctors diagnose, or identify, an ailment that is not immediately obvious by first studying the patient's case history, a report that tells them about the person's previous state of health and what problems they might expect. Next they make a physical examination of the patient's body to try and locate the position and state of an injury or infection. If necessary,

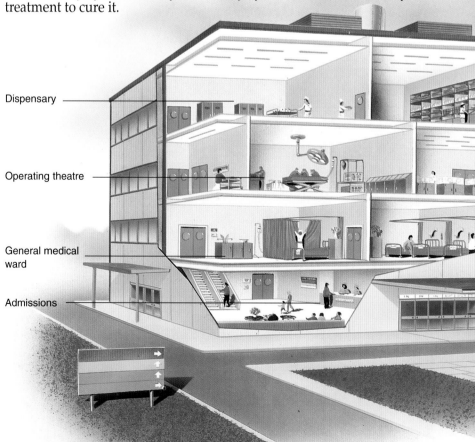

Dispensary

Operating theatre

General medical ward

Admissions

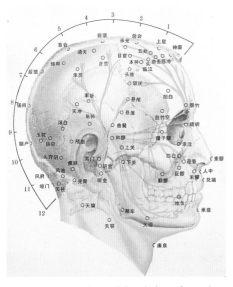

Acupuncture charts (above) *show the various places on the body where needles should be inserted to relieve the relevant disorder.*

ALTERNATIVE MEDICINE

Some forms of alternative medicine are based on ancient practices, such as acupuncture, which developed in ancient China. It can reduce pain by pricking the skin with needles at critical points on the body.

In homeopathy, an illness is treated with small quantities of the drug that would induce the same illness in a healthy person.

In osteopathy the bones and muscles are manipulated to remove pain, which is often caused by lesions.

Many primitive peoples relied on their local witch doctor or medicine man to cure them with herbal potions or secret magic powers. Some herbal medicines are still used.

North American Indian medicine man (above) *Many early civilizations and peoples relied on witch doctors to cure them.*

they arrange for special medical tests to be carried out, such as X-rays, or blood, urine or tissue analysis. Scanning techniques (see below) are used to investigate internal disorders such as tumours.

TREATMENT

Doctors may prescribe drugs to help the body fight infection and repair damaged tissues. Drugs are made from natural substances such as plants, or synthetically from

chemicals, and are classified according to their effect on the body. There are drugs to fight bacteria, prevent infectious diseases, affect the heart and the bloodstream, or affect the nervous system and so on.

If the best treatment involves surgery, the patient will go into hospital to have the damaged or diseased parts removed or repaired. Transplant surgery is now available, in which entire organs can be replaced. Laser surgery uses an

intense beam of light to cut or repair tissue. With micro-surgery even the tiniest nerve endings can be reconnected. Nuclear medicine, which uses radioactive materials, is used in both diagnosis and treatment. Radiotherapy is often used to treat cancer. While patients are in a critical condition they are given intensive care, where the combined use of drugs, life-support machines and accurate monitoring systems may enable them to start a good recovery.

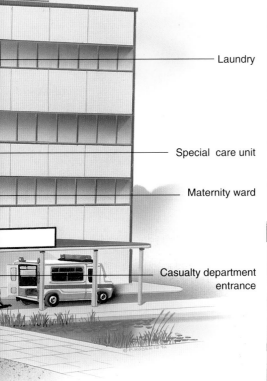

Laundry

Special care unit

Maternity ward

Casualty department entrance

SCANNING TECHNIQUES

X-ray diagnosis has been revolutionized by the CAT (computerized axial tomography) scanner . The scanner (below) moves around the patient producing a detailed picture of a cross-section of any part of the body. A close series of scans can be used to build up a 3D image showing the extent of a tumour, for example, as it shows both bone and soft tissue clearly. The NMR scanner

works by nuclear magnetic resonance, using radio waves and powerful magnets. It can be used for examining brain tissue (below).

The PET (positron emission tomography) scanner picks up signals from a radioactive substance injected into the patient. It can be used to study the behaviour of cells in different parts of the body while they are in action.

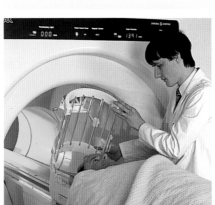

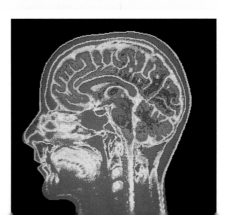

THEATRE & FILM

Theatre is one of the oldest forms of entertainment; cinema is one of the newest. But they both usually depend on telling a story or demonstrating a theme using actors.With theatre, each performance is live and different, but cinema can create spectacular special effects.

THE AGE OF SHAKESPEARE

It was in the 1570s that the first real theatres appeared. In England, there were *wooden-Os* like the Globe Theatre in London (above). These were round wooden buildings with the stage and an audience pit in the centre, open to the sky. Here noisy and enthusiastic crowds watched professional actors perform the dramatic new plays of playwrights like Shakespeare, Christopher Marlowe (1564-1593) and Ben Jonson (1572-1637).

In Spain, people crammed into open courtyard theatres called *corrales*. This time is called the 'golden age' of Spanish drama, for thousands of wonderful plays were written and performed. One of the most famous writers was Lope de Vega (1562-1635) who wrote plays such as *El Perro del Hortelano (The Dog in a Manger)*.

THEATRE

Plays were staged in Ancient Greece over 2500 years ago. In the Middle Ages, early dramas were often religious and staged in churches. For instance, *mystery plays* told Bible stories in a dramatic and colourful way.

In England and Spain, the first real theatres were built in the age of William Shakespeare (1564-1616) who wrote such famous plays as *Hamlet* and *Romeo and Juliet*. These theatres, though, were open-air; it was not until the late 1600s that theatres were roofed.

Many early plays were about heroes and kings and were set in exotic locations. But in the last 100 years, playwrights have written more about ordinary characters and situations. In the 1960s, many plays were *kitchen sink* dramas, showing life in very ordinary homes.

Stage and lights Today, banks of lights help the actors create the right atmosphere. Lights called *floods* give an overall light; *spotlights* and *profiles* focus on a particular spot; *fresnels* and *parcans* give something in between. Lights can be made any colour with a filter or *gel* in front of the lens.

The stage in older theatres is often set behind a large frame called the *proscenium arch*, and curtains or *tabs* open to reveal it at the start of the play. In many modern theatres, the stage is surrounded by the audience on three sides (*thrust stage*) or all four (*in-the-round*).

CINEMA

Frenchman Louis le Prince made the first moving pictures in Washington Heights, New York in 1885-7, and the first cinema was built in Georgia, USA, in 1895. By

CLASSICAL THEATRE

In the days of Ancient Greece and Rome, thousands of people went to see dramas in huge open-air theatres like the one in Athens (right). Actors usually wore huge masks. They performed not only comedies, but also tragedies with terrible deeds and strong emotions. The first great writer of tragedies was Aeschylus (525-456 BC), who is famous for his three plays about the hero Orestes. Equally powerful are the dramas of Sophocles (497-405 BC) and Euripides (485-406 BC). Sophocles' play *Oedipus Rex* is about a king who unwittingly kills his own father and marries his mother. Euripides' *Medea* is the tragedy of a woman who kills her own children.

SPECIAL EFFECTS

Film-makers have always used tricks to show things they could not film for real, such as a ship sinking. One technique is the *travelling matte*, used to make Superman fly. First, actors are filmed against a blue background to make a *matte*, that 'travels' across the screen. The matte masks off where the actors were while the real background is filmed. Background and actor shots are then merged. Now, film-makers can produce spectacular effects using computers. Computer screen techniques merge computer-driven models, actors and real scenes together so smoothly it is impossible to tell which is which.

1912, thousands of people in the USA were paying a nickel (5 cents) to see films in the *nickelodeons*, as cinemas were called. Many of the early films were made in Hollywood, California, because good weather was needed for filming. Hollywood has remained the centre of the American film industry ever since.

Early films were in black-and-white only, and were silent. A piano or organ in the cinema provided music to go with the film, and the actor's words appeared in writing on the screen. The first *talkies*, movies in which actors spoke, came with *The Jazz Singer* in 1927. Colour arrived soon after, though it was rarely used until the 1950s, when the Eastman-color process superseded Technicolor. In the 1970s, the invention of high-quality all-round sound systems made films like *Star Wars* incredibly dramatic by giving audiences the impression they were in the middle of a battle.

EARLY MOVIE STARS

There have been movie stars as long as there have been movies. In the days of the silents in the 1920s, the most famous stars were comics such as Buster Keaton

Shirley Temple

Humphrey Bogart

and Charlie Chaplin. Chaplin endeared himself to millions with his shabby tramp character with a bowler hat and walking stick. Beautiful women like Mary Pickford and Carole Lombard gave Hollywood and movies an aura of glamour which they have never lost. But many silent movie stars failed to make the transition to talkies.

One of the first talkies stars was German actress Marlene Dietrich who made her name in the film *Blue Angel* (1930).

Perhaps the most famous of all stars was Marilyn Monroe (1926-1962). Her sad death of an overdose in 1962 has made her a symbol of the way the movie industry can exploit youth and beauty ruthlessly.

Marilyn Monroe

An early Chaplin movie poster

Arnold Schwarzenegger

Stone Age people first painted animals such as this bison on cave walls nearly 30,000 years ago.

FINE ART

People have painted pictures and created shapes for pleasure and inspiration since prehistoric times, and every civilization and culture has its own style of painting and sculpture.

CAVE ART

The world's oldest works of art date back some 30,000 years to the Stone Age. There are many small stone sculptures of rotund women called Venus figurines dating from over 20,000 years ago. There are also many ancient paintings in the caves of southern France and northern Spain. The earliest of these dates back nearly 30,000 years. Those at the most famous sites – Lascaux in France and Altamira in Spain – were painted between 15,000 and 10,000 years ago.

These remarkable paintings were painted with a stick and paints ground from coloured earths and clays, such as iron oxide and yellow ochre, giving mostly browns and reds. They usually show deer, bison, horses, wild cattle, mammoths, woolly rhinoceroses and various other animals. Only occasionally do the cave artists paint humans and other subjects.

WESTERN ART

When people in Europe and America talk of *fine art*, they are usually talking of paintings and sculptures made in Europe and America over the last 700 years. Of course, many beautiful paintings and sculptures have been made elsewhere but they are not part of the same tradition.

Medieval painting In the Middle Ages, artists painted mainly on wood panels for churches, or directly on church walls, and their paintings show scenes from the life of Christ and the saints. They are clear and full of rich colours, but to us look a little flat, cartoon-like and unnatural. But around 1300, the Italian artist Giotto (1267-1337) began to paint figures and landscapes in a much more natural, lifelike style and others followed suit. For the first time, people seemed to have a definite shape beneath their loose clothes.

The Renaissance was one of the greatest periods in the history of art, especially in Italy. The artists of the Renaissance were fascinated by the pure, beautifully proportioned art of Ancient Greece and Rome, and also by the world around them.

In Masaccio's (1401-28) paintings, figures seem to be drawn from life for the first time. Artists such as Piero della Francesca (1420-92) and Leon Alberti (1404-72) showed how to use *perspective*, the way lines converge in the distance. Leonardo da Vinci (1452-1519) studied human anatomy to make his figures more realistic. The Renaissance reached its height in the early 16th century when Michelangelo (1475-1564), Raphael (1483-1520) and the architect Bramante (1444-1514) were working in Rome.

The 1600s Towards the end of the 16th century, artists began to abandon the classical purity of the

CLASSICAL IDEALS

The *classical* art of Ancient Greece and Rome has had a deep and lasting influence on western art. In the Renaissance in particular, artists like Alberti and Donatello went to Rome to study the ancient ruins and statues and copy the clear, calm and elegant style of the classical artists. Michelangelo's figures for the ceiling of the Sistine Chapel (left) have some of the grandeur of classical heroes.

Pigments The paints in the artist's palette get their colour from pigments. Up until the 1800s, pigments were made from naturally occurring minerals and plants. Since 1856, pigments have been made from synthetic dyes.

PAINTS

Paintings are done with oil or acrylic paints, watercolours or as *frescos* on wet plaster. Early Renaissance painters mixed pigments with egg white (*tempera*), later they mixed them with linseed oil (*oils*).

Renaissance and adopt a more dramatic, energetic style. Rubens (1577-1640) and Velasquez (1599-1660) painted ordinary people rather than heroes and saints, and in Holland, artists like Vermeer (1632-75) painted peaceful indoor scenes in perfect detail.

Portraits and landscapes In the 1700s rich people began to order pictures to decorate their houses – like Boucher's (1703-70) flowery

THE IMPRESSIONISTS

In the 1870s, a group of French artists called the Impressionists painted some of the most popular of all pictures. Their bright, softly coloured landscapes and scenes from French life were an attempt to get away from the studied detail of most paintings and capture the spontaneous, indistinct way we really see the world, which is why they are called Impressionists. The most famous are Monet (1840-1926), Renoir (1841-1919), and Degas (1834-1917).

interiors and Gainsborough's (1727-88) portraits. In the early 1800s, many artists reacted against reason and intellect, in favour of expressing personal feelings, painting passionate romantic dramas – Géricault (1791-1824) and Delacroix (1798-1863) – and moody landscapes – Constable (1776-1837) and Turner (1775-1851). By the 1850s, artists such as Courbet (1819-77) preferred a more realistic approach and more down-to-earth subjects.

SCULPTURE

One of the most famous early sculptors was Donatello (1386-1466) whose lithe statue of David was the first life-size bronze of the Renaissance. Michelangelo also made a statue of David, only his is much more muscular and carved from marble like many of his great sculptures. Perhaps the most famous sculptor since the Renaissance is the Frenchman Auguste Rodin (1840-1917) whose statues such as *The Thinker* and *The Kiss* seem to be almost frozen from life.

Before the 20th century, sculptors concentrated mostly on making realistic statues of people and animals. Now most sculptors make abstract or semi-abstract sculptures. Henry Moore's (1898-1986) sculptures are smooth, organic, figures with holes in them.

Few major modern artists paint realistic scenes; most paint abstracts. Cubists like Picasso (1881-1973) broke up scenes into different shapes. With artists such as Kandinsky (1866-1944) colour and form were more important than the subject (right).

POP ART

In the 1960s young artists like David Hockney (1937-) and Andy Warhol (1926-87) felt abstract art was irrelevant to modern life and tried to develop a popular style, called Pop Art. This is a painting by David Hockney (left) called *A bigger splash*.

Michelangelo's giant David was carved in Florence in 1501, and still stands there today.

MUSIC

There are rock music and rap music, classical and choral, jazz and jive, swing and salsa and many other kinds of music, but all music is basically sounds organized into notes and rhythms.

MUSICAL NOTATION

When writing down music, musicians use *musical notation*. This shows every aspect of the music, so that another musician can play the piece perfectly by simply reading it. The notes are written in order on two *staves*, each with five ruled lines. The lower stave (the *bass clef*) is for low notes; the upper (the *treble clef*) for high notes.

The pitch of each note is shown by its position on the stave. Its length is shown in a simple code. A whole note lasting four beats (a *semibreve*) is a white dot; a half note lasting two beats (*minim*) is a white dot with a tail; a quarter note lasting one beat (*crotchet*) is a black dot with a tail; an eighth note (*quaver*) has a flag on the tail; and so on. The tune is split into short periods called *bars*. For an even rhythm there must always be the same number of beats in a bar.

Music is written in a key, shown by symbols at the beginning of each stave. The key system is based on sequences of notes called major or minor scales.

CLASSICAL AND ORCHESTRAL MUSIC

The roots of classical and orchestral music lie in medieval monasteries where monks sang chants called *plainsong* that echoed hauntingly off the stone walls. In the 1100s, monks began to build up the sound by singing a second then later a third tune at the same time. This is called *polyphony*, meaning many sounds. In Reims in France, Machaut (1300-77) wrote rhythmic music in this form. Most polyphonic music was *vocal* (for singing) and composers like Palestrina (1525-94) and Monteverdi (1567-1643) wrote wonderful vocal *masses* (for church services) and *madrigals* (to entertain lords and ladies).

In the 1500s, people began to play polyphonic music on instruments such as *viols* (a kind of violin) and lutes – especially for the popular new dances like the *pavan* and *galliarde*. Then, as musicians became more skilled, composers like Monteverdi began to write brilliantly expressive music for solo voices and chorus.

Baroque and classical In the 1600s, composers began to write in *harmony* – that is, based on *chords* (groups of notes that sound right together) rather than parallel tunes. And for the new groups of professional musicians, they wrote elaborate instrumental pieces called *sonatas* and *concertos* – none finer than those of German composer JS Bach (1685-1750). In the 1700s, the groups grew into

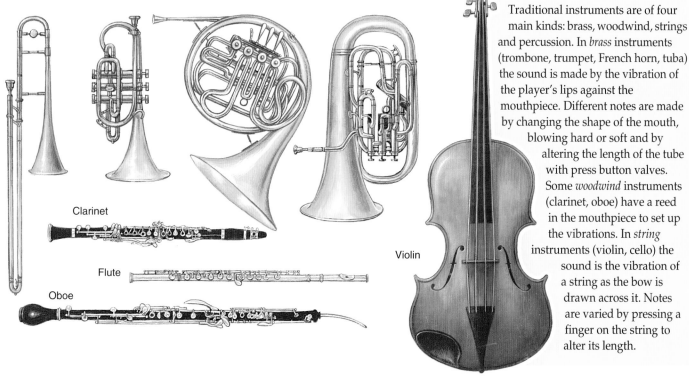

Trombone   Trumpet   French horn   Tuba

Clarinet

Flute

Oboe

Violin

INSTRUMENTS

Traditional instruments are of four main kinds: brass, woodwind, strings and percussion. In *brass* instruments (trombone, trumpet, French horn, tuba) the sound is made by the vibration of the player's lips against the mouthpiece. Different notes are made by changing the shape of the mouth, blowing hard or soft and by altering the length of the tube with press button valves. Some *woodwind* instruments (clarinet, oboe) have a reed in the mouthpiece to set up the vibrations. In *string* instruments (violin, cello) the sound is the vibration of a string as the bow is drawn across it. Notes are varied by pressing a finger on the string to alter its length.

ROCK AND RAP

Today's chart music and dance rhythms have their roots in the music of Black Americans – especially in the jazz and *blues* (sad, rhythmic songs) played in the saloon bars of New Orleans in the late 1800s. In the 1950s, Black guitar groups played frantic *rock'n'roll*. When taken up by Whites like Buddy Holly and Elvis Presley, it became the focus of many teenager's lives. In the 1960s, the simple pace of rock'n'roll matured into the varied *rock* of groups like the Beatles. But by the 1990s, popular music was led once again by the energetic dance beats like *rap* and *house* that emerged from Black neighbourhoods in the 1980s.

Miles Davis (1926-92) was a great jazz trumpeter. He played bebop in the 1940s, and later became famous for his jazz-rock fusions.

orchestras and the music became ever more structured, with each piece following a set formula. Symphonies, which were really sonatas for orchestra, almost always began with a fast section, had a slow middle and a fast end. Mozart (1756-91) used these rigid *classical* structures to create some of the most beautiful orchestral music ever written.

Romantic and modern Classical music was elegant and refined, but in the early 1800s, Beethoven

(1770-1827) began to write moody, passionate pieces on a grand scale. Beethoven's fluid *Romantic* music paved the way for the dazzling piano music of Chopin and Liszt. Some romantic composers such as the Russian Tchaikovsky (1840-93) were inspired partly by the folk music of their own countries.

Early this century, composers such as Stravinsky (1882-1971) and Bartok (1881-1945) began to appreciate how *dissonance* (notes that clash) can create a dramatic, exciting sound.

KEYBOARDS

Keyboard instruments have been popular for over 400 years because they can play chords of up to ten notes simultaneously. Harpsichords dominated music in the 1600s and 1700s, and in the 1800s and 1900s composers like Chopin (1810-49) and Rachmaninov (1873-1943) wrote for the loud and increasingly popular grand piano. Now modern and extremely versatile electronic keyboards and synthesizers are featured in all kinds of music.

THE ORCHESTRA

There are various kinds of orchestra ranging from small string orchestras to huge symphony orchestras with 90 or more players. The first orchestras appeared in the 17th century and were small often haphazard groups, held

together by the harpsichord or organ. By the time of Mozart, the harpsichord and organ had gone and the orchestra had a standard form with 40 or so players grouped into strings, woodwind, brass and percussion. Throughout the 19th

century, the orchestra got bigger and bigger, and composers like Richard Strauss wrote grand pieces demanding huge brass sections. Recently, exotic percussion and electric synthesizers have been added to the sound.

First and second violins — Clarinets, flutes — Horns — Bassoons, oboes — Double basses — Trumpets — Violas, cellos — Trombones, tubas — Percussion

THE BRITISH ISLES

There are over 4000 islands in the British Isles, and over 20,000 kilometres of coastline, but there are just two main islands, Great Britain and Ireland, and two nations, the United Kingdom and the Republic of Ireland.

ABOUT THE BRITISH ISLES
Area: 314,329 sq km
Population: UK 58,080,000
Republic of Ireland 3,516,000
Highest point: Ben Nevis, 1343m
Longest river: Shannon, 370km

COUNTRIES
UK (England, Wales, Scotland and province of Northern Ireland), Republic of Ireland.

ECONOMY
Farming: Intensive, mechanized farming supplies two thirds of Britain's food needs. Livestock rearing is important in the west and Ireland.
Natural resources: But for oil in the North Sea and coal, Britain has few resources and has to rely heavily on trade.
Industry: The UK is not the manufacturer it once was, though making cars and lorries is still important. More than half the labour force now works in service industries – especially since 1980.

GOVERNMENT
The UK has a monarch, but the country is run by a government formed from the party which has a majority in the House of Commons. The leader of this party is the Prime Minister. The Republic of Ireland has a president with little power. The country is run by the *Taoiseach* (Prime Minister) and Cabinet nominated by the *Dáil* (House).

LANGUAGES
Most people speak English. In Ireland, Scotland and Wales many people speak Irish, Scots Gaelic and Welsh respectively.

RELIGION
Anglican Protestants are in the majority in the UK, Roman Catholics in Ireland. There are other religions too, including Islam, Hinduism and Judaism.

SPORT
Football, rugby and cricket are popular.

THE UNITED KINGDOM
The United Kingdom is really four countries – England, Scotland, Wales and Northern Ireland.

Of the four, England is the biggest and most densely populated – a lush country of rolling hills and rich farmland. The south east, with its grassy ridges and broad valleys is especially heavily populated and intensively farmed. Dairy farming is predominant in the west and south west. In the north, many people live in big industrial cities. But there are less densely populated uplands here too.

Wales is a land of hills and sheep farms, except for the south where industry is important and coal was once mined in great quantity. Scotland is mainly wild moors and valleys, and most people live in the central lowlands around Glasgow and Edinburgh. A third of Northern Ireland's people live in Belfast. The rest are scattered through its hills and valleys, or around Lough Neagh, the UK's biggest lake.

The people Many English people are descended from the Angles, Saxons and Normans who invaded in the Middle Ages. Many Scots, Irish, and Welsh are descended from Celts who lived in Britain before the early Middle Ages. But over the centuries, many peoples have come here, creating a rich mix of cultures and nationalities. This century, immigrants have come from Europe, Asia and the Caribbean.

After the empire In the 1800s, Britain was rich and powerful. It was at the forefront of the Industrial Revolution, ruling a vast overseas empire stretching around the world and including India, Australia and Canada. This century, however, the empire has gradually broken up, replaced by a voluntary Commonwealth of Nations, and the country's economic might has declined.

After World War II, a Labour government *nationalized* many industries (brought them under

Sheep auction in Wales
Sheep were the mainstay of the British economy in the Middle Ages. They are still important in Wales.

Digging peat Peat (partially rotted and compacted plants) is used as a fuel and fertilizer, but the destruction of peat bogs in Ireland is a problem.

The Houses of Parliament (Westminster Palace) in London, the home of the English government, completed in 1860.

Blackpool, with its long sandy beach and amusements, has long been a popular holiday resort for people from all over the country.

LONDON

Along with Tokyo and New York, London is one of the world's big three financial and commercial centres, and trade all over the world stands or falls by money deals in the City – the 'square mile' at the heart of London's financial business. It is also a major cultural centre, with more theatres and galleries than any other city, and millions of tourists come each year to see its historic buildings, such as the Tower of London, St Paul's Cathedral and Buckingham Palace. In the 1800s, it was for a long time the world's biggest city. Since then, many other cities have overtaken it, and its population is actually dwindling slowly as people move out into the suburbs.

government control), introduced a *welfare state* to help the needy, and created the world's first free national health service. The country still had economic problems, however. And some thought the nationalized industries, such as coal mining and iron and steel, were large and inefficient.

Recent years In 1979, a Conservative government led by Margaret Thatcher was elected. During the following years, many nationalized industries were privatized, and trade union rights were curtailed. Then, in 1997, the Labour Party led by Tony Blair won a landslide victory, but only having given up many of its traditional socialist policies.

Since 1973, the UK has been a member of the the European Union which has had a major influence on British politics.

THE REPUBLIC OF IRELAND

Rain makes Ireland's grass so green that it is known as the 'emerald isle'. But the country's past is far from jewel-like. From 1172 it was under English domination and most Irish were desperately poor. In the 1840s millions died when the potato crop failed; millions more emigrated to the USA.

England partitioned Ireland in 1920, taking six counties of the province of Ulster into the UK. In 1922, after a bitter war of independence, the Irish Free State was born. The Republic of Ireland (Eire) emerged in 1948. Since then, Eire has become more prosperous, but it remains largely rural and many young people still leave to find work in England. Joining the EC in 1973, though, seems to have brought considerable benefits to the country.

NORTHERN IRELAND

While most people in Eire are Roman Catholics, the majority in Northern Ireland are Protestant, descended from Scots settlers who came here in the 17th century. This is partly why, when Eire became independent in 1922, Ulster stayed part of the UK. In the 1960s, protests by the Catholic minority against discrimination led to violent bombing and murder campaigns by both sides. In 1969, British troops were sent in to try to restore peace. In 1972, the UK government imposed direct rule from Westminster.

DID YOU KNOW?
The British flag, often called the Union Jack, is a combination of the old flags of England, Ireland and Scotland.
Britain is the world's eighth biggest island – Greenland is the biggest.
The amount of steel used in North Sea oil platforms would build over 200 Eiffel Towers.
Great Britain got its name long ago, not because the country was great, but because it is bigger than Lesser Britain (Brittany in France).
There are more Welsh speakers in Patagonia, Argentina than in Wales.
Lloyd's insurance organization was founded in a London coffee house in about 1688.

Glencoe, Scotland
There were once many crofts (small farms) in the Highlands. But in the 1800s, many crofters were evicted to make way for sheep farms in the Highland Clearances. Now the Highlands are empty and crofts like this are rare.

NORTHERN EUROPE

Sweden, Norway, Denmark and Finland are among the most northerly inhabited countries in the world. The far north is well within the Arctic Circle and, though the sun shines here at midnight in summer, winters are dark all day long.

ABOUT NORTHERN EUROPE
Area: 1,154,261 sq km
Population: 22,963,000
Highest point: Glittertind, Norway, 2472m
Longest river: Glomma, Norway, 598km

COUNTRIES
Denmark, Finland, Norway, Sweden.

ECONOMY
Farming: Except in Denmark only a small area can be farmed. Denmark's modern farms produce dairy products and bacon.
Natural resources: Norway, Sweden and Finland have huge timber industries and use hydroelectric power. Sweden has iron ore, Norway oil and North Sea fishing.
Industry: Industry is well-developed, in Sweden especially, where industries based on its iron ore are important. Norway is one of world's leading shipping countries.

GOVERNMENT
All but Finland are monarchies, run by elected governments. Finland is a republic.

LANGUAGES
Each country has its own language: all but Finnish are closely related.

DID YOU KNOW?
Finland has over 60,000 lakes.
Sweden's socialist prime minister Olof Palme was murdered in 1986.
Homes in Stockholm are heated by water used for cooling at power stations.
One third of Denmark is small islands – 482 of them.
Sweden spends 60% of its gross domestic product on welfare and public services, more than any other country.
The people of Ornskodsvik in Sweden compete to eat rotten herrings.

THE LAND
Sweden, Norway, Denmark and Finland are often known as Scandinavia. In the west, it is rugged and mountainous. The icecaps and glaciers on the high plateaus are tiny remnants of the vast sheets of ice and glaciers that once covered northern Europe – gouging deep inlets called *fjords* ('fee-ords') out of the Norwegian coast and leaving Sweden and Finland with thousands of lakes. Towns are few, and most people live along the coast earning a living by fishing, or from forestry.

Southern Sweden and Denmark are much gentler landscapes with rich farmland on the sands and gravels deposited by the ice. Farming in Denmark is intense and highly mechanized.

THE PEOPLE
Fifty years ago, these countries were relatively poor. But the people now enjoy one of the highest standards of living in the world. They have made the most of their resources – hydroelectric (water) power, timber and iron ore – with high-quality manufacturing. Sweden is famous for precision machine parts and cars such as Volvo. Denmark exports fine food all over Europe.

These countries are well known for their enlightened attitudes and generous welfare systems. Norway and Sweden, for instance, gave women the vote well over 100 years ago, long before most other European countries. They also award the annual Nobel Prizes for sciences, literature and peace.

THE LAPPS
The Lapps of the far north of Norway, Sweden and Finland are traditional hunters, fishermen and herdsmen. There are about 40,000 of them and they have their own language and way of life. Many are reindeer herders who live in reindeer skin tents and follow their animals from winter grazing grounds on the northern forest fringes to summer pastures high on the fells of Lapland. The herds were badly affected by the nuclear accident at Chernobyl in 1986, and many Lapps have now abandoned their reindeer to live in modern towns.

Sogne Fjord in Norway is one of the biggest of the huge fjords carved out by glaciers long ago. Fjords have very steep sides, and the water in them is often thousands of metres deep. Sogne Fjord, the longest, winds 204km inland from the North Sea.

GERMANY, AUSTRIA & SWITZERLAND

The German-speaking countries in the centre of Europe – Germany, Austria and Switzerland – stretch from the high Alpine mountains in the south to the shores of the Baltic and North Sea. They are among the world's richest countries.

GERMANY

Much of north Germany is flat, with heath and marsh as well as rich farmland. The south is mostly thickly wooded hills and mountains, such as the Black Forest and the Harz Mountains, climbing to the high peaks of the Alps. Down from the Alps flow two great rivers, the Danube and the Rhine. The Rhine is a vital transport link, and much of Germany's industry is focused on it, especially around its tributary, the Ruhr. Today, though, new industry is moving to attractive cities in the south, like Stuttgart.

Divided and united When World War II ended in 1945, Germany lay in ruins and was divided in two.

East Germany came under the control of the Soviet Union as a communist country; while *West* Germany and half the old capital – Berlin (inside East Germany) – became a federal republic. The two halves of Berlin were separated by a huge concrete wall from 1961 until 1989.

West Germany staged a remarkable recovery. Indeed, its economy boomed so much its people were soon among the richest in the world. Germany became famous for its technology and quality products, such as BMW cars, and it is a key country in the European Union.

Yet when the Berlin Wall was taken down in 1989, the German 'economic miracle' was beginning to falter. East and West Germany were reunited as one country in 1990, and a few Germans began to worry that the cost of reunification – and in particular the levels of unemployment in former East Germany – might end their prosperity. All the same, Germany is still a very rich country.

ABOUT GERMANY
Area: 356,840 sq km
Population: 79,754,000
Highest point: Zugspitze, 2963m
Longest river: Danube, 2859km

ECONOMY
Farming: Farming employs only 1% of the workforce, yet provides two-thirds of Germany's food, especially in meat, dairy products, wheat, sugar beet and wine.
Natural resources: Germany has valuable forests and coal reserves, but imports most of its energy as oil and gas.
Industry: Germany is the world's third biggest manufacturing nation, behind only the USA and Japan.

GOVERNMENT
Germany is a federal republic, which means the various regions, or *Länder*, such as Bavaria, have considerable power. There are two government houses – the *Bundestag* elected nationwide by proportional representation (page 183), and the *Bundesrat* consisting of representatives of the Länder. The head of government is the Chancellor.

The Matterhorn, (left) at 4477m, one of Switzerland's highest peaks. The spectacular scenery of the Alps attracts many visitors each year, especially to fashionable ski resorts such as St Moritz.

Bavaria (below) in southern Germany is a land of pine forests and fairy tale castles – and also industry.

The beautiful city of Salzburg (above), in Austria, is the birthplace of Mozart.

SWITZERLAND & AUSTRIA
Switzerland and Austria are beautiful, mountainous countries, with peaks in Switzerland rising over 4000m. Both are also wealthy, especially Switzerland, which has grown rich from banking and making small, valuable things like watches. Yet they are very different. Switzerland has always been strictly neutral in wars, which is why many peace conferences are held in Geneva. It also has many French, Italian and Romansch speaking people, as well as Germans. Austria is all that remains of a once-huge empire (page 142).

ABOUT FRANCE & LOW COUNTRIES
Area: 616,429 sq km
Population: 80,415,400
Highest point: Mont Blanc, 4807m
Longest river: Rhine 1320km

Economy
Farming: France is Europe's biggest food producer after Russia. The Netherlands is intensively farmed, with dairy farming on the polder lands and flowers near the coast.
Natural resources: France and Belgium have natural resources, including coal and iron ore. The Netherlands relies on trade.
Industry: French industries include textiles, chemicals, steel, aircraft and car-making.

Government
France is a republic headed by a president. Belgium and the Netherlands have monarchs, Luxembourg a Grand Duke.

Religion
France and Belgium are mainly Catholic; the Dutch are half Catholic, half Protestant.

Language
Dutch in the Netherlands; Flemish and French in Belgium; French in France.

DID YOU KNOW?
The Eiffel Tower in Paris, built in 1889 entirely of iron girders, is 300m high.
Rotterdam handles over 1 million tonnes of cargo every day.
Italy produces 28% of the world's wine, more than France (25%).
Amsterdam has 80km of canals.
The EU is administered by the European Commission, based in Brussels.
The European Court of Justice in Luxembourg hears disputes on EU laws.
The European Parliament is based in Strasbourg in France.

FRANCE & THE LOW COUNTRIES

Stretching from the rugged Atlantic coast of Brittany to the Côte d'Azur on the Mediterranean, France is Europe's biggest country after Russia. The Low Countries – Belgium, the Netherlands and Luxembourg – are among its smallest.

FRANCE

France is a rural country with small towns, villages and old farmhouses scattered through the countryside. Industry is concentrated in a few big cities like Paris, Lyon, Lille and Marseilles. In the centre are the rugged hills and volcanic pinnacles of the Massif Central, with the Mediterranean coast to the south, where grapes, fruit and vegetables are grown in the warm sun. The low, rolling countryside of the north and west is cooler, and here the main crops are cereals and sugar beet. The highest mountains are the Alps in the south east and the Pyrenees along the Spanish border.

France has recovered from the trauma of German occupation in World War II to become a driving force in the European Union. Modernization of industry has made it the world's fourth largest industrial power after the USA, Japan and Germany.

THE LOW COUNTRIES

Belgium, the Netherlands and Luxembourg are small but densely populated, with ancient market towns and big industrial cities and ports such as Rotterdam, one of the world's largest and most modern. But for the hills of the Ardennes in southern Belgium, most of the region is low-lying, especially in the Netherlands where banks called *dykes* play a vital role in protecting the land from flooding.

Tulip fields (left)
The polders (drained land) of the Netherlands are famous for tulips.

Lace-making (right)
Belgium has been a centre for weaving and lace-making since the Middle Ages.

The european union
Western European countries are joined politically and economically in the *European Union (EU)*. Originally there were 6 members – France, West Germany, Italy and the Low Countries. Now there are 15, including Portugal, the UK, Ireland, Spain, Denmark and Greece, and more may join. The EU has created a single 'market' with nothing to stop trade and people moving between member countries.

French cheeses (below) The French are known for their love of fine food, and French farmers make many wonderful cheeses.

SPAIN, PORTUGAL & ITALY

Spain, Portugal and Italy are three of the great nations of southern Europe, famous for their long and distinguished histories, their architecture and their wines. The climate ranges from the icy mountainous areas of northern Italy to the semi-arid interior region of Spain.

THE IBERIAN PENINSULA

Spain and Portugal are two separate, independent nations occupying the Iberian Peninsula, a large outcrop of land in southwestern Europe. To the northeast the mountain range of the Pyrenees separates them from the rest of Europe. On the western coast lies the Atlantic ocean, while the calmer waters of the Mediterranean warm the eastern shores.

Spain is one of Europe's largest wine-producing areas and also one of the most mountainous. Most of its land area consists of the Meseta, a high plateau dotted with mountains. Each year millions of tourists visit the country.

Portugal is one of the oldest nations in Europe but also now one of the poorest. Its history as an independent country goes back to the 12th century. In the 15th and 16th centuries, Portuguese explorers led many of Europe's voyages of discovery. Portugal's main exports include clothing, textiles, paper and wine.

ITALY

Italy is also a mountainous land, but it has rich farming soil in the north. It has much more industry than either Spain or Portugal. In the northern 'industrial triangle', bounded by Turin, Milan and Livorno, there is much heavy industry, including car-manufacturing. Southern Italy is much poorer.

REGIONS OF SPAIN

Spain is divided into 17 political regions, each with its own Parliament. When the 1992 Summer Olympics were held in Barcelona in the northeast Catalan area, many local songs and dances of Catalonia were performed at the magnificent opening ceremony.

ABOUT ITALY
Area: 301,245 sq km
Population: 57,838,000
ECONOMY
Farming: Fruits, cereals, grapes and beef.
Industries: Clothing, food and wine, engineering, car-making, chemicals, tourism.

ABOUT SPAIN
Area: 504,750 sq km
Population: 38,479,000
ECONOMY
Farming: Citrus fruits, olives, grapes
Industries: Engineering, textiles, wine-making, tourism

ABOUT PORTUGAL
Area: 91,630 sq km
Population: 10,525,000
ECONOMY
Farming: Grapes, tomatoes, pigs
Industries: Textiles, food, paper and wine

GOVERNMENTS
Italy and Portugal are republics with elected presidents. Spain is a democracy with a parliament and a monarch.

DID YOU KNOW?
The volcanoes of Etna and Vesuvius in Italy are still active and sometimes erupt.
The state of Vatican City in Rome is the smallest state in the world to receive the ambassadors of other nations. It is the home of the Pope, who is the head of the state.
Two of Spain's provinces lie about 1300km to the south west of mainland Spain. These are the Canary Islands off the coast of Africa. They did not get their name from the bird, but from the Latin word canis (dog), after the dogs which once infested the islands.

Port (above), the fortified sweet wine which originated in the valley of the river Douro in Portugal, loaded in barrels on board a sailing vessel in a Portuguese harbour.

Venice (left) is built on 117 islands off the coast of Italy. More than 150 canals twist among the islands. Venice contains some of the most beautiful buildings in Italy.

SOUTHERN & EASTERN EUROPE

Until the end of the 1980s, almost all southern and eastern Europe, from Poland to Albania, formed part of the communist world. The collapse of communist rule is bringing dramatic changes to every country.

ABOUT SOUTHERN & EASTERN EUROPE
Area: 1,307,795 sq km
Population: 133,309,000
Highest point: Musala, Bulgaria 2925m
Longest river: Danube, 2859km

COUNTRIES
Croatia, Slovenia, Bosnia, Yugoslavia, Macedonia, Albania, Czech Republic, Slovakia, Hungary, Bulgaria, Greece, Romania, Poland.

ECONOMY
Farming: Many people still work on the land, especially in Bulgaria and Albania, growing cereals and sugar beet. Southern countries grow grapes and olives.
Natural resources: Most countries have coal reserves, especially Poland, but few other mineral resources – except chromium ore in Albania and copper in Poland.
Industry: Poland, Hungary, Romania, Czech Republic and Slovakia are heavily industrialized, with the emphasis on making heavy machines, cars and chemicals.

GOVERNMENT
Most of these countries were recently under communist rule; now only Albania is. Most now have democratic governments. But the changeover has uncovered national differences in countries united under the communists, such as former Yugoslavia.

LANGUAGES
In most countries, people speak their own Slavic or German language. Hungarians speak Magyar. Greeks speak Greek and Romanians speak a language like Latin. But there are many different languages spoken throughout the region.

RELIGION
In Greece, Bulgaria and Romania, most people belong to Orthodox Churches (page 191). Many people in Bosnia, Albania and Bulgaria are Muslim. Elsewhere most people are Roman Catholic.

THE LAND
Eastern Europe stretches from the Baltic in the north to the Aegean Sea and Adriatic Sea in the south and the Black Sea in the east.

Eastern Europe is a land of thickly wooded mountains and vast, open plains. Running through the centre are the beautiful Carpathian mountains and the Transylvanian Alps of Romania, said to be home of the legendary Count Dracula.

On the Polish side of the mountains lies the North European plain, with wide heaths and marshes near the coast and fertile land further south around Warsaw and Lodz. On the poor heathland soils, farmers grow oats, rye and potatoes; on the richer soils, wheat, barley and sugar beet.

Between the southern arms of the mountains are three broad and fertile basins centring on the Czech Republic (page 211) city of Prague, on Budapest in Hungary and on Bucharest in Romania. Here,
winters are cold but summers are warm, and farmers grow maize, sunflowers and tobacco. On south-facing slopes, there are vineyards and orchards. The great river Danube winds across the wide Hungarian and Romanian plains, cutting through the Transylvanian Alps between these two plains in a deep gorge called the Iron Gates. Ships using the Danube bypass the Iron Gates' dangerous rapids through the Sip Canal.

Southern Europe, often called the Balkans, is rugged and mountainous. Mt Musala in Bulgaria towers to 2925m; Mt Olympus in Greece is only 8m shorter. Because the rock is often porous limestone (page 94), the scant summer rainfall sinks into the ground rapidly, leaving much of the mountains arid and fit only for grazing sheep and goats.

Many southern Europeans live near the sea – along the jagged and broken Adriatic and Greek coasts,

Romanian church Most people in Romania belong to the Romanian Orthodox Church, and churches look rather like those in Russia.

Prague, the historic capital of the Czech Republic on the banks of the Vltava river, is one of Europe's most beautiful cities.

and on the thousands of islands that are dotted throughout the Aegean Sea. The weather is warm here, and each summer brings millions of tourists, drawn by the sun, the beautiful scenery and beaches and the ruins of Ancient Greece.

THE PEOPLE

Southern and eastern Europe contains a rich mixture of peoples. But they have been torn this way and that so often by the surrounding powerful countries that individual cultures are often hard to identify.

At the turn of the century, nearly all the area was under the domination of four great Empires: the Ottoman Turks, the German empire of Prussia, the Austrian empire, and the Russian empire. When these broke up after World War I, Poland, Czechoslovakia, Hungary and other nations briefly enjoyed independence before they were occupied first by Germany and then by the Soviet Union at the end of World War II. Afterwards, most eastern

Budapest was a grand city famous for its stylish coffee bars when Hungary was part of the Austrian Empire in the 19th century.

Modern Athens is very different from its ancient counterpart. It is a noisy, bustling city with air so polluted that most cars are only allowed into the city on alternate days.

European countries were run by communist governments under the control of the Soviet Union and remained so until 1989-1990, when revolutions forced out the communists.

The communist era left a turmoil of political and economic problems which may take decades to sort out. First of all, there is the problem of where to draw boundaries. Under communism, Czechia and Slovakia were united as Czechoslovakia, but in 1993 they split up again. Czechoslovakia has become the Czech Republic and Slovakia. Similarly, Croatia, Macedonia, Slovenia, and Bosnia-Herzegovina have broken away from Yugoslavia. Sorting out this problem has caused many bitter conflicts.

Secondly, heavy industries had been built up under the communists in countries like Poland and Czechoslovakia to supply the Soviet Union. With the collapse of the communists, these industries have no one to supply. They also cause a great deal of pollution. Krakow in Poland is thought to be the dirtiest city in Europe.

People in the east of Europe are generally very poor compared to people in the west, and the new democratic governments of countries like the Czech Republic and Hungary are hoping to become full members of the European Union, to benefit from its wealth.

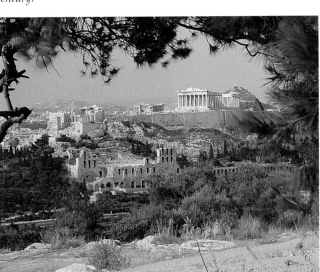

SOLIDARITY AND LECH WALESA

When Poland's communist government imposed high price rises in 1981, Gdansk shipyard workers led by Lech Walesa protested. The protest movement spread like wildfire, gaining 10 million members and the name *Solidarity*. Polish leader Wojciech Jaruzelski banned Solidarity and had Walesa arrested. But Solidarity had the support of the West and the economy was in a mess. Solidarity carried on protesting, and in 1989 Jaruzelski was forced to lift the ban. In the elections that year, Solidarity swept to victory, and the communist party was dissolved in 1990. Solidarity failed to solve the country's economic problems and in 1990 Walesa stood for election as president and was voted in.

INDEPENDENT GREECE

In 1820, Greece had been languishing under the rule of the Ottoman Turks for nearly 400 years, and the glories of Ancient Athens were long past. That year, however, the people of Greece began a hard war to gain independence. The struggle caught the imagination of people all over Europe, including the romantic poet Lord Byron, who came to fight for the Greeks. When British and French fleets sunk the Turkish sultan's fleet at Navarino Bay in 1827, the sultan was forced to grant Greece independence. In 1981, Greece joined the European Community.

DID YOU KNOW?

Lech Walesa, leader of Solidarity, was the first union leader to win the Nobel Peace Prize.
Nicolae Ceausescu, dictator of Romania from 1967 till his death in 1989, planned to wipe out every Romanian village to increase farmland.
There are over 270,000 nomadic Romany people in Bulgaria.
Bulgarian is written in the Cyrillic (Russian) alphabet; Greek is written in the Greek alphabet.
Budapest has Europe's largest bus factory. Until 100 years ago, Budapest was two towns, Buda and Pest, separated by the Danube river.

THE FORMER SOVIET UNION

Until 1991, the whole of Northern Asia and the far eastern part of Europe was a single country, the Soviet Union, stretching almost 9000km from the Baltic to the Bering seas. Now it has split into 15 separate republics, of which the largest, the Russian Federation or Russia, is still by far the biggest country in the world.

ABOUT THE FORMER SOVIET UNION
Area: 22,402,200 sq km
Population: 286,700,000
Highest point: Mount Garmo in the Pamir range, Tajikistan, 7495m
Longest river: Yenisey-Angara, 5550km

COUNTRIES
Armenia, Moldova, Estonia, Latvia, Lithuania, Georgia, Azerbaijan, Tajikistan, Kyrgyzstan, Belarus, Uzbekistan, Ukraine, Kazakhstan, Russia, Turkmenistan

ECONOMY
Farming: This varies greatly from the mountainous Arctic regions of the north to the sub-tropical Black Sea climate in the south.
Main crops: apples, barley, cotton, dairy products, maize, potatoes, rye, sugar beet, wheat, wool.
Livestock: reindeer, horses, cattle, sheep, pigs.
Natural resources: There are great deposits of oil, natural gas, coal, asbestos, manganese, silver, tin and zinc.
Industry: Steel-making, oil refining, timber, chemicals and cotton manufacturing.

GOVERNMENT
Until 1991, power in the Union of Soviet Socialist Republics (USSR) was in the hands of the Communist Party, which ran the national government in the capital, Moscow. The 15 republics of the USSR each had their own local governments which were also communist controlled. Then, in December 1991, the USSR was dissolved and the republics became independent countries. Some of these nations have joined in a loose alliance known as the Commonwealth of Independent States, which has no central governing body.

LANGUAGES
More than 80 languages are spoken among the nations of the former Soviet Union, and some 70 dialects. Russian is the most common language, spoken by about 52% of the population.

THE LAND
The countries of the former Soviet Union vary greatly in their climate and landforms. To the north, bordering on the Arctic, there is the great, cold treeless plain, known as the *tundra.* For much of the year the land here is frozen over. A little farther south the tundra slowly gives way to the *taiga,* millions of square kilometres of conifer forests. Farther south still are the *steppes,* the great grazing grasslands of central Asia. Around the Black Sea, a popular holiday spot, the climate is sub-tropical and all sorts of fruit may be grown. At the extreme southern end of the region there are mountain ranges. The former Soviet Union is bounded by a number of countries.

In the west, it shares boundaries with Finland, Norway, Poland, Slovakia, Romania, Turkey and Iran. To the south are four countries: Afghanistan, Mongolia, China and North Korea.

THE PEOPLE
The people of the 15 countries have always been fiercely independent. Even before the break-up of the Soviet Union, they had been demanding their independence. Each country has its own language and traditions, but the main types of language spoken are Slavonic, Turkic, Armenian, Uralic and Georgian. It is estimated that more than 260 million people speak one of the Slavonic dialects.

GEORGIA
Georgia probably has the most pleasant climate of all the countries of the former Soviet Union and is a popular tourist area. It borders the Black Sea with its continental climate and shares a boundary with Turkey. There are many holiday resorts along the coast of the Black Sea. However, Georgia has suffered from some ethnic conflict in recent years. The country has large deposits of manganese and coal and houses a number of oil refineries.

Nomadic sheep herders (left) *follow a traditional way of life in what used to be the Soviet Republic of Kyrgyzstan.*

The Kremlin Palace (right) *was the symbol of communist power in the Soviet Union until its break-up in 1991.*

Religion (above) *was discouraged in the former Soviet Union, but all the world's major faiths were practised within its boundaries.*

The people of Northern Asia (right) *take a great pride in their national costumes.*

COMMUNICATIONS

In such a vast and difficult area, communications have always been a problem. For hundreds of years, merchants tried to solve the problem of moving the vast wealth of northern Asia to markets in the west and east. One of the first trade routes was the old Silk Road from China to Europe. Today the city of Tashkent in Uzbekistan, on the site of the old Silk Road, is a modern city with over two million inhabitants and is the centre of the area's cotton industry.

Another attempt to open up the region was the construction of the trans-Siberian railway, covering a distance of 9298km on an eight-day journey from Moscow to the Pacific coast. Before the break-up of the Soviet Union, a great pipeline from Siberia to Europe was constructed to pump the huge supplies of oil found in the region to markets in the west.

Nevertheless, for a region enormously wealthy in oil, grain and natural gas, the problem of transporting these items to markets overseas remains a difficult one for the farmers, miners and engineers.

WILDLIFE

The northern part of the region abounds in animals trapped and hunted for their fur, including sable, ermine, bear, fox and beaver. There are also herds of reindeer. Further south, lakes and seas abound in fish and shellfish, such as salmon, sturgeon, herring, carp and crabs.

RUSSIA

The country of Russia stretches from the Arctic Ocean to sub-tropical regions in the south. It has the longest Arctic coastline in the world. It also extends into Europe in the west and as far as the Pacific coast to the east. It covers an area of 17,078,005 sq km and has a population of 148 million. Its iron, steel and engineering industries are the most productive of all the former states of the USSR, yet in its northern regions reindeer rearing is a major commercial activity. Russia has the largest deposits of oil in the former Soviet Union and Europe as well as huge timber-producing forests. The Volga, a great navigable river, flows through it to the Caspian Sea.

END OF THE SOVIET UNION

When the break-up of the Soviet Union was announced in 1991, the leaders of the two most powerful countries, President Boris Yeltsin of Russia and President Leonid Kravchuk of the Ukraine, issued a statement which said: 'The USSR, as a subject of international law and a geopolitical reality, ceases to exist.' The idea was that the 15 countries should become completely responsible for their own futures. Unfortunately, it was not so simple, for the Soviet system had ensured that everything from the army to the telephone system was interlinked. Unravelling such problems will take many years. Disputes over who owns what are already bitter.

DID YOU KNOW?
The former Soviet Union contains the world's largest and deepest lakes.
The Caspian Sea, located between Russia, Azerbaijan, Turkmenistan and Kazakhstan, is a salt-water lake of 371,000 sq km.
Lake Baykal in Russia is more than 1600m deep. It contains 20% of the Earth's supply of fresh water. More than 300 rivers flow into Lake Baykal, but only one flows out of it.
Parts of Siberia in Russia are among the world's coldest places. There have been temperatures of almost –68°C recorded here.

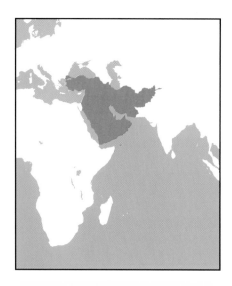

ABOUT THE MIDDLE EAST
Area: 6,180,746 sq km
Population: 176,535,000
Highest point: Demavend, Iran, 5601m
Longest river: Euphrates, 2815km

COUNTRIES
Bahrain, Lebanon, Qatar, Kuwait, Israel, United Arab Emirates, Jordan, Syria, Oman, Iraq, Yemen, Turkey, Iran, Saudi Arabia.

ECONOMY
Farming: Where land can be irrigated, dates, fruit, cotton, lentils and cereals are grown. Israel is famous for Jaffa oranges. Oman grows trees for frankincense.
Natural resources: Oil reserves are huge. Israel is famous for cut diamonds, Lebanon for other gems.
Industry: Only Israel has much industry that is not entirely oil-based, though Syria, Turkey, Iraq and Iran are well on the way to being industrialized.

GOVERNMENT
Many of the Arab countries of the Middle East – that is, all but Israel – are dominated by Islamic traditions, and ruled by kings or emirs, sultans and sheikhs who have absolute power. Yemen is a socialist republic. Turkey is also a republic, but it has often been run by army generals. Iraq is also a republic, ruled by President Saddam Hussein. Israel is a western-style republic.

LANGUAGES
Arabic is spoken in all the Islamic countries, except for Iran, where Farsi (Persian) is spoken, and Turkey, where they speak Turkish. In Israel, Jews speak Hebrew.

RELIGION
Islam is the dominant religion throughout the Arab world. Lebanon has many Christians; Israel is mostly Jewish.

SPORT
Sport is not popular but football is played.

THE MIDDLE EAST

It was in the Middle East, over 10,000 years ago, that people first learned to farm and later built the first cities. Persian, Byzantine and Islamic empires dominated the area in their time, but until the recent discovery of oil much of it was very poor.

THE LAND
Much of the Middle East is hot, dry, rocky desert where people are few and far between. Indeed, vast areas, like the Rub' al Khali or 'Empty Quarter' in southern Arabia are completely uninhabited. There are high mountains, too, such as the Asir mountains of Saudi Arabia and Yemen by the Red Sea and the plateaus of Turkey and Iran, where winters can be bitterly cold. But there is also a crescent of fertile land running westwards through Iraq by the Tigris and Euphrates rivers and south into Lebanon and Israel. It is in this crescent that the ruins of the world's oldest cities are found.

IRAN
Iran has a history dating back thousands of years. Until 1935, it was known as Persia and the last Shah (emperor) of Persia was overthrown only in 1979 by a popular revolution, led by Muslim leader Ayatollah Ruhollah Khomeini.

The revolution was provoked not only by the Shah's oppressive rule but also by his westernization of the country, which many Muslims felt violated Islamic law. When Khomeini came to power, he halted the westernization of Iran and declared a republic based upon fundamental Islamic principles (page 126). Iran's relationship with

Oil (right) has brought wealth to many poor Arab countries, such as Bahrain and Kuwait.

A Bedouin on a camel (left) stands before the Treasury building at the city of Petra in Jordan. Petra was the capital of the ancient kingdom of Nabataea.

THE DEAD SEA
The Dead Sea on the Israel-Jordan border is the lowest point on Earth, 396m below the level of the Red Sea. It is also the world's saltiest sea. Although regularly replenished with fresh water by the River Jordan, it steadily evaporates in the hot sun, leaving the water incredibly salty. The saltiness not only kills all life, which is why it is called the Dead Sea, but also makes the water so dense it is almost impossible to sink – people float so easily they can lie on their backs in the water reading a newspaper or drinking tea!

the western powers deteriorated. Soon after, long-standing territorial disputes over the Shatt al Arab region spurred Iraq to invade, starting an eight-year war that cost both sides dearly. In 1989, Khomeini died, the country elected its first president, and attitudes to the West began to soften.

The 1979 revolution reversed the rapid industrialization of Iran under the Shah – paid for by the country's huge oil reserves. Oil continues to play a large part in the country's fortunes, but people are now looking more to small-scale farming, manufacturing, trading and making Persian carpets, rather than heavy industry.

Yemeni woman *The people of Yemen are among the world's poorest, with an income per head just 3% of the United Arab Emirates.*

The Church of St Mary Magdalene *on the Mount of Olives in Jerusalem (right).*

ISRAEL

Despite its brief history and lack of natural resources, Israel is one of the most developed countries in the Middle East – thanks to foreign aid (mainly from the USA) and its own people's determination. Israel was set up by the UN in 1948 to provide a permanent home for the Jews, and since then the country has thrived economically. Irrigation and soil conservation has helped the country produce most of its own food, and industry makes chemicals and machines for export. But Israel's will to succeed has brought it into constant and bitter contact with its Arab neighbours, especially over the Palestinian

Mecca in Saudi Arabia is the birthplace of Muhammad, and every Muslim tries to visit it once in a lifetime.

refugees living in the West Bank area invaded by Israel in 1967 (page 148).

THE ARAB STATES

Oil has turned many Arab countries into some of the richest in the world. The people of the United Arab Emirates, Bahrain and Kuwait have a higher income per head than anyone but Americans.

Wealth from oil sales is being used to develop new airports, roads, factories, schools and hospitals, as well as provide a luxurious lifestyle for a powerful few. *Desalination plants* have also been built in many places to improve the water supply by taking the salt out of sea water. Many people from Europe and neighbouring Asian countries are here to work on these projects and the foreign influence has had a noticeable effect on lifestyles.

All the Arab states have regular contact with the western nations through business and through the oil trade organization OPEC. All the same, most Arabs are committed Muslims and retain their traditions. Arab businessmen often attend meetings in traditional flowing robes and women are still expected to hide themselves in the Islamic way.

JERUSALEM'S SACRED SITES

Jerusalem is not only one of the oldest cities in the world, dating back at least 6000 years; it also contains sites sacred to Christians, Muslims and Jews. In 1967, the Israelis occupied the city, removed the barriers set up by the Arabs between the Arab and Israeli halves of the city and made it their capital. It has long been a source of conflict. A trouble spot is the Temple Mount, holy to both Muslims and Jews. One side is the Wailing Wall, the most holy Jewish site; on top is the Al Aqsa mosque on the spot where Muhammad ascended into heaven. Some radical Jews wish to replace the mosque with a Jewish temple.

DID YOU KNOW?
Muhammad turned to pray first to Jerusalem, not Mecca, in reverence to Abraham. But when Jews refused to accept Muhammad's claim that Abraham was a Muslim, he faced Mecca instead, where Abraham built the Kaaba shrine, the holiest place in Islam.
The oil wells of Kuwait produced 1,150,000 barrels of oil per day before the invasion by Iraq.
Jericho in Palestine is the world's oldest town – at least 10,000 years old.
The Suez Canal, linking the Mediterranean and Red Seas, was first opened in 1869. It is 162km long.

NORTH AMERICA

The United States of America is the richest and most powerful nation in the world. Over 250 million people live here, and it covers a vast area of North America, from the freezing wastes of Alaska to the hot and steamy Everglades (marshes) of Florida. Canada is even bigger. In fact, it is the second largest country in the world, but it has a population of just 28 million.

ABOUT NORTH AMERICA
Area: 19,285,515 sq km
Population: 284,000,000
Highest point: Mt McKinley, Alaska, 6914m
Longest river: Mississippi-Missouri, 6020km

COUNTRIES
United States of America, Canada.

ECONOMY
Farming: More than 25% of the USA is pasture, and huge numbers of beef cattle are raised. Agriculture is heavily mechanized and produces surpluses for export. Main crops are maize, wheat, soya beans, cotton.
Natural resources: The USA has rich natural resources and is self-sufficient in all but oil, chemicals and newsprint. It is the world's second largest timber producer.
Industry: The USA manufactures just about everything, in huge quantities, from iron and steel to computers. Cars remain very important.

GOVERNMENT
The USA is the world's oldest democratic republic and is governed by a president, two Houses of Congress and the Judiciary, in accordance with the Constitution of 1788 (page 138). Canada has been independent from Britain since 1931. Its government, like Britain's, is led by a prime minister, whose party has a majority in the Commons, one of two houses of parliament. The PM is 'appointed' by the British monarch.

LANGUAGES
Numerous languages are spoken in the USA, but English is predominant, as it is in Canada, but for French-speaking Quebec.

RELIGION
Most North Americans are Christians, belonging to one of many different churches.

SPORT
Sports are very popular in North America and the three big sports are baseball, basketball and American football.

THE LAND
The rugged Rocky Mountains stretch nearly 5000km down the west of North America from Alaska to Mexico. In the wetter north, there are thickly forested slopes and snowy peaks climbing to over 6000m. Much of the dry south is scorching desert with salt flats and deep canyons.

Beyond the Rockies, a vast plain stretches east for thousands of kilometres to the Appalachian Mountains and north to the old hard rocks of the Canadian Shield. In the drier west of this plain is the grassland of the Great Plains, where millions of cattle and sheep graze on ranches. In the heart lie the flat prairies, where wheat grows in fields stretching as far as the eye can see. Further south is the cotton belt, either side of the great Mississippi river. And in the middle of the continent are the five Great Lakes – Superior, Michigan, Huron, Erie and Ontario, among the largest lakes in the world.

East of the Appalachians is the Atlantic coastal plain, where Europeans first settled. This area is still very densely populated and includes the huge city of New York, with a population of over 17 million.

THE PEOPLE
Long before the first Europeans arrived, North America was the home of Indians, or Native Americans, as they are now called. There were once hundreds of different Indian tribes, each with their own customs and way of life, from the Pawnee, who lived in domed earth huts, to the Cheyenne, who lived in tall tents called tepees and hunted buffalo. But from 1620 on, more and more people came from Europe to settle here and pushed further westwards, wiping out the Indians as they went (page 138). Now most remaining Indians live in special reservations in the south west and in the mountains.

At first, European settlers came mainly from

Totem poles had sacred meaning for the Indians – the original inhabitants of North America.

Inuits have lived in the frozen north of Canada for thousands of years, hunting for seals, fish and caribou (reindeer).

Britain, which is why most North Americans speak English – except in parts of Canada, where French is spoken. But from 1840 on, immigrants began to arrive from all over Europe. Immigration is now restricted, although poor people from Latin America often cross the United States border illegally.

Racial tension The mixture of cultures and nationalities earned the USA the name 'Melting Pot', but the mix is far from easy and the country is beset by racial tensions, especially in cities such as Los Angeles, New York and Chicago, where there are many poor people of different races. The wealth and prejudices of many white people, for instance, excites the anger of the black descendants of Africans brought there as slaves, and also of poor *Hispanics* (people from Latin America), Puerto Ricans and others.

Lifestyles vary greatly across the continent, from the traditional life of the Inuits of northern Canada, who live by hunting and fishing, to the hustle and bustle of New York, where life goes on 24 hours a day. The small towns of middle America are known for their conservative views; the warm coast of California attracts the young and rich.

THE WEALTH OF AMERICA

With a wealth of natural resources and a large, energetic population, the USA has dominated the world economy since the end of World War II. For a while, in the 1950s and 1960s, the USA cornered more than 25% of the world market in manufactured goods, and Americans earned more money, ate more food, used more energy and drove more cars than anyone else in the world.

Now, the American economy has lost ground to countries such as Japan, Germany and Korea, and the country sustains its high standard of living partly by borrowing money on a massive scale. It also has to import huge amounts of energy, mainly in the form of oil, to keep its millions of motor cars on the road.

The government and business people worry about the state of the economy, what to do about rising imports from Japan and how to keep Americans rich. Others worry about the effects of America's debt on the rest of the world and about the drain its huge consumption of food, energy and other resources places on our planet.

The Grand Canyon in Arizona is 450km long, up to 20km wide and 1615m deep. The Colorado River runs along the bottom.

Houston, Texas is one of the fastest-growing cities in the USA, and home to the US space agency NASA's Johnson Space Center.

THE STATES

The USA is not a single country like Brazil or Canada, but a *federation* or group of 50 separate states, such as Texas and Alaska, each represented by a star on the country's flag, known as the 'Stars and Stripes'. Originally there were just 13 states on the Atlantic coast, but as Americans spread westwards during the 19th century, new states were added. All but two of the states are grouped together between the Atlantic and Pacific oceans. The other two are Alaska, on the far northwest tip of North America, and Hawaii – a group of islands in the Pacific. Alaska is the largest state. Hawaii is the youngest, joining only in 1959.

NEW YORK

New York is North America's largest city, with a population of over 17 million. Its spectacular skyline of skyscrapers is among the most famous in the world. The first skyscraper was the Flatiron building, built in 1902. Other big skyscrapers include the Empire State Building (381m tall), for 40 years the tallest building in the world, and the even taller twin-tower World Trade Center (415m tall). The city was founded in 1624 as New Amsterdam by Dutchman Peter Minuit, who bought the island now called Manhattan from the Indians for cloth, beads and trinkets worth just $24. Minuit thought he was buying 89 sq km of land; in fact it was only 57 sq km, but proved to be a bargain. The English seized New Amsterdam and renamed it New York in 1664.

DID YOU KNOW?

Four cities were rivals to be Canada's capital in 1858 – Quebec, Montreal, Kingston and Toronto. But Queen Victoria chose Ottawa, then 4 years old.

The border between the USA and Canada is the longest in the world, stretching over 6000km.

The hottest place in the USA is Death Valley, where it soars above 50°C.

Americans eat 45,000 burgers every minute.

Over 1 million litres of water pour over the Niagara Falls every second.

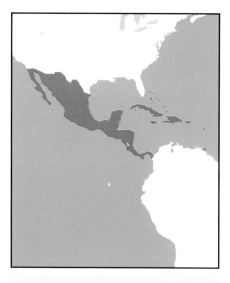

CENTRAL AMERICA & THE CARIBBEAN

Central America is the narrow strip of land that joins North America to South America. In Panama, where the Panama Canal links the Caribbean Sea to the Pacific Ocean, it is just 85km wide. Stretching away westwards in a great arc 4000 km long are the hundreds of tropical islands of the Caribbean.

ABOUT CENTRAL AMERICA AND THE CARIBBEAN

Area: Central America 2,471,984 sq km
Population: Central America 106,569,000
Highest point: Citlaltépetl, Mexico, 5699m
Longest river: Rio Grande, 3034km

COUNTRIES

Central America: El Salvador, Belize, Costa Rica, Panama, Guatemala, Honduras, Nicaragua, Mexico. *Caribbean:* includes Barbados, Antigua & Barbuda, Dominica, Martinique, Trinidad & Tobago, Puerto Rico, Jamaica, the Bahamas, Grenada, Haiti, Dominican Republic, Cuba.

ECONOMY

Farming: Coffee, cotton, bananas, and, in the Caribbean, sugar cane for export. People grow maize and wheat for food.
Natural resources: Only Mexico and Trinidad have oil and gas. Mexico is the world's leading producer of silver.
Industry: Mexico has growing chemical, motor and textile industries.

GOVERNMENT

All countries but Cuba have governments elected by popular vote. The USA invaded Panama in 1989, Grenada in 1983 and helps keep right-wing governments in power. US backing for Contra rebels in Nicaragua undermined the socialist Sandinista regime, aiding its defeat in the 1990 elections.

LANGUAGES

Some people speak native languages, but 90% of Central Americans speak Spanish. English is common in the Caribbean.

RELIGION

The major religion is Christianity (Roman Catholic), though there are Protestants too. Many Jamaicans are Rastafarians.

SPORT

Soccer is popular in Central America, cricket on the islands of the Caribbean.

CENTRAL AMERICA

Central America is a land of sea and mountains. The peaks of the Sierra Madre stretch from Mexico to Honduras, towering in places to over 5500m. Yet the sea is rarely far away. High up, the climate is cool, but down near the coast there are steamy, tropical jungles, and the marshes of the Caribbean coast, including the aptly named Mosquito Coast, are especially hot and sticky. Most people live on the cooler Pacific slopes, or in Mexico and Costa Rica, in the high *mesetas* (tablelands) between the mountains, growing coffee, cotton and bananas on the steep hillsides.

Natural disasters are frequent in Central America. Hurricanes batter the Caribbean coast each summer. Barely a year goes by without a major earthquake. And Mexico contains the world's biggest active volcanoes, including Popocatepetl (5452m), Ixtaccihuatl (5286m) and Citlaltépetl (5699m).

The people It was here that Columbus landed on his historic voyages in the 1490s (page 135), and the Spanish began to settle soon after. Yet the Maya and other early civilizations had flourished here for thousands of years. The coming of the Spanish decimated the native peoples living here. In 1519, there were 25 million Indians in Mexico alone; by 1600 there were just one million. Those that survived lived in semi-slavery. There are still many native peoples in Central America, especially in Guatemala, but the majority of people are *mestizos*, descended from both native peoples and Spaniards.

Poverty The people of Central America are among the world's poorest. Most work the land, growing food for themselves or labouring on the coffee plantations. Despite land reform in Nicaragua and Mexico, much of

Sweet slavery Most of the Caribbean people are descendants of slaves brought from Africa to work on the sugar plantations. Many still have to work growing sugar cane for export.

A fruit market in Grenada shows just some of the range of tropical fruits and vegetables grown in the Caribbean – including mangoes, yams, coconuts, pineapples and bananas.

the land still belongs to a rich few. Much is also devoted to 'cash crops' – crops that can be sold abroad like coffee and sugar – rather than food.

In the 1970s, Mexico began to exploit its oil and gas resources, and Mexican peasants flocked to the cities to find work in the new industries. Mexico City, in particular, grew so fast that it is now the largest city in the world, with a population of 19 million. Many poor Mexicans and other Central Americans try to sneak past the border patrols into the USA to find a better living there.

Nearly all the countries in Central America have been torn apart by revolution and civil war at some time – Mexico, Honduras and Costa Rica earlier this century and Nicaragua until 1990. Fighting ended in El Salvador in 1992, and there was unrest in Panama. Belize alone has been relatively peaceful.

THE CARIBBEAN ISLANDS
The islands dotted through the blue waters of the Caribbean are often called the West Indies or Antilles. Some are just rocky outcrops. Some are large and varied, with high mountains and rolling hills. The biggest are Cuba, Jamaica and Hispaniola. Hispaniola is split into two countries: Haiti and the Dominican Republic.

Hurricanes are a constant hazard on these islands. Bad storms, such as Hurricane David in 1980, bring devastation with their ferocious winds and the terrible floods that often follow.

The people Just as in Central America, native peoples such as Arawaks and Caribs once lived in the Caribbean. But most died soon after the arrival of Europeans, from disease, physical abuse and despair. The Caribbean people of today are mostly descended from black Africans, brought by Europeans in the 17th and 18th centuries as slaves to work on the sugar plantations. As a result, most people speak English or French, or a local version of these languages.

Although the people of the Caribbean were actually freed from slavery over a century ago, most were left with very little and remain poor. Even today, many work on large sugar and coffee plantations for low wages.

More than half the Caribbean people work on the land. Some work on the plantations and farm their own plot as well, to provide food for their families. Only on a few islands, such as Puerto Rico, is there much industry. In recent years, the tourists who come for the warm weather and clear seas have helped bring in extra money.

JAMAICAN MUSIC
Music has always been important to the poor black people of Kingston, Jamaica. In the 1960s, they began to develop their own styles, partly based on American soul. First there was *ska* and *rock steady*, promoted by the Trojan record label and played by groups like Toots and the Maytals. Then from the late 1960s on, there was reggae with its strong, springy deep bass rhythm and hypnotic vocals. Reggae songs were often highly political or about the Rastafarian religion. The most famous reggae group was Bob Marley and the Wailers.

CUBA
In the late 1800s Cuba was a Spanish colony inhabited by Spanish immigrants and freed African slaves. It gained its independence in 1903, but for the next 50 years most Cubans lived in poverty under a series of corrupt dictatorships, ending with that of Fulgencio Batista. Batista was overthrown by a revolution led by Fidel Castro in 1959.

Castro seized all American property, promised Cubans freedom and made Cuba a communist country. He survived a US-backed attempt to invade the island at the Bay of Pigs in 1961, and, helped by massive Soviet aid in the 1960s and 70s, gave Cuba a good education and health service. He also sent Cuban troops abroad to support revolutions in Latin America and Africa, notably Angola. But his dictatorial control is not liked by all Cubans.

Mayan Woman (left) In Mexico, Guatemala and Honduras, the Mayan people number over 2 million.
The Panama Canal (below) has been a source of conflict since it was built in 1914. It is now controlled by the USA, but control goes to Panama in 2000.

Mayan pyramid (below) The Maya left behind many traces of their remarkable civilization (page 123), including this pyramid in the jungle.

DID YOU KNOW?

Teotihuacan, near Mexico City, with its vast pyramids, is one of the best preserved of all ancient cities. At its height in AD 300, 100,000 lived here.
Paracutin, a 300m volcano of ash in Mexico, grew from nothing in a year.
Haiti is one of the poorest countries in the world.
Mexico owes over 100 billion dollars – over half its gross domestic product.
The Mexican population quadrupled between 1940 and 1990.
The people of Martinique and Guadeloupe vote in French elections.

SOUTH AMERICA

South America is the fourth largest continent. Its northern shores are washed by the warm tropical waters of the Caribbean Sea, while its southern tip, Cape Horn, reaches within less than 1000km of the Antarctic Circle. There are twelve independent nations on the continent, many of them very poor. The largest, Brazil, occupies nearly half of the land.

ABOUT SOUTH AMERICA
Area: 17,611,000 sq km
Population: 283,519,000
Highest point: Aconcagua, Argentina, 6960m
Longest river: Amazon, 6515km

COUNTRIES
From smallest to largest: French Guiana, Surinam, Uruguay, Guyana, Paraguay, Ecuador, Chile, Venezuela, Bolivia, Colombia, Peru, Argentina and Brazil.

ECONOMY
Farming: Only 5% of the land is used for growing crops, chief among which are maize, wheat and rice. Brazil and Colombia are the world's leading coffee exporters.
Natural resources: South America has great mineral wealth – much still unexplored. Venezuela is rich in oil. Chile is the world's largest copper producer after the USA.
Industry: Industry is beginning to develop, especially in Brazil, which is the world's fifth largest car maker.

GOVERNMENT
Much of South America was freed from Spanish rule by Simon Bolivar in the 1820s. Since then many countries have been ruled by harsh military dictators – overthrown every so often by revolution – such as Pinochet in Chile. Most countries are now moving towards democracy.

LANGUAGES
Most South Americans speak the languages of the European conquerors: Portuguese in Brazil and Spanish elsewhere. Ten million still speak a native language; half of them Quechua, the language of the Inca empire.

RELIGION
Most non-native peoples are Roman Catholics, but native peoples have their own beliefs.

SPORTS
Football is popular in the cities.

THE ANDES AND THE AMAZON
South America is dominated by two huge natural features. All down the west are the lofty Andes mountains, making Ecuador, Peru and Bolivia among the world's highest countries. No capital city is higher than La Paz in Bolivia at 3600m. Flowing east to the Atlantic through the rainforests of Brazil, is the mighty Amazon river. The Amazon carries more water than any other river and is 20km wide in places.

South of the Amazon lies the high Brazilian Plateau, where most Brazilians live. Further south in Argentina, cattle are reared on grassy plains called *pampas*. Further south still, sheep graze on the dry, windswept tablelands of Patagonia. Sandwiched between the Andes and the Pacific is Chile, over 4200km long, yet nowhere wider than 430km.

THE PEOPLE
Before its conquest by the Spanish and Portuguese in the 16th century, South America was home to many native peoples. Millions died after the Europeans arrived – some killed by their conquerors, some by European diseases to which they had no resistance and some from cruel treatment. Many who survived married the Spanish settlers who came to seek their fortune. Their descendants are called *mestizos*. Between 1518 and 1850, seven million African slaves were brought here and between 1850 and 1930 12 million more Europeans arrived.

Today there is a mixture of many different races in South America, especially in large cities. Even so,

The statue of Christ the Redeemer, high on Mount Corcovado, overlooks Rio de Janeiro, a major port of Brazil.

there are native villages in the Andes with only one race, and in the Amazon there are still native tribes that have had little contact with the world outside.

A POOR CONTINENT

South America has the fastest growing population in the world, and most people are poor. In the country, much of the land is in vast estates called *latifundia* owned by a rich few. So millions of people are moving to fast-growing cities like São Paulo. But there is often no work or even homes for them here, and thousands sleep rough or live in *favelas* (shanty towns) in houses made from scrap. Industry is growing in some South American

The Uru, an ancient Indian people, live on floating mats of dried reeds on Lake Titicaca, high in the Andes between Bolivia and Peru.

A tributary of the Amazon wends its way through the Brazilian rainforest, which is the largest tropical rainforest in the world.

countries, especially Brazil, and these may create wealth in time. But growth is slow because many governments owe so much money to banks in America, Europe and Japan that they cannot afford to pay for new developments.

THE TROPICAL RAINFOREST

The Amazon forests are being cut for wood and burned to make way for farms, roads and mines at the alarming rate of 260 sq km a day. In the 1980s alone, nearly 7% of Brazil's rainforest was destroyed. As a result, the last forest-dwelling Indian tribes are threatened with extinction, along with countless species of plants and animals, and the Earth's atmosphere may suffer irreparable damage.

PERONISM

From 1946 to 1955, Argentina was ruled by President Juan Peron. Peron and his young wife Eva were popular with the poor, industrialists and churchmen. To push through his ideal of a strong, rich Argentina – called *Peronism* – he gave himself dictatorial powers and crushed all opposition. But the economy did not prosper, and when Eva died in 1952, his support dwindled. In 1955, he was driven out by a military coup. Peronism was still popular, though, and in 1973, Peron came back as president – only to die a year later. His third wife, Isabel, took over, but was thrown out by the military in 1976.

THE FALKLANDS

The Falklands are islands off the coast of Argentina, known as the Malvinas by Argentinians. They have been ruled by Britain since 1833, and the 2000 islanders speak English. But Argentinians say they belong to Argentina. After a long series of talks, Argentinian troops seized the islands' capital Port Stanley on 3 April 1982. The British launched an all-out attack by sea and air and, after two months of war in which many soldiers from both sides died, recaptured the islands on 14 June. Now 4000 British troops are stationed on the islands to guard against further invasion.

DID YOU KNOW?

Tutunendo, Colombia, with an average yearly rainfall of 1177cm, is the rainiest place in the world.

The driest place in the world is the Atacama desert in Chile. Average yearly rainfall: 0.00mm.

The highest waterfall in the world is Angel Falls in Venezuela, 979m high.

Ecuador is so called because it is crossed by the equator (in Spanish: ecuador).

The trade in illegal drugs (chiefly cocaine) in Bolivia and Colombia is so large that it is thought to earn more money than all legal trade.

Through the Amazon's mouth flows a fifth of all the world's river water.

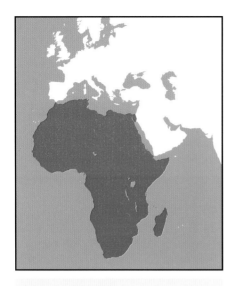

AFRICA

Africa is the world's second largest continent, stretching 8000km from the Mediterranean in the north to the Cape of Good Hope in the south. It is also the warmest, for the Equator runs right through the middle, and temperatures in the Sahara desert are the highest on Earth.

ABOUT AFRICA
Area: 30,335,000 sq km
Population: 650,000,000
Highest point: Kilimanjaro, Tanzania, 5895m
Longest river: Nile, 6695km

COUNTRIES
With population over 7 million: Algeria, Angola, Burkina Faso, Cameroon, Egypt, Ethiopia, Ghana, Ivory Coast, Kenya, Madagascar, Malawi, Mali, Morocco, Mozambique, Niger, Nigeria, Rwanda, Senegal, Somalia, South Africa, Sudan, Tanzania, Tunisia, Uganda, Zaire, Zambia, Zimbabwe.
There are also 26 smaller countries.

ECONOMY
Farming: Most Africans grow food for themselves – cassava, yams and bananas in the wetter areas, corn in drier areas. But more and more land is now used for cash crops for export, including cocoa, oil-palm, bananas, groundnuts, coffee and rubber.
Natural resources: South Africa has huge deposits of copper, diamonds and gold. Oil has made Libya and west African countries such as Nigeria rich by African standards.
Industry: Industry is developed barely anywhere but South Africa and Egypt.

GOVERNMENT
Colonial rule left Africa in chaos. Many countries have unstable European-style governments torn by tensions between tribal groups or dominated by a powerful few. Many west African countries, such as Niger and Burkina Faso, are under military governments. Egypt, Congo and Angola are socialist republics.

LANGUAGES
1300 languages are spoken in Africa – more than in any other continent.

RELIGION
Many Africans hold to traditional beliefs. North Africa is mainly Muslim. Christianity is common south of the Sahara.

THE LAND
Most of Africa is an immense plateau, punctuated here and there by mountain ranges, such as the Ruwenzori, in Uganda. In the east, the plateau is broken by the Great Rift Valley, which runs all the way from the Red Sea down into Malawi and contains such vast lakes as Rudolf and Tanganyika.

Along the tropics lie two great deserts: the Kalahari in the south and the vast Sahara in the north, stretching 5500km from the Atlantic to the Red Sea. But along the Equator in west and central Africa, there are dense green tropical forests. Much of the rest of Africa is savanna grassland and bush country roamed by elephants, antelopes, lions, giraffes, zebras and many other creatures.

Where people live Much of the land is so hot and dry, and the soil so thin, that in many places Africans have always led a nomadic or semi-nomadic lifestyle. Some continually move from place to place with their herds, looking for fresh pastures. Others clear the land of trees and grow crops for a few years, then leave the land to recover. This is called *shifting cultivation*. Only in the north, along the Nile valley and in the fertile coastal strip, is the land more permanently settled.

More than 70 per cent of Africa's population is rural and many Africans live just as they have for thousands of years, in tiny hut villages, often with less than 50 inhabitants. But over the past 30 years or so, as more and more land has been taken up for cash crops, millions of Africans have headed for growing cities, such as Cairo in Egypt and Abidjan in Ivory Coast.

THE PEOPLE
Africa has been inhabited by humans far longer than anywhere else in the world, and many remarkable cultures and civilizations have come and gone, including that of Ancient Egypt (page 116), Mali and Zimbabwe. Today in Africa, there is an

Millions of Africans live in small villages like the one shown below. People exchange the food they have grown for clothing and other things.

The Tuareg are are among the few people who can stand the blazing sun of the Sahara desert. They are wanderers who live in tents and herd camels and goats.

The Masai are tall, slender nomadic herders from Kenya. They paint themselves with red ochre and wear elaborate brass collars and bracelets and bead necklaces.

enormous variety of cultures and races. In the north, countries such as Algeria, Morocco and Egypt are mainly Arabic. South of the Sahara, most people are black Africans, but there are 800 or more different ethnic groups, each with its own unique culture and lifestyle.

Unfortunately, when the colonial powers of Europe carved Africa into nations, they largely ignored these differences. All over the continent, national boundaries cut right across tribal lands – separating peoples and leaving many small groups isolated in countries dominated by different, maybe hostile tribes. This is one reason why so many African countries have been ravaged by bloody civil wars, or fallen into the hands of dictators, such as Emperor Bokassa of the Central African Republic and Idi Amin of Uganda.

Sorghum is a kind of corn grown widely in the drier areas around the edges of the forests. It is used to make bread.

Gold is South Africa's main export. Some black South Africans travel huge distances each day to work in the Transvaal mines.

POVERTY AND FAMINE

Africa contains the most desperately poor people in the world. The GNP (page 186) of the USA for every person is nearly $20,000; Chad's is $163, Malawi's is $160, and Ethiopia's is just $120. Even in countries that earn a good deal, like South Africa, many live in dire poverty, crowded into ramshackle huts with no furniture, no power and ragged clothes.

Worse still, millions of Africans are now starving to death; many more are suffering malnutrition. Since 1980, the effects of war and overuse of land have been made worse by a series of droughts. People in Ethiopia, Sudan, Somalia and Mozambique, in particular, have suffered terrible famines. Thousands of African men, women and children are dying of hunger even as you read this.

THE SAHARA

The Sahara desert is vast, covering an area larger than the entire United States of America. It gets less than 100mm of rain each year, and shade temperatures often reach a scorching 50°C during the day, only to fall almost to freezing at night. Over 70% of the desert is coarse gravel; only 15% is rolling sand dunes. But the desert is far from lifeless; it provides a home for two million people – some are wandering herders, but most are farmers living on oases, where they grow date palms and other crops.

MOZAMBIQUE

Few people in Africa can have suffered more than the inhabitants of Mozambique. For 470 years, the country was a colony of Portugal. White *prazeros* snatched all the land, keeping the people in slavery. When the Portuguese were finally thrown out in 1975, the country became a socialist republic. At once, a guerrilla group called Renamo began waging a terror campaign against the socialists that has killed and maimed many innocent people. People lived in constant fear, their children were abducted and 5 million were forced from their homes. Even while a series of droughts plagued the country, Renamo destroyed crops and food aid. Renamo's campaign of terror may now be at an end, but many thousands of people are still dying of hunger.

DID YOU KNOW?
Africa's largest lake, covering almost 70,000 sq km, is Lake Victoria.
7.7 million litres of water flow every second over the Victoria Falls on the Zambia-Zimbabwe border.
Zimbabwe is named after the ruined ancient stone city of Great Zimbabwe that flourished there 500 years ago.
The summit of Mount Kilimanjaro is always covered in snow.
The Nile is the world's longest river flowing 6695km to the Mediterrranean Sea.
The University of Fez in Morocco was founded in AD 859.

ABOUT INDIA & ITS NEIGHBOURS
Area: 4,235,204 sq km
Population: 1,082,264,000
Highest point: K2, Pakistan, 8611m
Longest river: Indus, 3180km

COUNTRIES
Sri Lanka, Bangladesh, Pakistan, India.

ECONOMY
Farming: Two-thirds of the population grow their own food, mainly rice and wheat; cash crops include sugar cane, tea, cotton, oilseed and jute.
Natural resources: India's coal reserves give energy for industry. It also has diamonds, aluminium, copper and iron ore.
Industry: India is the 10th biggest industrial nation. Textiles are important, but the emphasis is now on heavy industry, including iron and steel, vehicles and machine tools and pharmaceuticals.

GOVERNMENT
India is the world's largest democracy, but for many years, until Rajiv Gandhi was assassinated in 1991, the Gandhi family had a stranglehold on power. In 1971, East Pakistan broke away from West Pakistan to become Bangladesh. Pakistan is a democracy, too, but the army has often had a high degree of control, especially under General Zia, who was killed in 1988.

LANGUAGES
Well over 30 languages and 1500 dialects are spoken. Hindi and English are the main languages in India, Punjabi and Urdu in Pakistan, and Bengali in Bangladesh.

RELIGION
Many religions are practised, but India is 83% Hindu; Pakistan and Bangladesh are mostly Muslim. Sri Lanka is mainly Buddhist.

SPORT
Cricket is immensely popular.

INDIA

Separated from the rest of Asia by the towering peaks of the Himalayas, the Indian sub-continent – including India, Pakistan and Bangladesh – is one of the most heavily populated regions in the world, with a civilization dating back 5000 years.

THE LAND
The northern wall of India is the Himalayas, the highest mountains in the world, where rich Indians often escape from the summer heat. To the south are the fertile plains around the Indus and Ganges rivers, heavily farmed and densely populated. India's biggest cities are here, including Delhi and Calcutta. Further south is the scrub and thorn of the Deccan, a vast upland with hills either side called the Ghats.

Much of India is hot; summers average 30°C in places. Monsoon rains (page 86) bring welcome water, and irrigation helps to grow crops in quite dry areas. But drought is common, and because the rain tends to come at once, so are floods, especially in low-lying Bangladesh.

THE GANDHIS
Mahatma Gandhi campaigned for India's independence. From 1966 to 1977 Indira Gandhi (no relation of Mahatma) was prime minister, and again from 1980 to 1984. After she was killed in 1984, her son Rajiv became prime minister. He too was murdered in 1991.

THE PEOPLE
After 50 years of independence, India is still living with the effects of British rule. English is, with Hindi, the official language; government and business run much as they did under the British. Even new cars are often old British designs. More worryingly, there is still tension over the way independence created two countries, India and East and West Pakistan, from a huge range of peoples with little in common. East Pakistan split from the West to form Bangladesh in 1971. The Sikhs' fight to split from India led to the murder of India's Prime Minister, Indira Gandhi, in 1984. Yet even though many Indians are poor, India can grow enough food to feed itself, and industry is developing steadily.

Elephants are highly regarded by most Indians, but they have long been used for work such as lifting logs.

The River Ganges is thought holy by the Hindus and there are especially holy places along its length. This is one at Varanasi (Benares).

SOUTH EAST ASIA

Warm and damp, South East Asia is a fertile part of the world where Hindu and Buddhist kings once built giant temples in the forests. Today some countries are thriving on new industry while others try to live with the scars of some of the most terrible wars of recent history.

THE LAND

South East Asia is an area of mountains, islands and wide plains. The climate is warm, and monsoons bring rain from June to October. Mountains thick with forest range from Myanmar (Burma), through Laos, Thailand and Vietnam. In between are fertile plains and deltas where most people live – around the Irrawaddy river in Myanmar, the Chao Phraya in Thailand and the Mekong in Cambodia and Vietnam. South lies the peninsula of Malaysia, stretching out into the South China Sea, and the 3700 volcanic islands of Indonesia beyond. Much of Indonesia is tropical rainforest, but the plains in between are densely populated.

THE PEOPLE

South East Asia has a long history and a wide mix of people. Most people in the north are poor and live by growing rice, especially in Laos, Myanmar and Vietnam, or, in Malaysia and Myanmar, by tapping trees for rubber. In the south, Singapore and Indonesia especially, manufacturing industry has developed under the leadership of Singapore's Lee Kuan Yew and now Goh Chok Teng, and Indonesia's Suharto.

THE KILLING FIELDS

Laos, Vietnam and Cambodia were once French colonies, and the end of French rule in the 1950s led to years of suffering and war – nowhere more so than in Cambodia. Here, the military regime supported by the USA was toppled in 1975, after a bloody struggle, by the Khmer Rouge guerrillas. At once, victorious leader Pol Pot forced 2 million Cambodians into the country and slaughtered them in the fields. Pol Pot was himself overthrown by the Vietnamese in 1978. After elections in 1993, the Cambodians reinstated their king.

In Indonesia, the construction of hillside terraces ensures every inch of land is used for rice cultivation (left).

The traditional dances of S E Asia are graceful and precise – every gesture and movement has a particular meaning (below).

ABOUT SOUTH EAST ASIA
Area: 4,188,259 sq km
Population: 713,025,000
Highest point: Hkakado Razi, Myanmar (formerly Burma), 5881m
Longest river: Mekong, 4425km

COUNTRIES
Singapore, Cambodia, Laos, Vietnam, Malaysia, Myanmar (formerly Burma), Indonesia, Philippines.

ECONOMY
Farming: Over three-quarters of the population grow rice to eat themselves.
Natural resources: Malaysia relies heavily on its rubber, tin and oil resources. Indonesia has rich but barely developed sources of oil, gas, tin, nickel and copper.
Industry: Industry is growing rapidly in Indonesia, Malaysia and Singapore, but elsewhere it is barely developed.

GOVERNMENT
Both Laos and Vietnam are one-party communist states, though officially their governments are elected by popular vote. Myanmar is a republic. Thailand has a king and a democratically elected government like Britain. Malaysia's king is elected, but power is in the hands of an elite few. Singapore is under the rule of the People's Action Party. Indonesia is ruled by the right-wing dictatorship of General Suharto. In Cambodia, the monarchy was restored in 1993.

LANGUAGES
Thai is the main language in Thailand, Vietnamese in Vietnam, Khmer in Cambodia, Burmese in Myanmar. But there are many others spoken, including over 250 languages in Indonesia.

RELIGION
Cambodia, Vietnam, Thailand and Myanmar are mainly Buddhist; Indonesia, and Malaysia are mainly Muslim.

DID YOU KNOW?
The walls of the 12th century temple of Angkor Wat, in the ancient capital of the Khmer empire in Cambodia, are over 1.5 km long.
Thailand's capital is called Bangkok by foreigners, but its real name has over 17 words, beginning 'Krungthep', which is why it is known as Krung Thep.
Thousands of Vietnamese have risked their lives in flimsy boats to find a better life elsewhere. Many of these boat people have been sent back.

AUSTRALASIA & THE SOUTH PACIFIC

Australasia and the South Pacific, sometimes known as Oceania, is a collection of more than 10,000 islands dotted through the Pacific Ocean, the world's biggest ocean. They stretch almost a third of the way round the world, 14,000km from Western Australia to Easter Island.

ABOUT AUSTRALASIA & THE SOUTH PACIFIC

Area: 8,510,000 sq km; Australia, 7,682,300 sq km; New Zealand 265,150 sq km; Papua New Guinea (PNG), 462,840 sq km
Population: 26,000,000; Australia, 17,086,197; New Zealand, 3,390,000; PNG, 3,699,000
Highest point: Mt Wilhelm, PNG, 4509m
Longest river: Murray-Darling, 3750km

COUNTRIES

Nauru,Tuvalu, Tonga, Kiribati, Western Samoa, Vanuatu, Fiji, Solomon Islands and many other island groups, New Zealand, PNG and Australia.

ECONOMY

Farming: Millions of sheep are raised for wool in Australia. New Zealand is the world's largest exporter of lamb and dairy produce, and the second largest exporter of wool. The Pacific Islands rely heavily on coconuts.
Natural resources: Australia has extensive mineral resources, including iron, silver and aluminium. PNG has big copper and gold mines on the island of Bougainville.
Industry: Industry is only really developed in Australia.

GOVERNMENT

Australia, New Zealand, PNG and the Solomon Islands were once British colonies. They now have their own parliaments and are effectively independent, but the British queen is queen here too, and is represented in each country by a Governor General who appoints the Prime Minister. Tonga and Western Samoa have their own king and parliament. Fiji and Vanuatu are republics.

LANGUAGES AND RELIGION

English is widely spoken everywhere, but many Pacific Islanders, the Aborigines of Australia and the Maoris of New Zealand have their own languages. The same is true of religion. The English church dominates, but there are many native religions.

AUSTRALIA

Australia is the world's smallest continent but its sixth largest country. Much of the country is dry and thinly populated. Most people live in the moist south east, in New South Wales and Victoria, where the biggest cities (Sydney and Melbourne) are. They also live along the east coast in Queensland and around Perth in the extreme south west. But much of the rest of Australia is virtually uninhabited.

In the east, the Great Dividing Range divides the relatively damp coastal plain from the much drier outback, where millions of sheep and cattle are grazed on vast ranches called *stations*. Beyond the outback lies the vast desert heart of the continent, stretching almost all the way to the west coast.

The people Hunters called Aborigines have lived in Australia for 40,000 years. When the British arrived in the late 1700s, the Aborigines were driven from their homes into the dry interior. Troubles brought by the British – including disease, massacre and the loss of their traditional hunting grounds – have left the Aborigines few in number and dispirited. Many now live in poverty in the southern cities.

THE GREAT BARRIER REEF

The Great Barrier Reef is one of the world's most extraordinary natural features. It is a maze of 2500 coral reefs covering an area of 207,000 sq km and stretching for 2000km along Australia's north east coast. The corals themselves are beautiful and multi-coloured and they are home to a fabulous variety of tropical fish. There are important marine biological research stations on Heron Island and Lizard Island, and the reef is visited by thousands of divers. The reef is now officially protected, but the pressure of visitors is causing problems.

Papua New Guinea has many thousands of native tribes, living their own lives in the tropical forests in the mountains, as they have done for 50,000 years. More than 700 different languages are spoken on PNG – a quarter of all the world's languages – although most people also speak Motu or a kind of English called 'Pidgin'.

Ayers Rock, in the heart of Australia, is a massive sandstone formation popular with tourists – and is also sacred to the Aborigines.

Sheep shearing in the Australian outback. Australia exports more wool than any other country in the world.

BOUGAINVILLE GOLD

The island of Bougainville, in PNG, has rich copper and gold deposits. When the natives agreed in 1967 to let their land be mined, they were told it would make them rich. But the giant Panguna mine ruined the island and destroyed hunting grounds, and the natives got barely one per cent of the profits, for most went to CRA Ltd of Australia. The natives' Bougainville Revolutionary Army (BRA) began a bombing campaign against CRA in 1988 and the mine was forced to close. The BRA demanded independence from PNG. A ceasefire was agreed in 1991.

Few of the original British and Irish settlers wanted to go to Australia. Most were people convicted of minor crimes and shipped out in terrible conditions on sailing ships called *transports*. But the discovery of gold and silver in the 19th century, and the prospect of a clean and healthy life in Australia's warm environment, gradually attracted more and more white immigrants.

Now Australia is a wealthy country with its own character and lifestyle. There is an emphasis on outdoor pursuits, such as surfing, tennis and barbecues, but Australia also has a reputation for making outstanding films and prominence in many other cultural activities. Some people are worried, though, that Australia's prosperity may suffer as a result of competition from Japan.

The Sydney Opera House with the Harbour Bridge in the background is a famous Australian landmark.

NEW ZEALAND

New Zealand is a green, mountainous country, divided into two islands. It was first settled by Maoris less than 1000 years ago. The British arrived in the mid-1800s and began to fell the forests to create large ranches, for cattle on the north island and sheep on the south. Exports of lamb, wool and dairy products have kept the country's small, young population fairly prosperous.

PACIFIC ISLANDS

The Pacific islands are often divided into three, according to the kind of people who live there: Melanesia in the west; Micronesia in the north; and Polynesia in the east. Most islands remain under the control of powerful nations such as the USA, France, the UK and Australia.

COCONUTS

The coconut has become crucial to the economy of many Pacific Islands, especially the Solomon Islands, Vanuatu and Fiji, and is often the main export. Seedling coconut palms are planted in rows on large plantations and harvested after 7–12 years. They provide more than food and drink. Soap, margarine and make-up is made from coconut oil, and the fibres of the husk are used for mats, ropes and brushes.

DID YOU KNOW?

There are 20 sheep and three cows to every human in New Zealand.

Over half of all New Zealanders are under 30 years old.

Aborigines believe they have animal, plant and human ancestors who created the world in the 'Dreamtime'.

Bikini is not only the name of a two-piece swimsuit, but also a Pacific atoll where nuclear bombs were tested.

Broken Hill in New South Wales, Australia, is the site of the world's biggest silver mine.

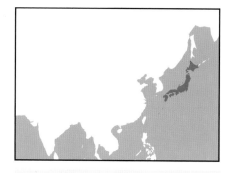

ABOUT JAPAN
Area: 377,801 sq km
Population: 123,612,000
Capital: Tokyo
Population: 11,680,000
Highest point: Mt Fuji, 3776m

ECONOMY
Farming: Only 15% of the land is good for growing crops. The main crop is rice.
Fishing: The Japanese fishing industry is one of the largest in the world.
Natural resources: Japan has few resources and relies on imports of oil and iron ore.
Industry: Japan is famous for its electronic goods, such as personal stereos. It also makes a lot of steel, half the world's ships and more cars than any other country in the world.

GOVERNMENT
For centuries, Japan was ruled by an emperor. But in 1946 it became a democracy. There is still an emperor, but the country is run by a parliament.

RELIGION
Most Japanese are Shintoists or Buddhists, but Confucianism is a strong influence.

LANGUAGE
Japanese.

DID YOU KNOW?
The Seikan railway tunnel linking Honshu to Hokkaido is the longest in the world (54km).
The Bullet Train gets from Tokyo to Fukuoka (1176km) in under 6 hours.
Buildings in Tokyo are knocked down to make way for new ones every 6 years or so.
Japanese children do 5 hours of homework a day at the age of 7.
The Japanese writing system uses over 3000 characters.

Tokyo streets are among the most polluted in the world, and traffic policemen must wear masks.

JAPAN

Japan is made up of four large islands – Hokkaido, Honshu, Shikoku and Kyushu – and nearly 4000 small ones. 75 per cent of Japanese people live on Honshu, the largest island, but the most densely populated island is Kyushu, which is linked to Honshu by railway tunnels.

MOUNTAINS AND CITIES
Japan is a very mountainous country, with steep, forested slopes, fast-flowing rivers and several volcanoes, including the famous and beautiful Mount Fuji. Most Japanese people are crowded onto the narrow plains beside the seashore and along the river valleys. Indeed nine out of ten Japanese people live in cities. Tokyo is the fourth largest city in the world, and the pace of life here is frantic. Over 40 million people live in Tokyo and its suburbs and there is so little space that most people live in very small flats.

JAPAN TODAY
Japan was defeated in World War II and two of its major cities, Hiroshima and Nagasaki, were destroyed by American atomic bombs. Since then, however, the country has become rich. The Japanese are hard workers, exporting a great many products and Japan is now the world's largest economy, recently overtaking even the USA. Japanese cities are very modern, with most homes full of all kinds of electronic gadgets. But the Japanese are also proud of their traditional culture and religion.

SHOGUNS AND SAMURAI
From 1254 to 1868, Japan was effectively ruled not by the emperor, but by strong military leaders called *shoguns*. Each shogun was served by a powerful brotherhood of warriors called *samurai*. The samurai had a very strict code of honour, called the *Bushido* ('the way of the warrior'). If they were dishonoured, samurai were expected to commit *hara-kiri* (suicide) – usually by falling on to their long, curved steel swords.

COMPANY WORKERS
Japanese workers tend to work for the same company all their lives. Workers often take holidays together, exercise together and may even sing the company song every day. Managers are so proud of their business that they often spend many evenings working. However, the pressures such a regime of hard work can bring are too much for some people, and Japan has a high suicide rate.

CHINA

With more than 1000 million (one billion) citizens, the People's Republic of China is the most populous country on Earth. One out of every five people alive today is Chinese. China is also the third largest country in the world.

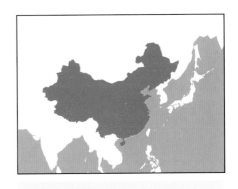

AN OLD FARMING COUNTRY

China is a huge and varied country, ranging from the lofty Himalayan mountains in the west – the world's highest – to the vast empty Gobi desert in the north and the green plains of the east by the Yellow and Yangtze rivers, where most people live. Chinese cities date back over 3500 years (page 122) and cities today, such as Beijing and Shanghai, are among the world's largest. Yet four out of five Chinese still live in the countryside, many growing rice in flooded fields called paddies.

CHINESE MEDICINE

Although China has adopted modern surgical and drug treatments from the West, it has its own tradition of medicine dating back thousands of years. Chinese chemists sell a wide range of herbal and other natural remedies. Many people are helped by acupuncture, an ancient healing and pain-relieving system, involving sticking thin needles into the skin in any of some 800 specific points.

COMMUNIST CHINA

Until this century, China was ruled by emperors, and the country had changed little for 3000 years. But in 1911, the last emperor was forced from the throne. In 1949, after a long struggle, the communists came to power, led by Mao Zedong. Now people in the country live and work on huge farming communes and people in cities work in big factories. Life for the Chinese has improved greatly under communism; disease is much rarer, nearly all can read and write, and China is now a major industrial power. But there is little freedom. Many Chinese are in jail for their political beliefs, and calls for more democracy are crushed – as they were in Beijing's Tiananmen Square in 1989, when many students and workers were killed.

ABOUT CHINA
Area: 9,597,000 sq km
Population: 1,088,870,000
Capital: Beijing (Peking)
Longest river: Yangtze, 6380km
Highest mountain Everest, 8848m

ECONOMY
Farming: 800 million Chinese are involved in farming, growing rice, wheat, corn, kaoliang (a cereal like sorghum), sweet potatoes, tea and much more besides. Pigs and poultry are common.
Fishing: The Chinese catch a great deal of freshwater fish in the big rivers of the east.
Natural resources: China has huge coal reserves, is a major oil producer and has vast potential for hydroelectricity. It also has large sources of metal ores.
Industry: China's industry is mostly heavy, but more bicycles are made in China than all the rest of the world.

GOVERNMENT
China is one of the world's few remaining communist countries and is under the control of a president and the party leaders.

RELIGION
Before Communism, most Chinese practised a mixture of Confucianism, Taoism and Buddhism.

The Hall of Prayer for Good Harvests
Built in 1420 for the emperors, this is part of the Temple of Heaven in Beijing.

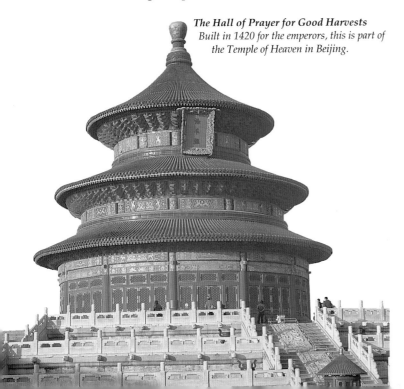

Rice paddies and fish farming along the Jingbao River, Guangxi province in south China. In the valleys of the south and east, every available piece of land is farmed, and steep hillsides are often carved into terraces for growing rice and other crops.

FACTS & FIGURES

This section is included for general interest and to expand the information presented in the rest of the book. It contains lists, for example of the world's longest rivers and highest mountains, short descriptions of famous people and an up-to-date map of the world.

CONTINENTS OF THE WORLD

CONTINENT	AREA (square km)
EURASIA	54,106,000
EUROPE	10,498,000
ASIA	43,608,000
AFRICA	30,335,000
NORTH & CENTRAL AMERICA	25,349,000
SOUTH AMERICA	17,611,000
ANTARCTICA	13,340,000
AUSTRALASIA	8,923,000

LAKES

LAKE	AREA (square km)
CASPIAN SEA	371,000
LAKE SUPERIOR	83,270
LAKE VICTORIA	68,800
LAKE HURON	60,700
LAKE MICHIGAN	58,020
LAKE TANGANYIKA	32,900
GREAT BEAR LAKE	31,790
LAKE BAYKAL	30,500

OCEANS AND SEAS

OCEAN	AREA (square km)
PACIFIC OCEAN	165,384,000
ATLANTIC OCEAN	82,217,000
INDIAN OCEAN	73,481,000
ARCTIC OCEAN	14,056,000

SEAS	AREA (square km)
MEDITERRANEAN SEA	2,505,000
SOUTH CHINA SEA	2,318,000
BERING SEA	2,269,000
CARIBBEAN SEA	1,943,000
GULF OF MEXICO	1,544,000
SEA OF OKHOTSK	1,528,000
EAST CHINA SEA	1,248,000
HUDSON BAY	1,233,300
SEA OF JAPAN	1,008,000
NORTH SEA	575,000
BLACK SEA	461,000
BALTIC SEA	422,000
RED SEA	438,000
YELLOW SEA	404,000

ISLANDS

ISLAND	AREA (square km)
GREENLAND	2,175,600
NEW GUINEA	808,510
BORNEO	757,050
MADAGASCAR	594,180
SUMATRA	524,100
BAFFIN ISLAND	476,070
HONSHU	230,456
GREAT BRITAIN	229,870
ELLESMERE ISLAND	212,690
VICTORIA ISLAND	212,200

MOUNTAINS

MOUNTAIN	HEIGHT (m)
EVEREST	8848
K2	8611
KANGCHENJUNGA	8586
MAKALU	8463
CHO OYU	8201
DHAULAGIRI	8167
MANASLU	8163
NANGA PARBAT	8125
ANNAPURNA	8091
GASHERBRUM	8068

LONGEST RIVERS AND HIGHEST MOUNTAINS BY CONTINENT

CONTINENT	RIVER	LENGTH (km)	MOUNTAIN	HEIGHT (m)
NORTH AMERICA	MISSISSIPPI	6020	McKINLEY	6194
SOUTH AMERICA	AMAZON	6515	ACONCAGUA	6960
EURASIA	YANGTZE	6380	EVEREST	8848
EUROPE	VOLGA	3688	EL'BRUS	5642
ASIA	YANGTZE	6380	EVEREST	8848
AFRICA	NILE	6695	KILIMANJARO	5895
AUSTRALASIA	MURRAY-DARLING	3750	COOK	3764
ANTARCTICA	—	—	VINSON MASSIF	5140

RIVERS

RIVER	LENGTH (km)
NILE	6695
AMAZON	6515
YANGTZE	6380
MISSISSIPPI-MISSOURI	6020
YENISEI	5550
YELLOW	5464
OB'-IRTYSH	5409
CONGO	4667
PARANA	4500
MEKONG	4425

SOLAR SYSTEM

PLANET	DIAMETER AT EQUATOR (km)	AVERAGE DISTANCE FROM THE SUN (mkm)
MERCURY	4878	60
VENUS	12,104	108
EARTH	12,756	149.6
MARS	6794	228
JUPITER	142,800	778
SATURN	120,000	1427
URANUS	51,800	2870
NEPTUNE	49,500	4497
PLUTO	2500	5900

BRIGHTEST STARS IN THE SKY

STAR	CONSTELLATION	MAGNITUDE
SIRIUS	CANIS MAJOR	−1.5
CANOPUS	CARINA (S)	−0.7
RIGIL KENTAURUS	CENTAURUS (S)	−0.3
ARCTURUS	BOÖTES	0.0
VEGA	LYRA	0.0
CAPELLA	AURIGA	0.1
RIGEL	ORION	0.1
PROCYON	CANIS MINOR	0.4
BETELGEUSE	ORION	0.4
ACHERNAR	ERIDANUS)	0.5

(S) = southern hemisphere constellation, not visible from northern hemisphere

GEOLOGICAL TIMETABLE

ERA	PERIOD	PERIOD BEGAN (mya)	VERTEBRATES	INVERTEBRATES	PLANTS
CENOZOIC	QUATERNARY	2	HOMINIDS APPEAR	ARTHROPODS AND MOLLUSCS ABUNDANT	
	TERTIARY	66	MAMMALS EMERGE, DINOSAURS EXTINCT	MODERN GROUPS EMERGE	
MESOZOIC	CRETACEOUS	144	DINOSAURS DOMINANT	AMMONOIDS EXTINCT	FLOWERING PLANTS
	JURASSIC	208	BIRDS EMERGE	MODERN CRUSTACEANS EMERGE, AMMONOIDS ABUNDANT	
	TRIASSIC	245	REPTILES FLOURISH, DINOSAURS EMERGE	MARINE FORMS DECLINE	
PALAEOZOIC	PERMIAN	286	AMPHIBIANS DECLINE	TRILOBITES EXTINCT	CONIFERS EMERGE
	CARBONIFEROUS	360	REPTILES EMERGE		
	DEVONIAN	408	AMPHIBIANS EMERGE, FISH ABUNDANT	INSECTS EMERGE	MOSSES, HORSETAILS, FERNS EMERGE
	SILURIAN	438	FISH EMERGE	TRILOBITES DECLINE, BRACHIOPODS ABUNDANT	
	ORDOVICIAN	505			FIRST LAND PLANTS EMERGE
	CAMBRIAN	570		MOST INVERTEBRATE PHYLLA PRESENT, TRILOBITES AND BRACHIOPODS FLOURISH	

WORLD MAP

This map shows the positions and names of the countries of the world. Illustrating the world at such a small scale means it is impossible to show capital cities, major rivers and other geographical features. For this and other information you should consult a good quality atlas.

1 BELIZE
2 GUATEMALA
3 HONDURAS
4 EL SALVADOR
5 NICARAGUA
6 COSTA RICA
7 PANAMA
8 JAMAICA
9 HAITI
10 DOMINICAN REPUBLIC
11 CUBA
12 VENEZUELA
13 GUYANA
14 SURINAM
15 FRENCH GUIANA
16 PARAGUAY
17 URUGUAY
18 PORTUGAL
19 MOROCCO
20 WESTERN SAHARA
21 MAURITANIA
22 SENEGAL
23 THE GAMBIA
24 GUINEA-BISSAU
25 GUINEA
26 SIERRA LEONE
27 LIBERIA
28 IVORY COAST
29 BURKINA FASO
30 GHANA
31 TOGO
32 BENIN
33 EQUATORIAL GUINEA
34 GABON
35 CAMEROON
36 CONGO
37 CENTRAL AFRICAN REPUBLIC
38 UGANDA
39 RWANDA

40 BURUNDI
41 SOMALIA
42 KENYA
43 TANZANIA
44 MOZAMBIQUE
45 MALAWI
46 ZAMBIA
47 ZIMBABWE
48 BOTSWANA
49 SWAZILAND
50 LESOTHO
51 ANDORRA
52 LUXEMBOURG
53 BELGIUM
54 THE NETHERLANDS
55 DENMARK
56 GERMANY
57 POLAND
58 LITHUANIA

59 LATVIA
60 ESTONIA
61 BELARUS
62 CZECH REPUBLIC
63 SLOVAKIA
64 AUSTRIA
65 SWITZERLAND
66 ITALY
67 LIECHTENSTEIN
68 HUNGARY
69 SLOVENIA
70 CROATIA
71 BOSNIA-HERZEGOVINA
72 YUGOSLAVIA
73 MACEDONIA
74 MONACO
75 TUNISIA
76 MALTA
77 ALBANIA
78 GREECE

79	BULGARIA	88	LEBANON	97	UZBEKISTAN	106 THAILAND
80	ROMANIA	89	GEORGIA	98	TAJIKISTAN	107 CAMBODIA (KAMPUCHEA)
81	MOLDOVA	90	AZERBAIJAN	99	KYRGYZSTAN	108 VIETNAM
82	TURKEY	91	ARMENIA	100	AFGHANISTAN	109 BRUNEI
83	CYPRUS	92	KUWAIT	101	NEPAL	110 SINGAPORE
84	ISRAEL	93	BAHRAIN	102	BHUTAN	111 PAPUA NEW GUINEA
85	JORDAN	94	QATAR	103	BANGLADESH	112 TAIWAN
86	DJIBOUTI	95	UNITED ARAB EMIRATES	104	MYANMAR	113 SOUTH KOREA
87	SYRIA	96	TURKMENISTAN	105	LAOS	114 NORTH KOREA

235

ARTISTS

Name	Lived	Place of birth	Achievement
LEONARDO da Vinci	1452-1519	Vinci, Italy	Leonardo was a great painter and illustrator, as well as a fine sculptor, architect, scientist and engineer. He was ahead of his time in his sketches of mechanical objects, such as submarines, aircraft and tanks, but he is probably best known for his painting of the *Mona Lisa*.
MICHELANGELO (Michelangelo di Lodovico Buonarroti Simoni)	1475-1564	Caprese, Italy	A devout Christian, Michelangelo was also an exceptionally talented architect, sculptor and painter, best known for his sculpture of *David* and for painting the ceiling of the Sistine Chapel in the Vatican, which shows stories from the Old Testament, including *The Creation, Adam and Eve* and *Noah and the Flood*.
RAPHAEL (Raffaello Sanzio)	1483-1520	Urbino, Italy	Influenced by the works of Michelangelo and Leonardo, Raphael worked in the Vatican, painting hundreds of religious pictures on its walls. They are particularly admired for their three-dimensional effect and for their natural and realistic characters.
Peter Paul RUBENS	1577-1640	Siegen, Germany	Rubens was internationally famous as a portrait painter. He also painted large battle and crowd scenes, taken from the Bible or ancient mythology. The people in these scenes appear fat to us now, but a full figure was a sign of beauty at that time.
REMBRANDT (Rembrandt Harmenszoon van Rijn)	1606-69	Leiden, The Netherlands	Rembrandt was a fashionable portrait painter, who did not always paint his subjects in a flattering light, but painted so skilfully that people flocked to him. He also painted religious themes, such as the story of *Saul and David*.

Jan VERMEER	1632-75	Delft, The Netherlands	Painting only 2 or 3 pictures a year, Vermeer worked from his home town of Delft. He liked to paint people inside their own homes and his paintings show well the texture of the floors, ceilings and furniture of the background and give an impression of calm.
Francisco GOYA (Francisco José de Goya y Lucientes)	1746-1828	Fuendetodos, Spain	Goya's paintings were used as models for the huge royal tapestries made in Madrid. In 1786 he was appointed court painter to King Charles IV. An ear infection left him stone deaf in 1792, and from then on his private work often showed examples of pain and suffering, though his court pictures were still bright and colourful.
Joseph Mallord William TURNER	1775-1851	London, England	Turner believed that everything in a painting could be shown by light and colour, rather than by line and shape. He painted many romantic landscapes, using a technique that gave an impression of the scene, rather than a definite outline. His ideas inspired other painters, especially in France, and gave rise to the *Impressionist* style of art.
Paul CEZANNE	1839-1906	Aix-en-Provence, France	As a painter, Cézanne was very interested in the geometric shape of the scene or object he was painting and experimented with ways of showing these shapes simply by using colour. He was an important influence on Picasso and the *Cubist* movement in art.
Pierre-Auguste RENOIR	1841-1919	Limoges, France	Renoir started out as a ceramicist — decorating pieces of china before they were glazed. His style of painting changed after he saw an Impressionist painting by Monet, and he soon became one of the leading Impressionist painters.

Henri MATISSE	1869-1954	Le Cateau, France	Matisse believed that colours and shapes in painting were beautiful in themselves, and did not need to be used in a realistic way. His landscape scenes were admired, but when he painted his wife with a green nose, people were shocked and Matisse and his fellow artists were described as *fauves*, which means 'wild beasts'. The name still exists to describe the movement inspired by his style of painting.
Pablo Ruiz y PICASSO	1881-1973	Málaga, Spain	Picasso invented a new style of painting, known as *Cubism* — so-called because he combined the angles from which he viewed natural subjects into a series of cubic geometrical surfaces. The colours he used in his early work, which is known as his 'blue period', gave many of his paintings a sad look. He was also a sculptor, a ceramicist and a print designer and is regarded as one of the greatest artists of this century.
David HOCKNEY	born 1937	Bradford, England	Hockney's paintings show bright, clear colours and simple shapes and have been copied a lot in advertisements, making him one of this century's best-known painters. An art form he invented called 'photocopy art' uses a series of enlarged photocopied images to suggest movement.

EXPLORERS

Marco POLO	c.1254-1324	Venice, Italy	Aged 17, Polo travelled with his father and uncle to the court of Kublai Khan in China. Here he worked for the Khan as an ambassador, travelling all over Europe. His written account of the wonders of the Orient inspired future explorers, such as Columbus.

CHENG HO	c.1371-1435	K'unming, China	The admiral Cheng Ho was sent by the emperor Ch'eng-Tsu on 7 expeditions by sea to areas outside the boundaries of the Chinese empire, such as South East Asia, India, the Persian Gulf and the African coast. His fleets of up to 63 ships covered huge distances in record-breaking times.
Christopher COLUMBUS	1451-1506	Genoa, Italy	Unlike most people of his time, Columbus believed the world was round and not flat. It was already possible to reach countries like India by travelling east from Europe, but he wanted to see if it was also possible to reach India by travelling west. In 1492 his first expedition sailed west across the Atlantic and after 10 weeks reached San Salvador Island, in the Bahamas. Although he never found the western sea route to India, Columbus was the first European to have discovered what became known as the West Indies.
Amerigo VESPUCCI	1454-1512	Florence, Italy	Vespucci joined an expedition to the Caribbean in 1499 and, on his arrival back in Italy, he claimed that he had discovered the continent of America long before Columbus. Although his claim was false, his first name, Amerigo, led to the naming of America.
Vasco DA GAMA	c.1460-1524	Sines, Portugal	Da Gama led an expedition of 3 ships from Portugal to the southern tip of the African continent. This had already been done before, but Da Gama was the first to use the strong westerly winds to help him sail safely around the tip. He then went on to discover the route from there to India, by hiring the skills of an Arab navigator to guide his fleet across the Indian Ocean. Da Gama's newly-discovered route to India established new trading links with the East.

Francisco PIZARRO	c.1475-1541	Trujillo, Spain	Pizarro travelled to the empire of the Incas in South America – rumoured to be full of gold. The Incas lived in modern-day Peru and were ruled by their king, Atahualpa. Pizarro captured and killed the king, and the Incas surrendered to the Spanish, who became the rulers of Peru.
Hernán CORTES	1485-1547	Medellín, Spain	In 1519 Cortés led an expedition to Mexico, where Montezuma ruled over the empire of the Aztecs. On seeing the Spanish on horseback, the Aztecs believed Cortés was a god. In the capital, Tenochtitlán, Cortés captured Montezuma, and after much fighting the Aztecs surrendered. The empire was then declared Spanish.
Daniel BOONE	1734-c.1820	Pennsylvania, USA	Boone explored the interior of North America at a time when most settlements were restricted to the east coast. He was a 'frontiersman' – hunting, trapping and tracking for survival in unknown territory. He published an account of his adventures in 1784.
David LIVINGSTONE	1813-73	Blantyre, Scotland	Livingstone was a missionary and explorer of Africa. He wanted to open more east–west trade routes across the African continent so that the message of the missionaries could more easily be spread. He explored the River Zambezi and discovered the Victoria Falls. He also searched for the source of the River Nile.
Richard BURTON	1821-90	Torquay, England	Burton was a very gifted linguist, able to speak over 30 languages. He explored Arabia disguised as a Muslim, then set out with John Hanning Speke to search for the source of the River Nile. They discovered Lake Tanganyika, but argued over the source of the Nile.

| Henry Morton STANLEY | 1841-1904 | Denbigh, Wales | As a top journalist in the USA, Stanley was sent to Africa to look for Livingstone, who was reported missing. He succeeded in his mission, greeting Livingstone on the shores of Lake Tanganyika. |

KINGS & QUEENS

CANDRAGUPTA MAURYA	(ruled c.321-c.297 BC)	India	Candragupta was a powerful Indian general who made himself king. Leading a vast army, he expanded his empire to such an extent that it covered three quarters of the Indian sub-continent.
CLEOPATRA	69-30 BC (ruled 51-30 BC)	Egypt	This beautiful Queen of Egypt had a love affair with Julius Caesar and, after his death in 44 BC, with his heir as ruler of Rome, Mark Antony. She and Antony were defeated in battle by Augustus and both committed suicide.
CHARLEMAGNE	AD 742-814 (ruled AD 786-814)	France	Charlemagne was king at a time when Europe was divided into a collection of many states. He conquered so much land that his kingdom doubled in size and he fulfilled his ambition of creating a single united empire.
HARUN AR-RASHID	AD 766-809	Iran	Harun ar-Rashid was caliph of Baghdad, a religious and political leader of a Muslim ruling family called the Abassids. The magnificent wealth of his court has been written about in the tales of the *Arabian Nights*.
FERDINAND & ISABELLA	1452-1516 1451-1504	Spain	Ferdinand and Isabella each inherited separate thrones within Spain and, when they married, Spain was unified for the first time. Together they made an effective team, and they set up the ruthless 'Spanish Inquisition', which aimed to convert all Spain's subjects to Catholicism.

HENRY VIII	1491-1547 (ruled 1509-1547)	Greenwich, England	King Henry VIII was determined to secure a male heir to the throne and when his first wife, Catherine of Aragon, produced only a daughter he granted himself a divorce. This, and his subsequent marriage to Anne Boleyn led to the act of Supremacy, making Henry supreme head of the Church in England. Although Henry married 5 more times, he had only one son who survived childhood, Edward VI.
ELIZABETH I	1533-1603 (ruled 1558-1603)	Greenwich, England	Queen Elizabeth I was the daughter of Henry VIII and his second wife, Anne Boleyn. She angered the king of Spain when she re-established the Church of England and they sent a huge fleet of ships, the Spanish Armada, to attack Britain. The Armada was defeated by Elizabeth's ships, but more so by the weather. Elizabeth never married, despite having many suitors.
LOUIS XIV	1638-1715 (ruled 1643-1715)	St Germain, France	Louis XIV dissolved the parliament and declared himself the sole ruler of France. He lived in a magnificent palace at Versailles, which he had built himself, and encouraged artists, musicians and writers to his court. His nickname was 'The Sun King'. He would not tolerate any religion other than Catholicism and persecuted the Huguenots (French Protestants).
PETER the Great	1672-1725 (ruled 1682-1725)	Moscow, Russia	Peter brought Russia out of its isolation by following the example of Western countries and modernizing Russian industry, the army and the navy, and reducing the power of the aristocracy. He was interested in art and literature and organized the translation of many foreign books into Russian. He also built a new capital city at St Petersburg.

CATHERINE the Great	1729-96 (ruled 1762-96)	Stettin, Prussia (now Poland)	Catherine wanted to open up Russia to the influence of Western ideas and culture. She created new schools and universities, and was influenced by the French thinker Voltaire, who encouraged her in her aim to rule Russia for the benefit of all its people. She was forced to abandon her ideals, however, by the Russian nobility, who threatened civil war, but she fought successful campaigns abroad and won territory for Russia.
MARIE-ANTOINETTE	1755-93 (ruled 1774-93)	Vienna, Austria	Married to King Louis XVI of France and daughter of the empress of Austria, Marie Antoinette was unpopular in France, especially after the French Revolution in 1789, when the poor people showed their anger against the aristocracy for years of poverty and suffering. Although she tried to escape Paris with her family, she was caught and taken prisoner with her husband, the king. Within a year both were executed.
VICTORIA	1819-1901 (ruled 1837-1901)	London, England	During Victoria's 64-year long reign, Britain changed greatly from a rural to an industrial nation, and built up a huge empire that covered a quarter of the world. The power of the monarch became less important and the country was ruled by Parliament. Victoria had 9 children and was known as the 'Grandmother of Europe' because so many of her descendants married into European royal families.
Mad King LUDWIG	1845-86 (ruled 1864-86)	Munich, Germany	King Ludwig II of Bavaria was declared insane in 1886. He was never interested in state affairs and spent his time pursuing his interests in music and architecture and spending money having 'fairy-tale' castles built on the banks of the River Rhine. He was found drowned soon after he was declared insane.

MUSICIANS

Johann Sebastian BACH	1685-1750	Eisenach, Saxony	As a member of a very musical family, Bach was first trained by his father, practising the harpsichord, violin and organ. He worked as a church musician and composed two main kinds of music: sacred (for the church) and secular (for concerts).
Wolfgang Amadeus MOZART	1756-91	Salzburg, Austria	Mozart was an infant prodigy, giving piano and violin concerts all over Europe at the age of 6. By the time he died, at the age of 35, he had written over 150 orchestral works, several operas – including *The Marriage of Figaro*, *Don Giovanni* and *The Magic Flute* – and some church works. He is regarded by many as the greatest classical composer to have lived.
Ludwig van BEETHOVEN	1770-1827	Bonn, Germany	Beethoven was a composer of piano, orchestral and chamber music. He started to go deaf in 1798 and by the time he was 50, he could hear almost nothing at all. He could still compose as he was able to 'hear music in his head', but his music became more inward-looking, and came to be appreciated only after his death. He wrote 9 great symphonies, 17 string quartets and 32 piano sonatas.
Frédéric CHOPIN	1810-49	Zelazowa Wola, near Warsaw, Poland	Chopin settled in Paris when he was 21, but much of his music is based on Polish folksongs and dances. The music he wrote consists mainly of short pieces written for the piano.
Franz LISZT	1811-86	Raiding, Hungary	Liszt became famous all over Europe for his piano playing. He also came to be greatly respected for his orchestral pieces, which were inspired by such themes as gardens, waterfalls and dancing devils. He also wrote fine choral music.

Giuseppe VERDI	1813-1901	La Roncole, Italy	Verdi was a composer of operas. His first successful opera was *Nabucco*, followed by another 20 operas, which brought him fame worldwide.
Richard WAGNER	1813-83	Leipzig, Germany	A great admirer of Shakespeare's plays and Beethoven's music, Wagner wrote 'music-dramas', which were plays set to music. His masterpiece was the 15-hour long *Ring of the Nibelung* and the theatre that was built for it at Bayreuth in Germany is still used every year for a huge festival.
Johann STRAUSS II	1825-99	Vienna, Austria	Son of Johann Strauss I, Strauss came from a very musical family. He was nicknamed 'The Waltz King' because of the 400 waltzes that he wrote, many of which became popular favourites.
Johannes BRAHMS	1833-97	Hamburg, Germany	Although from a poor family, Brahms learnt the piano, practising 7-8 hours a day. His playing and composing were greatly admired, along with that of his rival, Wagner. He became famous for the large-scale symphonic music he wrote, but he preferred the smaller-scale pieces that he wrote for himself and his friends to play.
Pyotr Ilyich TCHAIKOVSKY	1840-93	Votkinsk, Russia	Tchaikovsky is known chiefly for his ballets, such as *Swan Lake* and *The Nutcracker*, which he based on fairy tales, and for his symphonies and operas. He was a rather unstable personality, largely rescued by the patronage of an aristocratic lady, Nadyezhda von Meck.
Giacomo PUCCINI	1858-1924	Lucca, Italy	Puccini is famous throughout the world for his operas, including three of the most popular ever written, *Madame Butterfly*, *La Bohème*, and *Tosca*.

Igor STRAVINSKY	1882-1971	Oranienbaum, Russia	Stravinsky wrote ballets and operas which were unpopular when they were first heard, partly because they were quite different from what people were used to. But over time, people began to admire his music, especially his 2 most exciting works, *Petrushka* and *The Rite of Spring*.
Billie HOLIDAY	1915-59	Baltimore, USA	After an unhappy and deprived childhood and adolescence, Billie Holiday started singing in clubs in Harlem. She appeared with Count Basie and Artie Shaw in the late 1930s. She then pursued a solo career. She died of heroin addiction.
Elvis PRESLEY	1935-77	Tupelo, USA	Presley began making records in 1953, when he recorded *Heartbreak Hotel* for his mother's birthday. From then on he became a star, with 26 of his recorded singles becoming hits. His stage performances are legendary and won him thousands of fans, and he also acted in films. Presley became a drug addict, and he died of a heart attack aged 42.
THE BEATLES: John LENNON Paul McCARTNEY George HARRISON Ringo STARR (born Richard Starkey)	1940-80 born 1942 born 1943 born 1940	Liverpool, England	Formed in 1960, The Beatles became the world's best-known pop group, with 17 of their 28 songs reaching number 1 in the pop charts. Lennon and McCartney were the 2 main songwriters and some of their best-known songs include: *A Hard Day's Night*, *Paperback Writer* and *Hey Jude*. The group broke up in 1971. In 1980 Lennon was shot dead.
Robert Nesta (Bob) MARLEY	1945-81	St Ann, Jamaica	Together with his band, The Wailers, which formed in 1964, Bob Marley became world famous for his reggae music. He wrote and sang songs about love, politics and religion, and many of them have become classics of reggae music. He died of cancer in 1981.

SOCIAL REFORMERS & SAINTS

ST FRANCIS of Assisi (Giovanni di Barnardone)	c.1181-1226	Assisi, Italy	Son of a rich family, St Francis gave up his wealth to follow a life of poverty, charity and Christianity. He believed that all creatures on Earth should be treated equally and his way of life led to the founding of a new order of monks called the Franciscans.
Florence NIGHTINGALE	1820-1910	Florence, Italy	Nightingale trained as a nurse at a time when there were very few professional nurses in England. She looked after British soldiers injured in the Crimean War, where she became known as 'the lady with the lamp' because every night she visited each patient, with a lamp in her hand, making sure he was as comfortable as possible.
Emmeline PANKHURST	1858-1928	Manchester, England	Pankhurst and her 2 daughters campaigned for women's rights at a time when British women were not allowed to vote. They chained themselves to railings in protest at the treatment women received, and when imprisoned for their actions, continued protesting by going on hunger strike. Their actions helped secure improved conditions for women in Britain. British women were granted the vote in 1918.
Mohandas Karamchand GANDHI	1869-1948	Porbandar, India	At a time when India was under British rule, Gandhi played a vital role in gaining India its independence. He used a policy of non-violence and encouraged his followers to protest passively by using methods such as hunger strikes and non-payment of taxes. He was known to his many admirers as 'Mahatma' (great soul) and after his assassination by a Hindu fanatic he was greatly mourned.

MOTHER TERESA of Calcutta (Agnes Gonxha Bojaxhiu)	1910-1997	Skopje, Macedonia	Mother Teresa was a nun who trained as a teacher and a nurse. She opened the first school for poor children in Calcutta, in India. She founded a sisterhood called the Missionaries of Charity, which runs schools, hospitals and orphanages all over the world.
Martin Luther KING	1929-68	Atlanta, Georgia, USA	King grew up in the USA at a time when black people were segregated from whites. He campaigned for equal rights for blacks using non-violent methods of protest. He was assassinated while speaking in Tennessee, but the message he preached resulted in improved conditions for black Americans.

THINKERS

BUDDHA (Gautama Siddhartha)	c.563-483 BC	Kapilavastu, Nepal	Gautama's wealthy parents prevented him from seeing anything upsetting. He first learnt about sickness and death when he was 29. This changed his life and he was determined to find out why such misery existed. Through meditation he concluded that humans' craving for love, wealth and power was the root of their unhappiness. His followers called him 'Buddha' (the enlightened one) and Buddhism, followed by over 300 million people today, teaches believers to give up worldly desires in a quest for inner peace.
CONFUCIUS (Kongfuzi)	551-479 BC	Lu, Shandong, China	Confucius was interested in what 'goodness' was and whether it could be taught and learned. He travelled widely teaching people that we are all born good and that we must try to remain so. His followers developed his ideas into a way of life called Confucianism, which was used throughout China for 2500 years until it was abolished in 1966.

PLATO (Platon)	c.427-347 BC	Athens, Greece	Plato was a pupil of Socrates and later became a teacher of philosophy (the search for wisdom) himself. He believed that perfection in everything is possible, but that human vision causes things to seem imperfect. He wrote many books, and in one of them, *The Republic*, he talks about the ideal state. His views are still taught today.
ARISTOTLE (Aristoteles)	384-322 BC	Stagira, Greece	As a boy, Aristotle studied everything in nature and later he lectured on the 4 elements (earth, fire, air, water), from which he said everything was made. He also wrote books on law, politics, religion and human nature. He became world famous and his teaching affected scholars worldwide. His ideas were rediscovered in the Middle Ages.
Niccolò MACHIAVELLI	1469-1527	Florence, Italy	Machiavelli believed that a ruler must do anything necessary in order to secure the health and safety of the state. His book, *The Prince*, caused people to think that he supported evil and treachery in the interest of the state, and the word 'machiavellian' today describes anyone who is cunning and selfish.
Martin LUTHER	1483-1546	Eisleben, Saxony	Luther, a Roman Catholic monk, was shocked by the corruption of the Roman Catholic Church, especially by the sale of 'indulgences' granting people freedom from punishment in Hell. Luther said that only God could free someone from punishment for sin. Despite angering the Pope, Luther set in motion the Reformation, a movement to change the Church. He translated the Bible from Latin to German and wrote prayers and hymns that could be understood by ordinary people. Protestantism came into being gradually after Luther's excommunication in 1521.

René DESCARTES	1596-1650	La Haye, Touraine, France	Descartes believed that understanding could be acquired through logic. He also believed that everything is made of either mind or matter, but that humans are unique as they have a mind and are also made of matter (material substance) which is controlled by the mind. His view of life was summed up in the phrase, *Cogito ergo sum* – 'I think, therefore I am.'
VOLTAIRE (François-Marie Arouet)	1694-1778	Paris, France	Voltaire criticized the way people in France were not allowed to follow religious or political beliefs that were not approved by the state. For this he was imprisoned and, on his release, he gave lectures saying that people were entitled to hold their own beliefs. He was one of the great philosophers of the Age of Reason. He also wrote essays and plays.
Benjamin FRANKLIN	1706-90	Boston, Massachusetts, USA	Franklin was the inventor of bifocal lenses and of a lightning conductor that carried electricity harmlessly into the earth. He was also a thinker, believing that people should try to help and understand each other. He led an active life as a town councillor and when America became independent in 1792, he was a member of the committee that wrote the Constitution – the rules by which Americans still live today.
Mary WOLLSTONECRAFT	1759-97	London, England	Wollstonecraft believed in equality and social reform and she supported the French revolutionaries who rebelled against the aristocracy in 1789. She published a book in their defence which scandalized the society of her day. She also believed in equality for women, arguing that girls should be educated as well as boys, and her book *Vindication of the Rights of Women* claimed that women were equal to men.

Henry David THOREAU	1817-62	Concord, Massachusetts, USA	Thoreau felt great strength in solitude and in the presence of God all around him. He spent 2 years living alone in a wood and later wrote a book, *Walden*, about his experience, which inspired many people to take holidays in wild and unpopulated areas, hoping to 'discover themselves' as he had done.
Karl MARX	1818-83	Trier, Prussia	Marx's ideas form the basis of modern-day communism. He said that the system of poor people working for rich people was unfair and that all the workers of a country should take businesses and property into their own hands and run a state in which everyone was equal. He wrote several books, many of which caused riots, and he was expelled from one country after another. His two books *Capital* and *The Communist Manifesto* describe his revolutionary ideas.
Sigmund FREUD	1856-1939	Freiberg, Moravia	Freud's ideas on the way our mind works have profoundly influenced the way we treat mental illnesses today. The Austrian scholar believed we should study the way our minds have evolved since birth, looking at the influences of our family, friends and society, and in the importance of childhood sexual experiences. He called his work 'psychoanalysis' (logical study of the mind).
Carl JUNG	1875-1961	Basel, Switzerland	Jung believed that the unconscious mind has an effect on the conscious mind. He also thought that people keep in their unconscious mind some memory of the past human race and that this affects their actions. He believed that dreams and religious faith show the unconscious mind ruling the conscious. He classified people as *extrovert* (outgoing) or *introvert* (inward-looking).

LEADERS

ALEXANDER the Great	c.356-323 BC	Pella, Greece	Alexander united the warring Greek states and led them to victory against the huge Persian empire, in a campaign that took him to the borders of India. He died at the age of 32 in Babylon.
SHIH Huang-ti (Shih Huangdi)	c.259-210 BC	China	Chinese emperor who ordered the building of the Great Wall of China. When Shih Huang Ti died he was buried in a vast underground tomb protected by thousands of lifesize terracotta soldiers.
HANNIBAL	247-c.183 BC	Carthage, North Africa	Hannibal led the Carthaginian army against the Romans in the Second Punic War, crossing the Alps to invade Italy from the north. Hannibal was forced to return home with his army when the Roman general Scipio attacked Carthage. Hannibal later committed suicide to avoid capture.
SPARTACUS	died 71 BC	Thrace	Spartacus was a Greek who became a gladiator after being captured by the Romans. He led a revolt against Rome but was ultimately unsuccessful and was captured and crucified.
Julius CAESAR	100-44 BC	Rome, Italy	Caesar was a politician and brilliant army general who invaded Britain in 55–54 BC. He defeated Pompey in a civil war, but was murdered outside the Roman Senate on the Ides of March (March 15th) 44 BC.
BOUDICCA (Boadicea)	died AD 62	East Anglia, Britain	Boudicca was a queen who led her tribe of Ancient Britons, the Iceni, in a revolt against Roman rule in Britain. To start with she was successful, but her army was eventually defeated and Boudicca poisoned herself.

ALFRED the Great	849-99	Wantage, England	King of the kingdom of Wessex, Alfred fought the Danish invaders, eventually defeating them at the Battle of Edington. When the fighting was over, Alfred encouraged learning in his kingdom.
GENGHIS Khan	c.1162-1227	Dulun-Boldaq, Mongolia	Genghis Khan made himself leader of all the warlike Mongol people. Having unified the tribes he led them on an invasion of China. He founded the massive Mongol empire which stretched from the Baltic Sea to the Pacific Ocean.
George WASHINGTON	1732-99	Pope's Creek, Virginia, USA	George Washington was commander in chief of the colonists' army that fought against the British in the American War of Independence. Six years after the war was over he was elected the first president of the United States.
TOUSSAINT-L'OUVERTURE (François Dominique Toussaint)	c.1743-1803	St Domingue (now Haiti), Caribbean	A great revolutionary leader in St Domingue, who fought to keep his people free from slavery. He successfully drove out both the British and the Spanish. He was later tricked and captured by the French, who took him to France, where he was imprisoned and died.
NAPOLEON Bonaparte	1769-1821	Ajaccio, Corsica	Napoleon created the largest European empire since the Romans. Its collapse began with Napoleon's defeat at Leipzig (1813), and was sealed at the Battle of Waterloo (1815) where the French were defeated by the British and Prussian armies.
Giuseppe GARIBALDI	1807-82	Nice, France	Garibaldi led his patriots in a guerrilla war against the Austrian and French armies in Italy (1848-9, 1851). He successfully conquered Sicily and Naples and helped form the emerging kingdom of Italy (1860).

GERONIMO (Goyathlay)	1829-1908	No-Doyohn Canyon, New Mexico, USA	Geronimo was chief of the Apache tribe of Amerindians. He fought continually against the white settlers and the United States army until his eventual capture in Sonora, in 1886.
Vladimir Ilyich LENIN (Vladimir Ilyich Ulyanov)	1870-1924	Simbirsk, Russia	Lenin returned from exile abroad to lead the communist revolution in Russia in 1917. He led the new Soviet Union until his death.
Joseph STALIN (Josif Vissarionovich Dzugashvili)	1879-1953	Gori, Georgia	Stalin was a ruthless and single-minded dictator who led the Soviet Union from 1924 to 1953. He led his country in their victory over Germany and her allies in World War II and established it as a world power.
Adolf HITLER	1889-1945	Braunau am Inn, Austria	Hitler became leader of the German Nazi party in 1921, and Chancellor of Germany in 1933. He led his country into war against the allies. He directed the war and established the concentration camps where six million Jews and others were murdered.
Francisco FRANCO	1892-1975	El Ferrol, Spain	Franco fought for the fascist forces against the Republicans in the Spanish Civil War (1936-9), eventually becoming their leader. The Republican government was defeated, and Franco established a dictatorship in 1939.
MAO Zedong (Mao Tse Tung)	1893-1976	Shaoshan, Hunan, China	Mao led China in its fight against Japanese invasion during World War II. He was one of the founders of the People's Republic of China. He led the country until his death.
Ernesto (Che) GUEVARA	1928-67	Rosario, Argentina	Che Guevara developed the use of guerrilla warfare as a tool of revolution and played a major part in Fidel Castro's revolution in Cuba.

POLITICIANS

Cardinal RICHELIEU (Armand-Jean du Plessis)	1585-1642	Paris, France	As a cardinal of the Roman Catholic church Richelieu was a powerful man. He was principal minister to Louis XIII, and virtually ruled France from 1624 to 1642, strengthening the monarchy in France, and the role of France in Europe.
Thomas JEFFERSON	1743-1826	Shadwell, Virginia, USA	Thomas Jefferson wrote the Declaration of Independence, which became the basis for the constitution of the United States. He was the third president of the US (1801-9). He was responsible for the purchase of Louisiana from France.
Maximilien ROBESPIERRE	1758-94	Arras, France	One of the most famous leaders of the French Revolution, he instigated 'the Terror' under which anyone might be arrested, tried and executed. In 1794 he was executed himself, by the guillotine to which he had sent so many of his countrymen.
William PITT (the Younger)	1759-1806	Hayes, Kent, England	Prime minister from 1783 to 1801 and from 1804 to 1806, Pitt made important changes to the tax laws. From 1793 he focused his attention on the wars with revolutionary France and on ensuring a similar revolution did not occur in Britain.
Benjamin DISRAELI (Lord Beaconsfield)	1804-81	London, England	Prime minister in 1868 and from 1874 to 1880, Disraeli introduced the second Reform Act, increasing the number of people allowed to vote. His government did much to improve housing conditions in towns.
Prince Otto von BISMARCK	1815-98	Schönhausen, Prussia	Called the Iron Chancellor, Bismarck was prime minister of Prussia from 1862 to 1890, during which time he defeated Austria and France, and united all of Germany.

Sun Yat-sen (SUN I'xian)	1866-1925	Zhangshan, Guangdong Province, China	Sun Yat-sen struggled to overthrow China's ruling dynasty. To escape the police, he fled China, and while abroad he met Lenin (see page 254). He was invited back to China in 1911 to be its first president.
Winston Spencer CHURCHILL	1874-1965	Blenheim Palace, Oxfordshire, England	Churchill is most famous as the wartime leader of Britain from 1940 to 1945. He wrote a history of World War II, for which he won the Nobel Prize for Literature in 1953, and *A History of the English-Speaking Peoples.*
Franklin Delano ROOSEVELT	1882-1945	Hyde Park, New York State, USA	As thirty-second president of the United States, Roosevelt instituted major reforms, known as the New Deal, to counter the economic depression of the 1930s. He led the USA into World War II, but died before victory.
Jawaharlal NEHRU	1889-1964	Allahabad, India	Nehru was a supporter of Mahatma Gandhi, and worked hard to bring about Indian independence. He became the first prime minister of independent India in 1947, and remained so until his death.
Indira GANDHI	1917-84	Allahabad, India	Indira Gandhi was the only daughter of Jawaharlal Nehru (see above). She too entered politics and became prime minister of India in1966, a post she held until 1977, and again from 1980 to 1984. In 1984 she was murdered by one of her own bodyguards.
Mikhail GORBACHEV	born 1931	Privolnoye, Russia	Gorbachev became leader of the USSR in 1985. He instituted *perestroika*, to improve the country's economic efficiency, *glasnost*, to make it more honest, and *demokratizatsiya*, to make it more democratic. He was awarded the Nobel Peace Prize in 1990. He was deposed in 1991.

SCIENTISTS

SCIENTISTS

ARCHIMEDES	c.287-212 BC	Syracuse, Sicily	Mathematician, engineer and teacher. Discovered the principle of levers.
Nicholas COPERNICUS	1473-1543	Torún, Poland	Proposed the theory that the planets orbit the Sun.
GALILEO Galilei	1564-1642	Pisa, Italy	First to use a telescope to make astronomical observations, including the discovery of Jupiter's moons.
Anton van LEEUWENHOEK	1632-1723	Delft, The Netherlands	First to realize the scientific benefits of the microscope.
Isaac NEWTON	1642-1727	Woolsthorpe, Lincolnshire, England	Discovered that white light is made up of colours; worked out the laws of gravity, and the three laws of motion.
Antoine-Laurent LAVOISIER	1743-94	Paris, France	Explained the process of burning.
Michael FARADAY	1791-1867	London, England	Experimented with electro-magnetism, leading to the invention of the transformer, dynamo and electric motor.
Charles DARWIN	1809-82	Shrewsbury, England	Proposed the theory of evolution.
James Clerk MAXWELL	1831-79	Edinburgh, Scotland	Suggested that light is made up of waves, and predicted the discovery of other such waves.
Marie CURIE	1867-1934	Warsaw, Poland	Discovered a new radioactive element, called radium.
Guglielmo MARCONI	1874-1937	Bologna, Italy	Pioneered work on the sending and receiving of radio waves.
Albert EINSTEIN	1879-1955	Ulm, Germany	Proposed the theory of relativity.

WRITERS

HOMER	believed to be 9th or 8th century BC	Greece	Homer wrote two long 'epic' poems, the *Iliad* and the *Odyssey*, about the heroes and gods of ancient Greece.
DANTE Alighieri	1265-1321	Florence, Italy	Wrote *The Divine Comedy*, describing the author's imagined journey through hell, purgatory and paradise.
Geoffrey CHAUCER	c.1342-1400	London, England	Most famous for his collection of stories, *The Canterbury Tales*, told by pilgrims journeying to Canterbury.
Miguel de CERVANTES	1547-1616	Alcalá, Spain	Cervantes' wrote about Don Quixote, who set off with his squire, Sancho Panza, to live a chivalrous life.
William SHAKESPEARE	1564-1616	Stratford-upon-Avon, England	The world's best-known writer. Among his most famous plays are the tragedies *Hamlet*, *King Lear*, *Othello* and *Macbeth*. He also wrote a collection of poems, called Sonnets, mostly on the theme of love.
John MILTON	1608-74	London, England	Milton wrote many poems including *Paradise Lost*, describing the temptation of Adam and Eve by the fallen angels.
Jane AUSTEN	1775-1817	Steventon, England	Her books give a feeling of being part of the scene she is describing. The most famous are *Pride and Prejudice*, *Sense and Sensibility* and *Emma*.
Victor HUGO	1802-85	Besançon, France	French poet, novelist and playwright. He led the romantic movement in France. Perhaps his most famous work is *Les Misérables*.
Hans Christian ANDERSEN	1805-75	Odense, Denmark	Andersen wrote many fairy stories. Among the best are *The Ugly Duckling*, *The Tin Soldier* and *The Snow Queen*.

Charles DICKENS	1812-70	Portsmouth, England	Famous for his descriptions of life for the poor in Victorian Britain.
Charlotte BRONTË Emily BRONTË Anne BRONTË	1816-55 1818-48 1820-49	Thornton, England	Their books included: *Jane Eyre* (Charlotte); *Wuthering Heights* (Emily) and *Agnes Grey* (Anne).
Leo TOLSTOY	1828-1910	Yasnaya Polyana, Russia	Tolstoy was a great writer but also ran a school for peasant children on his family estate. His most famous books are *War and Peace* and *Anna Karenina*.
Lewis CARROLL (real name Charles Dodgson)	1832-98	Daresbury, England	Lewis Carroll wrote two of the most famous stories for children, *Alice's Adventures in Wonderland* and *Alice Through the Looking-Glass*.
Robert Louis STEVENSON	1850-94	Edinburgh, Scotland	Stevenson wrote exciting adventure stories for children, including *Treasure Island* and *Kidnapped*.
A A MILNE	1882-1956	London, England	Milne was the creator of Christopher Robin, and his friends Winnie the Pooh, Piglet, Owl, Tigger, Rabbit, Eyore, Kanga and Roo.
J R R TOLKIEN	1892-1973	Bloemfontein, South Africa	Tolkien's fantasy tales of hobbits, elves and orcs are popular all over the world. His most famous are *The Hobbit* and *The Lord of the Rings*.
F Scott FITZGERALD	1896-1940	St Paul, Minnesota, USA	Fitzgerald is remembered for his portrayal of the American Jazz Age (the 1920s) in stories like *The Great Gatsby*, *The Beautiful and the Damned* and *Tender is the Night*.
Roald DAHL	1916-90	Llandaff, Wales	For today's children, Roald Dahl is perhaps the most popular author in the world. His famous book, *Charlie and the Chocolate Factory* is one of the best-selling children's books of all time.

216, 218, 220, 222, 224, 225, 226, 228, 229
Relativity, Theory of, 79
Rembrandt 236
Renaissance 132–133, 200–201
Renoir, Pierre-Auguste, 201, 237
Replication 10
Reptiles 23, 36–37, 106–107, 108
Republics 182
Resistance 153
Respiration (plants) 57
Rhinocerus 27, 109
Rhizomes 60
Rhythm 202–203
Richard I, King, (The Lionheart) 127
Richelieu, Cardinal, 255
Richter scale 92
Ring of Fire 92
Ring of the Nibelung 245
Rite of Spring, The, 246
Rivers 98–99
Robespierre, Maximilien, 136, 255
Robots 177
Rock music 202–203
Rock 'n' Roll 203
Rocket locomotive 169
Rockets 74, 155
Rocks 94–95
Rocky Mountains 91, 216
Rodin, Auguste, 201
Roemer, Ole, 79
Roman Catholics 191, 210–211, 220, 242, 249
Roman empire 124, 192
Roman law system 188–189
Romania 210
Rome 120, 195, 198, 200
Romeo and Juliet 198
Röntgen, Wilhelm, 167
Roosevelt, Franklin D, 149, 256
Roots 56–57
Rossby waves 89
Roundheads 134
Rousseau 182
Rubens, Peter Paul, 201, 236
Rubies 95
Rudolf, Lake, 222
Ruminants 30
Russell, Henry, 77
Russia 212–213
Russian empire 211
Russian language 193
Russian Revolution 145
Ruwenzori mountains 222
Rwanda 222

S

Sahara desert 222–223
Saints 247–248
Saladin 127
Samurai 228
San Andreas Fault 91,92
Sancho Panza 258
Sandhoppers 54
Sandstone 94
Sanskrit 192–193
Satellites 74, 181
Saturn 75, 81
Saudi Arabia 214
Saurischians 105
Sauropods 105
Savanna grassland 222
Saxons 124, 204
Scandinavia 206
Scanning 197
Schist 94–95
Schouten 135
Scorpions 22, 52–53
Scotland 204–205
Scots 124
Scribes 194
Sea anemones 54
Sea birds 34–35
Sea cucumber 55
Seals 29
Seas 86–87
Seashore 54
Seasons 85
Sea urchin 55
Seawise Giant 172
Sedimentary rocks 94
Seeds 58–59
Seljuks 127
Semiconductors 176
Senegal 222
Sense and Sensibility 258
Senses 16–17
Serbia 144
Serica 173
Seven Wonders of the World 115
Sex organs 20–21
Sexual intercourse 21
Shadows 160
Shah, The, 214–215
Shakespeare, William, 198, 258
Shanghai 229
Shares 185
Sheep 44–45, 205
Shifting cultivation 222
Shih Huang Ti 252

Shinto, Shintoists, 191, 228
Ships 172–173
Shoguns 228
Shrews 26
Shrubs 60–61
Siberia 213
Sidereal day 84
Silicates 95
Silicon chips 177
Silk 70
Silkworms 122
Singapore 225
Sistine Chapel 132, 200, 236
Sky 88
Skylab 75
Skyscrapers 217
Slaves 139, 141
Slovenia 210
Slugs 53
Smallpox 166
Smallpox virus 13
Smell 17
Smith, Adam, 184
Smith, Francis, 173
Snails 52–53
Snakes 23, 36–37
Snow-line 86
Snow Queen, The, 258
Social contract 182
Socialists 183
Socrates 249
Solar day 84
Solar energy power 96–97, 181
Solar System 73, 74–75, 80–81
Solid Rocket boosters (SRBs) 74
'Solidarity' 211
Solids 151
Solomon Islands 226
Somalia 186–187, 222–223
Sonnets 258
Sound 162
Sound recording 180
Sound waves 162, 180
South Africa 222–223
South America (see America, South)
South Pole 86
Southern hemisphere 76–77
Spacecraft 74–75
Space probes 74–75, 81
Space shuttle 74–75
Space Transportation System (STS) 74
Spanish Armada 133, 173, 242
Spanish Civil War 254

269

ACKNOWLEDGEMENTS

PICTURE SOURCES

The publishers would like to thank the following for permission to reproduce photographs:

(T = Top, B = Bottom, C = Centre, L = Left, R = Right)

AEA Technology 174B;

Allsport 16;

Ancient Art and Architecture Collection 93, 116, 119 and cover, 122T&C, 126T, 166R, 200BR;

Sue Baker 70/71B, 94/95B;

Barnaby's Picture Library 133 BL;

The Bridgeman Art Library 129, 132T&B, 139TL, 165B, 201C, (© Academia de San Fernando, Madrid) 133BR, (© ADAGP Paris and DACS, London 1992) 201L, (Biblioteca National, Turin) 132C, (Bibliothèque Nationale, Paris) 71, (University of Oxford, Bodleian Library) 70, 118B, 164T, (Forbes Magazine) 136T, (Gallerica Academia, Florence), 201BR (Germanisches National Museum, Nuremburg) 133TR, (Greek Museum, Newcastle on Tyne) 112B, (Guildhall Library) 140C, (Hammerby House, Upsala) 135TL, (Harrogate Museums) 134, (Musée Condé) 131TR, (Museum of Antiquities, Newcastle on Tyne)112T, (National Army Museum) 141BR, (Worshipful Company of Clockmakers, London) 84B; The Bridgeman Art Library/Giraudon 136C&B, 200BL, 201TR&B;

British Film Institute 199CL&CR&BC&BL;

The British Museum 114T;

BT Pictures, © British Telecommunications plc 181;

Britstock-IFA Ltd 224C;

Neill Bruce Photographic 166B;

J Allan Cash Photolibrary 221B;

C M Dixon 121T;

Editions Alecto 128T;

Ivan Lapper/English Heritage 128B;

Pete Addis/The Environmental Picture Library 13;

Mary Evans Picture Library 127R, 137T&B, 140B, 144B;

E T Archive 167B, (British Museum) 114B;

First Independent Films 199T;

Werner Forman Archive (Museo Nationale, Rome) 123, (National Museum Copenhagen) 125BR;

Fotomas Index 131TL, 135TR;

French Railways/Jean Marc Fabro 169;

Colin Garratt's Steam Locomotives of the World Photo Library 169;

The Ronald Grant Archive 199R;

Robert Harding Picture Library 68TL, 69BL, 86, 87, 192, 205TL, 207BL, 209B, 216CR, 217BR, 218BL, 224B, 225BR, 229BR;

Michael Holford 118T, 127L, 130, 131B, 191T, 193, 194, 195, 200T;

Holt Studios Ltd 69R, 223BR;

The Hulton Deutsche Collection 135B, 137C, 139TR&B, 140T, 141BL,143BL, 144T&BL&BR, 145C&B, 147T&BR, 164B, 165TL, 166L, 184, 188;

The Hutchison Library 24BL, 187T&C&BL&BC, 189T, 219TL&BL;

Impact Photos 183T;

International Stock Exchange Photo Library 189B;

David King Collection 145T, 146BR;

L Freed/Magnum Photos 148C;
P J Griffiths/Magnum Photos 149B;

NASA 74;

NHPA 23, 24, 25, 29 and back cover, 49, 51, 53, 61, 64, 65, 66B, 67;

NHM Picture Library 90, 104;

Peter Newark's Historical Pictures 129T, 133TL, 141T, 144C, 146T&BL, 147BL, 197TR;

Ronnie O'Brien 156;

Oxford Scientific Films Ltd 22, 47, 52, 98C, 102B, 103T;

Panos Pictures 98T;

Planet Earth Pictures 31, 42;

Millbrook House Collection 169;

Railways and Steam Locomotives of the World Milepost 92½ 171;

Redferns 180, 203TL&TR;

Rex Features Ltd 148T&B, 149T&C, 182, 183B, 212, 213TL&TR, 216;

Ann Ronan Picture Library 126B, 196;

The Royal Photographic Society, Bath 178;

Science Photo Library 9, 10, 11, 12, 19, 20T, 58, 67T, 72, 73, 74T, 75, 76, 77, 78, 79, 81, 88, 89, 92, 93, 97, 98B, 99, 102, 103B&R, 151, 161, 162, 164C, 167TL&TR, 174T, 175, 176T, 177, 178, 197TL&B;

South American Pictures 221T;

Staatliche Museen zu Berlin, Vorderasintisches Museen – PK 115;

Tony Stone Worldwide 11, 20L, 68B, 84T, 97, 113BR, 121B, 122B, 176B, 184T, 187BR, 198, 201TL, 204BL& BR, 205TR&B, 206, 207TL&R, 208TL&TR&B, 209T, 210L&R, 211L&R, 213B, 214, 215, 217BL, 218BR, 219BR, 220, 222, 223T, 225BL, 226, 227, 228, 229BL;

TRH Pictures 170T, 171BR ;

The Board of Trinity College Dublin 124;

TRRL Photography and Video Section 153;

Dr A C Waltham 91, 94, 95, 191B;

York Archaeological Trust Picture Library 125T&C&BL;

Zefa Picture Library 138, 185, 189C.

Every effort has been made to contact the holders of copyright material, but if any have been inadvertently overlooked the publishers will be pleased to make any necessary amendments.

ILLUSTRATORS

Arcana: John Fox, Greg Stewart;

Norman Arlot;

Peter Bull Art Studio;

Tony Hanaford;

David Lewis Management: Martyn Andrews, Oriol Bath, Christopher Brown, Robert Cook, David Cuzik, Jeremy Ford, Sue Hall, Bob Harvey, Philip Roberts, David John Rowe, Peter Walsh, Ross Watton, Tracy Wayte;

Martin Woodward

Greg Whyte; Strawberrie Donnelly; Braz Atkins

First published in 1992 by HarperCollinsChildren's Books, an imprint of HarperCollins Publishers Ltd
77–85 Fulham Palace Road
Hammersmith, London W6 8JB
Reprinted 1993, 1996, 1997 (with revisions), 1998
This paperback edition published in the UK in 2000

The HarperCollins website address is:
www.fireandwater.com

ISBN: 0-00-710155-4

Printed and bound in Slovenia